Contents Table

~ Welcome & What You'll Learn

Section A: Foundations of Service Management

- Chapter 1: Introduction to Service Management
- Chapter 2: Evolution of IT Service Management (ITSM)
- Chapter 3: The ITIL 4 Framework Overview
- Chapter 4: Key Concepts and Terminology

Section B: Four Dimensions of Service Management

- Chapter 5: Organizations and People
- Chapter 6: Information and Technology
- Chapter 7: Partners and Suppliers
- Chapter 8: Value Streams and Processes

Section C: Guiding Principles of ITIL 4

- Chapter 9: Focus on Value
- Chapter 10: Start Where You Are
- Chapter 11: Progress Iteratively with Feedback
- Chapter 12: Collaborate and Promote Visibility
- Chapter 13: Think and Work Holistically
- Chapter 14: Keep It Simple and Practical
- Chapter 15: Optimize and Automate

Section D: The ITIL Service Value System (SVS)

- Chapter 16: Understanding the Service Value Chain
- Chapter 17: Governance
- Chapter 18: Practices
- Chapter 19: Continual Improvement

Section E: ITIL Management Practices

- Chapter 20: General Management Practices
- Chapter 21: Service Management Practices
- Chapter 22: Technical Management Practices

Section F: ITIL 4 and Practical Implementation

- Chapter 23: Adopting ITIL 4 in Your Organization
- Chapter 24: Measuring and Demonstrating Success
- Chapter 25: Case Studies and Real-World Examples

Appendices

- Appendix A: Glossary of Key Terms

- Appendix B: ITIL Exam Preparation Tips
- Appendix C: Further Reading and Resources
- Appendix D: ITIL Certifications

~ Conclusion

Welcome & What You'll Learn

Welcome to "The ITIL 4 Service Management Handbook: A Practical Guide to Four Dimensions, Guiding Principles, Service Value System, and Best Practices." Whether you're new to the world of service management or a seasoned IT professional, this book is designed to equip you with a deep understanding of ITIL 4 and the practical skills needed to implement it successfully.

Why ITIL 4 Matters

In today's fast-paced digital world, organizations rely on IT services more than ever before. The ability to deliver high-quality, efficient, and value-driven services is critical for success. ITIL 4, the latest evolution of the IT Infrastructure Library, provides a comprehensive framework for managing and improving IT services throughout their entire lifecycle.

By adopting ITIL 4, organizations can:

- **Enhance customer satisfaction:** Deliver services that meet or exceed customer expectations.
- **Optimize costs:** Streamline processes, eliminate waste, and improve resource utilization.
- **Increase agility:** Adapt quickly to changing business needs and market demands.
- **Mitigate risks:** Identify and address potential problems before they impact service delivery.
- **Foster collaboration:** Break down silos and encourage communication between teams.

What This Book Will Teach You

This handbook is your roadmap to mastering ITIL 4. Throughout its pages, we will explore:

- **The Fundamentals:** We'll start with the basics of service management, tracing the evolution of IT service management (ITSM) and outlining the key concepts and terminology of ITIL 4.
- **The Four Dimensions:** We'll delve into the four dimensions that underpin successful service management: organizations and people, information and technology, partners and suppliers, and value streams and processes.
- **Guiding Principles:** You'll discover the seven guiding principles that form the foundation of ITIL 4, enabling you to make informed decisions and drive continual improvement.
- **Service Value System (SVS):** We'll explore the SVS, which provides a holistic model for creating, delivering, and managing value through IT services.
- **ITIL Practices:** You'll learn about the management practices recommended by ITIL 4, categorized into general management, service management, and technical management practices.
- **Practical Implementation:** We'll provide guidance on how to adopt ITIL 4 within your organization, measure success, and learn from real-world case studies.

Who This Book Is For

This book is for anyone involved in the delivery and management of IT services, including:

- IT managers and leaders
- Service delivery professionals
- IT operations teams
- Business analysts
- Consultants
- Students and anyone interested in IT service management

How to Use This Book

You can read this book from cover to cover to gain a comprehensive understanding of ITIL 4, or you can focus on specific chapters based on your interests and needs. We encourage you to use the numerous examples, diagrams, and real-world scenarios to apply the concepts you learn to your own organization.

We hope this book will be a valuable resource as you embark on your ITIL 4 journey. Let's get started!

Section A:
Foundations of Service Management

Introduction to Service Management

Outline

- Defining Services and Service Management
- Importance of Service Management in Today's Business Landscape
- The Relationship Between Services and Products
- Types of Services
- Service Provider Types
- Challenges and Opportunities in Service Management
- Chapter Summary

Defining Services and Service Management

In the simplest terms, a **service** is an act or performance offered by one party to another. However, this definition doesn't fully capture the nuances that set services apart from physical products. Let's delve deeper:

Key Characteristics of Services:

1. **Intangibility:** Unlike products you can touch and hold, services are intangible experiences. You can't physically grasp a haircut, a software update, or a financial consultation.
2. **Heterogeneity:** Services are inherently variable. The quality of a service can differ from one instance to the next, even when provided by the same person or organization.
3. **Inseparability:** Services are often produced and consumed simultaneously. The customer is typically present and involved in the service experience (think of a restaurant meal or a live concert).
4. **Perishability:** Services cannot be stored or inventoried like products. An empty seat on a plane or an unused hour of a consultant's time represents lost revenue.

These characteristics create unique challenges and opportunities for service providers. That's where **service management** comes in.

Service Management: The Holistic Approach

Service management is a set of specialized organizational capabilities for providing value to customers in the form of services. It encompasses the entire lifecycle of a service, from conception to retirement.

Key Goals of Service Management:

- **Customer Satisfaction:** Ensuring that services meet or exceed customer expectations in terms of quality, reliability, and timeliness.
- **Efficiency:** Optimizing the use of resources (people, technology, processes) to deliver services at the lowest possible cost.

- **Effectiveness:** Achieving desired outcomes through the delivery of services that contribute to business goals.
- **Continual Improvement:** Identifying and implementing opportunities to enhance the quality, efficiency, and effectiveness of services over time.

Service Management Activities:

Service management involves a wide range of activities, including:

- **Service Strategy:** Defining the organization's approach to service delivery, aligning services with business goals, and creating a value proposition for customers.
- **Service Design:** Developing new services or enhancing existing ones, taking into consideration factors such as functionality, usability, cost, and risk.
- **Service Transition:** Implementing and deploying new or changed services, ensuring a smooth transition from development to production.
- **Service Operation:** Managing and maintaining services in production, including incident management, problem management, change management, and request fulfillment.
- **Continual Service Improvement:** Identifying and implementing opportunities to enhance service quality, efficiency, and effectiveness based on data and feedback.

In Summary:

Services are intangible, variable, inseparable, and perishable offerings that play a vital role in today's economy. Service management is the discipline of planning, designing, delivering, operating, and controlling services to create value for both customers and organizations.

Importance of Service Management in Today's Business Landscape

Service management has evolved from a support function to a critical driver of business success. Here's why it plays a pivotal role in today's dynamic business landscape:

Increasing Reliance on Services for Revenue and Customer Satisfaction:

In the modern economy, services have become the primary engine for revenue generation and customer engagement. Companies across industries, from technology and finance to healthcare and retail, are increasingly focused on delivering exceptional service experiences to differentiate themselves and foster customer loyalty. This shift towards a service-oriented economy underscores the importance of effective service management to meet rising customer expectations and maintain a competitive edge.

Competitive Advantage through Efficiency, Effectiveness, and Customer-Centricity:

Service management provides organizations with a structured framework to streamline operations, reduce costs, and enhance service quality. By implementing best practices in incident management, problem management, change management, and request fulfillment, businesses can ensure efficient and reliable service delivery. Effective service management also focuses on understanding and anticipating customer needs, leading to improved customer satisfaction and stronger relationships. In a crowded marketplace, these capabilities translate into a distinct competitive advantage.

Impact of Digital Transformation on Service Management:

The digital age has revolutionized service management. Technologies like cloud computing, mobile devices, and social media have empowered customers and raised their expectations for seamless, personalized, and on-demand service experiences. In response, organizations are leveraging digital tools to automate routine tasks, enable self-service options, and gain valuable insights from data analytics. Artificial intelligence (AI) and machine learning are also transforming service management by predicting customer behavior, personalizing interactions, and resolving issues proactively. Organizations that embrace these digital advancements can streamline operations, enhance customer experiences, and stay ahead of the curve.

In conclusion, service management is no longer just a back-office function; it is a strategic imperative for businesses seeking to thrive in the digital age. By focusing on efficiency, effectiveness, and customer-centricity, organizations can leverage service management to drive innovation, growth, and long-term success.

The Relationship Between Services and Products

The traditional distinction between services and products is becoming increasingly blurred. While pure services and pure products exist, many offerings combine elements of both in what is called a product-service bundle. Let's explore these categories:

Examples:

- **Pure Services:** These offerings consist entirely of intangible activities or performances. Examples include haircuts, legal consultations, financial advice, and online education.
- **Pure Products:** These are tangible items that customers purchase and own. Examples include clothing, electronics, cars, and furniture.
- **Product-Service Bundles:** These offerings combine a tangible product with one or more associated services. Examples include smartphones with data plans, cars with maintenance contracts, and software with customer support.

The Servitization Trend

The servitization trend refers to the growing tendency for manufacturers to expand their offerings beyond pure products and include services as an integral part of their value proposition. This shift is driven by several factors:

- **Increased Competition:** In many industries, product differentiation is becoming more difficult, leading companies to seek new ways to stand out by offering complementary services.
- **Changing Customer Preferences:** Customers increasingly value convenience, customization, and experiences, all of which can be enhanced through services.
- **Recurring Revenue Streams:** Services can provide a source of recurring revenue, which is more stable and predictable than one-time product sales.

Implications for Service Management

The servitization trend has significant implications for service management:

- **Expanded Scope:** Service management is no longer confined to pure service providers. Manufacturers must now develop expertise in service design, delivery, and management.
- **Integrated Approach:** Product and service development must be closely aligned to ensure a seamless customer experience.
- **New Skills and Competencies:** Service management requires a different set of skills and competencies than product management, including customer relationship management, service level agreement (SLA) negotiation, and incident resolution.
- **Data-Driven Insights:** Data analytics plays a crucial role in understanding customer needs, optimizing service delivery, and identifying opportunities for improvement.

In Summary:

The relationship between services and products is complex and evolving. While pure services and pure products still exist, product-service bundles are becoming increasingly common. This shift towards servitization requires organizations to rethink their approach to service management, embracing an integrated, customer-centric perspective to deliver value in the form of both products and services.

Types of Services

Services can be categorized based on various criteria, such as the target audience, the nature of the service, and the provider. Let's explore some common types:

1. Business-to-Consumer (B2C) Services:

These services are offered directly to individual consumers for personal use or consumption. B2C services span a wide range of industries and needs, including:

- **Retail:** Shopping experiences, both in-store and online, offering products and services like fashion, electronics, groceries, and home goods.
- **Healthcare:** Medical consultations, treatments, surgeries, diagnostic tests, and preventative care services.
- **Entertainment:** Movies, concerts, theater performances, streaming platforms, amusement parks, and other leisure activities.
- **Hospitality:** Accommodation, dining, and travel-related services such as hotels, restaurants, airlines, and travel agencies.
- **Financial Services:** Banking, insurance, investment advice, and personal financial planning.

2. Business-to-Business (B2B) Services:

These services are provided by one business to another to support their operations, enhance their performance, or achieve their objectives. B2B services are often more complex and specialized than B2C services and include:

- **Consulting:** Expert advice and guidance on various business functions such as strategy, marketing, finance, and technology.
- **Information Technology (IT):** Software development, cybersecurity, cloud computing, data analytics, and IT infrastructure management.
- **Professional Services:** Legal counsel, accounting, auditing, tax preparation, and other specialized services.
- **Marketing and Advertising:** Market research, branding, advertising campaigns, public relations, and digital marketing strategies.
- **Logistics and Supply Chain:** Transportation, warehousing, inventory management, and supply chain optimization.

3. Internal Services:

These services are provided within an organization to support its internal operations and functions. They are often essential for maintaining productivity, efficiency, and employee satisfaction and include:

- **IT Support:** Help desk services, troubleshooting, software installation, and hardware maintenance.
- **Human Resources (HR):** Recruitment, onboarding, training, performance management, benefits administration, and employee relations.
- **Finance and Accounting:** Budgeting, financial reporting, accounts payable and receivable, payroll, and tax compliance.
- **Facilities Management:** Building maintenance, cleaning, security, and other services related to the physical workplace.

4. Public Services:

These services are provided by the government or other public entities to meet the needs of citizens and society as a whole. Public services are often considered essential for quality of life and include:

- **Education:** Public schools, universities, libraries, and other educational programs.
- **Transportation:** Public transportation systems like buses, trains, subways, and infrastructure like roads and airports.
- **Healthcare:** Public hospitals, clinics, and health insurance programs.
- **Utilities:** Electricity, gas, water, sewage, and waste management services.
- **Emergency Services:** Police, fire, and ambulance services.
- **Social Services:** Welfare programs, child protection, and housing assistance.

This categorization of services is not mutually exclusive. Some services may fall into multiple categories, and the lines between them can be blurred. However, understanding these different types can help service providers tailor their offerings to meet the specific needs of their target customers and achieve their business goals.

Service Provider Types

The landscape of service providers is diverse, with various models catering to different organizational needs. Let's break down the key types:

1. **Internal Service Providers:**

These are departments or teams within an organization that provide services to other internal departments or business units. They function as in-house experts, offering support and solutions tailored to the organization's specific requirements.

Examples:

- **IT Department:** Provides technical support, software development, and infrastructure management services to other departments.
- **Human Resources (HR) Department:** Offers recruitment, onboarding, training, and employee relations services.
- **Finance Department:** Handles budgeting, accounting, financial reporting, and payroll services.

Benefits:

- **Greater Control:** Organizations have direct control over the quality and delivery of services.
- **Customization:** Services can be tailored to meet the specific needs of internal customers.
- **Confidentiality:** Sensitive information remains within the organization.

Challenges:

- **Cost:** Maintaining internal service providers can be expensive, especially for smaller organizations.
- **Limited Expertise:** Internal teams may lack specialized skills or knowledge in certain areas.
- **Potential for Bias:** Internal providers may prioritize certain departments or projects over others.
2. **External Service Providers:**

These are third-party vendors, contractors, or outsourcers that provide services to organizations on a contractual basis. They specialize in specific areas and offer expertise that may not be available in-house.

Examples:

- **IT Consulting Firms:** Provide specialized IT services such as cybersecurity, cloud migration, or software development.

- **Marketing Agencies:** Offer expertise in market research, branding, advertising, and digital marketing.
- **Legal Firms:** Provide legal counsel, representation, and advice on various legal matters.

Benefits:

- **Cost-Effective:** Outsourcing can often be more cost-effective than maintaining internal teams.
- **Specialized Expertise:** External providers offer specialized skills and knowledge in their respective fields.
- **Scalability:** Services can be easily scaled up or down based on demand.

Challenges:

- **Loss of Control:** Organizations have less control over the quality and delivery of services.
- **Communication Barriers:** Coordinating with external providers can be challenging, especially across different time zones or cultures.
- **Data Security Risks:** Sharing sensitive information with external providers requires careful management and risk mitigation.
3. **Shared Service Providers:**

These are centralized functions within an organization that provide services to multiple business units or departments. They aim to streamline operations, reduce costs, and standardize processes.

Examples:

- **Shared IT Services:** Centralized IT support, infrastructure management, and application development.
- **Shared HR Services:** Centralized recruitment, onboarding, training, and payroll processing.
- **Shared Finance Services:** Centralized accounting, financial reporting, and accounts payable/receivable.

Benefits:

- **Cost Savings:** Consolidation of resources and elimination of redundancies lead to cost savings.
- **Standardization:** Processes are standardized across business units, leading to improved efficiency and consistency.
- **Improved Service Quality:** Centralized functions can focus on developing specialized expertise and delivering high-quality services.

Challenges:

- **Lack of Customization:** Standardized services may not fully meet the specific needs of individual business units.
- **Resistance to Change:** Implementing shared services often requires significant organizational change, which can be met with resistance.
- **Governance:** Effective governance mechanisms are necessary to ensure accountability and alignment with business goals.

Understanding these different service provider types allows organizations to make informed decisions about how to best meet their service needs, considering factors such as cost, expertise, control, and scalability.

Challenges and Opportunities in Service Management

Service management is a dynamic field that presents both significant challenges and exciting opportunities for organizations. Understanding these complexities is essential for harnessing the full potential of service management.

Challenges in Service Management:

1. **Managing Intangible Assets:**
   - Services are intangible, making them difficult to quantify, standardize, and control.
   - Measuring service quality and demonstrating value to customers can be challenging.
   - Ensuring consistent service delivery across different channels and touchpoints requires careful planning and coordination.
2. **Ensuring Customer Satisfaction:**
   - Customer expectations are constantly evolving, making it difficult to anticipate and meet their needs consistently.
   - Service experiences are subjective, and what satisfies one customer may not satisfy another.
   - Maintaining a customer-centric approach requires ongoing feedback, analysis, and adaptation.
3. **Maintaining Consistent Service Quality:**
   - Service quality can be affected by various factors, including human error, technology failures, and external disruptions.
   - Establishing and enforcing service level agreements (SLAs) is essential for managing expectations and ensuring accountability.
   - Continual monitoring and improvement are necessary to identify and address any deviations from agreed-upon service standards.

Opportunities in Service Management:

1. **Innovation and Growth:**
   - Effective service management can drive innovation by fostering a culture of continuous improvement and customer-centricity.
   - New technologies like AI, automation, and self-service portals can be leveraged to enhance service delivery and create new revenue streams.
   - Service management can contribute to business growth by improving customer retention, attracting new customers, and expanding into new markets.
2. **Differentiation and Competitive Advantage:**
   - Exceptional service experiences can differentiate a company from its competitors and create a loyal customer base.
   - Investing in service management can lead to improved efficiency, reduced costs, and enhanced agility, all of which contribute to a competitive edge.
   - Organizations that prioritize service management are often seen as more reliable, trustworthy, and customer-focused.
3. **Alignment with Business Strategy and Objectives:**
   - Service management should not be an isolated function but an integral part of the overall business strategy.
   - Aligning service management with business goals ensures that services are designed and delivered in a way that supports the organization's mission and vision.
   - This alignment fosters collaboration between different departments, promotes a shared understanding of customer needs, and drives a unified approach to value creation.

In Summary:

While service management presents various challenges, it also offers significant opportunities for organizations to innovate, grow, and differentiate themselves. By embracing a customer-centric approach, leveraging technology, and aligning service management with business strategy, organizations can overcome the challenges and unlock the full potential of their services.

Looking Ahead:

As the service economy continues to evolve, the importance of service management will only grow. By proactively addressing challenges and seizing opportunities, organizations can position themselves for success in an increasingly competitive and customer-driven market.

Chapter Summary

In this chapter, we introduced the fundamental concepts of service management, laying the groundwork for your journey into the ITIL 4 framework. Here's a recap of the key points:

- **Services vs. Products:** We explored the defining characteristics of services—intangibility, heterogeneity, inseparability, and perishability—and how they differ from physical products. We also discussed the rise of product-service bundles and the growing trend of servitization, where manufacturers are incorporating services into their offerings.
- **Defining Service Management:** You learned that service management is a holistic discipline encompassing the planning, design, delivery, operation, and control of services to meet customer and organizational goals.
- **The Importance of Service Management:** We highlighted the pivotal role service management plays in today's business landscape, particularly in driving revenue, ensuring customer satisfaction, and creating a competitive advantage. We also discussed the impact of digital transformation on service management, including the rise of self-service, automation, and AI.
- **Types of Services:** You were introduced to various types of services, categorized by target audience (B2C, B2B), organizational function (internal services), and societal impact (public services).
- **Service Provider Types:** We explored the different models for delivering services, including internal providers, external providers, and shared service providers, each with its own advantages and challenges.
- **Challenges and Opportunities:** Finally, we discussed the unique challenges service management faces—such as managing intangible assets and ensuring consistent quality—and the vast opportunities it presents for innovation, growth, and differentiation.

With this foundation in place, you're well-prepared to delve deeper into the ITIL 4 framework, starting with its evolution from previous versions. In the next chapter, we will trace the history of IT Service Management (ITSM) and how it has led to the development of the modern ITIL 4 approach.

Evolution of IT Service Management (ITSM)

Outline

- Early Days of IT Service Management
- The Rise of ITIL
- ITIL v2 and v3: Expanding the Framework
- Shift to ITIL 4: A New Paradigm
- The Impact of Agile and DevOps
- Chapter Summary

Early Days of IT Service Management

In the early days of computing, IT service management (ITSM) was largely focused on the technology itself. The primary concern was ensuring that the hardware and software functioned correctly, with little emphasis on the services they provided or the needs of the users.

Technology-Centric Focus:

IT departments were primarily responsible for maintaining and troubleshooting the technical infrastructure, such as mainframes, servers, and networks. This often led to a reactive approach, where IT teams would only address issues as they arose, resulting in downtime, disruptions, and frustrated users.

Challenges of Growing Complexity:

As organizations adopted more sophisticated technologies and IT environments became increasingly complex and distributed, the limitations of this technology-centric approach became apparent. The challenges included:

- **Lack of Standardization:** Each IT team had its own processes and procedures, leading to inconsistencies and inefficiencies.
- **Poor Communication:** Communication between IT and other business functions was often siloed, resulting in misunderstandings and delays.
- **User Dissatisfaction:** Users often felt neglected, as IT teams focused primarily on technology rather than their needs and expectations.
- **Rising Costs:** The reactive approach to IT management was costly, as it focused on fixing problems rather than preventing them.

Emergence of ITIL as a Standardized Framework:

To address these challenges, a standardized framework for IT service management was needed. The IT Infrastructure Library (ITIL) emerged in the late 1980s as a set of best practices for IT service management. Developed by the UK government's Central Computer and Telecommunications Agency (CCTA), ITIL provided a structured approach to managing IT services throughout their lifecycle.

ITIL's core principles include:

- **Process Orientation:** ITIL defines a set of processes that cover all aspects of IT service management, from strategy to design, transition, operation, and continual improvement.
- **Customer Focus:** ITIL emphasizes the importance of understanding and meeting customer needs, ensuring that IT services deliver value to the business.
- **Continual Improvement:** ITIL promotes a culture of continuous improvement, encouraging organizations to regularly assess and enhance their IT services.

The adoption of ITIL by organizations worldwide led to significant improvements in IT service management. It provided a common language and framework for IT professionals, facilitated communication and collaboration, and helped organizations deliver more reliable, efficient, and customer-focused IT services.

The emergence of ITIL marked a turning point in the evolution of IT service management, shifting the focus from technology to service delivery and customer value. It paved the way for further developments in the field, leading to the modern ITIL 4 framework that we will explore in the following chapters.

The Rise of ITIL

The IT Infrastructure Library (ITIL) emerged as a beacon of standardization in the often chaotic landscape of IT service management. Its roots trace back to the 1980s, when the UK government's Central Computer and Telecommunications Agency (CCTA) recognized the need for a structured approach to managing IT services.

Origins in the UK Government:

The CCTA, tasked with overseeing IT operations across government agencies, developed ITIL as a set of best practices to streamline IT service delivery and improve efficiency. The initial focus was on government agencies, but the framework's value quickly became apparent to the private sector as well.

Core Principles of ITIL:

ITIL's success stems from its emphasis on several core principles:

1. **Process Orientation:** ITIL emphasizes the importance of well-defined and documented processes for managing IT services. These processes cover all aspects of the service lifecycle, from strategy and design to operation and improvement.
2. **Customer Focus:** ITIL places the customer at the center of IT service management. It stresses the need to understand and meet customer needs, ensuring that IT services deliver value to the business and its stakeholders.
3. **Continual Improvement:** ITIL promotes a culture of continuous improvement, encouraging organizations to regularly assess their IT services and identify opportunities for enhancement.

Widespread Adoption and De Facto Standard:

ITIL's comprehensive and practical approach resonated with organizations worldwide. Its adoption spread rapidly across industries and geographies, establishing ITIL as the de facto standard for IT service management. By the early 2000s, ITIL had become the most widely used ITSM framework globally.

Several factors contributed to ITIL's widespread adoption:

- **Vendor Neutrality:** ITIL is not tied to any specific technology or vendor, making it adaptable to diverse IT environments.
- **Flexibility:** ITIL provides a flexible framework that can be tailored to the specific needs and goals of an organization.
- **Proven Success:** Numerous organizations have reported significant improvements in IT service quality, efficiency, and customer satisfaction after adopting ITIL.
- **Professional Certification:** The availability of ITIL certifications has further fueled its adoption, as professionals seek to demonstrate their expertise in IT service management.

The rise of ITIL transformed the way organizations approach IT service management. It provided a common language and framework, enabling IT professionals to communicate effectively and collaborate across teams and departments. By standardizing processes, aligning IT with business goals, and promoting continuous improvement, ITIL has played a pivotal role in elevating the maturity and effectiveness of IT service management worldwide.

ITIL v2 and v3: Expanding the Framework

Building upon the foundations of the original ITIL framework, versions 2 and 3 introduced significant updates and refinements that further solidified ITIL's position as the leading ITSM framework.

Key Updates and Enhancements:

- **New Processes:** ITIL v2 and v3 introduced several new processes, including Demand Management, Service Catalog Management, and Knowledge Management, expanding the scope of ITIL's guidance and addressing emerging challenges in IT service delivery.
- **Revised Processes:** Existing processes were refined and updated to reflect evolving best practices and industry trends. For example, Incident Management and Problem Management were enhanced to provide more detailed guidance on incident resolution and root cause analysis.
- **Expanded Terminology:** New concepts and terminology were introduced to clarify and enhance ITIL's vocabulary. This included terms like Service Asset and Configuration Item (CI), which became fundamental building blocks of the framework.
- **Greater Emphasis on Measurement:** ITIL v2 and v3 placed increased emphasis on the importance of measuring and monitoring IT services to ensure they meet agreed-upon targets and deliver value to the business.

Introduction of the Service Lifecycle:

One of the most significant changes in ITIL v3 was the introduction of the Service Lifecycle concept. This model provided a structured approach to managing IT services throughout their entire lifecycle, from strategy to design, transition, operation, and continual improvement. Each stage of the lifecycle was supported by a set of processes, roles, and responsibilities, providing a clear roadmap for IT service management.

The Service Lifecycle model helped organizations:

- **Visualize the entire service lifecycle:** Gain a holistic view of IT service management, from conception to retirement.
- **Identify key activities and dependencies:** Understand the interdependencies between different stages of the service lifecycle.
- **Manage services more effectively:** Apply appropriate processes and practices at each stage of the lifecycle to achieve desired outcomes.

Increased Emphasis on Alignment with Business Goals:

ITIL v2 and v3 also emphasized the importance of aligning IT services with business goals and delivering value to customers. This shift in focus from a purely technical perspective to a more business-oriented approach recognized the critical role that IT plays in supporting organizational objectives.

Key aspects of this shift included:

- **Value Creation:** ITIL encouraged organizations to view IT services as a means to create value for the business, rather than just a cost center.
- **Business Relationship Management:** The establishment of strong relationships between IT and business stakeholders became a priority to ensure IT services meet business needs.
- **Service Level Management:** ITIL v3 expanded on the concept of Service Level Agreements (SLAs) to ensure that IT services meet agreed-upon performance targets and deliver value to customers.

In conclusion, ITIL v2 and v3 represented a significant evolution of the framework, expanding its scope, refining its processes, and emphasizing the importance of alignment with business goals. These versions laid the groundwork for the latest iteration, ITIL 4, which embraces a more holistic and adaptable approach to IT service management in the digital age.

Shift to ITIL 4: A New Paradigm

ITIL 4, released in 2019, marked a significant paradigm shift in the ITIL framework. It represents a comprehensive update designed to address the evolving needs of modern businesses operating in a rapidly changing digital landscape.

Key Drivers Behind ITIL 4 Development:

1. **Digital Transformation:** The digital age brought about rapid technological advancements, such as cloud computing, mobile devices, and big data. ITIL 4 was designed to adapt to these changes and provide guidance on managing IT services in a digital-first world.
2. **Emerging Technologies and Methodologies:** The rise of Agile, DevOps, and Lean methodologies challenged the traditional, process-heavy approach of ITIL v3. ITIL 4 sought to integrate these new ways of working, emphasizing flexibility, collaboration, and rapid value delivery.
3. **Customer-Centricity:** Customer expectations continued to rise, demanding more personalized and seamless service experiences. ITIL 4 recognized the need for a more customer-centric approach, focusing on value co-creation and customer journey optimization.
4. **Holistic Approach:** ITIL v3's focus on processes, while valuable, sometimes led to siloed thinking. ITIL 4 adopted a more holistic approach, recognizing the interconnectedness of various elements within an organization and the need for a broader perspective.

Shift from Process-Centric to Holistic and Flexible Approach:

ITIL 4 moved away from the rigid, process-centric model of ITIL v3 towards a more flexible and adaptable approach. It emphasizes the importance of collaboration, value co-creation, and adaptability to meet the evolving needs of businesses and customers.

This shift is reflected in several key changes:

- **Focus on Value:** ITIL 4 places greater emphasis on value creation, encouraging organizations to focus on outcomes rather than just outputs.
- **Guiding Principles:** ITIL 4 introduces seven guiding principles that provide a foundation for decision-making and action, promoting a more holistic and adaptable approach to IT service management.
- **Practices:** ITIL 4 replaces the processes of ITIL v3 with a set of 34 management practices, offering more flexibility and allowing organizations to tailor their approach to their specific needs.

Introduction of Core Components:

ITIL 4 introduced three core components that form the foundation of the framework:

1. **Service Value System (SVS):** The SVS is a holistic model that describes how all the components and activities of an organization work together to facilitate value creation through IT-enabled services.
2. **Four Dimensions of Service Management:** These dimensions – organizations and people, information and technology, partners and suppliers, and value streams and processes – provide a comprehensive view of the factors that contribute to successful service management.
3. **Guiding Principles:** The seven guiding principles, such as "Focus on Value," "Start Where You Are," and "Collaborate and Promote Visibility," guide decision-making and actions in IT service management.

In Summary:

ITIL 4 represents a significant evolution of the ITIL framework, adapting to the digital age and embracing new ways of working. By shifting from a process-centric to a more holistic and flexible approach, ITIL 4 empowers organizations to deliver value, adapt to change, and achieve sustainable success in the dynamic world of IT service management.

The Impact of Agile and DevOps

Agile and DevOps methodologies have significantly influenced the evolution of ITIL 4, injecting a new dynamism and responsiveness into the framework.

Influence of Agile and DevOps on ITIL 4:

- **Faster Delivery:** Agile's iterative approach and DevOps' emphasis on automation and continuous delivery align with ITIL 4's focus on rapid value creation. This enables organizations to deliver IT services and updates more frequently, responding quickly to changing business needs and customer demands.
- **Increased Collaboration:** Both Agile and DevOps promote collaboration between development, operations, and other teams, breaking down silos and fostering a culture of shared responsibility. ITIL 4 echoes this emphasis, recognizing the importance of cross-functional collaboration for successful service management.
- **Continuous Feedback Loops:** Agile and DevOps advocate for short feedback loops and continuous improvement through regular retrospectives and post-incident reviews. ITIL 4 incorporates this feedback-driven approach into its continual service improvement model, ensuring that services are constantly evaluated and enhanced based on real-world data and user feedback.

Integration of ITIL Practices with Agile and DevOps Principles:

ITIL 4 seamlessly integrates with Agile and DevOps principles, creating a more streamlined and responsive approach to IT service management. For example:

- **Change Management:** ITIL's change management practices can be adapted to Agile's iterative development cycles, enabling faster and more frequent changes while maintaining control and minimizing risk.
- **Incident Management:** DevOps practices like blameless post-incident reviews can be incorporated into ITIL's incident management process to foster a learning culture and drive continuous improvement.
- **Problem Management:** Agile's focus on root cause analysis and prevention aligns with ITIL's problem management practices, helping organizations identify and address underlying issues before they impact service quality.

Benefits of Adopting an Agile and DevOps Mindset with ITIL 4:

By embracing Agile and DevOps principles in conjunction with ITIL 4, organizations can achieve significant benefits:

- **Improved Time-to-Market:** Faster delivery cycles enable organizations to launch new services and updates quickly, gaining a competitive edge.
- **Enhanced Customer Satisfaction:** Continuous feedback loops and rapid response to incidents and requests lead to improved customer satisfaction and loyalty.
- **Greater Organizational Agility:** The ability to adapt quickly to changing market conditions and business needs ensures that IT services remain relevant and valuable.
- **Increased Efficiency and Productivity:** Automation, collaboration, and streamlined processes lead to increased efficiency and productivity across IT teams.

Incorporating Agile and DevOps principles into ITIL 4 creates a powerful synergy, combining the structured guidance of ITIL with the flexibility and responsiveness of modern development and operations practices. This integrated approach enables organizations to deliver high-quality, customer-centric IT services in a fast-paced and ever-changing digital landscape.

Chapter Summary

In this chapter, we traced the evolution of IT service management (ITSM), from its early, technology-focused days to the modern, holistic approach embodied in ITIL 4. Here's a recap of the key points covered:

- **Early Days of ITSM:** We explored the initial emphasis on technology management and the challenges this posed as IT environments grew more complex. This highlighted the need for a standardized framework like ITIL.
- **The Rise of ITIL:** We delved into the origins of ITIL, its core principles of process orientation, customer focus, and continual improvement, and its widespread adoption as the de facto standard for ITSM.
- **ITIL v2 and v3:** We discussed the key updates and enhancements introduced in ITIL v2 and v3, including the addition of new processes, the introduction of the Service Lifecycle concept, and the increased emphasis on aligning IT services with business goals.
- **Shift to ITIL 4:** We examined the factors driving the development of ITIL 4, such as digital transformation, emerging technologies, and the need for a more holistic approach. We also highlighted the key changes in ITIL 4, including the shift from processes to practices, the introduction of the Service Value System and Guiding Principles, and the focus on value co-creation.
- **Impact of Agile and DevOps:** We discussed the influence of Agile and DevOps methodologies on ITIL 4, emphasizing their contribution to faster delivery, increased collaboration, and continuous feedback loops. We also explored the integration of ITIL practices with Agile and DevOps principles and the benefits of adopting this integrated approach.

Understanding the evolution of ITSM and the progression of ITIL provides valuable context for appreciating the current state of IT service management. It also highlights the importance of continuous learning and adaptation in this dynamic field.

In the next chapter, we will take a closer look at the ITIL 4 framework, providing a comprehensive overview of its structure, components, and key concepts. This will lay the foundation for your understanding of how ITIL 4 can be applied to improve IT service management in your organization.

The ITIL 4 Framework Overview

Outline

- The ITIL 4 Service Value System (SVS)
- The Four Dimensions of Service Management
- The ITIL Guiding Principles
- The ITIL Practices
- The ITIL Continual Improvement Model
- Chapter Summary

The ITIL 4 Service Value System (SVS)

The ITIL 4 Service Value System (SVS) is the heart of the ITIL 4 framework. It's a comprehensive, flexible model that illustrates how all the elements of an organization – its people, processes, information, technology, and partners – work together to co-create value through IT-enabled services.

The SVS shifts the focus from individual processes to the overall system, emphasizing the importance of collaboration, integration, and adaptability to achieve desired outcomes. Let's break down the key components of the SVS:

1. **Opportunity/Demand:** The SVS is triggered by opportunities or demands, which can be internal or external. An internal opportunity might be a need to streamline a business process, while an external demand could be a customer request for a new product feature.
2. **Guiding Principles:** The seven ITIL guiding principles (Focus on Value, Start Where You Are, Progress Iteratively with Feedback, Collaborate and Promote Visibility, Think and Work Holistically, Keep It Simple and Practical, Optimize and Automate) act as a compass, providing guidance for decision-making and actions throughout the entire SVS.
3. **Governance:** Governance ensures that the SVS operates effectively and aligns with the organization's strategic objectives. It involves establishing clear roles, responsibilities, and decision-making processes, as well as measuring and evaluating performance against defined goals.
4. **Service Value Chain:** This is the core of the SVS, representing the series of interconnected activities that transform inputs (demands and opportunities) into outputs (valuable services). The six key activities in the Service Value Chain are:
   - **Plan:** Strategize and coordinate efforts.
   - **Improve:** Continually assess and enhance the SVS.
   - **Engage:** Collaborate with stakeholders and understand their needs.
   - **Design & Transition:** Create and implement new or changed services.
   - **Obtain/Build:** Ensure the availability of necessary resources.
   - **Deliver & Support:** Ensure the smooth operation and support of services.
5. **Practices:** ITIL 4 defines 34 management practices, which are sets of organizational resources designed for performing work or accomplishing an objective. These practices cover various areas of service management, from incident management and problem management to relationship management and supplier management.
6. **Continual Improvement:** The SVS is designed to be a learning and adaptive system. Continual Improvement is an ongoing cycle of identifying opportunities for enhancement, planning and implementing changes, and measuring the effectiveness of those changes. It ensures that the SVS remains aligned with evolving business needs and customer expectations.

The SVS in Action:

In practice, the SVS operates as a dynamic and interconnected system. A customer request (demand) triggers the Service Value Chain, which engages various practices to plan, design, deliver, and support the service. Throughout this process, the guiding principles guide decision-making, and governance ensures alignment with organizational objectives. Feedback loops and continual improvement mechanisms ensure that the SVS adapts to changing circumstances and delivers increasing value over time.

By understanding and applying the SVS, organizations can achieve a more holistic and integrated approach to IT service management, ensuring that their services are not only efficient and effective but also aligned with strategic goals and focused on delivering value to customers and stakeholders.

The Four Dimensions of Service Management

The Four Dimensions of Service Management in ITIL 4 provide a holistic view of the key factors that contribute to the successful creation and delivery of IT-enabled services. Each dimension plays a crucial role in the Service Value System (SVS), and their interaction is essential for achieving desired outcomes.

1. **Organizations and People:**

This dimension focuses on the human aspects of service management, including the roles, responsibilities, skills, and culture of the people involved. It emphasizes the importance of leadership, communication, collaboration, and a customer-centric mindset.

- **Key Considerations:**
  - Organizational structure and governance
  - Roles and responsibilities of individuals and teams
  - Skills and competencies required for service management
  - Culture and values that support service excellence
  - Leadership and management practices

2. **Information and Technology:**

This dimension encompasses the information, knowledge, and technologies that underpin service management activities. It includes the tools, systems, data, and information management processes used to support service delivery.

- **Key Considerations:**
  - Information and knowledge management systems
  - IT infrastructure and applications
  - Data analytics and reporting
  - Security and privacy considerations
  - Technology trends and innovations

3. **Partners and Suppliers:**

This dimension recognizes that organizations rarely operate in isolation. They often rely on external partners and suppliers to deliver services. This dimension focuses on managing these relationships effectively to ensure seamless service delivery.

- **Key Considerations:**
  - Partner and supplier selection and onboarding
  - Contract management and performance monitoring
  - Relationship management and collaboration
  - Risk management and contingency planning
  - Integration of partner and supplier services

4. **Value Streams and Processes:**

This dimension encompasses the end-to-end activities that create and deliver value to customers through services. It includes the design, development, transition, operation, and continual improvement of services.

- **Key Considerations:**
  - Service design and development methodologies
  - Service transition and deployment processes
  - Service operation and support practices
  - Continual improvement initiatives
  - Value stream mapping and optimization

Interaction and Interdependence of Dimensions:

The four dimensions of service management are interconnected and interdependent. For example:

- **Organizations and people** need the right **information and technology** to perform their roles effectively.
- **Partners and suppliers** must be integrated into the **value streams and processes** to ensure seamless service delivery.
- The **culture and values** of the **organization and people** influence how **information and technology** are used.
- The **value streams and processes** must be designed to leverage the strengths of **partners and suppliers**.

A **balanced and holistic approach** to service management is essential to ensure that all four dimensions are considered and addressed effectively. This requires a deep understanding of how each dimension contributes to value creation and how they interact with each other. By taking a holistic approach, organizations can optimize their service management capabilities, improve customer satisfaction, and achieve their business goals.

The ITIL Guiding Principles

ITIL 4 introduces seven Guiding Principles that serve as a philosophical and practical foundation for successful service management. These principles are designed to be universal and applicable across all industries, organizational structures, and levels of IT maturity. Let's delve into each principle and how it can guide decision-making and actions within the Service Value System (SVS):

1. **Focus on Value:**
- **Explanation:** Every activity within the SVS should contribute to the creation and delivery of value for customers and stakeholders. This involves understanding their needs, prioritizing initiatives that deliver the greatest impact, and measuring outcomes to ensure that value is being realized.
- **Practical Guidance:** When making decisions, always ask, "How will this action create or enhance value for our customers and stakeholders?" Prioritize projects and initiatives that have a clear and measurable impact on value creation.
2. **Start Where You Are:**
- **Explanation:** Rather than starting from scratch, ITIL 4 encourages organizations to assess their current state and build upon their existing strengths and capabilities. This approach saves time and resources, reduces risk, and leverages the knowledge and experience already present within the organization.
- **Practical Guidance:** Before implementing any changes, conduct a thorough assessment of your current IT service management practices. Identify areas for improvement and prioritize actions based on the potential value they can deliver.
3. **Progress Iteratively with Feedback:**
- **Explanation:** ITIL 4 advocates for an iterative approach to improvement, making small, incremental changes and gathering feedback along the way. This allows organizations to adapt quickly, learn

from their mistakes, and continuously improve their services based on real-world data and user feedback.

- **Practical Guidance:** Break down large projects into smaller, manageable phases. Implement changes incrementally, gather feedback from users and stakeholders, and use that feedback to refine and improve your approach.

4. **Collaborate and Promote Visibility:**

- **Explanation:** Effective service management requires collaboration and communication across teams, departments, and even organizations. ITIL 4 emphasizes the importance of breaking down silos, promoting transparency, and sharing information to foster trust, alignment, and a shared understanding of goals and priorities.
- **Practical Guidance:** Encourage open communication and collaboration between teams involved in service management. Use tools and technologies that facilitate information sharing and visibility across the organization.

5. **Think and Work Holistically:**

- **Explanation:** ITIL 4 recognizes that IT services are part of a larger system that includes people, processes, information, technology, and partners. To achieve optimal outcomes, it's important to consider the impact of decisions and actions on the entire system, not just on individual components.
- **Practical Guidance:** When making decisions, consider the broader context and potential impacts on all aspects of the SVS. Encourage cross-functional collaboration and a systems thinking approach to problem-solving.

6. **Keep It Simple and Practical:**

- **Explanation:** ITIL 4 emphasizes the importance of simplicity and practicality. Avoid unnecessary complexity, streamline processes, and focus on solutions that deliver real value. The goal is to make IT service management easier and more efficient, not more cumbersome.
- **Practical Guidance:** When designing or improving processes, ask yourself, "Is this the simplest way to achieve our desired outcome?" Eliminate unnecessary steps, automate repetitive tasks, and use plain language in documentation and communication.

7. **Optimize and Automate:**

- **Explanation:** ITIL 4 encourages organizations to leverage technology to optimize and automate tasks and processes. This frees up human resources for more complex and value-adding activities, improves efficiency, and reduces the risk of errors.
- **Practical Guidance:** Identify opportunities for automation within the SVS. Implement tools and technologies that can streamline processes, automate routine tasks, and provide valuable insights into service performance.

The ITIL Practices

ITIL 4 introduces a comprehensive set of 34 management practices, providing a toolbox of resources that organizations can leverage to support their service management activities. These practices are not prescriptive processes; rather, they offer flexible guidance on how to organize and manage work to achieve desired outcomes.

The practices are categorized into three groups:

1. **General Management Practices:** These practices apply to the entire organization and support various aspects of business operations, including strategy, risk management, information security, and organizational change management.
2. **Service Management Practices:** These practices focus on the specific activities involved in managing IT services throughout their lifecycle, from design and development to delivery and support.
3. **Technical Management Practices:** These practices deal with the technical aspects of IT service management, such as infrastructure management, software development and management, and deployment management.

Brief Overview of Each Practice:

Practice Category	Practice Name	Purpose	Key Activities	Relationship to Service Value Chain
General Management	Strategy management	Ensure that services align with business goals	Develop and maintain a service strategy, portfolio management	Plan
	Portfolio management	Manage the lifecycle of services and investments	Prioritize investments, balance risk and reward	Plan
	Architecture management	Design and maintain a holistic architecture	Define and document architecture principles, assess and mitigate risks	Design & Transition
	Service financial management	Manage the financial aspects of services	Budgeting, accounting, charging, and cost optimization	Obtain/Build, Deliver & Support
	Workforce and talent management	Attract, develop, and retain talent	Recruitment, onboarding, training, performance management	Organizations & People
	Continual improvement	Embed a culture of continual improvement	Identify and implement improvements, measure and report on progress	Improve
	Measurement and reporting	Monitor and report on service performance	Define metrics, collect data, analyze results, and provide insights	Improve
	Risk management	Identify, assess, and manage risks	Risk identification, analysis, evaluation, and treatment	Plan, Design & Transition, Deliver & Support
	Information security management	Protect information assets from unauthorized access, use, disclosure, disruption,	Develop and implement information security policies and procedures, conduct risk	Information & Technology

		modification, or destruction	assessments, and implement controls	
	Knowledge management	Capture, store, share, and reuse knowledge	Create and maintain a knowledge base, promote knowledge sharing, and foster a learning culture	Organizations & People
	Organizational change management	Manage the people side of change	Develop and implement change plans, communicate effectively, and address resistance to change	Organizations & People
Service Management	Service request management	Manage the fulfillment of service requests	Receive, log, prioritize, and fulfill service requests	Deliver & Support
	Incident management	Restore normal service operation as quickly as possible	Detect, log, classify, prioritize, diagnose, resolve, and close incidents	Deliver & Support
	Problem management	Eliminate recurring incidents and minimize the impact of incidents that cannot be prevented	Identify, analyze, and resolve root causes of incidents	Deliver & Support
	Service desk	Single point of contact for users	Provide information, advice, and support to users	Deliver & Support
	Monitoring and event management	Monitor the status of IT infrastructure and applications	Detect and respond to events, identify trends, and proactively address potential issues	Deliver & Support
	Service level management	Ensure that services meet agreed-upon targets	Define, negotiate, monitor, report, and review SLAs	Engage

	Service configuration management	Maintain accurate and reliable information about configuration items	Identify, track, and control changes to CIs	Deliver & Support
	IT asset management	Manage the lifecycle of IT assets	Track and manage IT assets, optimize utilization, and dispose of assets responsibly	Obtain/Build
	Supplier management	Manage relationships with suppliers	Select, onboard, manage, and evaluate suppliers	Partners & Suppliers
Technical Management	Deployment management	Move new or changed hardware, software, documentation, processes, or any other component to live environments.	Plan, schedule, coordinate, and implement deployments	Design & Transition

Flexibility and Integration:

ITIL 4 recognizes that not all practices will be relevant or applicable to every organization. The framework encourages organizations to adopt the practices that best align with their specific needs, goals, and context. It also emphasizes the importance of integrating ITIL practices with other frameworks and methodologies, such as Agile and DevOps, to create a seamless and effective approach to IT service management.

The ITIL Continual Improvement Model

The ITIL Continual Improvement Model is a cornerstone of the ITIL 4 framework, embodying the philosophy that service management is an ongoing journey, not a destination. It provides a structured approach for organizations to continually enhance their services, processes, and practices, ultimately driving greater value for customers and stakeholders.

The Cyclical Nature of Continual Improvement:

The ITIL Continual Improvement Model is a cyclical process that consists of the following steps:

1. **What is the vision?** Define the direction and objectives of the improvement initiative, ensuring alignment with the organization's strategic goals and customer needs.
2. **Where are we now?** Assess the current state of the service, process, or practice, identifying strengths, weaknesses, and areas for improvement. This may involve collecting data, analyzing performance metrics, and gathering feedback from stakeholders.
3. **Where do we want to be?** Define specific, measurable targets for improvement, establishing clear objectives that align with the overall vision.
4. **How do we get there?** Develop a plan of action, outlining the steps, resources, and timelines required to achieve the improvement targets. This may involve implementing new technologies, redesigning processes, or providing additional training to staff.

5. **Take action:** Implement the planned improvements, ensuring effective communication and coordination across teams and stakeholders.
6. **Did we get there?** Evaluate the effectiveness of the improvements by measuring performance against the defined targets. This may involve collecting and analyzing data, gathering feedback from users, and conducting post-implementation reviews.
7. **How do we keep the momentum going?** Identify further opportunities for improvement and initiate a new cycle of the continual improvement process. This step ensures that the organization maintains a continuous focus on improvement and adapts to changing needs and circumstances.

Establishing a Culture of Continual Improvement:

A successful continual improvement initiative requires more than just following a process. It requires a cultural shift within the organization, where everyone is encouraged to contribute ideas, challenge the status quo, and embrace change.

To foster a culture of continual improvement, organizations should:

- **Promote a learning mindset:** Encourage employees to learn from mistakes, share knowledge, and experiment with new approaches.
- **Empower employees:** Give employees the authority and resources to identify and implement improvements within their areas of responsibility.
- **Recognize and reward contributions:** Celebrate successes and acknowledge the contributions of individuals and teams who drive improvement initiatives.
- **Lead by example:** Senior leaders should actively participate in and champion continual improvement efforts.

The Role of Data and Metrics:

Data and metrics play a critical role in the continual improvement process. They provide objective evidence of performance, help identify areas for improvement, and enable organizations to measure the effectiveness of their efforts.

To leverage data and metrics effectively, organizations should:

- **Define clear metrics:** Establish relevant and measurable metrics that align with improvement goals.
- **Collect and analyze data:** Regularly collect and analyze data to track performance, identify trends, and uncover insights.
- **Use data to inform decisions:** Use data-driven insights to inform decision-making and prioritize improvement actions.
- **Communicate results:** Share performance data and improvement results with stakeholders to demonstrate progress and foster transparency.

By embracing the ITIL Continual Improvement Model, establishing a culture of continual improvement, and leveraging data and metrics, organizations can ensure that their IT services are continuously evolving and improving to meet the changing needs of their customers and stakeholders.

Chapter Summary

In this chapter, we explored the key elements of the ITIL 4 framework, providing you with a comprehensive overview of its structure and core components. Here's a summary of what we covered:

- **The Service Value System (SVS):** We delved into the heart of ITIL 4, the SVS, explaining how it illustrates the interconnectedness of various organizational elements in creating value through IT-enabled services. You learned about the key components of the SVS, including opportunity/demand, guiding principles, governance, the service value chain, practices, and continual improvement.

- **The Four Dimensions of Service Management:** We explored the four dimensions that provide a holistic perspective on service management: organizations and people, information and technology, partners and suppliers, and value streams and processes. We emphasized the importance of considering all these dimensions in a balanced way to achieve successful service delivery.
- **The ITIL Guiding Principles:** You were introduced to the seven guiding principles that serve as the philosophical and practical foundation of ITIL 4. These principles offer valuable guidance for decision-making and actions throughout the SVS, helping organizations adapt ITIL to their specific needs.
- **The ITIL Practices:** We provided a brief overview of the 34 management practices in ITIL 4, categorized as general management, service management, and technical management. You learned that these practices are flexible and adaptable, allowing organizations to choose the ones that best suit their requirements.
- **The ITIL Continual Improvement Model:** We explained the cyclical nature of continual improvement and its importance in driving ongoing service enhancement. You learned about the steps involved in the process, the importance of establishing a culture of continual improvement, and the role of data and metrics in measuring progress.

With this overview of the ITIL 4 framework, you now have a solid foundation to explore the specific practices and concepts in more detail. The following chapters will delve into each dimension, guiding principle, and practice, providing you with the knowledge and tools to implement ITIL 4 effectively in your organization.

Key Concepts and Terminology

Outline

- Service
- Service Offering
- Service Relationship Management
- Configuration Item (CI)
- Change
- Event
- Incident
- Problem
- Known Error
- Value
- Outcome
- Cost
- Risk
- Utility
- Warranty
- Chapter Summary

Service

A **service** is an act or performance offered by one party to another. It is a means of delivering value to customers by facilitating outcomes that customers want to achieve without the ownership of specific costs and risks. In essence, a service is a collaborative effort between the service provider and the customer, where both parties contribute to the creation of value.

Key Characteristics of a Service:

1. **Intangibility:** Services are intangible. Unlike physical products that can be touched or seen, services are often experienced, felt, or perceived. This makes it challenging to measure and evaluate service quality, as it relies on subjective customer perceptions.
2. **Heterogeneity:** Services are inherently variable and can differ in quality from one instance to another, even when provided by the same provider. This variability is due to the involvement of people in service delivery, as well as the unique circumstances of each customer interaction.
3. **Inseparability:** Services are often produced and consumed simultaneously. The customer is typically present and involved in the service process, influencing its outcome. This means that the service provider and the customer must collaborate effectively to ensure a positive service experience.
4. **Perishability:** Services cannot be stored or inventoried for later use. An unused hotel room, an empty seat on a plane, or an unutilized hour of consulting time cannot be recovered and represents lost revenue.

Service vs. Product:

While both services and products aim to deliver value to customers, there are fundamental differences between them:

Characteristic	Service	Product
Nature	Intangible	Tangible

Ownership	Not owned, experienced	Owned and possessed
Production and Consumption	Simultaneous	Separated
Variability	High (heterogeneous)	Low (standardized)
Storability	Not storable (perishable)	Storable (inventory)

In the real world, the distinction between services and products is not always clear-cut. Many offerings combine elements of both in what is called a product-service bundle. For example, a smartphone is a tangible product, but the data plan and customer support associated with it are services.

Understanding the unique characteristics of services is crucial for effective service management. It allows organizations to tailor their approaches to service design, delivery, and improvement, ensuring that they meet customer expectations, deliver value, and achieve their business goals.

Service Offering

A service offering is a formal description of one or more services, designed to address the needs of a specific target consumer group. It's essentially a package that outlines the value proposition of the service, clarifying what the customer can expect to receive and under what conditions.

Structure of a Service Offering:

A well-defined service offering typically includes the following elements:

1. **Service Description:** A clear and concise description of the service being offered, highlighting its features, benefits, and intended outcomes. This description should be tailored to the target audience and clearly communicate the value proposition.
2. **Service Level Agreement (SLA):** A formal agreement between the service provider and the customer that defines the expected level of service, including performance metrics, availability, reliability, and responsiveness. SLAs provide a clear framework for managing customer expectations and ensuring accountability.
3. **Pricing:** The cost of the service, which can be structured in various ways, such as fixed fees, usage-based pricing, subscription models, or tiered pricing based on different service levels. The pricing model should be transparent and align with the perceived value of the service.
4. **Delivery Options:** The methods by which the service will be delivered, such as online, on-site, or through a combination of channels. The delivery options should be convenient and accessible for the target customer group.
5. **Terms and Conditions:** The legal and contractual terms governing the service relationship, including liability, warranties, dispute resolution, and termination clauses.

Additional Considerations:

- **Target Audience:** A service offering should be tailored to the specific needs, preferences, and expectations of the target customer group. This may involve segmenting the market and creating different service offerings for different customer segments.
- **Value Proposition:** The service offering should clearly articulate the value that the customer will receive from the service, highlighting how it will address their pain points, solve their problems, or help them achieve their goals.
- **Competitive Differentiation:** The service offering should differentiate the service from competitors, highlighting its unique features, benefits, or delivery mechanisms.
- **Continuous Improvement:** Service offerings should not be static. They should be regularly reviewed and updated based on customer feedback, market trends, and evolving business needs.

Example:

Consider a cloud storage service offering for small businesses. The service description might highlight features like secure file storage, collaboration tools, and automatic backups. The SLA could specify uptime guarantees, data recovery procedures, and response times for support requests. The pricing model might be a monthly subscription based on storage capacity, with additional fees for premium features. The delivery options could include web-based access, mobile apps, and desktop sync clients.

By clearly defining and communicating these elements, a service offering can effectively attract customers, manage their expectations, and build a strong foundation for a successful service relationship.

Service Relationship Management

Service Relationship Management (SRM) encompasses the activities, processes, and communication mechanisms that organizations use to establish and nurture mutually beneficial relationships between service providers and service consumers. It's the strategic approach that ensures a focus on customer value, satisfaction, and overall service experience.

Activities Involved in Service Relationship Management:

1. **Relationship Establishment:** The initial phase involves understanding the customer's needs, establishing clear communication channels, and setting expectations regarding service delivery, SLAs, and support.
2. **Ongoing Engagement:** Regular communication and interaction with customers through various channels like surveys, feedback mechanisms, and account management meetings. This helps in understanding evolving needs, addressing concerns promptly, and ensuring a positive customer experience.
3. **Service Level Management:** Monitoring and managing service performance against agreed-upon SLAs, identifying potential issues proactively, and taking corrective actions to maintain service quality.
4. **Incident and Request Management:** Promptly addressing customer incidents and requests, resolving issues efficiently, and providing timely updates to keep customers informed and satisfied.
5. **Continual Improvement:** Regularly reviewing the service relationship, gathering feedback from customers, and identifying opportunities for improvement to enhance service delivery and value.
6. **Relationship Expansion:** Exploring opportunities to expand the service relationship by offering additional services, upselling, or cross-selling relevant products.

Focus on Understanding Customer Needs, Managing Expectations, and Ensuring Satisfaction:

SRM places the customer at the center of service delivery. It emphasizes:

- **Understanding Customer Needs:** Engaging in active listening, conducting surveys, and analyzing customer feedback to gain insights into their needs, preferences, and expectations.
- **Managing Expectations:** Setting realistic expectations with customers regarding service delivery, SLAs, and support through clear communication and transparent agreements.
- **Ensuring Customer Satisfaction:** Regularly measuring customer satisfaction through surveys, feedback mechanisms, and other tools. Addressing any dissatisfaction promptly and taking proactive steps to improve the service experience.

Benefits of Effective Service Relationship Management:

- **Enhanced Customer Satisfaction:** Building strong relationships with customers leads to increased loyalty, repeat business, and positive word-of-mouth recommendations.
- **Improved Service Quality:** Regular communication and feedback loops help identify and address issues proactively, leading to improved service quality.

- **Increased Revenue:** Strong customer relationships can lead to upselling and cross-selling opportunities, generating additional revenue for the service provider.
- **Reduced Costs:** Proactive problem resolution and efficient incident management can reduce the cost of service delivery.
- **Competitive Advantage:** Exceptional service experiences can differentiate a company from its competitors and create a loyal customer base.

By focusing on building strong, collaborative relationships with customers, service providers can create a win-win situation where both parties benefit from improved service quality, increased satisfaction, and long-term value.

Configuration Item (CI)

A **Configuration Item (CI)** is any component or asset that needs to be managed to deliver an IT service. CIs are the building blocks of IT services, and understanding their relationships and dependencies is crucial for effective service management.

Examples of Configuration Items (CIs):

CIs can be tangible or intangible and include a wide range of elements, such as:

- **Hardware:** Servers, desktops, laptops, network devices, storage devices, mobile devices, printers, etc.
- **Software:** Operating systems, applications, databases, middleware, firmware, etc.
- **Documentation:** User manuals, technical specifications, design documents, process flows, etc.
- **Processes:** Incident management processes, change management processes, service request fulfillment processes, etc.
- **People:** Employees, contractors, customers, and other stakeholders involved in service delivery.
- **Contracts and Agreements:** Service level agreements (SLAs), vendor contracts, licenses, etc.

Importance of Tracking and Managing CIs throughout their Lifecycle:

Tracking and managing CIs throughout their lifecycle (from creation or acquisition to retirement) is essential for several reasons:

- **Maintaining Service Availability:** CIs play a critical role in service delivery. By tracking and managing their status, performance, and relationships, organizations can proactively identify and address potential issues that could impact service availability.
- **Supporting Change Management:** Changes to CIs can have a significant impact on services. By tracking CIs, organizations can assess the potential impact of changes, plan and implement changes effectively, and minimize the risk of disruptions.
- **Facilitating Incident and Problem Management:** When incidents or problems occur, knowing the configuration of the affected services can help IT teams quickly diagnose and resolve issues.
- **Optimizing Resource Utilization:** By tracking CIs, organizations can gain insights into how resources are being used, identify underutilized assets, and optimize resource allocation.
- **Ensuring Compliance:** In regulated industries, tracking and managing CIs is often required to demonstrate compliance with regulatory requirements.

How CIs are Managed:

CIs are typically managed using a Configuration Management System (CMS). A CMS is a database or repository that stores information about CIs, including their attributes, relationships, and history. The CMS allows IT teams to track changes to CIs, assess the impact of those changes, and maintain accurate and up-to-date records.

In summary, Configuration Items are the fundamental building blocks of IT services. Effectively tracking and managing CIs throughout their lifecycle is essential for ensuring service availability, supporting change management, facilitating incident and problem management, optimizing resource utilization, and ensuring compliance.

Change

In the context of ITIL, a **change** is defined as the addition, modification, or removal of anything that could have a direct or indirect effect on services. This could involve changes to hardware, software, documentation, processes, or even roles and responsibilities within an organization.

Changes are an inevitable part of IT service management. They are necessary for adapting to evolving business needs, implementing new technologies, fixing problems, and improving service quality. However, changes also carry inherent risks. If not managed properly, they can lead to service disruptions, outages, security breaches, and other negative consequences.

Importance of Change Management:

Change management is a critical process that helps organizations manage the lifecycle of changes from inception to implementation. It involves assessing the potential impact of changes, planning and coordinating their implementation, and minimizing the associated risks.

Key benefits of effective change management include:

- **Minimizing Risk:** Change management helps identify and assess potential risks associated with changes, enabling organizations to take proactive measures to mitigate those risks and minimize the likelihood of negative impacts.
- **Ensuring Smooth and Effective Implementation:** By carefully planning and coordinating changes, organizations can ensure that they are implemented smoothly and effectively, with minimal disruption to services.
- **Maintaining Service Stability:** Change management helps maintain the stability and reliability of IT services by ensuring that changes are thoroughly tested and validated before being deployed to the live environment.
- **Improving Communication and Collaboration:** Change management promotes communication and collaboration between different teams and stakeholders involved in the change process, ensuring that everyone is informed and aligned.
- **Enhancing Efficiency and Productivity:** By streamlining the change process and minimizing the risk of errors and rework, change management can improve the overall efficiency and productivity of IT operations.

Change management is a vital component of ITIL, enabling organizations to adapt to change while maintaining service quality and stability. By implementing robust change management processes, organizations can effectively manage the risks associated with change and ensure that changes are implemented in a controlled and coordinated manner. This ultimately leads to improved service delivery, increased customer satisfaction, and enhanced business performance.

As we've seen, change management is crucial for minimizing risks and ensuring that changes to IT services are implemented smoothly and effectively.

Event

In the context of ITIL, an **event** is defined as any detectable or discernible change of state that has significance for the management of a service or other configuration item (CI). Events can be generated by various sources, including hardware, software, networks, environmental sensors, security systems, or even user actions.

Examples of Events:

- A server's CPU utilization exceeding a predefined threshold.
- A network switch going offline.
- A user logging into a system.
- A security system detecting a potential intrusion.
- A scheduled backup completing successfully.

Events vs. Incidents:

While all incidents are events, not all events are incidents. The key difference lies in their impact on services.

- **Event:** An event is a neutral occurrence that may or may not have an impact on service quality or availability. It is simply a change of state that has been detected and recorded.
- **Incident:** An incident is an unplanned interruption to a service or reduction in the quality of a service. It is an event that negatively affects the operation of a service and requires action to be taken.

Why Events Matter:

Although not all events are incidents, they are still important for service management. By monitoring and analyzing events, organizations can:

- **Detect Potential Issues Proactively:** Events can serve as early warning signs of potential problems, allowing IT teams to take corrective action before an incident occurs. For example, a sudden increase in disk usage on a server could indicate a potential storage issue that needs to be addressed.
- **Gain Insights into Service Performance:** Analyzing event patterns can provide valuable insights into service performance, utilization, and trends. This information can be used to optimize service delivery, identify areas for improvement, and make informed decisions about resource allocation.
- **Improve Security:** Monitoring security events can help detect and respond to potential threats, such as unauthorized access attempts or malware infections.

In Summary:

Events are a valuable source of information for service management. By effectively monitoring, analyzing, and responding to events, organizations can proactively identify and address potential problems, gain insights into service performance, and improve the overall quality and reliability of their IT services.

Events provide essential data for managing IT services. By understanding the types and significance of events, organizations can utilize this information to improve service delivery, enhance security, and ensure optimal performance.

Incident

An **incident** is a disruption or degradation of the quality of an IT service. It is an unplanned event that negatively impacts the operation of a service and requires immediate attention to restore normal functionality.

Examples of Incidents:

- A server crash causing a website to become unavailable.
- A network outage preventing employees from accessing email.
- A software bug causing an application to malfunction.
- A security breach exposing sensitive data.

Importance of Incident Management:

Incident management is a critical process within ITIL that focuses on the swift detection, logging, categorization, prioritization, diagnosis, resolution, and closure of incidents. It aims to restore normal service operation as quickly as possible and minimize the impact on business operations.

Effective incident management is crucial for several reasons:

- **Minimizing Business Impact:** Incidents can cause significant disruptions to business operations, leading to lost productivity, revenue loss, and reputational damage. Prompt resolution of incidents helps minimize these negative impacts.
- **Ensuring Customer Satisfaction:** Quick and efficient resolution of incidents demonstrates a commitment to customer service and helps maintain customer satisfaction and loyalty.
- **Improving Service Quality:** Incident management provides valuable insights into the root causes of service disruptions, allowing organizations to identify and address underlying problems to prevent future incidents.
- **Optimizing Resource Utilization:** By streamlining the incident resolution process and prioritizing critical incidents, organizations can ensure that resources are used effectively and efficiently.

Key Activities in Incident Management:

1. **Incident Identification and Logging:** Incidents are detected through various channels, such as user reports, monitoring tools, or automated alerts. They are then logged into an incident management system, which captures relevant details such as the nature of the incident, its impact, and the time it was reported.
2. **Incident Categorization and Prioritization:** Incidents are categorized based on their type and impact, and then prioritized based on their urgency and severity. This ensures that critical incidents receive immediate attention.
3. **Incident Diagnosis and Resolution:** IT support teams investigate incidents, diagnose the root cause, and implement appropriate solutions to restore service.
4. **Incident Closure and Communication:** Once the incident is resolved, it is closed in the incident management system. Customers and stakeholders are notified about the resolution and any preventive measures taken to avoid similar incidents in the future.

By following these steps and continuously improving their incident management processes, organizations can effectively manage incidents, minimize their impact, and ensure the smooth delivery of IT services.

Problem

A **problem** in ITIL is defined as the underlying cause, or potential cause, of one or more incidents. It is a condition or situation that, if left unaddressed, could lead to recurring or multiple incidents. Problems are often more complex and difficult to diagnose than incidents, as they may not be immediately apparent when an incident occurs.

Examples of Problems:

- A faulty network configuration causing intermittent connectivity issues.
- A bug in a software application causing frequent crashes.
- A hardware failure leading to multiple system outages.
- A lack of user training leading to repeated user errors and support requests.

Role of Problem Management:

Problem management is a proactive ITIL process that focuses on identifying and addressing the root causes of incidents to prevent them from recurring. It involves a systematic approach to investigating and analyzing incidents, identifying trends and patterns, and implementing corrective actions to eliminate or minimize the underlying problems.

Key activities in problem management include:

1. **Problem Detection and Logging:** Identifying potential problems based on incident data, error logs, user feedback, or other sources. Problems are then logged into a problem management system, capturing relevant details such as the symptoms, impact, and potential causes.
2. **Problem Categorization and Prioritization:** Problems are categorized based on their type and impact, and then prioritized based on their potential to disrupt services or cause harm to the organization.
3. **Problem Investigation and Diagnosis:** IT teams investigate problems, analyze data, and conduct root cause analysis to determine the underlying causes of incidents. This may involve reviewing logs, interviewing users, and testing systems.
4. **Problem Resolution and Closure:** Once the root cause is identified, corrective actions are taken to address the problem and prevent future incidents. This may involve fixing bugs, applying patches, updating configurations, or providing additional training. The problem is then closed in the problem management system.

Benefits of Problem Management:

- **Reduced Incident Volume:** By addressing the root causes of incidents, problem management can significantly reduce the number of incidents that occur, leading to improved service stability and availability.
- **Improved Service Quality:** By preventing recurring incidents and minimizing their impact, problem management can enhance the overall quality and reliability of IT services.
- **Increased Efficiency:** Problem management can help streamline IT operations by eliminating the need to repeatedly address the same issues.
- **Cost Savings:** By preventing incidents and reducing downtime, problem management can lead to significant cost savings for organizations.

In summary, problem management is a proactive and systematic approach to identifying and addressing the root causes of incidents. By focusing on problem prevention and resolution, organizations can improve service quality, reduce costs, and enhance customer satisfaction.

Known Error

A **known error** in ITIL refers to a problem that has been analyzed and understood, but for which a full resolution or permanent fix is not yet available or implemented. In other words, it's a problem whose root cause has been identified, but the solution is either not immediately feasible, too costly, or requires extensive testing and validation before being implemented.

Documentation and Tracking:

Known errors are typically documented in a Known Error Database (KEDB). This database contains information about the problem, its symptoms, potential workarounds, and the status of the permanent fix. The KEDB serves as a valuable resource for IT support teams, helping them quickly identify and diagnose similar incidents and apply known workarounds.

Workarounds:

In the absence of a permanent fix, workarounds are often implemented to mitigate the impact of known errors. A workaround is a temporary solution or procedure that bypasses or minimizes the effect of the problem. Workarounds can be simple or complex, depending on the nature of the problem and the available resources.

Examples of Workarounds:

- Restarting a service or application to temporarily resolve a malfunction.
- Modifying a configuration setting to avoid triggering a bug.
- Using an alternative software tool or feature to achieve the desired outcome.
- Providing manual workarounds to users until a permanent fix is available.

Importance of Known Error Management:

Managing known errors is an important part of problem management. By documenting and tracking known errors, organizations can:

- **Reduce Incident Resolution Time:** When a known error is identified, IT support teams can quickly apply a workaround, reducing the time and effort required to resolve incidents.
- **Improve Customer Satisfaction:** By providing workarounds, organizations can minimize the impact of known errors on users and maintain service quality.
- **Prioritize Problem Resolution:** The KEDB helps prioritize problem-solving efforts, ensuring that resources are allocated to address the most impactful known errors first.
- **Facilitate Knowledge Sharing:** The KEDB serves as a central repository of knowledge about known errors, allowing IT teams to share information and learn from each other's experiences.

While workarounds provide temporary relief, it's important to remember that they are not a substitute for a permanent fix. Organizations should strive to develop and implement permanent solutions as soon as possible to eliminate the underlying problems and prevent recurring incidents.

Value

In the context of ITIL 4, **value** is defined as the perceived benefits, usefulness, and importance of something. It's a concept that is central to service management, as the ultimate goal of any service is to create value for its customers and stakeholders.

Subjectivity of Value:

It's important to note that value is not a fixed or objective measure. It is subjective and can vary greatly depending on the individual or organization perceiving it. What one customer considers valuable, another may not. This is because value is based on individual needs, preferences, and priorities.

For example, a customer may value a service based on its:

- **Functionality:** Does the service provide the features and capabilities that the customer needs?
- **Reliability:** Does the service perform consistently and reliably over time?
- **Usability:** Is the service easy to use and understand?
- **Cost:** Is the service affordable and does it provide good value for money?
- **Responsiveness:** Does the service provider respond quickly and effectively to requests and issues?

Importance of Understanding Customer Value Perceptions:

Understanding customer value perceptions is crucial for successful service design and delivery. By understanding what customers value, organizations can:

- **Design Services that Meet Customer Needs:** Services can be designed with features and benefits that align with customer expectations and deliver the value they seek.
- **Set Appropriate Pricing:** Pricing can be structured in a way that reflects the perceived value of the service to the customer.

- **Manage Customer Expectations:** Clear communication about service offerings and service level agreements can help manage customer expectations and ensure satisfaction.
- **Continuously Improve Services:** By collecting and analyzing customer feedback, organizations can identify areas for improvement and enhance the value they deliver over time.

Examples:

- A cloud storage service might be valuable to one customer because of its large storage capacity, while another customer might value its collaboration features more.
- A technical support service might be valuable to one customer because of its fast response times, while another customer might value its knowledgeable and friendly staff more.

By recognizing that value is subjective and varies from customer to customer, service providers can tailor their offerings and communication to better meet individual needs and preferences. This customer-centric approach is key to building strong relationships, increasing customer satisfaction, and ultimately driving business success.

Outcome

In ITIL 4, an **outcome** is defined as a result for a stakeholder enabled by one or more outputs. Outcomes are the ultimate goals that customers and stakeholders seek to achieve by utilizing a service. They represent the change in state or condition that the service facilitates.

Outputs vs. Outcomes:

While related, outputs and outcomes are distinct concepts:

- **Outputs:** These are the tangible or intangible deliverables of a service. Outputs are what the service provider produces or provides to the customer.
- **Outcomes:** These are the results or changes experienced by the customer or stakeholder as a consequence of using the service. Outcomes are the reason why customers engage with the service in the first place.

Examples:

- **Service:** Online training course
    - **Output:** Course materials, videos, quizzes, completion certificate.
    - **Outcome:** New knowledge and skills acquired by the student, improved job performance, career advancement.
- **Service:** Cloud storage service
    - **Output:** Secure storage space, file sharing capabilities, backup and recovery features.
    - **Outcome:** Protection of valuable data, improved collaboration among team members, peace of mind knowing data is safe.
- **Service:** IT help desk support
    - **Output:** Resolved incidents, answered queries, provided information.
    - **Outcome:** Reduced downtime, increased productivity, minimized frustration for users.

Importance of Focusing on Outcomes:

While outputs are important for service delivery, focusing solely on them can lead to a narrow, provider-centric view. Organizations that prioritize outcomes adopt a customer-centric approach, understanding that the ultimate goal is to help customers achieve their desired results.

Focusing on outcomes has several benefits:

- **Enhanced Customer Satisfaction:** When services are designed and delivered with a clear focus on outcomes, they are more likely to meet customer expectations and lead to higher satisfaction levels.
- **Improved Service Value:** By understanding and aligning services with customer outcomes, organizations can ensure that their services deliver real value to customers and stakeholders.
- **Increased Business Relevance:** Focusing on outcomes helps ensure that IT services are aligned with the overall business goals and objectives of the organization.
- **Greater Innovation:** By understanding customer outcomes, organizations can identify new opportunities for innovation and develop services that deliver greater value.

In Summary:

Outcomes are the desired results that customers seek to achieve through the use of a service. While outputs are the deliverables of the service, outcomes are the ultimate value that customers receive. By prioritizing outcomes, organizations can ensure that their services are not only efficient and effective but also meaningful and impactful for their customers.

Cost

In the context of ITIL and service management, **cost** refers to the amount of money spent on a particular activity, resource, or service. Understanding and managing costs is crucial for ensuring the financial viability and sustainability of IT services.

Types of Costs Associated with IT Services:

1. **Direct Costs:** These are costs that can be directly attributed to the delivery of a specific service. They are often easily measurable and traceable.
   - **Examples:**
     - Hardware costs (servers, storage, network devices)
     - Software licenses
     - Salaries of IT staff directly involved in service delivery
     - Training and certification expenses
     - Travel and accommodation costs for on-site support
2. **Indirect Costs:** These are costs that are not directly tied to a specific service but are necessary for the overall operation of IT services. They can be more difficult to measure and allocate.
   - **Examples:**
     - Rent and utilities for IT facilities
     - General IT administration and management expenses
     - Depreciation of IT assets
     - Shared service costs (e.g., HR, finance)
     - Security and compliance costs
3. **Opportunity Costs:** These are the potential benefits or value that an organization foregoes by choosing one course of action over another. In the context of IT services, opportunity costs might arise from decisions like:
   - **Choosing one technology over another:** The chosen technology might be cheaper upfront, but it could lead to higher maintenance costs or missed opportunities for innovation in the long run.
   - **Investing in one service improvement project over another:** The chosen project might deliver immediate benefits, but it could delay the implementation of a more strategic initiative with greater long-term value.

Importance of Cost Management in ITIL:

Effective cost management is a key aspect of ITIL. It involves:

- **Cost Identification and Allocation:** Accurately identifying and allocating costs to specific services or activities.
- **Cost Budgeting and Forecasting:** Developing budgets and forecasts for IT services to ensure that spending is aligned with organizational goals and available resources.
- **Cost Optimization:** Continuously seeking ways to reduce costs without compromising service quality or performance. This can involve streamlining processes, automating tasks, negotiating better contracts with suppliers, and optimizing resource utilization.
- **Cost Reporting and Transparency:** Providing regular reports on IT service costs to stakeholders, ensuring transparency and accountability.

By effectively managing costs, organizations can ensure the financial sustainability of their IT services, optimize resource utilization, and maximize the value delivered to customers and stakeholders.

Risk

In the context of ITIL, **risk** is defined as a possible event that could cause harm or loss, or make it more difficult to achieve objectives. Risks can be associated with any aspect of service management, from service design and delivery to operations and support.

Types of Risks:

Risks can be categorized in various ways:

- **Technical Risks:** These relate to the technology used to deliver services, such as hardware failures, software bugs, security vulnerabilities, or data breaches.
- **Operational Risks:** These relate to the processes and procedures used to manage services, such as human error, lack of documentation, or inadequate training.
- **Financial Risks:** These relate to the financial aspects of service delivery, such as cost overruns, budget cuts, or unexpected expenses.
- **External Risks:** These arise from factors outside the organization's control, such as natural disasters, regulatory changes, or economic downturns.
- **Reputational Risks:** These relate to the potential damage to an organization's reputation due to service disruptions, security breaches, or negative publicity.

Risk Management in ITIL:

Risk management is a critical practice within ITIL that involves identifying, assessing, and mitigating risks. It is an ongoing process that should be integrated into all aspects of service management.

The risk management process typically involves the following steps:

1. **Risk Identification:** This involves identifying potential risks that could affect the organization's ability to deliver services or achieve its objectives. This can be done through brainstorming sessions, risk assessments, or analyzing historical data.
2. **Risk Assessment:** Once risks have been identified, they need to be assessed in terms of their probability of occurrence and potential impact. This helps prioritize risks and allocate resources to address the most significant ones.
3. **Risk Mitigation:** This involves developing and implementing strategies to reduce the probability or impact of risks. Risk mitigation strategies can include:
   - **Risk Avoidance:** Eliminating the risk altogether by avoiding the activity or situation that creates the risk.
   - **Risk Reduction:** Taking steps to reduce the probability or impact of the risk, such as implementing security controls or backup procedures.
   - **Risk Transfer:** Transferring the risk to a third party, such as through insurance or outsourcing.

     ○ **Risk Acceptance:** Accepting the risk if the potential impact is low or the cost of mitigation is too high.
4. **Risk Monitoring and Review:** Risks need to be continuously monitored and reviewed to ensure that mitigation strategies are effective and to identify any new or emerging risks.

Importance of Risk Management:

Effective risk management is essential for ensuring the resilience and continuity of IT services. By proactively identifying and addressing risks, organizations can:

- **Minimize Service Disruptions:** By mitigating risks, organizations can reduce the likelihood of service disruptions, outages, and security breaches.
- **Protect Organizational Assets:** Risk management helps protect the organization's valuable assets, such as data, infrastructure, and reputation.
- **Improve Decision Making:** By providing a clear understanding of risks and their potential impact, risk management helps organizations make informed decisions about resource allocation and investment priorities.
- **Enhance Stakeholder Confidence:** Demonstrating a commitment to risk management can build confidence among customers, employees, and investors.

By incorporating risk management into their ITIL practices, organizations can build a more resilient and adaptable IT service management system, capable of responding effectively to unexpected events and minimizing their impact on business operations.

Utility

In ITIL 4, **utility** refers to the functionality offered by a product or service to meet a particular need. It's essentially the "fit for purpose" aspect of a service, determining whether it does what it's supposed to do and fulfills the intended objectives.

To have utility, a service must:

1. **Support the Performance of the Consumer:** This means the service enables the customer to achieve specific goals or tasks more effectively or efficiently. For example, a project management software tool that helps teams collaborate and track progress supports their performance in completing projects.
2. **Remove Constraints from the Consumer:** The service eliminates obstacles or limitations that hinder the customer's ability to perform certain activities. For instance, a cloud storage service removes the constraint of limited local storage space, allowing users to store and access files from anywhere.

In many cases, a service does both – it supports performance and removes constraints. A good example is a CRM (Customer Relationship Management) system, which not only enables sales teams to manage customer interactions more efficiently but also removes the constraint of manual data entry and tracking.

Key Considerations:

When assessing the utility of a service, consider the following:

- **Functional Requirements:** Does the service provide the necessary features and capabilities to meet the customer's needs?
- **Usability:** Is the service user-friendly and easy to learn?
- **Reliability:** Does the service perform consistently and reliably?
- **Performance:** Does the service meet performance expectations in terms of speed, accuracy, and responsiveness?
- **Compatibility:** Is the service compatible with the customer's existing systems and infrastructure?

Utility and Value:

Utility is a crucial component of value, but it's not the only factor. A service can be highly functional and meet all the customer's needs, yet still fail to deliver value if it's too expensive, difficult to use, or unreliable. Therefore, it's important to consider utility alongside other factors like warranty (fitness for use), cost, and risk when assessing the overall value proposition of a service.

Warranty

In the realm of ITIL, warranty refers to the assurance that a product or service will meet agreed-upon requirements. It focuses on how the service performs and is used to determine whether a service is "fit for use." This concept ensures that the service not only does what it's supposed to do (utility) but also does it in a way that meets the customer's expectations regarding reliability, availability, security, and other performance factors.

Warranty in Service Level Agreements (SLAs):

Warranties are typically defined and documented in Service Level Agreements (SLAs), which are formal agreements between service providers and customers. SLAs outline the expected level of service, including:

- **Availability:** The percentage of time the service is expected to be available for use.
- **Capacity:** The maximum amount of work or demand the service can handle.
- **Continuity:** The ability of the service to continue operating during and after disruptions or disasters.
- **Security:** The measures in place to protect the service and its data from unauthorized access, use, disclosure, disruption, modification, or destruction.
- **Performance:** The speed, accuracy, and responsiveness of the service.

SLAs often include specific metrics and targets for each of these areas, along with penalties or remedies if the service provider fails to meet the agreed-upon levels.

Importance of Warranty:

Warranty is a critical aspect of service management because it directly impacts customer satisfaction and trust. When a service consistently meets or exceeds its warranty requirements, customers are more likely to be satisfied with the service and continue using it. On the other hand, if a service fails to meet its warranty obligations, it can lead to customer dissatisfaction, complaints, and even contract termination.

By clearly defining warranty requirements in SLAs and actively monitoring service performance against those requirements, service providers can:

- **Manage Customer Expectations:** Set clear expectations with customers about the level of service they can expect.
- **Ensure Accountability:** Hold themselves accountable for delivering on their promises and meeting agreed-upon service levels.
- **Build Trust:** Demonstrate a commitment to providing high-quality, reliable services that meet customer needs.
- **Drive Continual Improvement:** Identify areas where service performance can be improved and take proactive measures to enhance service quality.

In summary, warranty is the assurance that a service will meet agreed-upon requirements, typically defined in SLAs. It focuses on how the service performs and is essential for building trust, managing expectations, and ensuring customer satisfaction. By prioritizing warranty, service providers can deliver services that are not only fit for purpose (utility) but also fit for use, providing value to customers and achieving business objectives.

Chapter Summary

In this chapter, we delved into the key concepts and terminology that form the foundation of ITIL 4 service management. Understanding these concepts is essential for effectively navigating the ITIL framework and applying it to real-world scenarios. Here's a recap of the key points covered:

- **Service:** We defined a service as a means of delivering value to customers by facilitating outcomes without the customer having to manage specific costs and risks. We highlighted its key characteristics (intangible, heterogeneous, inseparable, perishable) and differentiated it from a product.
- **Service Offering:** You learned that a service offering is a formal description of one or more services designed to meet the needs of a target consumer group. We discussed the structure of a service offering, including the service description, SLA, pricing, delivery options, and terms and conditions.
- **Service Relationship Management:** We explored the activities involved in establishing and nurturing relationships between service providers and consumers. You learned that SRM focuses on understanding customer needs, managing expectations, and ensuring customer satisfaction.
- **Configuration Item (CI):** We defined a CI as any component that needs to be managed to deliver an IT service and provided examples such as hardware, software, documentation, and processes. You learned the importance of tracking and managing CIs throughout their lifecycle.
- **Change, Event, Incident, Problem, and Known Error:** We defined these key terms and explained their significance in IT service management. You learned how they are interconnected and how effectively managing them contributes to service stability and quality.
- **Value, Outcome, Cost, and Risk:** We discussed these important concepts that underpin ITIL 4. You learned that value is the perceived benefits of something, outcomes are the results achieved through using a service, cost is the amount spent on an activity or resource, and risk is a potential event that could cause harm or loss.
- **Utility and Warranty:** You learned that utility is the functionality of a service to meet a particular need ("fit for purpose"), while warranty assures that the service will meet agreed-upon requirements ("fit for use").

With a solid understanding of these key concepts and terminology, you are now equipped to explore the next sections of the book, which will delve into the four dimensions of service management, the guiding principles of ITIL 4, and the ITIL Service Value System. These sections will provide you with a deeper understanding of how ITIL 4 can be applied to effectively manage and improve IT services in your organization.

Section B:
Four Dimensions of Service Management

Organizations and People

Outline

- The Importance of Organizations and People in Service Management
- Organizational Culture and Structure
- Roles and Responsibilities
- Skills and Competencies
- Communication and Collaboration
- Leadership and Management
- Motivation and Empowerment
- Workforce and Talent Management
- Chapter Summary

The Importance of Organizations and People in Service Management

In the world of IT service management (ITSM), it's easy to get caught up in the technical complexities of hardware, software, and processes. However, ITIL 4 emphasizes that organizations and people are the true driving force behind successful service delivery.

People: The Heart of Service Management

People are the ones who design, develop, deliver, and improve IT services. They are the ones who interact with customers, solve problems, and ensure that services meet the needs of the business. Without skilled, motivated, and engaged people, even the most sophisticated technology and processes will fail to deliver the desired outcomes.

The human element is particularly important in the context of ITIL 4, which emphasizes collaboration, value co-creation, and adaptability. These principles rely on the ability of individuals and teams to work together effectively, share knowledge, and make decisions that benefit both the customer and the organization.

Creating a Positive and Supportive Work Environment

To maximize the potential of their people, organizations need to create a positive and supportive work environment that fosters collaboration, innovation, and customer focus. This involves:

- **Clear Roles and Responsibilities:** Defining clear roles and responsibilities for each individual and team helps to ensure accountability, minimize duplication of effort, and promote efficient collaboration.
- **Open Communication:** Encouraging open communication and feedback channels allows employees to share ideas, raise concerns, and collaborate effectively.
- **Empowerment:** Empowering employees to make decisions and take ownership of their work fosters a sense of responsibility and encourages innovation.

- **Recognition and Rewards:** Recognizing and rewarding good performance motivates employees and reinforces desired behaviors.
- **Continuous Learning and Development:** Providing opportunities for training and development helps employees stay up-to-date with the latest technologies and best practices, enhancing their skills and knowledge.

The Role of Organizational Culture and Structure

Organizational culture and structure play a significant role in shaping the behavior and performance of individuals and teams. A positive culture that values collaboration, innovation, and customer focus can significantly enhance service management capabilities.

Similarly, the organizational structure can either facilitate or hinder effective service management. A flexible and adaptable structure that encourages cross-functional collaboration and empowers teams to make decisions can be a key enabler of service excellence.

In Summary:

Organizations and people are the most critical components of the ITIL 4 Service Value System. By investing in their people, fostering a positive work environment, and creating a culture of collaboration and innovation, organizations can unlock the full potential of their IT service management capabilities and deliver exceptional value to their customers.

Organizational Culture and Structure

The way an organization is structured and the culture it fosters significantly impact its ability to deliver effective IT services. Let's delve into the relationship between organizational culture, structure, and service management.

Impact of Organizational Culture on Service Management

Organizational culture encompasses the shared values, beliefs, and behaviors that shape how employees interact with each other and with customers. A culture that prioritizes customer centricity, continuous improvement, and collaboration can create a fertile ground for successful service management.

- **Customer Centricity:** A customer-centric culture places the needs and expectations of customers at the forefront of all activities. It encourages employees to empathize with customers, actively seek their feedback, and go the extra mile to ensure their satisfaction. This focus on customer value is essential for designing and delivering services that meet and exceed customer expectations.
- **Continuous Improvement:** A culture of continuous improvement fosters a mindset of learning, experimentation, and adaptation. It encourages employees to identify opportunities for improvement, challenge the status quo, and embrace change. This mindset is crucial for staying ahead of the curve in the fast-paced world of IT and ensuring that services remain relevant and valuable.
- **Collaboration:** Collaboration is key to breaking down silos, promoting knowledge sharing, and fostering innovation. A collaborative culture encourages employees to work together across teams and departments, leveraging their diverse skills and perspectives to solve problems and deliver better services.

Different Organizational Structures and Their Implications

The way an organization is structured can either facilitate or hinder effective service management. Different organizational structures have varying implications for communication, decision-making, and collaboration, all of which are crucial for IT service delivery.

- **Hierarchical Structure:** This traditional structure is characterized by clear lines of authority and control. While it can provide stability and order, it may also lead to slow decision-making and hinder collaboration across departments.
- **Flat Structure:** This structure minimizes levels of management, empowering employees with more autonomy and decision-making authority. It can foster faster decision-making and greater collaboration, but it may also create challenges in terms of coordination and control.
- **Matrix Structure:** This structure combines functional and project-based teams, allowing for greater flexibility and resource sharing. However, it can also lead to conflicting priorities and challenges in managing dual reporting lines.

Benefits of a Flexible and Adaptable Organizational Structure:

In today's rapidly changing business environment, a flexible and adaptable organizational structure is essential for success. ITIL 4 emphasizes the need for organizations to be agile and responsive to changing customer needs and market demands.

A flexible structure allows organizations to:

- **Respond quickly to change:** Adapt to new technologies, market trends, and customer expectations.
- **Empower employees:** Encourage innovation and initiative by giving employees greater autonomy and decision-making authority.
- **Foster collaboration:** Break down silos and promote cross-functional collaboration to solve problems and deliver better services.
- **Optimize resource utilization:** Deploy resources effectively to meet changing business priorities.

By fostering a customer-centric culture and adopting a flexible and adaptable organizational structure, organizations can create an environment where IT service management thrives, ultimately leading to improved service quality, enhanced customer satisfaction, and greater business value.

Roles and Responsibilities

In the ITIL 4 framework, roles are not rigidly defined as in previous versions. Instead, the emphasis is on flexibility and adaptability, allowing organizations to tailor roles to their specific needs and context. However, some common roles are typically involved in IT service management, each with distinct responsibilities:

1. **Service Owner:**
- **Responsibilities:**
    - Overall accountability for a specific service.
    - Defining and maintaining the service's vision, strategy, and objectives.
    - Ensuring the service meets customer and stakeholder needs and delivers value.
    - Managing the service's lifecycle, from design and transition to operation and improvement.
    - Representing the service to stakeholders and ensuring their interests are considered.
    - Monitoring and reporting on service performance, including service level agreements (SLAs).
- **Importance of Accountability:** The service owner is ultimately responsible for the success of the service. Clear accountability ensures that someone is in charge of driving the service forward and making decisions that align with organizational goals.
2. **Service Manager:**
- **Responsibilities:**
    - Operational management of a specific service.
    - Planning, coordinating, and overseeing service delivery and support activities.
    - Ensuring that the service meets its SLAs and performance targets.
    - Managing service resources, including people, technology, and processes.
    - Resolving service issues and escalations.

- ○ Reporting on service performance to the service owner and other stakeholders.
- **Importance of Defined Ownership:** The service manager is responsible for the day-to-day operation of the service. Having a clearly defined owner for each service ensures that there is someone responsible for its performance and continuous improvement.
3. **Process Owner:**
- **Responsibilities:**
  - ○ Responsible for a specific process within the Service Value System (SVS).
  - ○ Defining, documenting, and maintaining the process, ensuring that it aligns with the overall service management strategy.
  - ○ Monitoring and improving the process's performance.
  - ○ Ensuring that the process is being followed consistently and effectively.
  - ○ Providing training and guidance to process users.
- **Importance of Accountability:** The process owner is accountable for the performance and effectiveness of their process. This ensures that processes are continuously reviewed and improved, leading to better service delivery.
4. **Service Desk Agent:**
- **Responsibilities:**
  - ○ The first point of contact for users seeking help or reporting incidents.
  - ○ Logging and categorizing incidents and service requests.
  - ○ Providing initial support and troubleshooting.
  - ○ Escalating complex issues to higher-level support teams.
  - ○ Keeping users informed about the status of their incidents and requests.
- **Importance of Coordination:** The service desk is the central hub for communication between users and IT. Effective coordination between service desk agents and other IT teams is essential for ensuring timely and efficient resolution of incidents and requests.

Need for Role Clarity and Effective Coordination:

Clear roles and responsibilities are essential for avoiding confusion, duplication of effort, and conflicts. When everyone knows what is expected of them, they can focus on their specific tasks and contribute to the overall success of service management.

Effective coordination between different roles is also crucial. Service owners, service managers, process owners, and service desk agents need to work together seamlessly to ensure that services are designed, delivered, and supported effectively. This requires clear communication channels, regular meetings, and a shared understanding of goals and priorities.

Skills and Competencies

In the dynamic landscape of IT service management, a diverse set of skills and competencies is crucial for individuals and teams to thrive. These skills not only ensure the effective delivery of IT services but also contribute to a positive customer experience and overall business success.

Key Skills and Competencies for Successful Service Management:

1. **Technical Expertise:**
- Understanding of IT infrastructure, applications, and technologies.
- Proficiency in troubleshooting and problem-solving technical issues.
- Knowledge of ITIL practices and processes.
- Ability to apply technical knowledge to practical situations.
2. **Communication Skills:**
- Clear and effective written and verbal communication.
- Active listening skills and the ability to understand and empathize with others.
- Interpersonal skills to build rapport and trust with customers and stakeholders.

- Ability to communicate technical information to non-technical audiences.
- Proficiency in using various communication channels (e.g., email, phone, chat, video).

3. **Problem-Solving Abilities:**
- Analytical and critical thinking skills to diagnose and resolve problems.
- Ability to gather and analyze information from various sources.
- Creativity and resourcefulness in developing solutions.
- Decision-making skills to evaluate options and choose the best course of action.

4. **Customer Service Skills:**
- A customer-centric mindset and a focus on delivering value to customers.
- Patience, empathy, and professionalism in dealing with customer inquiries and complaints.
- Ability to manage customer expectations and resolve conflicts.
- Proactive approach to anticipating and addressing customer needs.

5. **Collaboration and Teamwork:**
- Ability to work effectively with others in a team environment.
- Interpersonal skills to build positive relationships and trust.
- Willingness to share knowledge and collaborate to achieve common goals.
- Flexibility and adaptability to work with diverse teams and personalities.

Strategies for Developing and Enhancing Skills:

Organizations can utilize various strategies to develop and enhance these skills within their workforce:

- **Training and Certification:** Provide formal training programs and encourage employees to obtain certifications in ITIL and other relevant areas.
- **Mentoring and Coaching:** Pair less experienced employees with more experienced mentors or coaches to facilitate knowledge transfer and skill development.
- **Job Rotation and Cross-Training:** Allow employees to experience different roles and functions within the organization to broaden their skills and perspectives.
- **Knowledge Sharing Platforms:** Create online forums, wikis, or knowledge bases where employees can share information, best practices, and lessons learned.
- **Regular Feedback and Performance Reviews:** Provide regular feedback to employees on their performance, highlighting areas for improvement and recognizing achievements.

Importance of Continuous Learning and Development:

The field of IT service management is constantly evolving, with new technologies, methodologies, and best practices emerging regularly. To remain competitive and effective, it's crucial for individuals and organizations to embrace continuous learning and development.

This involves staying up-to-date with the latest industry trends, attending conferences and workshops, reading relevant publications, and participating in online communities. By investing in continuous learning and development, organizations can ensure that their workforce remains skilled, adaptable, and equipped to deliver high-quality IT services in the ever-changing digital landscape.

Communication and Collaboration

In the realm of IT service management (ITSM), effective communication and collaboration are not merely desirable traits; they are essential ingredients for success. They serve as the lifeblood of the Service Value System (SVS), enabling smooth operations, informed decision-making, and a unified focus on delivering value to customers.

Importance of Effective Communication and Collaboration:

- **Within IT Teams:** Clear communication and collaboration within IT teams are crucial for coordinating activities, sharing knowledge, resolving issues efficiently, and maintaining a cohesive team environment. When teams communicate openly and effectively, they can identify potential problems early on, work together to find solutions, and avoid misunderstandings that can lead to delays or errors.

- **Across Departments and Stakeholders:** IT service management is not an isolated function; it involves interactions with various departments and stakeholders, such as business units, customers, suppliers, and partners. Effective communication and collaboration across these boundaries ensure that IT services align with business goals, meet customer expectations, and leverage the expertise of external partners.

Tools and Techniques for Fostering Communication and Collaboration:

A variety of tools and techniques can be employed to foster communication and collaboration in service management:

- **Regular Meetings:** Schedule regular team meetings, cross-functional meetings, and stakeholder meetings to discuss progress, challenges, and opportunities.
- **Status Reports:** Provide regular updates on service performance, project status, and key initiatives to keep everyone informed and aligned.
- **Knowledge Sharing Platforms:** Create wikis, knowledge bases, or online forums where employees can share information, best practices, and lessons learned.
- **Feedback Mechanisms:** Establish formal and informal feedback channels to gather input from customers, stakeholders, and employees. This can be done through surveys, interviews, focus groups, or suggestion boxes.
- **Visual Management Tools:** Use visual tools like Kanban boards or dashboards to track progress, visualize workflows, and identify bottlenecks.
- **Communication Technologies:** Leverage modern communication technologies like instant messaging, video conferencing, and collaboration platforms to facilitate real-time communication and collaboration across teams and locations.

The Role of Communication in Managing Customer Expectations, Building Trust, and Resolving Conflicts:

Communication plays a critical role in managing customer expectations. Clear, timely, and transparent communication helps set realistic expectations, build trust, and ensure that customers feel heard and valued. When customers understand what to expect from a service and are kept informed about its performance, they are more likely to be satisfied, even if issues arise.

Open communication is also essential for resolving conflicts that may arise between IT and other departments, or between IT and customers. By fostering a culture of open dialogue and constructive feedback, organizations can address issues promptly, prevent misunderstandings, and maintain positive working relationships.

In Conclusion:

Effective communication and collaboration are the linchpins of successful IT service management. They enable organizations to break down silos, align with business goals, and deliver services that meet and exceed customer expectations. By investing in communication and collaboration tools and fostering a culture of openness and transparency, organizations can build stronger relationships with customers, improve service quality, and achieve sustainable success.

Leadership and Management

Effective leadership and management are vital catalysts for success in any organization, and IT service management is no exception. Leaders and managers play distinct but complementary roles in shaping the direction, culture, and performance of IT teams.

The Importance of Strong Leadership:

Strong leadership is essential for setting the vision and direction for IT service management. Leaders must articulate a compelling vision that aligns with the organization's strategic goals and inspires employees to deliver excellent service. This vision should encompass:

- **Customer Centricity:** Leaders must instill a customer-centric mindset throughout the organization, emphasizing the importance of understanding and meeting customer needs.
- **Value Creation:** Leaders should focus on creating value through IT services, aligning them with business objectives and measuring their impact on overall performance.
- **Continuous Improvement:** Leaders need to foster a culture of continuous improvement, encouraging employees to challenge the status quo, experiment with new approaches, and learn from mistakes.
- **Collaboration:** Leaders should promote collaboration and communication across teams and departments, breaking down silos and fostering a shared sense of purpose.

The Role of Managers:

While leaders set the vision, managers are responsible for translating that vision into action. They provide guidance, support, and resources to their teams, empowering them to deliver excellent service. Key responsibilities of managers include:

- **Setting Clear Goals and Expectations:** Managers define clear goals and expectations for their teams, ensuring alignment with the overall service management strategy.
- **Providing Resources and Support:** Managers ensure that their teams have the necessary resources, tools, and training to perform their roles effectively.
- **Fostering a Positive Work Environment:** Managers create a positive and collaborative work environment where employees feel valued, supported, and empowered to contribute their best work.
- **Monitoring and Evaluating Performance:** Managers regularly monitor and evaluate team and individual performance, providing feedback and coaching to help employees improve.
- **Resolving Conflicts and Addressing Issues:** Managers proactively address conflicts and issues within their teams, promoting a healthy and productive work environment.

Commitment to Continuous Improvement and Leading by Example:

Both leaders and managers must demonstrate a commitment to continuous improvement. This involves actively participating in improvement initiatives, seeking feedback from customers and employees, and leading by example. When leaders and managers model the behaviors they expect from their teams, it reinforces a culture of continuous improvement and sets a high standard for service excellence.

In Summary:

Leadership and management are two sides of the same coin in IT service management. Leaders set the vision and direction, while managers translate that vision into action. Both roles are essential for creating a high-performing service management organization that delivers value to customers, contributes to business success, and adapts to the ever-changing demands of the digital age.

Motivation and Empowerment

In the realm of IT service management, motivated and empowered employees are the key to unlocking a higher level of service excellence. When individuals feel valued, trusted, and capable, they are more likely to take ownership of their work, go above and beyond to meet customer needs, and proactively contribute ideas for improvement.

The Importance of Motivation and Empowerment:

- **Increased Engagement:** Motivated employees are more engaged in their work, leading to increased productivity, better problem-solving, and higher quality service delivery.
- **Ownership and Accountability:** Empowered employees take ownership of their responsibilities, proactively seek solutions to challenges, and hold themselves accountable for outcomes.
- **Innovation and Continuous Improvement:** A culture of empowerment encourages employees to share ideas, experiment with new approaches, and contribute to a continuous improvement cycle.
- **Customer Focus:** Motivated and empowered employees are more likely to prioritize customer needs, go the extra mile to resolve issues, and build strong relationships with customers.

Strategies for Motivating Employees:

There are many ways to motivate employees in IT service management. Here are a few key strategies:

1. **Recognition and Rewards:** Recognize and reward employees for their contributions and achievements. This could include verbal praise, written acknowledgments, bonuses, promotions, or other forms of recognition.
2. **Growth and Development Opportunities:** Provide opportunities for employees to learn new skills, take on challenging assignments, and advance their careers. This could involve offering training programs, mentoring, or opportunities to work on high-profile projects.
3. **Clear Goals and Expectations:** Clearly define goals and expectations for employees, providing them with a sense of direction and purpose. This helps them understand how their work contributes to the overall success of the organization and motivates them to achieve their best.
4. **Feedback and Communication:** Provide regular feedback on performance, both positive and constructive. Open communication channels create a safe space for employees to share ideas, concerns, and suggestions.
5. **Autonomy and Trust:** Give employees the freedom and flexibility to make decisions and solve problems within their areas of responsibility. Trusting employees to do their jobs fosters a sense of ownership and accountability.
6. **Positive Work Environment:** Create a positive and supportive work environment where employees feel valued, respected, and appreciated. This can include team-building activities, social events, and opportunities for fun and relaxation.

The Role of Empowerment in Fostering Innovation and Continuous Improvement:

Empowerment is a key driver of innovation and continuous improvement. When employees feel empowered to make decisions and take initiative, they are more likely to identify opportunities for improvement and come up with creative solutions.

Empowered employees are also more willing to experiment with new approaches, take risks, and learn from their mistakes. This experimentation and learning are essential for driving innovation and continuous improvement within the organization.

By fostering a culture of empowerment, organizations can tap into the creativity and ingenuity of their employees, leading to new and improved ways of delivering IT services, enhanced customer experiences, and greater business value.

Workforce and Talent Management

Workforce and Talent Management is a critical aspect of ITIL 4, recognizing that the people within an organization are its most valuable asset. In the context of service management, this involves strategically managing and developing the workforce to ensure the organization has the right people, with the right skills, in the right roles, to effectively support its business objectives.

Challenges in Attracting, Developing, and Retaining Talent:

The IT service management field faces several challenges in attracting, developing, and retaining talent:

1. **Skills Gap:** The rapid pace of technological change creates a constant need for new skills and competencies. Organizations struggle to find individuals with the right mix of technical, interpersonal, and business skills.
2. **Competition:** Demand for skilled IT professionals often outstrips supply, leading to fierce competition for talent. Companies must offer attractive compensation packages and career development opportunities to remain competitive.
3. **Changing Workforce Demographics:** The workforce is becoming increasingly diverse, with different generations having varying expectations and preferences. Organizations need to adapt their talent management strategies to cater to the needs of a multi-generational workforce.
4. **Burnout and Attrition:** The high-pressure nature of IT service management can lead to burnout and attrition. Organizations need to create a supportive and engaging work environment that fosters well-being and promotes long-term retention.

Strategies for Building a Strong and Diverse Workforce:

To overcome these challenges and build a strong and diverse workforce, organizations can implement the following strategies:

1. **Competitive Compensation and Benefits:** Offering competitive salaries, bonuses, and benefits packages is essential for attracting and retaining top talent. Consider offering additional perks like flexible work arrangements, tuition reimbursement, or professional development opportunities.
2. **Career Advancement Opportunities:** Providing clear career paths and opportunities for growth and development can help retain employees and motivate them to excel in their roles. Encourage employees to take on new challenges, learn new skills, and expand their responsibilities.
3. **Positive and Inclusive Work Environment:** Foster a positive and inclusive work culture where employees feel valued, respected, and supported. This can be achieved through open communication, recognition of achievements, team-building activities, and initiatives that promote diversity and inclusion.
4. **Continuous Learning and Development:** Invest in ongoing training and development programs to equip employees with the latest skills and knowledge. Offer opportunities for professional certifications, workshops, conferences, and online courses.
5. **Mentoring and Coaching:** Establish mentoring and coaching programs to provide guidance and support to less experienced employees. This can help accelerate their development and foster a sense of belonging within the organization.
6. **Recruitment and Onboarding:** Develop effective recruitment strategies to attract diverse talent with the right skills and experience. Implement comprehensive onboarding programs to help new hires integrate into the organization and become productive quickly.

Importance of Investing in Employee Development and Succession Planning:

Investing in employee development is not just a nice-to-have; it's a strategic imperative for ensuring the long-term sustainability of an organization's service management capabilities. By developing a skilled and adaptable workforce, organizations can:

- **Maintain Service Continuity:** Ensure that there are qualified individuals to take over key roles and responsibilities in case of turnover or unexpected events.
- **Enhance Service Quality:** Continuously improve the quality and efficiency of IT services through the application of new skills and knowledge.
- **Drive Innovation:** Foster a culture of innovation by encouraging employees to experiment with new ideas and approaches.
- **Adapt to Change:** Quickly adapt to new technologies, market trends, and customer demands.

Succession planning is also critical for identifying and developing future leaders within the organization. By having a clear plan in place, organizations can ensure a smooth transition of leadership and maintain continuity of service management operations.

Chapter Summary

In this chapter, we explored the first dimension of ITIL 4's Service Value System (SVS): Organizations and People. This dimension underscores the critical role that people and organizational dynamics play in successful service management.

Here's a summary of the key points covered:

- **The Importance of Organizations and People:** We emphasized that people are the driving force behind IT service management. They are the ones who design, develop, deliver, and improve services. A positive and supportive work environment is essential for their success.
- **Organizational Culture and Structure:** We discussed how organizational culture, with its shared values and beliefs, significantly impacts service management. A culture that prioritizes customer centricity, continuous improvement, and collaboration is crucial. We also explored different organizational structures and their implications, highlighting the benefits of a flexible and adaptable structure in today's dynamic business landscape.
- **Roles and Responsibilities:** We described common roles in service management, including service owners, service managers, process owners, and service desk agents. We emphasized the importance of clear accountability and defined areas of ownership for each role.
- **Skills and Competencies:** You learned about the key skills and competencies required for success in IT service management, such as technical expertise, communication skills, problem-solving abilities, customer service skills, and collaboration skills. We also discussed strategies for developing and enhancing these skills within the workforce.
- **Communication and Collaboration:** We highlighted the importance of effective communication and collaboration both within IT teams and across different departments and stakeholders. We explored tools and techniques to foster communication and collaboration, emphasizing their role in managing customer expectations, building trust, and resolving conflicts.
- **Leadership and Management:** We discussed the critical role of leadership in setting the vision for service management and establishing a customer-centric culture. We also outlined the role of managers in providing guidance, support, and resources to their teams.
- **Motivation and Empowerment:** You learned about the importance of motivating and empowering employees to take ownership of their work, contribute ideas, and take initiative to improve service delivery. We discussed strategies for motivating employees and the role of empowerment in fostering innovation.
- **Workforce and Talent Management:** We highlighted the challenges of attracting, developing, and retaining talent in the IT service management field. We explored strategies for building a strong and diverse workforce, emphasizing the importance of investing in employee development and succession planning.

By understanding and applying the principles discussed in this chapter, organizations can create a high-performing and motivated workforce that is capable of delivering excellent IT services and driving business value. As we move forward, we will delve into the other three dimensions of the ITIL 4 SVS, further expanding your knowledge of this comprehensive framework.

Information and Technology

Outline

- The Role of Information and Technology in Service Management
- Types of Information
- Information Management
- Technology in Service Management
- Emerging Technologies and Trends
- IT Infrastructure and Architecture
- Information and Technology Risk Management
- Security and Privacy
- Chapter Summary

The Role of Information and Technology in Service Management

Information and technology are the twin pillars that underpin modern service management. They are deeply interwoven into every aspect of the Service Value System (SVS), driving efficiency, enabling innovation, and shaping the customer experience.

Information and Technology as the Backbone of Modern Service Delivery:

In today's digital age, information and technology are the backbone of service delivery. They enable the creation, delivery, and support of services in ways that were unimaginable just a few decades ago.

- **Digital Channels:** Technology has opened up a plethora of digital channels for service delivery, such as websites, mobile apps, social media, and chatbots. These channels provide customers with convenient access to information, self-service options, and support, enhancing their overall experience.
- **Data-Driven Insights:** Information, in the form of data, provides valuable insights into customer behavior, service performance, and operational efficiency. Organizations can leverage this data to make informed decisions, personalize services, and continuously improve their offerings.
- **Automation:** Technology enables the automation of repetitive tasks, freeing up human resources for more complex and value-adding activities. Automation can streamline processes, reduce errors, and improve response times, leading to enhanced efficiency and cost savings.

Enabling Automation, Efficiency, and Customer Self-Service:

Information and technology play a crucial role in enabling automation, efficiency, and customer self-service. Automation tools can handle routine tasks like password resets, order processing, and data entry, allowing service agents to focus on more complex issues that require human intervention.

Self-service portals and knowledge bases empower customers to find answers to their questions, resolve simple issues, and access information on their own, reducing the need for direct interaction with service agents. This not only improves efficiency but also enhances the customer experience by providing greater convenience and control.

Use of Information for Decision-Making, Improvement, and Performance Tracking:

Information is a powerful tool for decision-making, improvement, and performance tracking. Organizations can leverage data analytics to gain insights into customer preferences, identify trends, and measure the effectiveness of their services. This information can be used to make data-driven decisions about service design, resource allocation, and improvement initiatives.

Performance metrics and key performance indicators (KPIs) provide a way to track the progress of service management initiatives and measure their impact on business outcomes. By regularly monitoring and analyzing performance data, organizations can identify areas for improvement and take corrective actions to ensure that services continue to meet customer expectations and business goals.

Balancing Technological Advancement with Usability and Security:

While information and technology offer immense opportunities for improving service management, it's important to balance technological advancement with usability and security.

- **Usability:** Technology should be user-friendly and intuitive, enabling customers and employees to interact with services easily and effectively. Complex or cumbersome systems can lead to frustration and dissatisfaction.
- **Security:** Protecting sensitive information and ensuring the security of IT systems is paramount. Organizations must implement robust security measures, such as access controls, encryption, and vulnerability management, to safeguard data and prevent cyberattacks.

By striking the right balance between technological advancement, usability, and security, organizations can harness the power of information and technology to deliver exceptional service experiences, drive efficiency, and achieve their business objectives.

Types of Information

Information is the lifeblood of IT service management. It comes in various forms, each serving a unique purpose in enabling effective decision-making, optimizing operations, and delivering value to customers. Let's explore the different types of information that play a crucial role in the ITIL 4 framework:

1. **Operational Data:**

Operational data is real-time information about the current status and performance of IT systems and services. It provides a snapshot of how services are functioning at any given moment, enabling proactive monitoring and rapid response to issues.

- **Examples:**
    - Server uptime and downtime
    - Network traffic and bandwidth utilization
    - Application response times
    - Error logs and alerts
    - Service desk call volumes and resolution times
- **How it's used in Service Management:**
    - Real-time monitoring of service health
    - Incident detection and prioritization
    - Problem diagnosis and root cause analysis
    - Performance analysis and optimization
    - Capacity planning and resource allocation

2. **Configuration Data:**

Configuration data provides detailed information about the components that make up IT systems (Configuration Items or CIs) and their relationships. This data forms the basis for understanding how systems and services are built and how they interact.

- **Examples:**
    - Hardware specifications (e.g., CPU, memory, storage)
    - Software versions and dependencies
    - Network topology and configurations

- ○ Relationships between CIs (e.g., which applications run on which servers)
  - **How it's used in Service Management:**
    - ○ Change management (assessing impact of changes)
    - ○ Incident management (identifying affected components)
    - ○ Problem management (root cause analysis)
    - ○ Configuration management (maintaining accurate records)
3. **Service Knowledge:**

Service knowledge encompasses all information related to how IT services are designed, delivered, and supported. It includes technical documentation, process flows, troubleshooting guides, and best practices.

- **Examples:**
  - ○ Service level agreements (SLAs)
  - ○ Operational level agreements (OLAs)
  - ○ Work instructions and procedures
  - ○ Knowledge articles and FAQs
  - ○ Training materials
- **How it's used in Service Management:**
  - ○ Service design and development
  - ○ Service transition and deployment
  - ○ Service operation and support
  - ○ Knowledge sharing and collaboration
  - ○ Training and onboarding of new staff
4. **Business Information:**

Business information refers to data about the organization's customers, markets, and operations. This information provides context for IT service management, ensuring that services are aligned with business goals and customer needs.

- **Examples:**
  - ○ Customer demographics and preferences
  - ○ Market trends and competitor analysis
  - ○ Financial data and performance metrics
  - ○ Strategic plans and objectives
- **How it's used in Service Management:**
  - ○ Service strategy development
  - ○ Service portfolio management
  - ○ Demand management
  - ○ Service level management
  - ○ Business relationship management

By effectively managing these different types of information, organizations can gain valuable insights, make informed decisions, and continuously improve their IT services. This information-driven approach is essential for staying competitive in today's fast-paced digital landscape.

Information Management

Information management (IM) is the process of collecting, storing, organizing, protecting, and retrieving information in a way that supports effective decision-making, service delivery, and continuous improvement. In the context of ITIL 4, it plays a critical role in ensuring that the right information is available to the right people at the right time.

Importance of Effective Information Management:

- **Informed Decision-Making:** Information management provides accurate, timely, and relevant data that enables IT and business leaders to make informed decisions about service design, delivery, and improvement.
- **Efficient Service Delivery:** Access to the right information allows service teams to diagnose and resolve issues quickly, fulfill requests promptly, and proactively manage service risks.
- **Continual Improvement:** Information management enables organizations to track performance, identify trends, and measure the effectiveness of improvement initiatives, facilitating data-driven decision-making.
- **Risk Mitigation:** Proper information management helps protect sensitive data, mitigate security risks, and ensure compliance with regulatory requirements.
- **Customer Satisfaction:** By ensuring accurate and timely information is available to customers, information management can enhance their experience and build trust.

Key Processes Involved in Information Management:

1. **Data Collection:** Gathering data from various sources, such as IT systems, sensors, logs, surveys, and customer feedback.
2. **Data Storage:** Storing data in a secure, organized, and accessible manner, using appropriate databases, repositories, or cloud storage solutions.
3. **Data Processing and Analysis:** Transforming raw data into meaningful information through cleaning, validation, aggregation, and analysis. This may involve using tools like spreadsheets, statistical software, or data visualization platforms.
4. **Reporting and Visualization:** Presenting information in a clear, concise, and easily understandable format, using reports, dashboards, or visualizations.

Role of Information Management in Ensuring Data Quality, Accuracy, and Accessibility:

Information management is responsible for ensuring that data is:

- **Accurate:** Data should be correct and free from errors or inconsistencies.
- **Complete:** Data should include all necessary information and not omit any relevant details.
- **Consistent:** Data should be consistent across different systems and sources.
- **Timely:** Data should be available when it is needed for decision-making or action.
- **Relevant:** Data should be pertinent to the specific needs of users and stakeholders.
- **Accessible:** Data should be easily accessible to authorized users through appropriate channels and interfaces.

By maintaining data quality, accuracy, and accessibility, information management ensures that the information used for decision-making and service delivery is reliable and trustworthy.

Need for Appropriate Security Controls:

Information security is a critical aspect of information management. Organizations must implement appropriate security controls to protect sensitive data from unauthorized access, use, disclosure, disruption, modification, or destruction. These controls may include:

- **Access Controls:** Limiting access to sensitive data to authorized personnel only.
- **Encryption:** Protecting data in transit and at rest using encryption algorithms.
- **Intrusion Detection and Prevention Systems:** Monitoring networks and systems for suspicious activity and taking preventive measures.
- **Data Loss Prevention (DLP) Solutions:** Preventing the unauthorized transmission of sensitive data outside the organization.
- **Security Awareness Training:** Educating employees about security risks and best practices to protect sensitive information.

By implementing robust security controls, organizations can safeguard their information assets, maintain customer trust, and comply with regulatory requirements.

In conclusion, information management is a crucial enabler of effective IT service management. It empowers organizations to leverage information and technology to deliver high-quality services, make informed decisions, and continuously improve their operations.

Technology in Service Management

Technology is the engine that powers modern service management. It provides the tools and platforms that enable organizations to streamline processes, automate tasks, gather data-driven insights, and deliver seamless customer experiences.

Various Technologies Used in Service Management:

1. **IT Service Management (ITSM) Tools:** These comprehensive software suites provide a centralized platform for managing various aspects of service delivery, such as incident management, problem management, change management, service request fulfillment, and knowledge management. Popular ITSM tools include ServiceNow, Jira Service Management, BMC Remedy, and Ivanti.
2. **Knowledge Management Systems (KMS):** KMS platforms enable organizations to capture, store, organize, and share knowledge related to IT services. They provide a central repository of information, such as troubleshooting guides, how-to articles, and FAQs, that can be accessed by both service agents and customers. Examples of KMS tools include Confluence, SharePoint, and Guru.
3. **Self-Service Portals:** These web-based platforms allow customers to access information, request services, report incidents, and track the status of their requests without needing to interact directly with a service agent. Self-service portals can significantly improve customer satisfaction by providing 24/7 access to support and empowering customers to resolve issues on their own.
4. **Automation Platforms:** Automation platforms leverage technologies like robotic process automation (RPA), artificial intelligence (AI), and machine learning (ML) to automate repetitive tasks, streamline workflows, and improve efficiency. They can be used to automate tasks like password resets, incident routing, and data entry, freeing up service agents to focus on more complex and value-adding activities.
5. **Chatbots and Virtual Assistants:** These AI-powered tools can interact with customers through natural language, providing instant answers to questions, guiding them through self-service processes, and escalating complex issues to human agents.
6. **Monitoring and Observability Tools:** These tools provide real-time visibility into the health and performance of IT systems and services. They can detect anomalies, predict potential problems, and alert IT teams to take corrective action before an incident occurs.

Benefits of Using Technology in Service Management:

- **Improved Efficiency:** Automation and streamlined workflows reduce manual effort, eliminate errors, and speed up service delivery.
- **Enhanced Customer Experience:** Self-service portals, chatbots, and virtual assistants provide customers with convenient access to information and support, improving their overall experience.
- **Data-Driven Insights:** Technology enables the collection and analysis of vast amounts of data, providing valuable insights into service performance, customer behavior, and operational efficiency.
- **Proactive Problem Management:** Monitoring and observability tools help identify and address potential issues before they escalate into major incidents.
- **Cost Savings:** Automation and process optimization can lead to significant cost savings by reducing the need for manual intervention and minimizing downtime.

Challenges of Selecting, Implementing, and Maintaining Technology Solutions:

- **Cost:** The initial investment in technology can be significant, and there are ongoing costs for maintenance, upgrades, and support.
- **Complexity:** Implementing new technologies can be complex and disruptive, requiring careful planning and change management.
- **Integration:** Integrating new technologies with existing systems and processes can be challenging, especially in legacy environments.
- **User Adoption:** Ensuring that users adopt and embrace new technologies can be a hurdle, requiring effective training and communication.
- **Security:** Protecting sensitive data and ensuring the security of technology solutions is a critical concern, requiring robust security measures and ongoing vigilance.

Despite these challenges, the benefits of using technology in service management are undeniable. By carefully selecting and implementing the right tools, organizations can transform their service delivery, improve efficiency, enhance customer experiences, and gain a competitive advantage in the digital age.

Emerging Technologies and Trends

The landscape of IT service management is continuously evolving, driven by rapid advancements in technology. Emerging technologies like artificial intelligence (AI), machine learning (ML), big data, and automation are transforming the way services are designed, delivered, and supported. Let's explore their impact and the opportunities they present:

Impact of Emerging Technologies on Service Management:

1. **Artificial Intelligence (AI) and Machine Learning (ML):**
- **Automation:** AI and ML algorithms can automate repetitive and time-consuming tasks, such as ticket routing, incident classification, and password resets. This frees up service agents to focus on more complex issues that require human expertise.
- **Predictive Analytics:** By analyzing vast amounts of data, AI and ML can identify patterns and predict potential problems before they occur. This enables proactive problem management and reduces the impact of service disruptions.
- **Virtual Agents and Chatbots:** AI-powered virtual agents and chatbots can provide instant support to customers, answer questions, guide them through self-service processes, and even resolve simple issues. This improves customer satisfaction and reduces the workload on service desks.
- **Natural Language Processing (NLP):** NLP technology allows computers to understand and interpret human language, enabling more natural and intuitive interactions with chatbots and virtual assistants.
2. **Big Data:**
- **Data-Driven Insights:** Big data analytics can uncover hidden patterns, correlations, and trends in service data. These insights can be used to optimize service delivery, identify areas for improvement, and personalize the customer experience.
- **Performance Optimization:** By analyzing performance data, organizations can identify bottlenecks, optimize resource utilization, and improve service levels.
- **Predictive Maintenance:** Big data can be used to predict equipment failures and schedule maintenance proactively, reducing downtime and improving service availability.
3. **Automation:**
- **Streamlined Processes:** Automation can streamline workflows, eliminate manual steps, and reduce the risk of human error.
- **Faster Response Times:** Automated processes can respond to incidents and requests much faster than human agents, improving service levels.
- **Cost Savings:** Automation can lead to significant cost savings by reducing the need for manual labor and improving operational efficiency.

Potential Risks and Challenges:

While emerging technologies offer immense potential for improving service management, there are also some risks and challenges that need to be addressed:

- **Data Security and Privacy:** The use of AI, ML, and big data involves collecting and processing large amounts of sensitive information. Organizations must implement robust security measures to protect this data from unauthorized access, use, or disclosure.
- **Algorithm Bias:** AI and ML algorithms can sometimes exhibit bias, leading to discriminatory outcomes or unfair treatment of certain groups. Organizations need to be aware of this risk and take steps to mitigate it.
- **Cost and Complexity:** Implementing new technologies can be costly and complex, requiring significant investment in hardware, software, and training.
- **Change Management:** Introducing new technologies can disrupt existing workflows and processes, requiring careful change management to ensure a smooth transition.
- **Job Displacement:** Automation may lead to the displacement of some jobs, requiring organizations to reskill and retrain their workforce.

By carefully considering these risks and challenges, organizations can harness the power of emerging technologies to transform their service management practices, improve efficiency, enhance customer experiences, and drive innovation.

IT Infrastructure and Architecture

IT Infrastructure and Architecture are fundamental to the successful delivery of IT services. They provide the foundation upon which services are built, operated, and supported. A well-designed and managed infrastructure ensures the availability, reliability, and performance of IT services, while a sound architecture aligns technology with business goals, ensuring scalability and flexibility.

Importance of a Well-Designed and Managed IT Infrastructure:

- **Service Availability and Reliability:** A robust IT infrastructure ensures that services are available to users when they need them. It includes redundant systems, backup power, and disaster recovery plans to minimize downtime and ensure service continuity.
- **Service Performance and Capacity:** A well-managed infrastructure ensures that services perform optimally and can handle the expected workload. This involves monitoring performance metrics, capacity planning, and proactively addressing bottlenecks to prevent performance degradation.
- **Security and Compliance:** IT infrastructure plays a critical role in protecting sensitive data and ensuring compliance with security regulations. This includes implementing firewalls, intrusion detection systems, encryption, and other security measures.
- **Cost Efficiency:** A well-designed infrastructure can help organizations optimize resource utilization and reduce costs. This includes consolidating servers, virtualizing resources, and adopting cloud computing technologies.

Key Components of IT Infrastructure:

- **Hardware:** Servers, storage devices, network equipment (routers, switches, firewalls), desktops, laptops, mobile devices, and other physical components.
- **Software:** Operating systems, applications, databases, middleware, and other software components that run on the hardware.
- **Networks:** The physical and logical networks that connect devices and enable communication between them. This includes local area networks (LANs), wide area networks (WANs), and wireless networks.
- **Data Centers:** The facilities that house IT infrastructure, providing power, cooling, security, and other environmental controls.

Role of IT Architecture:

IT architecture is the blueprint for how IT infrastructure and components are organized and interconnected. It defines the standards, guidelines, and principles that govern the design and implementation of IT systems.

- **Alignment with Business Goals:** IT architecture ensures that technology investments align with the organization's strategic goals and objectives. This involves understanding business requirements, identifying technology solutions that can support those requirements, and designing a roadmap for implementation.
- **Scalability:** IT architecture ensures that IT systems can scale up or down to meet changing business needs. This involves designing systems that can handle increased workloads, adding new resources as needed, and optimizing performance to avoid bottlenecks.
- **Flexibility:** IT architecture provides a framework for adapting to new technologies and business models. This involves designing modular systems that can be easily modified or replaced, and adopting open standards that facilitate integration with other systems.
- **Cost Optimization:** IT architecture helps organizations optimize IT costs by identifying opportunities for consolidation, standardization, and automation.

In conclusion, IT infrastructure and architecture are the foundation of IT service management. They enable the delivery of reliable, secure, and high-performing IT services that align with business goals and can adapt to changing needs. By investing in a well-designed and managed infrastructure and a sound architecture, organizations can ensure the success of their IT service management initiatives and achieve their strategic objectives.

Information and Technology Risk Management

Information and Technology Risk Management (ITRM) is a critical discipline within the ITIL 4 framework that focuses on identifying, assessing, and mitigating risks associated with the use of information and technology within an organization. It's a proactive approach to safeguarding the confidentiality, integrity, and availability of information assets and ensuring the resilience of IT services.

The Need for ITRM:

IT systems and data are vulnerable to a wide range of threats, both internal and external. These threats can disrupt operations, compromise sensitive information, damage the organization's reputation, and result in significant financial losses. ITRM helps organizations proactively identify and address these risks, reducing the likelihood and impact of negative events.

Types of Risks in Information and Technology:

1. **Security Breaches:** Unauthorized access, data theft, ransomware attacks, malware infections, and other security incidents can expose sensitive information and disrupt operations.
2. **Data Loss:** Accidental deletion, hardware failures, natural disasters, and cyberattacks can lead to the loss of critical data, impacting business continuity and potentially causing financial losses.
3. **System Failures:** Hardware malfunctions, software bugs, power outages, and network disruptions can cause IT systems to fail, leading to downtime, lost productivity, and dissatisfied customers.
4. **Technology Obsolescence:** As technology evolves rapidly, older systems and software can become outdated, unsupported, and vulnerable to security risks. This can hinder innovation and limit the organization's ability to adapt to changing business needs.
5. **Third-Party Risks:** Organizations often rely on external vendors and suppliers for IT services and support. These third parties can introduce risks, such as data breaches, supply chain disruptions, or financial instability.
6. **Human Error:** Employees can inadvertently introduce risks through mistakes, negligence, or malicious actions. This can include accidental data deletion, misconfigured systems, or falling victim to phishing scams.

Importance of a Risk Management Plan:

A risk management plan is a documented strategy that outlines how an organization will identify, assess, and mitigate risks associated with information and technology. It provides a structured approach to proactively addressing potential threats and minimizing their impact on the organization.

A risk management plan typically includes:

- **Risk Assessment:** A systematic process for identifying and evaluating risks, including their likelihood and potential impact.
- **Risk Mitigation Strategies:** Actions that will be taken to reduce the probability or impact of identified risks. These strategies can include implementing security controls, backup procedures, disaster recovery plans, and employee training.
- **Risk Monitoring and Review:** Regularly reviewing and updating the risk management plan to ensure it remains relevant and effective in addressing emerging threats.
- **Incident Response Plan:** A predefined plan for responding to security incidents or other IT disruptions, outlining the steps to be taken to minimize damage and restore normal operations.

By having a well-defined risk management plan in place, organizations can proactively identify and address potential threats, reduce the likelihood and impact of incidents, and protect their valuable information and technology assets. This not only enhances the resilience of IT services but also fosters trust among customers, employees, and stakeholders.

Security and Privacy

Security and privacy are paramount concerns in the realm of information and technology (I&T). They are not merely technical considerations but ethical and legal imperatives that impact an organization's reputation, customer trust, and ultimately, its bottom line.

Critical Importance of Ensuring Security and Privacy:

Information and technology assets are the lifeblood of modern organizations. They encompass sensitive customer data, confidential business information, intellectual property, and critical operational systems. Breaches in security or privacy can have devastating consequences, including:

- **Financial Losses:** Data breaches can result in significant financial losses due to theft, fraud, regulatory fines, legal fees, and remediation costs.
- **Reputational Damage:** A security or privacy incident can severely damage an organization's reputation, eroding customer trust and loyalty.
- **Operational Disruptions:** Cyberattacks and data breaches can disrupt business operations, leading to downtime, lost productivity, and customer dissatisfaction.
- **Legal and Regulatory Penalties:** Non-compliance with data protection regulations can result in hefty fines and legal action.

Need for Robust Security Controls:

To safeguard information and technology assets, organizations must implement a multi-layered approach to security. This includes a combination of technical, administrative, and physical controls:

1. **Access Controls:** Restricting access to sensitive data and systems to authorized personnel only. This can be achieved through strong passwords, multi-factor authentication, role-based access controls, and regular access reviews.
2. **Encryption:** Protecting data in transit and at rest by converting it into an unreadable format. This ensures that even if data is intercepted or stolen, it cannot be easily accessed or used.

3. **Intrusion Detection and Prevention Systems (IDPS):** Monitoring networks and systems for suspicious activity and taking preventive measures to block unauthorized access or malicious attacks.
4. **Vulnerability Management:** Regularly scanning for and patching vulnerabilities in software and systems to prevent exploitation by attackers.
5. **Backup and Disaster Recovery:** Creating regular backups of critical data and having a disaster recovery plan in place to ensure business continuity in the event of a data loss or system failure.

Importance of Complying with Data Protection Regulations and Standards:

Organizations must comply with relevant data protection regulations and standards, such as the General Data Protection Regulation (GDPR) in the European Union, the California Consumer Privacy Act (CCPA), and industry-specific standards like the Payment Card Industry Data Security Standard (PCI DSS). Compliance not only helps avoid legal penalties but also demonstrates a commitment to protecting customer data and building trust.

Role of Employee Awareness and Training:

Employees play a crucial role in maintaining a secure environment. Even with the most robust security controls, human error can still lead to security breaches. Regular security awareness training is essential to educate employees about potential risks, such as phishing scams and social engineering attacks, and to teach them how to identify and report suspicious activity.

In Summary:

Ensuring the security and privacy of information and technology assets is not just an IT issue; it's a business imperative. By implementing robust security controls, complying with relevant regulations, and fostering a culture of security awareness, organizations can protect their valuable assets, maintain customer trust, and ensure the continuity of their operations.

Chapter Summary

In this chapter, we explored the second dimension of ITIL 4's Service Value System (SVS): Information and Technology. This dimension emphasizes the critical role that information and technology play in enabling effective and efficient service management.

Key takeaways from this chapter include:

- **The Backbone of Modern Service Delivery:** Information and technology are the essential infrastructure upon which modern service delivery is built. They enable digital channels, data-driven insights, and automation, all of which are essential for meeting customer expectations and achieving business goals.
- **Types of Information:** We discussed the various types of information that are crucial for service management, including operational data, configuration data, service knowledge, and business information. Each type of information serves a specific purpose in supporting decision-making, service delivery, and continuous improvement.
- **Information Management:** Effective information management is essential for ensuring that the right information is available to the right people at the right time. This involves processes such as data collection, storage, analysis, and reporting, as well as ensuring data quality, accuracy, and accessibility.
- **Technology in Service Management:** We explored the various technologies that are used in service management, such as ITSM tools, knowledge management systems, self-service portals, and automation platforms. These technologies can streamline processes, improve efficiency, and enhance the customer experience.

- **Emerging Technologies and Trends:** We discussed the impact of emerging technologies like AI, ML, and big data on service management. These technologies have the potential to revolutionize service delivery by automating tasks, personalizing experiences, and providing valuable insights from data.
- **IT Infrastructure and Architecture:** We emphasized the importance of a well-designed and managed IT infrastructure for supporting service delivery. The key components of IT infrastructure were outlined, along with the role of IT architecture in aligning technology with business goals and ensuring scalability and flexibility.
- **Information and Technology Risk Management:** We discussed the importance of identifying, assessing, and mitigating risks associated with information and technology. We explored the various types of risks that can arise and the need for a comprehensive risk management plan to address potential threats proactively.
- **Security and Privacy:** We highlighted the critical importance of ensuring the security and privacy of information and technology assets. This involves implementing robust security controls, complying with relevant data protection regulations, and fostering a culture of security awareness among employees.

By understanding and effectively managing information and technology, organizations can leverage these powerful tools to deliver high-quality services, meet customer expectations, and achieve their business objectives. As we move forward, we will delve into the remaining dimensions of the ITIL 4 SVS, further exploring the comprehensive nature of this framework.

Partners and Suppliers

Outline

- The Role of Partners and Suppliers in Service Management
- Types of Partner and Supplier Relationships
- The Partner and Supplier Management Practice
- Key Activities in Partner and Supplier Management
- Challenges in Partner and Supplier Management
- Strategies for Effective Partner and Supplier Management
- Chapter Summary

The Role of Partners and Suppliers in Service Management

In today's complex business landscape, organizations rarely operate in isolation. They increasingly rely on a network of **partners and suppliers** to deliver comprehensive IT services. These external entities play a crucial role in the Service Value System (SVS), contributing specialized skills, resources, and expertise that may not be available in-house.

Importance of Partners and Suppliers in Modern Service Delivery:

- **Access to Specialized Skills and Expertise:** Partners and suppliers often possess specialized skills and expertise in specific areas, such as cloud computing, cybersecurity, or application development. By collaborating with these experts, organizations can access the latest technologies and best practices without having to build those capabilities internally.
- **Resource Optimization:** Partnering with external entities allows organizations to leverage their resources more efficiently. Instead of investing in infrastructure, personnel, or software licenses, organizations can tap into the resources of partners and suppliers on an as-needed basis.
- **Increased Agility and Flexibility:** Partners and suppliers can provide the agility and flexibility needed to respond quickly to changing business needs and market demands. They can scale services up or down as required, helping organizations adapt to fluctuations in demand.
- **Cost Savings:** In some cases, partnering with external entities can be more cost-effective than building capabilities in-house. This is particularly true for specialized services or those that are not core to the organization's business.
- **Innovation:** Partners and suppliers can bring fresh perspectives and innovative ideas to the table, helping organizations identify new opportunities and stay ahead of the competition.

Contributions to the Service Value System (SVS):

Partners and suppliers contribute to the SVS in various ways:

- **Sourcing Components and Services:** They provide hardware, software, and other components that are essential for delivering IT services.
- **Providing Infrastructure:** They may host and manage IT infrastructure, such as data centers, servers, and networks.
- **Delivering End-User Support:** They can provide help desk support, training, and other services that directly benefit end users.
- **Managing Service Operations:** They may take responsibility for managing certain aspects of service operations, such as monitoring, maintenance, and incident resolution.
- **Driving Innovation:** They can collaborate with the organization to develop new services, improve existing ones, and explore emerging technologies.

Need for Effective Partner and Supplier Management:

To realize the full benefits of partnering with external entities, organizations need to establish effective partner and supplier management practices. This involves:

- **Clearly Defined Roles and Responsibilities:** Ensuring that both parties understand their roles and responsibilities in the service relationship.
- **Robust Contracts and Service Level Agreements (SLAs):** Establishing clear contractual agreements that define service levels, performance metrics, and remedies in case of non-compliance.
- **Regular Communication and Collaboration:** Maintaining open lines of communication and fostering collaboration to address issues, manage risks, and drive continuous improvement.
- **Performance Monitoring and Evaluation:** Tracking partner and supplier performance against agreed-upon metrics and taking corrective action as needed.
- **Risk Management:** Identifying and mitigating risks associated with relying on external entities, such as dependency, loss of control, and potential security breaches.

By developing strong partnerships with reliable and capable suppliers, organizations can enhance their service offerings, improve efficiency, and focus on their core competencies, ultimately delivering greater value to their customers and stakeholders.

Types of Partner and Supplier Relationships

Partner and supplier relationships exist on a spectrum, ranging from simple transactional interactions to deep, strategic partnerships. Each type of relationship has distinct characteristics, benefits, and considerations. Understanding these different types can help organizations choose the most appropriate approach for each partner and supplier.

1. **Transactional Relationships:**
- **Characteristics:** Primarily focused on the exchange of goods or services for payment. Minimal interaction beyond the transaction itself. Often involves standardized products or services with clearly defined terms and conditions.
- **Level of Collaboration, Trust, and Commitment:** Low. The relationship is primarily driven by price and convenience, with limited collaboration or trust between the parties.
- **Examples:** A company purchasing office supplies from a vendor, or a restaurant ordering ingredients from a food distributor.
2. **Operational Relationships:**
- **Characteristics:** Involves a more regular and ongoing interaction between the organization and the supplier. The focus is on ensuring that the supplier delivers products or services that meet the organization's operational needs.
- **Level of Collaboration, Trust, and Commitment:** Moderate. There is some level of collaboration and trust, as the organization relies on the supplier to meet its ongoing needs.
- **Examples:** A company outsourcing its IT help desk support, or a manufacturer contracting with a logistics provider to manage its supply chain.
3. **Value-Adding Relationships:**
- **Characteristics:** The supplier not only delivers products or services but also provides additional value through expertise, innovation, or process improvement. The relationship involves a deeper level of collaboration and information sharing.
- **Level of Collaboration, Trust, and Commitment:** High. There is a strong focus on collaboration and mutual benefit, with both parties working together to achieve shared goals.
- **Examples:** A software company partnering with a cloud provider to deliver a Software-as-a-Service (SaaS) solution, or a retailer working with a consultant to improve its customer experience.
4. **Strategic Partnerships:**

- **Characteristics:** The most advanced type of relationship, involving a long-term commitment and a high degree of collaboration and trust. Strategic partners work together to create new business opportunities, share risks and rewards, and drive innovation.
- **Level of Collaboration, Trust, and Commitment:** Very high. The relationship is characterized by deep trust, shared goals, and a long-term vision for mutual success.
- **Examples:** A pharmaceutical company partnering with a research institution to develop new drugs, or a technology company forming a strategic alliance with a competitor to jointly develop a new product.

Examples of Different Types of Partners and Suppliers:

- **Technology Vendors:** Provide hardware, software, and other technology products.
- **Outsourcers:** Take responsibility for managing specific functions or processes, such as IT support, payroll, or customer service.
- **Consultants:** Provide expert advice and guidance on various business issues.
- **Service Integrators:** Combine multiple services from different providers into a seamless end-to-end solution.

By understanding the different types of partner and supplier relationships, organizations can choose the most appropriate approach for each situation, ensuring that they get the most value out of their partnerships and achieve their strategic objectives.

The Partner and Supplier Management Practice

In ITIL 4, the **Partner and Supplier Management** practice is one of the 34 management practices that guide organizations in optimizing their interactions with external entities. It recognizes that in today's interconnected business landscape, organizations often rely on a network of partners and suppliers to deliver services effectively. This practice aims to ensure that these relationships are managed strategically, maximizing value and minimizing risk.

Purpose of Partner and Supplier Management:

The primary purpose of this practice is to ensure that the organization's partners and suppliers are managed in a way that supports the creation and delivery of value to customers and stakeholders. This involves:

- **Aligning with Organizational Goals:** Partners and suppliers should be selected and managed in a way that aligns with the organization's overall strategy, goals, and objectives.
- **Maximizing Value:** The practice aims to maximize the value derived from partner and supplier relationships by ensuring that they deliver high-quality products and services at a reasonable cost.
- **Minimizing Risk:** Partner and supplier relationships can introduce various risks, such as service disruptions, security breaches, and financial instability. This practice helps identify and mitigate these risks to protect the organization's interests.
- **Fostering Collaboration:** Building strong, collaborative relationships with partners and suppliers is essential for achieving mutual success. This involves open communication, trust, and a shared commitment to achieving common goals.
- **Driving Innovation:** Partner and supplier relationships can be a source of innovation, as they bring new ideas, technologies, and perspectives to the table. This practice encourages organizations to leverage these relationships to drive innovation and stay ahead of the competition.

Key Activities Involved:

1. **Partner and Supplier Strategy:** Developing a clear and comprehensive strategy for engaging with partners and suppliers, defining the types of relationships the organization wants to build, and establishing criteria for selecting partners and suppliers.

2. **Sourcing and Procurement:** Identifying potential partners and suppliers, evaluating their capabilities and offerings, and negotiating contracts that define roles, responsibilities, service levels, pricing, and other key terms.
3. **Contract Management:** Managing the ongoing relationship with partners and suppliers, ensuring compliance with contract terms, monitoring performance against agreed-upon service levels, and resolving any issues or disputes that may arise.
4. **Performance Management:** Establishing performance metrics and regularly monitoring and evaluating partner and supplier performance against these metrics. Providing feedback, recognizing achievements, and addressing any performance gaps.
5. **Relationship Management:** Building and maintaining strong, collaborative relationships with partners and suppliers based on trust, mutual respect, and open communication. This involves regular interaction, joint planning, and a focus on shared goals.
6. **Risk Management:** Identifying and assessing risks associated with partner and supplier relationships, such as dependency, performance issues, and security vulnerabilities. Developing and implementing risk mitigation strategies to minimize the impact of these risks.
7. **Continual Improvement:** Regularly reviewing and evaluating the effectiveness of partner and supplier management practices, identifying areas for improvement, and implementing changes to enhance the value and outcomes of these relationships.

Key Activities in Partner and Supplier Management

Effectively managing partners and suppliers requires a structured approach that encompasses various activities throughout the relationship lifecycle. Let's delve into the key activities involved in partner and supplier management within the ITIL 4 framework:

1. **Partner and Supplier Strategy:**

This foundational activity involves developing a clear and well-defined strategy for engaging with partners and suppliers. This strategy should be aligned with the organization's overall business goals and service management objectives. Key aspects of this strategy include:

- **Identifying Partner and Supplier Needs:** Determine the specific products, services, or capabilities that the organization needs from external entities.
- **Defining Relationship Types:** Decide on the appropriate types of relationships (transactional, operational, value-adding, or strategic) for different partners and suppliers based on their roles and contributions.
- **Establishing Selection Criteria:** Develop criteria for evaluating and selecting partners and suppliers, considering factors like cost, expertise, reputation, cultural fit, and alignment with organizational values.

2. **Sourcing and Procurement:**

This activity focuses on identifying potential partners and suppliers, evaluating their capabilities and offerings, and negotiating contracts that define the terms of the relationship.

- **Identifying Potential Partners and Suppliers:** Conduct market research, attend industry events, and network with other organizations to identify potential partners and suppliers.
- **Evaluating Capabilities and Offerings:** Assess the capabilities, experience, financial stability, and references of potential partners and suppliers.
- **Negotiating Contracts:** Negotiate contract terms that clearly define roles, responsibilities, service levels, pricing, payment terms, dispute resolution mechanisms, and exit clauses.

3. **Contract Management:**

Once contracts are in place, ongoing contract management is essential to ensure compliance with terms and conditions, monitor performance, and address any issues or disputes that may arise.

- **Monitoring Compliance:** Regularly review contracts to ensure that both parties are adhering to their obligations.
- **Tracking Performance:** Monitor partner and supplier performance against agreed-upon service levels and key performance indicators (KPIs).
- **Resolving Disputes:** Establish mechanisms for resolving disputes in a fair and timely manner, such as escalation procedures or mediation.

4. **Performance Management:**

Performance management involves setting clear performance expectations for partners and suppliers, regularly monitoring their performance against these expectations, and providing feedback to drive continuous improvement.

- **Establishing Performance Metrics:** Define clear and measurable metrics that align with the organization's goals and objectives.
- **Monitoring Performance:** Collect and analyze data to track partner and supplier performance against established metrics.
- **Providing Feedback:** Regularly communicate performance results to partners and suppliers, highlighting areas of strength and opportunities for improvement.
- **Taking Corrective Action:** When performance issues arise, work collaboratively with partners and suppliers to identify root causes and implement corrective actions.

5. **Relationship Management:**

Relationship management focuses on building and maintaining strong, collaborative relationships with partners and suppliers.

- **Building Trust:** Establish trust through open communication, transparency, and a focus on mutual benefit.
- **Regular Communication:** Maintain regular communication through meetings, reports, and other channels to discuss progress, challenges, and opportunities.
- **Joint Planning:** Involve partners and suppliers in the planning process to ensure their perspectives are considered and their needs are met.
- **Shared Goals:** Focus on shared goals and objectives, working together to achieve mutually beneficial outcomes.

By actively engaging in these key activities, organizations can establish and maintain productive relationships with partners and suppliers, ensuring that they contribute effectively to the creation and delivery of value.

Challenges in Partner and Supplier Management

Partner and supplier relationships can be complex and dynamic, presenting various challenges that organizations must navigate to ensure successful collaboration and value creation. These challenges can arise at any stage of the relationship, from initial selection to ongoing management, and can significantly impact service delivery and overall business performance.

Common Challenges:

1. **Communication Breakdowns:** Effective communication is crucial for any successful relationship, but miscommunication and misunderstandings can easily occur between organizations and their partners or suppliers. This can lead to delays, errors, and frustration on both sides. Language barriers, cultural differences, and differing communication styles can further exacerbate these challenges.
2. **Misaligned Expectations:** Unclear or misaligned expectations regarding roles, responsibilities, service levels, or deliverables can create friction and conflict. If expectations are not clearly defined and agreed upon upfront, it can lead to disappointment, disputes, and a breakdown in trust.

3. **Performance Issues:** Partners and suppliers may sometimes fail to meet their contractual obligations or service level agreements (SLAs). This could be due to various factors, such as inadequate resources, lack of expertise, or unforeseen circumstances. Performance issues can disrupt service delivery, impact customer satisfaction, and damage the organization's reputation.
4. **Conflicting Priorities:** Organizations and their partners or suppliers may have different priorities or goals, which can lead to conflicts of interest and disagreements over how resources should be allocated or how services should be delivered.
5. **Dependency and Lack of Control:** Relying on external entities for critical services can create a sense of dependency and loss of control. If a partner or supplier fails to deliver, it can significantly impact the organization's operations and ability to meet customer needs.
6. **Security and Compliance Risks:** Sharing sensitive information or systems with external parties can expose organizations to security and compliance risks. Data breaches, unauthorized access, and non-compliance with regulations can have severe consequences for the organization.

Proactive Identification and Mitigation of Challenges:

To minimize the impact of these challenges, organizations must take a proactive approach to partner and supplier management. This involves:

- **Establishing Clear Expectations:** Defining roles, responsibilities, service levels, and deliverables in detail during the contract negotiation phase.
- **Regular Communication and Feedback:** Maintaining open lines of communication with partners and suppliers, providing regular feedback, and addressing any issues or concerns promptly.
- **Performance Monitoring and Evaluation:** Establishing clear performance metrics and regularly monitoring and evaluating partner and supplier performance against these metrics.
- **Risk Assessment and Mitigation:** Identifying and assessing potential risks associated with each partner and supplier relationship, and developing mitigation strategies to address those risks.
- **Contingency Planning:** Having contingency plans in place to address potential disruptions or failures in partner and supplier services.

By proactively identifying and addressing these challenges, organizations can build stronger, more resilient relationships with their partners and suppliers, ensuring that they contribute effectively to the creation and delivery of value. This, in turn, will lead to improved service quality, increased customer satisfaction, and enhanced business performance.

Strategies for Effective Partner and Supplier Management

Establishing and maintaining successful partnerships with suppliers is a cornerstone of effective IT service management. It requires a strategic approach, clear communication, and a commitment to mutual benefit. Here are some practical tips and strategies for building and nurturing these relationships:

1. **Clearly Define Roles and Responsibilities:**
- **Develop Detailed Contracts and SLAs:** Ensure that contracts and service level agreements (SLAs) clearly define the roles, responsibilities, deliverables, and performance expectations of both parties. Leave no room for ambiguity or misinterpretation.
- **Regularly Review and Update Agreements:** As business needs and technology evolve, revisit and update agreements to reflect current requirements and ensure they remain relevant and effective.
2. **Foster Open and Transparent Communication:**
- **Establish Regular Communication Channels:** Schedule regular meetings, calls, or video conferences to discuss progress, address concerns, and share information.
- **Encourage Open Dialogue:** Create a safe space for both parties to express their opinions, raise concerns, and offer suggestions without fear of repercussions.

- **Provide Timely Feedback:** Give constructive feedback on performance, both positive and negative, to foster continuous improvement.
- **Utilize Technology:** Leverage communication and collaboration tools like email, instant messaging, video conferencing, and project management platforms to facilitate seamless communication and information sharing.

3. **Build Trust and Mutual Respect:**

- **Demonstrate Integrity and Fairness:** Act with integrity and fairness in all interactions, honoring commitments, and resolving disputes amicably.
- **Focus on Shared Goals:** Align interests and create a shared vision for success. Work collaboratively to achieve common objectives and celebrate mutual achievements.
- **Be Responsive and Proactive:** Address issues and concerns promptly, proactively seeking solutions, and demonstrating a willingness to go the extra mile.

4. **Establish Performance Metrics and Monitor Regularly:**

- **Define Key Performance Indicators (KPIs):** Identify relevant KPIs that align with the organization's goals and objectives, such as service availability, response times, customer satisfaction, and cost efficiency.
- **Track Performance Data:** Collect and analyze performance data regularly to assess whether partners and suppliers are meeting their obligations and delivering value as expected.
- **Use Performance Data to Drive Improvement:** Use performance data to identify areas for improvement, discuss them with partners and suppliers, and collaboratively develop action plans to address any shortcomings.

5. **Seek Strategic Partnerships:**

- **Look Beyond Transactional Relationships:** Instead of focusing solely on price, consider the long-term value that partners and suppliers can bring to the organization. Look for partners who share your vision, values, and commitment to innovation.
- **Invest in Building Relationships:** Allocate time and resources to building strong relationships with strategic partners. This can involve joint planning, knowledge sharing, and co-creation of new services or solutions.
- **Explore Opportunities for Mutual Growth:** Identify opportunities for collaboration that can benefit both parties, such as joint marketing initiatives, co-development of new products or services, or shared research and development efforts.

By adopting these strategies, organizations can create a network of strong, collaborative partnerships with suppliers that drive innovation, improve service quality, and deliver long-term value. These partnerships can become a source of competitive advantage, helping organizations stay ahead of the curve in the ever-evolving world of IT service management.

Chapter Summary

In this chapter, we explored the third dimension of the ITIL 4 Service Value System (SVS): Partners and Suppliers. Recognizing that modern service delivery often relies on external entities, we discussed the various ways partners and suppliers contribute to the SVS, ranging from sourcing components and providing infrastructure to delivering end-user support and driving innovation.

We delved into the different types of partner and supplier relationships, ranging from transactional to strategic, highlighting the varying levels of collaboration, trust, and commitment involved. We also examined the ITIL 4 Partner and Supplier Management practice, emphasizing its role in ensuring that these relationships are managed effectively to maximize value creation and minimize risks.

Key activities in partner and supplier management were explored in detail, including developing a clear strategy, sourcing and procurement, contract management, performance management, and relationship management. We acknowledged the common challenges organizations face in managing these relationships, such as communication breakdowns, misaligned expectations, and performance issues. We also discussed the inherent risks associated with relying on external entities, including dependency, loss of control, and potential security breaches.

To mitigate these challenges and risks, we provided practical tips and strategies for effective partner and supplier management. These strategies emphasize the importance of clear communication, shared goals, mutual trust, ongoing feedback, and the use of technology to facilitate collaboration. We concluded by emphasizing the benefits of establishing strategic partnerships that go beyond transactional interactions, fostering long-term value creation and mutual success.

Understanding the dynamics of partner and supplier relationships is crucial for organizations to leverage external expertise and resources effectively. By adopting a strategic and collaborative approach to partner and supplier management, organizations can enhance their service offerings, improve efficiency, and achieve their strategic objectives in the complex landscape of IT service management.

Value Streams and Processes

Outline

- Value Streams vs. Processes
- The ITIL Service Value Chain
- Value Stream Mapping
- Process Design and Management
- Workflow Automation and Optimization
- Measurement and Metrics
- Chapter Summary

Value Streams vs. Processes

While often used interchangeably, **value streams** and **processes** are distinct concepts in ITIL 4, each playing a specific role in service management. Understanding their differences is key to optimizing how organizations create and deliver value to customers.

Value Streams:

A value stream is a series of steps an organization undertakes to create and deliver products or services to the consumer. In the context of ITIL, a **value stream** represents the end-to-end set of activities that contribute to the creation and delivery of value to customers. It encompasses all the activities involved in transforming a customer request or need into a delivered outcome.

- **Key Characteristics:**
  - Customer-centric: Value streams focus on the customer's perspective, starting with their needs and ending with the realization of value.
  - Cross-functional: Value streams involve multiple functions and departments within the organization, breaking down silos and promoting collaboration.
  - Outcome-oriented: Value streams are focused on achieving specific outcomes that deliver value to customers.
- **Examples:**
  - **Request Fulfillment:** The entire journey from a customer placing a request for a new service to its successful delivery and ongoing support.
  - **Incident Resolution:** The steps taken to identify, diagnose, and resolve an incident that is disrupting a service.
  - **New Service Development:** The process of designing, developing, testing, and launching a new service.

Processes:

A **process** is a set of structured activities designed to achieve a specific objective. Processes are the building blocks of value streams, representing the individual steps or tasks that contribute to the overall delivery of value.

- **Key Characteristics:**
  - More granular: Processes are more focused and specific than value streams, addressing individual tasks or activities.
  - Repeatable: Processes are designed to be repeatable and consistent, ensuring standardized outcomes.

- Measurable: Processes can be measured and monitored to assess their efficiency and effectiveness.
- **Examples:**
  - **Logging an Incident:** The specific steps involved in recording details about an incident in a ticketing system.
  - **Diagnosing a Problem:** The analysis and investigation required to identify the root cause of an incident.
  - **Implementing a Change:** The steps involved in planning, testing, and deploying a change to an IT service.

The Relationship Between Value Streams and Processes:

Value streams are made up of multiple interconnected processes. Each process contributes to the overall value stream, but they can also be optimized individually to improve efficiency and effectiveness.

For example, within the "Request Fulfillment" value stream, there might be processes for:

1. Receiving and logging requests
2. Assessing and prioritizing requests
3. Approving and fulfilling requests
4. Communicating with the customer

By analyzing and optimizing these individual processes, organizations can improve the overall flow and efficiency of the value stream, leading to faster and more effective service delivery.

Understanding the distinction between value streams and processes is crucial for successful service management. By focusing on value streams, organizations can ensure that their efforts are aligned with customer needs and deliver the desired outcomes. At the same time, optimizing processes helps to improve efficiency, reduce waste, and enhance the overall effectiveness of the service delivery system.

The ITIL Service Value Chain

The ITIL Service Value Chain (SVC) is a core concept in ITIL 4, providing a flexible operating model for creating, delivering, and managing value through IT-enabled services. It comprises six key activities, each contributing to the overall goal of value realization for customers and stakeholders.

The Six Activities of the ITIL Service Value Chain:

1. **Plan:** This activity involves the strategic planning and coordination of all aspects of the service value chain. It encompasses the identification of opportunities and demands, the prioritization of initiatives, and the development of plans and policies to ensure the efficient and effective delivery of services.
2. **Improve:** Continual improvement is a fundamental principle of ITIL, and this activity focuses on identifying and implementing improvements across all areas of the service value chain. It involves analyzing performance data, gathering feedback from customers and stakeholders, and implementing changes to enhance service quality, efficiency, and effectiveness.
3. **Engage:** This activity centers on interacting and collaborating with stakeholders, both internal and external. It involves understanding their needs and expectations, building strong relationships, and ensuring that their perspectives are considered throughout the service lifecycle.
4. **Design and Transition:** This activity focuses on creating and implementing new or changed services. It involves designing service solutions that meet customer requirements, developing and testing new processes and technologies, and ensuring a smooth transition from development to production.

5. **Obtain/Build:** This activity ensures that the necessary resources are available to deliver and support services. It involves sourcing and acquiring components, software, and infrastructure, as well as building internal capabilities and competencies.
6. **Deliver and Support:** This activity is the core of service delivery, encompassing the day-to-day operation and support of services. It involves managing incidents and requests, fulfilling service orders, and ensuring that services meet agreed-upon service levels.

How Each Activity Contributes to Value Creation:

Each activity in the Service Value Chain plays a crucial role in creating and delivering value to customers and stakeholders.

- **Plan:** Ensures that services are aligned with business goals and customer needs, maximizing the potential for value creation.
- **Improve:** Continuously enhances service quality and efficiency, leading to increased customer satisfaction and greater value realization.
- **Engage:** Builds strong relationships with stakeholders, ensuring their needs are met and their feedback is incorporated into service improvement efforts.
- **Design and Transition:** Creates and implements new or changed services that address customer needs and deliver value in a timely and efficient manner.
- **Obtain/Build:** Ensures the availability of necessary resources, enabling the efficient and effective delivery of services.
- **Deliver and Support:** Provides the day-to-day operational support needed to ensure that services are available, reliable, and meet agreed-upon service levels.

The Importance of the Service Value Chain:

The Service Value Chain provides a holistic view of service management, highlighting the interconnectedness of different activities and the need for a coordinated approach. By understanding the entire value chain, organizations can identify and address bottlenecks, optimize processes, and ensure that every activity contributes to the ultimate goal of delivering value to customers.

Interconnectedness and Interdependence of Activities:

The activities in the Service Value Chain are not isolated; they are interconnected and interdependent. For example:

- The "Plan" activity informs the "Design and Transition" activity by identifying customer needs and setting strategic goals.
- The "Improve" activity uses feedback from the "Deliver and Support" activity to identify areas for improvement.
- The "Engage" activity ensures that stakeholders are involved throughout the value chain, providing input and feedback at every stage.

This interconnectedness highlights the importance of a holistic approach to service management. By considering the entire value chain, organizations can ensure that all activities work together seamlessly to create and deliver value to customers.

Value Stream Mapping

Value Stream Mapping (VSM) is a lean management technique used to analyze and improve the flow of work and information required to deliver a product or service to a customer. In the context of ITIL 4, VSM is a powerful tool for understanding, visualizing, and optimizing the end-to-end activities that constitute a service value stream.

Purpose of Value Stream Mapping:

The primary purpose of VSM is to:

- **Visualize the Flow:** Create a visual representation of the current state of the value stream, showing the steps involved, the time taken at each step, and the flow of information and materials.
- **Identify Waste and Bottlenecks:** Uncover areas of waste and inefficiency, such as delays, rework, unnecessary steps, and excess inventory. Pinpoint bottlenecks that impede the smooth flow of work.
- **Develop Improvement Plans:** Based on the analysis, develop targeted improvement plans to eliminate waste, streamline processes, and enhance the overall efficiency and effectiveness of the value stream.

Steps Involved in Value Stream Mapping:

1. **Select the Value Stream:** Identify the specific value stream you want to map. This could be any end-to-end activity that delivers value to a customer, such as incident resolution, request fulfillment, or new service development.
2. **Define the Scope:** Determine the starting and ending points of the value stream, as well as the boundaries of the analysis.
3. **Map the Current State:** Walk through the value stream and map out the steps involved, including the time taken at each step, the resources used, and the flow of information and materials. Use standard symbols and notations to create a visual representation of the current state.
4. **Identify Value-Adding and Non-Value-Adding Activities:** Distinguish between activities that directly contribute to value creation for the customer (value-adding) and those that don't (non-value-adding). Non-value-adding activities can be further classified as necessary waste (required but not directly adding value) and pure waste (unnecessary and should be eliminated).
5. **Analyze the Current State:** Identify bottlenecks, delays, rework, and other sources of waste. Calculate key metrics such as lead time, process time, and value-added time to quantify the efficiency of the value stream.
6. **Design the Future State:** Develop a vision for the ideal state of the value stream, eliminating waste, streamlining processes, and optimizing flow. This future state map serves as a roadmap for improvement initiatives.
7. **Develop an Improvement Plan:** Based on the analysis and the future state map, create a detailed plan outlining the specific actions, timelines, and responsibilities required to implement the desired improvements.
8. **Implement and Monitor:** Put the improvement plan into action and monitor its progress, making adjustments as needed. Regularly review and update the value stream map to track improvements and identify new opportunities for optimization.

Examples in IT Service Management:

- **Incident Management:** VSM can be used to map the incident resolution process, identifying bottlenecks in communication, diagnosis, or resolution, and implementing improvements to reduce response times and improve customer satisfaction.
- **Request Fulfillment:** VSM can help streamline the request fulfillment process, eliminating unnecessary steps, automating approvals, and reducing wait times.
- **New Service Development:** VSM can be used to map the end-to-end process of developing and launching new IT services, identifying areas where collaboration can be improved, bottlenecks can be removed, and time-to-market can be reduced.

By applying value stream mapping to IT service management processes, organizations can gain a deep understanding of how value is created, identify areas for improvement, and implement changes that lead to greater efficiency, effectiveness, and customer satisfaction.

Process Design and Management

In the context of ITIL 4, processes are structured sets of activities designed to accomplish a specific objective. They are the building blocks of value streams, which represent the end-to-end activities that create and deliver value to customers. Effective process design and management are crucial for ensuring that IT services are delivered efficiently, consistently, and in alignment with business needs and customer expectations.

Principles of Good Process Design:

1. **Clarity:** Processes should be clearly defined, with well-documented steps, inputs, outputs, roles, and responsibilities. This clarity ensures that everyone involved understands what needs to be done and how to do it.
2. **Efficiency:** Processes should be designed to minimize waste and maximize efficiency. This involves eliminating unnecessary steps, automating repetitive tasks, and optimizing the use of resources.
3. **Effectiveness:** Processes should be designed to achieve their intended objectives and deliver the desired outcomes. This requires a clear understanding of customer needs and expectations, as well as the ability to measure and monitor process performance.
4. **Customer Focus:** Processes should be designed with the customer in mind. This means considering their needs, preferences, and expectations throughout the design process and ensuring that the process delivers value from the customer's perspective.
5. **Adaptability:** Processes should be flexible and adaptable to changing circumstances. This involves regularly reviewing and updating processes to ensure they remain relevant and effective in the face of evolving business needs and technologies.

Importance of Documenting Processes and Ensuring Understanding:

Documenting processes is essential for ensuring consistency, repeatability, and continuous improvement. Well-documented processes provide a clear roadmap for how work should be done, reducing the risk of errors and misunderstandings.

It's also important to ensure that processes are understood and followed by all relevant stakeholders. This involves providing training and guidance to employees, communicating process changes effectively, and monitoring compliance.

The Need for Continuous Process Improvement:

Processes are not static; they need to evolve and adapt to changing business needs and customer expectations. Continuous process improvement (CPI) is a systematic approach to identifying, analyzing, and implementing improvements to processes. It involves:

1. **Identifying Improvement Opportunities:** Gathering data and feedback to identify areas where processes can be improved.
2. **Analyzing Root Causes:** Investigating the underlying causes of problems or inefficiencies in processes.
3. **Developing and Implementing Solutions:** Designing and implementing solutions that address the root causes of problems.
4. **Measuring and Monitoring Results:** Tracking the effectiveness of improvements and making adjustments as needed.

By embracing continuous process improvement, organizations can ensure that their processes remain aligned with business goals, deliver value to customers, and adapt to the ever-changing IT landscape.

In conclusion, effective process design and management are essential for delivering high-quality IT services. By following the principles of good process design, documenting processes clearly, and embracing continuous improvement, organizations can optimize their service delivery, enhance customer satisfaction, and achieve their business objectives.

Workflow Automation and Optimization

Workflow automation involves using technology to streamline and automate repetitive, manual tasks within a business process. In the context of IT service management, this can drastically improve efficiency, accuracy, and the overall service experience.

Benefits of Automating Workflows:

1. **Reduced Manual Effort:** Automating repetitive tasks frees up valuable human resources, allowing them to focus on more complex and strategic activities that require human judgment and creativity. This leads to increased productivity and job satisfaction.
2. **Minimized Errors:** Human errors are inevitable in manual processes. Automation eliminates the risk of human error, ensuring consistent and accurate execution of tasks. This improves data quality, reduces rework, and enhances service reliability.
3. **Improved Efficiency:** Automated workflows can complete tasks much faster than humans, accelerating service delivery and response times. This can lead to significant cost savings and improved customer satisfaction.
4. **Enhanced Compliance:** Automation ensures that processes are executed consistently according to predefined rules and regulations, reducing the risk of non-compliance.
5. **Increased Visibility and Control:** Automated workflows provide real-time visibility into process performance, enabling managers to track progress, identify bottlenecks, and make data-driven decisions to optimize processes.

Different Types of Workflow Automation Tools and Technologies:

- **Robotic Process Automation (RPA):** RPA software bots mimic human actions to automate repetitive, rule-based tasks. They can interact with applications, websites, and systems, performing tasks like data entry, form filling, and report generation.
- **Business Process Management (BPM) Systems:** BPM systems provide a comprehensive platform for designing, modeling, executing, monitoring, and optimizing business processes. They enable organizations to create end-to-end automated workflows that involve multiple systems and departments.
- **AI-Powered Chatbots:** AI-powered chatbots can automate customer interactions, providing instant responses to queries, guiding users through self-service processes, and escalating complex issues to human agents.
- **Orchestration and Integration Platforms:** These platforms allow for the seamless integration of different applications and systems, enabling the automation of complex workflows that involve multiple technologies.
- **Low-Code/No-Code Platforms:** These platforms allow business users to create and automate workflows without requiring extensive coding knowledge. They empower citizen developers to create customized solutions that meet their specific needs.

Importance of Considering Technical and Human Factors:

When implementing workflow automation, it's crucial to consider both technical and human factors.

- **Technical Factors:** Organizations need to choose the right automation tools and technologies that fit their specific needs and budget. They also need to ensure that the tools are compatible with their existing systems and infrastructure.
- **Human Factors:** Automation can significantly impact the roles and responsibilities of employees. Organizations need to provide adequate training and support to help employees adapt to the new workflows and technologies. It's also important to address any concerns or anxieties that employees may have about automation and its potential impact on their jobs.

In Summary:

Workflow automation and optimization are key enablers of efficiency, effectiveness, and customer satisfaction in IT service management. By leveraging the right tools and technologies and considering both technical and human factors, organizations can streamline processes, reduce costs, and deliver high-quality services that meet the evolving needs of their customers.

Measurement and Metrics

In ITIL 4, measurement and metrics are essential for understanding how well processes and value streams are performing, identifying areas for improvement, and demonstrating the value of IT services to the business. They provide objective data that can be used to make informed decisions, drive continuous improvement, and ensure that IT services align with business goals and customer expectations.

Importance of Measuring and Monitoring:

- **Performance Assessment:** Metrics allow organizations to assess the performance of their processes and value streams against defined targets and benchmarks. This helps identify areas where performance is lagging and where improvement efforts should be focused.
- **Identifying Improvement Opportunities:** By analyzing performance data, organizations can identify bottlenecks, inefficiencies, and other areas where processes can be optimized. This enables them to prioritize improvement initiatives and allocate resources effectively.
- **Demonstrating Value:** Metrics can be used to demonstrate the value that IT services deliver to the business. This can help justify investments in IT, secure funding for improvement initiatives, and build credibility with stakeholders.
- **Data-Driven Decision Making:** Metrics provide objective data that can be used to make informed decisions about service design, resource allocation, and investment priorities.
- **Continual Improvement:** Regular measurement and monitoring allow organizations to track the progress of improvement initiatives and ensure that they are achieving the desired results.

Key Metrics for Measuring Process Performance:

1. **Throughput:** The number of units of work (e.g., incidents, service requests) processed by a process or value stream within a given period.
2. **Cycle Time:** The average time it takes to complete a unit of work, from start to finish.
3. **Error Rates:** The percentage of errors or defects in the output of a process.
4. **Customer Satisfaction:** The level of satisfaction that customers have with the service, measured through surveys, feedback, or other means.
5. **Cost per Transaction:** The average cost of processing a single unit of work.
6. **Resource Utilization:** The percentage of time that resources (e.g., staff, equipment) are being used productively.

Using Metrics to Identify Improvement Opportunities and Track Effectiveness:

Metrics provide valuable insights that can be used to identify improvement opportunities and track the effectiveness of improvement initiatives. Here's how:

- **Analyzing Trends:** By tracking metrics over time, organizations can identify trends and patterns that may indicate areas for improvement. For example, a rising trend in incident resolution times could indicate a need for process optimization or additional resources.
- **Benchmarking:** Comparing performance metrics against industry benchmarks or internal targets can help identify areas where the organization is lagging behind and needs to catch up.
- **Root Cause Analysis:** When performance issues are identified, metrics can help pinpoint the root causes of the problems. This enables organizations to develop targeted solutions that address the underlying issues.

- **Measuring Improvement Impact:** By tracking metrics before and after implementing an improvement initiative, organizations can measure the impact of the change and determine its effectiveness.

By systematically measuring and monitoring processes and value streams, organizations can gain valuable insights into their performance, identify improvement opportunities, and ensure that their IT services are delivering the desired value to customers and stakeholders.

Chapter Summary

In this chapter, we delved into the fourth dimension of the ITIL 4 Service Value System (SVS): Value Streams and Processes. We explored how value streams represent the end-to-end activities that create and deliver value to customers, while processes are the smaller, more focused building blocks within those value streams.

Here's a summary of the key takeaways:

- **Value Streams vs. Processes:** You learned the distinction between these two concepts, recognizing that value streams focus on the big picture of delivering customer value, while processes break down the individual steps involved.
- **The ITIL Service Value Chain:** We explored the six core activities of the ITIL Service Value Chain (Plan, Improve, Engage, Design and Transition, Obtain/Build, Deliver and Support), emphasizing how each contributes to the creation and delivery of value. The Service Value Chain provides a holistic view of service management, highlighting the interconnectedness and interdependence of these activities.
- **Value Stream Mapping:** We discussed this powerful technique for visualizing and analyzing value streams. You learned the steps involved in value stream mapping, from selecting a value stream to developing and implementing improvement plans. We also illustrated how VSM can be applied to identify and eliminate waste in IT service management processes.
- **Process Design and Management:** We covered the principles of good process design, emphasizing clarity, efficiency, effectiveness, and customer focus. You learned the importance of documenting processes, ensuring their understanding by stakeholders, and continuously improving them to adapt to changing needs.
- **Workflow Automation and Optimization:** We explored the benefits of automating workflows, including reduced manual effort, minimized errors, and improved efficiency. We introduced various automation tools and technologies, such as RPA, BPM systems, and AI-powered chatbots. Importantly, we highlighted the need to consider both technical and human factors when implementing automation.
- **Measurement and Metrics:** We discussed the critical role of measurement and monitoring in ensuring that processes and value streams perform as expected and deliver value. You learned about key metrics like throughput, cycle time, error rates, and customer satisfaction, and how they can be used to identify improvement opportunities and track the effectiveness of initiatives.

By understanding and applying the concepts discussed in this chapter, you can gain a deeper appreciation for how value is created and delivered in IT service management. This knowledge empowers you to optimize processes, eliminate waste, and continuously improve the quality and efficiency of your services, ultimately leading to greater customer satisfaction and business success.

Section C:
Guiding Principles of ITIL 4

Focus on Value

Outline

- Understanding Value in Service Management
- The ITIL 4 Definition of Value
- Value Co-Creation
- Shifting from Outputs to Outcomes
- Understanding Stakeholder Needs and Expectations
- Prioritizing Value-Driven Activities
- Measuring and Demonstrating Value
- Chapter Summary

Understanding Value in Service Management

Value is the cornerstone of ITIL 4. It's the guiding light that steers every decision, action, and improvement within the framework. The entire Service Value System (SVS) is designed to facilitate the creation and delivery of value to customers and stakeholders.

The Central Role of Value in ITIL 4:

ITIL 4 shifts the focus of IT service management from purely technical outputs to value-driven outcomes. It recognizes that technology is not an end in itself but a means to an end – the end being the creation of value for the organization and its customers. This value-centric approach permeates every aspect of ITIL 4, from the guiding principles to the service value chain and the individual practices.

Value as Perceived Benefits, Usefulness, and Importance:

ITIL 4 defines value as "the perceived benefits, usefulness, and importance of something." It's important to note that value is subjective and can vary greatly from one stakeholder to another. What one customer values, another may not. This is because value is based on individual needs, preferences, and priorities.

For example:

- A customer might value a service for its reliability and responsiveness, while an IT manager might value it for its cost-effectiveness and scalability.
- A business stakeholder might value a service for its ability to drive revenue growth, while an employee might value it for its ease of use and productivity enhancements.

Focusing on Delivering Value, Not Just Technical Solutions:

IT service management should not be solely focused on providing technical solutions. While technical expertise is essential, it's equally important to understand the broader context in which services are delivered and the value they create for customers and stakeholders.

This requires a shift in mindset from a technology-centric approach to a customer-centric approach. IT service providers need to understand the needs and expectations of their customers and stakeholders, and design and deliver services that meet those needs in a way that is meaningful and valuable.

Aligning IT Services with Business Objectives:

To ensure that IT services contribute to the overall value proposition of the organization, they must be aligned with the organization's strategic goals and objectives. This means that IT service management decisions should not be made in isolation but in collaboration with business leaders and stakeholders.

By aligning IT services with business objectives, organizations can ensure that their investments in technology are delivering tangible benefits, such as increased revenue, improved customer satisfaction, reduced costs, and enhanced operational efficiency. This alignment also helps to build credibility and trust between IT and the rest of the organization, fostering a more collaborative and productive relationship.

In conclusion, understanding and focusing on value is the key to successful IT service management. By adopting a customer-centric approach, aligning IT services with business objectives, and co-creating value with customers and stakeholders, organizations can maximize the benefits of their IT investments and achieve their strategic goals.

The ITIL 4 Definition of Value

ITIL 4 defines **value** as "the perceived benefits, usefulness, and importance of something." This definition emphasizes that value is not solely about the features or capabilities of a service, but also encompasses the customer's or stakeholder's perception of its worth.

Key Components of Value in ITIL 4:

ITIL 4 breaks down the concept of value into two key components:

1. **Utility:** This refers to the functionality offered by a product or service to meet a particular need. It's about whether the service "fits the purpose" and delivers the specific capabilities that the customer or stakeholder requires.
2. **Warranty:** This refers to the assurance that a product or service will meet agreed-upon requirements. It's about whether the service is "fit for use" and performs reliably, securely, and according to the customer's expectations.

How Utility and Warranty Contribute to Value:

Utility and warranty are two sides of the same coin when it comes to value. A service may have high utility, offering all the features and functionality a customer needs, but if it's unreliable, difficult to use, or insecure, its overall value will be diminished. Conversely, a service may be highly reliable and secure, but if it lacks the necessary functionality or doesn't meet the customer's specific needs, its value will also be limited.

Therefore, to deliver maximum value, IT services must strike a balance between utility and warranty. They need to provide the right functionality (utility) and ensure that it works as expected (warranty). This involves considering factors such as:

- **Functionality:** Does the service offer the features and capabilities that customers need to achieve their desired outcomes?
- **Reliability:** Is the service available when needed and does it perform consistently?
- **Usability:** Is the service easy to use and understand?
- **Security:** Is the service protected from unauthorized access, use, disclosure, disruption, modification, or destruction?

- **Performance:** Does the service meet agreed-upon performance targets in terms of speed, accuracy, and responsiveness?
- **Cost:** Is the service cost-effective and does it provide good value for money?

Importance of Considering Both Utility and Warranty:

When designing and delivering IT services, it's crucial to consider both utility and warranty from the very beginning. This involves:

- **Understanding Customer Needs:** Engage with customers and stakeholders to understand their specific needs and expectations regarding both functionality and performance.
- **Designing for Utility and Warranty:** Design services that not only meet functional requirements but also incorporate features and measures that ensure reliability, security, and performance.
- **Testing and Validation:** Thoroughly test and validate services before deployment to ensure that they meet the defined warranty requirements.
- **Monitoring and Continuous Improvement:** Continuously monitor service performance and gather feedback from customers to identify opportunities for improvement and ensure that services continue to deliver value.

By prioritizing both utility and warranty, organizations can create IT services that are not only fit for purpose but also fit for use, providing maximum value to customers and stakeholders and driving business success.

Value Co-Creation

Value co-creation is a fundamental principle in ITIL 4, shifting the focus of service management from a provider-centric model to a collaborative one. It recognizes that value isn't solely delivered by the service provider but is actively created in partnership with the customer or stakeholder. This means that both parties play a vital role in defining, designing, and delivering services that meet the customer's unique needs and expectations.

How Service Providers and Customers Collaborate to Create Value:

- **Understanding Customer Needs:** The first step in value co-creation is to deeply understand the customer's needs, goals, and pain points. This involves actively listening to customers, seeking their feedback, and engaging them in meaningful conversations to uncover their underlying motivations and desired outcomes.
- **Jointly Defining Value:** Once customer needs are understood, service providers and customers can work together to define what value means in the context of their specific relationship. This involves identifying the desired outcomes, defining metrics for success, and establishing a shared understanding of what constitutes a valuable service experience.
- **Co-Designing Services:** Value co-creation extends to the design process, where customers are actively involved in shaping the service to meet their specific requirements. This can be done through workshops, focus groups, surveys, or other collaborative methods.
- **Iterative Development and Feedback:** Services are not created in a vacuum. They evolve through iterative development and continuous feedback. Customers are regularly engaged throughout the service lifecycle to provide feedback, suggest improvements, and validate that the service is delivering the desired value.
- **Shared Responsibility:** Value co-creation fosters a sense of shared responsibility for service success. Customers are not merely passive recipients of services but active participants in their creation and delivery.

Examples of Value Co-Creation in IT Service Management:

1. **Service Design Workshops:** Involving customers in service design workshops to gather input on their requirements, preferences, and expectations. This ensures that the service is designed from the outset with the customer's needs in mind.
2. **Customer Feedback Mechanisms:** Implementing feedback mechanisms such as surveys, focus groups, and online communities to gather continuous feedback from customers on their service experiences. This feedback can be used to identify areas for improvement and inform future service enhancements.
3. **Beta Testing and Pilot Programs:** Inviting customers to participate in beta testing or pilot programs for new services. This allows customers to provide valuable feedback and helps ensure that the service is ready for launch.
4. **Self-Service Portals and Knowledge Bases:** Providing customers with self-service tools and resources that empower them to find answers, resolve issues, and access information on their own. This not only improves efficiency but also enhances the customer experience by giving them greater control.
5. **Customer Advisory Boards:** Establishing customer advisory boards where customers can provide input on strategic direction, service priorities, and improvement initiatives. This fosters a deeper sense of partnership and collaboration.

By embracing value co-creation, IT service providers can shift from a transactional mindset to a relationship-oriented approach, where the focus is on building long-term partnerships with customers based on trust, collaboration, and mutual benefit. This approach not only leads to improved customer satisfaction but also drives innovation, efficiency, and ultimately, greater value for both the customer and the service provider.

Shifting from Outputs to Outcomes

ITIL 4 introduces a fundamental shift in perspective within service management: a move away from focusing on *outputs* (what is delivered) to *outcomes* (the results achieved). This shift in mindset is critical for ensuring that IT services truly meet the needs of customers and stakeholders, ultimately driving value creation.

Outputs vs. Outcomes: A Key Distinction

- **Outputs:** These are the tangible or intangible deliverables of a service. They are the things that the service provider produces or provides to the customer.
  - Examples: A deployed software application, a resolved incident, a completed training course, a generated report.
- **Outcomes:** These are the results or changes experienced by the customer or stakeholder as a consequence of using the service. Outcomes are the reason *why* customers engage with the service.
  - Examples: Increased revenue, improved productivity, reduced costs, enhanced customer satisfaction, mitigated risks.

ITIL 4's Emphasis on Outcomes:

ITIL 4 recognizes that while outputs are necessary for service delivery, they are not the ultimate goal. The true measure of success lies in the outcomes that services enable for customers and stakeholders.

This shift in focus from outputs to outcomes has several implications for IT service management:

- **Customer-Centricity:** It encourages a more customer-centric approach, where the focus is on understanding and meeting customer needs rather than simply delivering technical solutions.
- **Value Creation:** It emphasizes the importance of delivering value to customers, not just providing outputs.

- **Strategic Alignment:** It ensures that IT services are aligned with the overall business goals and objectives of the organization.
- **Continuous Improvement:** It promotes a continuous focus on improving service outcomes, rather than just optimizing processes for the sake of efficiency.

Examples of Applying the Shift in IT Service Management:

1. **Incident Management:**
   - **Output Focus:** Measuring success based on incident resolution times.
   - **Outcome Focus:** Measuring success based on the impact of incidents on business operations and customer satisfaction.
2. **Change Management:**
   - **Output Focus:** Focusing on the successful implementation of changes without disruption.
   - **Outcome Focus:** Measuring the impact of changes on business outcomes, such as increased efficiency or improved customer experience.
3. **Service Level Management:**
   - **Output Focus:** Monitoring compliance with service level agreements (SLAs).
   - **Outcome Focus:** Measuring the impact of service levels on customer satisfaction and business performance.

By shifting the focus from outputs to outcomes, IT service providers can ensure that their efforts are aligned with the needs of their customers and stakeholders, delivering tangible benefits to the business. This approach promotes a more collaborative, customer-centric, and value-driven approach to IT service management.

Understanding Stakeholder Needs and Expectations

ITIL 4 emphasizes the importance of adopting a stakeholder-centric approach to service management. Stakeholders are individuals or groups who have an interest or concern in an organization's services. They include customers, employees, partners, suppliers, investors, regulators, and the wider community. Understanding and meeting their diverse needs and expectations is crucial for delivering value and achieving long-term success.

Importance of Understanding Stakeholder Needs and Expectations:

- **Customer Satisfaction:** Customers are the primary recipients of IT services. Understanding their needs and expectations ensures that services are designed and delivered in a way that meets or exceeds their requirements, leading to higher satisfaction and loyalty.
- **Employee Engagement:** Employees are the ones who design, develop, deliver, and support IT services. Their engagement and motivation are essential for service excellence. Understanding their needs helps create a positive work environment, fosters collaboration, and drives innovation.
- **Partner and Supplier Collaboration:** Partners and suppliers play a vital role in the service value chain. Understanding their needs and expectations helps build strong, collaborative relationships that contribute to the successful delivery of services.
- **Business Alignment:** Understanding the needs of business stakeholders, such as executives, managers, and investors, ensures that IT services are aligned with the organization's strategic goals and objectives.
- **Regulatory Compliance:** Understanding the requirements of regulators and ensuring compliance with relevant laws and regulations protects the organization from legal and reputational risks.

Techniques for Gathering Feedback and Understanding Stakeholder Needs:

IT service providers can use a variety of techniques to gather feedback and understand stakeholder needs:

- **Surveys:** Conduct regular surveys to collect quantitative and qualitative data on stakeholder satisfaction, preferences, and expectations.
- **Interviews:** Conduct one-on-one interviews or focus groups to delve deeper into stakeholder needs and gather detailed feedback.
- **Feedback Mechanisms:** Implement feedback mechanisms such as suggestion boxes, online forums, or social media channels to encourage stakeholders to share their opinions and suggestions.
- **Observational Studies:** Observe how stakeholders use IT services in their daily work to gain insights into their needs and pain points.
- **Data Analysis:** Analyze data from various sources, such as service desk tickets, usage logs, and customer interactions, to identify patterns and trends in stakeholder behavior and preferences.

Importance of Ongoing Communication and Engagement:

Understanding stakeholder needs is not a one-time activity; it requires ongoing communication and engagement throughout the entire service lifecycle. This involves:

- **Regular Communication:** Providing regular updates on service performance, changes, and upcoming initiatives.
- **Transparent Communication:** Being open and honest about service limitations, challenges, and potential risks.
- **Active Listening:** Actively listening to stakeholder feedback, acknowledging their concerns, and taking their suggestions seriously.
- **Collaboration:** Involving stakeholders in service design, development, and improvement processes.
- **Building Relationships:** Establishing trust and rapport with stakeholders through regular interaction and open communication.

By actively engaging with stakeholders, IT service providers can build stronger relationships, gain valuable insights, and ensure that their services are continuously evolving to meet the changing needs of the people they serve.

Prioritizing Value-Driven Activities

In a world of finite resources and competing demands, prioritizing activities that deliver the most value is paramount for IT service management (ITSM). It ensures that resources are allocated effectively, efforts are focused on the most impactful initiatives, and the organization's overall goals are achieved.

Prioritization Strategies in ITSM:

1. **Align with Strategic Objectives:** The first step in prioritizing activities is to align them with the organization's strategic goals and objectives. This ensures that IT service management efforts are focused on initiatives that contribute to the overall success of the business.
2. **Understand Stakeholder Needs:** Engage with customers and stakeholders to understand their needs, expectations, and priorities. This helps identify which services and activities are most valuable from their perspective.
3. **Evaluate Potential Impact:** Assess the potential impact of different activities on key metrics like customer satisfaction, operational efficiency, revenue generation, and risk mitigation. Consider both short-term and long-term impacts.
4. **Consider Costs and Benefits:** Conduct a cost-benefit analysis to evaluate the financial implications of different options. Compare the costs of implementing an activity or initiative with the expected benefits to determine its overall value.

Techniques for Evaluating and Prioritizing Options:

- **Cost-Benefit Analysis:** A systematic approach to evaluating the costs and benefits of different options. It involves quantifying the costs and benefits in monetary terms and calculating the return on investment (ROI) for each option.
- **Impact Mapping:** A visual tool that helps map out the potential impact of different initiatives on various stakeholders and outcomes. It can help identify which initiatives are most likely to deliver the greatest value.
- **Prioritization Matrices:** These matrices use weighted criteria to evaluate and prioritize different options. The criteria can be customized based on the organization's specific needs and priorities.
- **MoSCoW Method:** This simple prioritization technique categorizes activities into four categories: Must Have, Should Have, Could Have, and Won't Have. This helps focus on the most critical activities first.
- **Weighted Shortest Job First (WSJF):** A prioritization model used in Agile and DevOps environments, which prioritizes tasks based on their business value, time criticality, and risk reduction/opportunity enablement.

Aligning ITSM Decisions with Business Strategy:

Prioritizing value-driven activities is not just about maximizing efficiency or minimizing costs. It's about ensuring that IT service management decisions align with the broader strategic objectives of the organization. This involves:

- **Understanding Business Goals:** IT leaders need to have a deep understanding of the organization's business goals and how IT services can contribute to their achievement.
- **Collaborating with Business Stakeholders:** Regular communication and collaboration with business stakeholders are essential to ensure that IT service management decisions are aligned with their needs and priorities.
- **Translating Business Objectives into IT Goals:** Business objectives need to be translated into specific IT goals and metrics that can be used to measure the success of IT service management initiatives.
- **Communicating the Value of IT:** IT leaders need to effectively communicate the value of IT services to business stakeholders, highlighting their contribution to achieving strategic goals and driving business outcomes.

By adopting a value-driven approach to prioritization, organizations can ensure that their IT service management efforts are focused on the most impactful initiatives, delivering maximum value to customers and stakeholders, and contributing to the overall success of the business.

Measuring and Demonstrating Value

In the ITIL 4 framework, the ability to measure and demonstrate the value that IT services deliver is paramount. It's not enough to simply provide services; organizations must prove that these services are making a tangible and positive impact on the business.

Importance of Measuring and Demonstrating Value:

- **Justifying Investments:** Measuring value provides concrete evidence of the return on investment (ROI) for IT services, justifying the resources allocated to them.
- **Securing Funding:** Demonstrating the value of IT can help secure funding for future projects and initiatives, as stakeholders are more likely to invest in areas that show a clear return.
- **Building Credibility:** By providing tangible evidence of value, IT departments can build credibility and trust with business leaders and stakeholders.
- **Driving Improvement:** Measuring value helps identify areas where services can be improved, allowing for more targeted and effective optimization efforts.
- **Aligning with Business Goals:** Demonstrating the value of IT services in the context of broader business goals ensures that IT is seen as a strategic partner, not just a cost center.

Approaches to Measuring Value:

There is no one-size-fits-all approach to measuring value, as it depends on the specific goals and context of each organization. However, some common approaches include:

1. **Cost Savings:** This involves quantifying the financial benefits of IT services, such as reduced operational costs, avoided expenses, or increased efficiency. Examples of cost-saving metrics include:
   - Reduced downtime
   - Decreased incident resolution time
   - Lowered support costs
   - Optimized resource utilization
2. **Revenue Generation:** This focuses on how IT services directly contribute to revenue generation, such as through increased sales, improved customer retention, or new product development. Examples of revenue-generating metrics include:
   - Increased customer lifetime value
   - Improved sales conversion rates
   - Faster time to market for new products
3. **Improved Customer Satisfaction:** This measures the impact of IT services on customer satisfaction and loyalty. Examples of customer satisfaction metrics include:
   - Net Promoter Score (NPS)
   - Customer satisfaction surveys
   - Reduced customer complaints
4. **Enhanced Productivity:** This assesses how IT services improve the productivity of employees and teams. Examples of productivity metrics include:
   - Increased employee output
   - Reduced time spent on manual tasks
   - Improved collaboration and communication

Examples of Metrics and Key Performance Indicators (KPIs):

- **Mean Time to Repair (MTTR):** The average time it takes to resolve an incident.
- **Customer Satisfaction (CSAT) Score:** A measure of how satisfied customers are with a service.
- **Net Promoter Score (NPS):** A measure of customer loyalty and willingness to recommend a service.
- **Return on Investment (ROI):** The financial return on an investment in IT services.
- **Employee Productivity:** The amount of work produced by employees in a given time period.
- **Service Availability:** The percentage of time a service is available to users.

Communicating the Value of IT Services to Stakeholders:

Effective communication of value is crucial for securing support and investment in IT services. When communicating with stakeholders, it's important to:

- **Use clear and concise language:** Avoid technical jargon and use language that stakeholders can easily understand.
- **Focus on business outcomes:** Explain how IT services contribute to the organization's strategic goals and objectives.
- **Provide concrete examples:** Use real-world examples and case studies to illustrate the value of IT services.
- **Use visuals:** Utilize graphs, charts, and dashboards to present data in a visually appealing and easy-to-understand format.
- **Tailor communication to the audience:** Understand the specific needs and interests of different stakeholders and tailor your communication accordingly.

By effectively measuring and demonstrating the value of IT services, organizations can ensure that their IT investments are aligned with business goals, deliver tangible benefits, and contribute to the overall success of the organization.

Chapter Summary

In this chapter, we explored the guiding principle of "Focus on Value," a core tenet of the ITIL 4 framework. We delved into the nuanced understanding of value in service management, recognizing its subjective nature and the importance of aligning it with the needs and perceptions of various stakeholders.

Key takeaways from this chapter include:

- **Value at the Core:** We highlighted how the concept of value permeates the entire ITIL 4 framework, guiding decisions and actions to ensure that services deliver meaningful benefits to customers and stakeholders.
- **Defining Value:** We dissected the ITIL 4 definition of value, emphasizing its two key components: utility (the functionality of a service) and warranty (the assurance that a service will meet agreed-upon requirements). We explained how both utility and warranty are crucial for delivering a complete value proposition.
- **Value Co-Creation:** We explored the collaborative nature of value creation, emphasizing that it is not solely delivered by the service provider but is co-created with the customer. We discussed how this can be achieved through active engagement, feedback mechanisms, and shared responsibility.
- **Shifting from Outputs to Outcomes:** We emphasized the importance of focusing on outcomes—the results that services enable for customers—rather than just outputs or deliverables. This shift ensures that IT services are truly aligned with customer needs and deliver meaningful value.
- **Understanding Stakeholder Needs:** We stressed the importance of understanding the diverse needs and expectations of all stakeholders, including customers, employees, partners, and suppliers. We discussed various techniques for gathering feedback and emphasized the need for ongoing communication and engagement.
- **Prioritizing Value-Driven Activities:** We explored how organizations can prioritize activities that deliver the greatest value by aligning with strategic objectives, understanding stakeholder needs, evaluating potential impact, and considering costs and benefits.
- **Measuring and Demonstrating Value:** We discussed the importance of measuring and demonstrating the value of IT services to justify investments, secure funding, and build credibility. We explored various approaches to measuring value, such as cost savings, revenue generation, improved customer satisfaction, and enhanced productivity, and provided examples of relevant metrics.

By internalizing the principle of "Focus on Value" and implementing the strategies discussed in this chapter, you can ensure that your IT service management efforts are not just about delivering technology solutions, but about creating meaningful value for your customers and stakeholders. This customer-centric and value-driven approach is the foundation for building successful and sustainable IT services in today's competitive landscape.

Start Where You Are

Outline

- Understanding the "Start Where You Are" Principle
- Assessing the Current State
- The Risks and Costs of Starting from Scratch
- Benefits of Building on Existing Foundations
- How to Start Where You Are
- Case Studies and Examples
- Chapter Summary

Understanding the "Start Where You Are" Principle

The "Start Where You Are" principle is a cornerstone of the ITIL 4 framework, embodying a pragmatic and efficient approach to service management. It encourages organizations to assess their current state, identify existing strengths, and build upon them rather than starting from scratch. This principle recognizes that every organization has unique strengths and resources that can be leveraged for improvement, making ITIL 4 adaptable to diverse contexts.

The Principle's Practicality and Efficiency:

This principle is rooted in practicality and efficiency. It acknowledges that starting from scratch is often unnecessary and can be counterproductive. By building on existing foundations, organizations can:

- **Save Time and Resources:** Reusing existing processes, tools, and knowledge eliminates the need to reinvent the wheel, saving valuable time and resources that can be better allocated to other areas.
- **Reduce Risk:** Starting with familiar practices and technologies reduces the risk of disruption and failure. Organizations can leverage their existing knowledge and experience to avoid common pitfalls and ensure a smoother transition to new ways of working.
- **Foster Buy-In:** Involving employees in the improvement process and leveraging their existing knowledge can increase engagement and buy-in, leading to a more successful implementation.
- **Preserve Organizational Knowledge:** Building on existing practices helps preserve valuable organizational knowledge and expertise, preventing the loss of institutional memory that can occur when starting from scratch.

Leveraging Existing Strengths and Capabilities:

The "Start Where You Are" principle encourages organizations to take stock of their current strengths and capabilities. This includes:

- **Processes:** Identify existing processes that are working well and can be built upon.
- **Tools and Technologies:** Assess existing tools and technologies to determine whether they can be leveraged or adapted for new initiatives.
- **Knowledge and Expertise:** Identify individuals or teams within the organization who possess valuable knowledge and expertise that can be leveraged.

By identifying and building upon these existing strengths, organizations can avoid unnecessary disruption, accelerate the adoption of ITIL 4, and create a more sustainable and effective service management system.

Assessing the Current State

Before embarking on any ITIL 4 implementation or improvement initiative, it is crucial to thoroughly assess the organization's current state of IT service management (ITSM). This assessment serves as a baseline for understanding existing strengths, weaknesses, and areas for improvement, enabling informed decision-making and a tailored approach to change.

Importance of Conducting a Thorough Assessment:

- **Identifying Strengths:** Recognizing existing strengths allows organizations to leverage their existing capabilities and build upon them, rather than starting from scratch. This can save time, resources, and reduce the risk of disruption.
- **Uncovering Weaknesses:** Identifying weaknesses or gaps in current practices is essential for prioritizing improvement efforts and allocating resources effectively.
- **Understanding the Current State:** A thorough assessment provides a clear picture of the organization's current ITSM maturity level, helping to set realistic expectations and goals for improvement.
- **Informing Decision Making:** Assessment results can inform decisions about which ITIL 4 practices to adopt, how to adapt them to the organization's specific needs, and where to focus improvement efforts.
- **Building Consensus:** Involving stakeholders in the assessment process can help build consensus and support for the implementation of ITIL 4.

Assessment Tools and Techniques:

Various tools and techniques can be used to assess the current state of ITSM:

1. **Maturity Models:** These models provide a structured framework for assessing the maturity level of different ITSM processes or capabilities. They typically define several levels of maturity, from basic to advanced, and provide criteria for evaluating each level.
2. **Gap Analyses:** These analyses compare the organization's current practices against industry best practices or ITIL 4 recommendations. They help identify gaps between the desired state and the current state, highlighting areas where improvements are needed.
3. **Benchmarking:** This involves comparing the organization's ITSM performance against that of other organizations in the same industry or with similar characteristics. Benchmarking can help identify areas where the organization is lagging behind and needs to catch up.
4. **Surveys and Interviews:** These tools can be used to gather qualitative feedback from employees, customers, and other stakeholders about their experiences with IT services and their perceptions of service quality.
5. **Data Analysis:** Analyzing data from various sources, such as incident records, service level agreements (SLAs), and customer satisfaction surveys, can provide quantitative insights into service performance and areas for improvement.

Involving Relevant Stakeholders in the Assessment Process:

It is important to involve relevant stakeholders in the assessment process to gain diverse perspectives and ensure that the assessment is comprehensive and accurate. Stakeholders can include:

- **IT Staff:** Service desk agents, support technicians, managers, and other IT personnel who are directly involved in service delivery.
- **Business Users:** Employees who use IT services in their daily work.
- **Customers:** External customers who rely on the organization's IT services.
- **Partners and Suppliers:** External entities that contribute to the delivery of IT services.
- **Senior Management:** Executives and managers who have a strategic interest in IT service management.

By involving a wide range of stakeholders, organizations can gain a more complete understanding of their current state of ITSM, identify areas for improvement, and build consensus for implementing changes. This collaborative approach also helps to ensure that the assessment results are accurate, relevant, and actionable.

The Risks and Costs of Starting from Scratch

While the prospect of a fresh start can be alluring, disregarding existing practices and capabilities when implementing new ITSM initiatives or adopting ITIL 4 can be fraught with risks and hidden costs.

Potential Risks:

1. **Disruption to Existing Services:** Implementing entirely new processes and tools can disrupt existing services, leading to downtime, errors, and frustrated customers. This can have a significant impact on business operations and productivity.
2. **Resistance to Change:** Employees who are accustomed to existing ways of working may resist new processes and technologies. This can lead to low morale, decreased productivity, and even sabotage of the new initiative.
3. **Loss of Knowledge and Expertise:** Discarding existing practices can result in the loss of valuable organizational knowledge and expertise. This can make it difficult to troubleshoot issues, understand historical context, and make informed decisions.
4. **Increased Risk of Failure:** Starting from scratch often involves a steep learning curve and increased risk of errors. Organizations may underestimate the complexity of the new initiative, leading to delays, cost overruns, and ultimately, failure to achieve desired outcomes.

Common Pitfalls of Ignoring Existing Practices:

- **Reinventing the Wheel:** Wasting time and resources developing new processes or tools that may already exist in some form within the organization.
- **Underestimating Complexity:** Oversimplifying the challenges of implementing new initiatives and underestimating the time and effort required.
- **Lack of Buy-In:** Failing to involve stakeholders in the decision-making process, leading to resistance and lack of support for the new initiative.
- **Disregarding Valuable Lessons:** Ignoring the lessons learned from past experiences and repeating the same mistakes.

Costs Associated with Starting from Scratch:

- **Financial Costs:** Investing in new tools, technologies, and training can be expensive. Organizations may also incur additional costs due to delays, rework, and lost productivity during the transition.
- **Opportunity Costs:** Starting from scratch can divert resources away from other important initiatives, delaying the realization of potential benefits and missed opportunities.
- **Reputational Costs:** Disruptions to services or failed implementations can damage the organization's reputation, leading to customer dissatisfaction and loss of trust.

Importance of Careful Evaluation:

Before deciding to start from scratch, organizations should carefully evaluate the costs and benefits of different approaches. This involves:

- **Assessing the Current State:** Conduct a thorough assessment of existing ITSM practices, processes, and capabilities to identify strengths and weaknesses.
- **Identifying Improvement Opportunities:** Based on the assessment, identify areas where improvements can be made without completely overhauling existing systems.

- **Considering Alternatives:** Explore different options for improvement, such as adapting existing processes, integrating new tools with existing systems, or phasing in changes gradually.
- **Weighing Costs and Benefits:** Carefully consider the financial, operational, and reputational costs of each option, as well as the potential benefits and risks.

By taking a thoughtful and measured approach, organizations can avoid the pitfalls of starting from scratch and maximize the value of their IT service management investments.

Benefits of Building on Existing Foundations

Adopting the "Start Where You Are" principle and building upon the organization's existing foundations when implementing ITIL 4 or other ITSM initiatives offers numerous advantages that can lead to a smoother, more efficient, and ultimately more successful transition.

1. Leveraging Existing Knowledge, Experience, and Resources:

- **Reduced Learning Curve:** Employees already possess valuable knowledge and experience with existing processes and tools. Building on this foundation reduces the need for extensive training and minimizes the learning curve associated with new practices.
- **Faster Implementation:** By leveraging existing resources and knowledge, organizations can avoid the time-consuming process of reinventing the wheel, accelerating the implementation of new initiatives.
- **Cost Savings:** Building on existing foundations can be more cost-effective than starting from scratch, as it eliminates the need to invest in new tools, technologies, and training materials. Organizations can redirect those resources to other critical areas.

2. Reduced Risk and Improved Success Rate:

- **Mitigated Disruption:** Building on existing practices helps to minimize disruption to existing services and workflows. This ensures that critical business operations continue uninterrupted during the transition.
- **Lower Risk of Failure:** Starting with familiar practices and technologies reduces the risk of errors, delays, and other issues that can derail an implementation.
- **Increased Adaptability:** Building on existing foundations allows organizations to tailor ITIL 4 practices to their specific context and needs, increasing the chances of successful adoption.

3. Fostering Ownership and Engagement:

- **Employee Empowerment:** Involving employees in the improvement process and leveraging their existing knowledge empowers them to take ownership of the changes. This fosters a sense of pride and engagement, increasing their motivation to contribute to the success of the initiative.
- **Increased Collaboration:** Building on existing practices encourages collaboration and knowledge sharing among teams. This can lead to the identification of innovative solutions and a more seamless integration of new practices.
- **Reduced Resistance to Change:** When employees feel that their existing knowledge and experience are valued, they are more likely to embrace change and support new initiatives.

In summary, the "Start Where You Are" principle offers a practical and effective approach to implementing ITIL 4 or other ITSM initiatives. By leveraging existing strengths, reducing risk, and fostering employee engagement, organizations can achieve a smoother, faster, and more successful transition to improved service management practices. This approach not only saves time and resources but also helps organizations maximize the value they derive from their IT investments.

How to Start Where You Are

Embracing the "Start Where You Are" principle in ITIL 4 implementation involves a systematic approach that leverages your organization's existing strengths and resources while paving the way for improvement. Here's a practical guide on how to put this principle into action:

1. **Identify and Document Existing Processes, Tools, and Resources:**
   - **Conduct a Thorough Inventory:** Begin by documenting all existing IT service management (ITSM) processes, tools, and resources. This includes formal and informal processes, software applications, hardware, knowledge bases, and even the expertise of your team members.
   - **Use Visual Aids:** Consider using flowcharts, diagrams, or other visual aids to represent the current state of your processes. This can help identify bottlenecks, redundancies, and opportunities for optimization.
2. **Assess Current Capabilities:**
   - **Baseline Assessment:** Evaluate the maturity and effectiveness of your existing ITSM practices. This can be done through self-assessments, maturity models, or external audits.
   - **Gap Analysis:** Compare your current state against the desired state defined by ITIL 4. Identify gaps or areas where your practices fall short of ITIL recommendations.
   - **Stakeholder Input:** Gather feedback from stakeholders, including IT staff, business users, and customers, to gain insights into their experiences and expectations.
3. **Prioritize Improvement Initiatives:**
   - **Impact and Feasibility:** Prioritize the identified gaps based on their potential impact on service quality, efficiency, and customer satisfaction, as well as their feasibility in terms of resources, time, and organizational readiness.
   - **Quick Wins:** Look for opportunities to achieve quick wins, such as addressing simple process bottlenecks or implementing minor improvements that can have a significant impact.
   - **Long-Term Goals:** Develop a roadmap for addressing more complex or strategic improvements over time.
4. **Adapt ITIL 4 Practices to Your Context:**
   - **Tailor to Your Needs:** ITIL 4 is a flexible framework. Don't feel obligated to adopt every practice verbatim. Instead, adapt the practices to fit your organization's unique context, culture, and maturity level.
   - **Start Small and Scale Up:** Begin with a few key practices that address your most pressing needs and gradually expand your implementation as you gain experience and confidence.
   - **Focus on Value:** Always keep the focus on delivering value to your customers and stakeholders. Prioritize improvements that have a clear and measurable impact on business outcomes.
5. **Continual Improvement:**
   - **Monitor and Measure:** Regularly monitor and measure the performance of your processes and services to identify areas for further improvement.
   - **Feedback Loop:** Establish a feedback loop with customers and stakeholders to gather insights and ensure that your services continue to meet their needs.
   - **Adapt and Evolve:** Continuously adapt and evolve your ITSM practices based on feedback, changing business needs, and emerging technologies.

Additional Tips:

- **Engage Leadership:** Secure leadership support for your ITIL 4 initiative. Their buy-in is crucial for success.
- **Communicate Effectively:** Communicate the goals, benefits, and progress of your initiative to all stakeholders to build support and manage expectations.
- **Celebrate Success:** Recognize and celebrate successes along the way to maintain momentum and motivation.

By following these steps and embracing the "Start Where You Are" principle, you can implement ITIL 4 in a way that is both practical and effective, leveraging your organization's existing strengths and resources to deliver high-quality IT services and achieve your business goals.

Case Studies and Examples

The "Start Where You Are" principle has proven to be a successful approach for numerous organizations across various industries, enabling them to seamlessly integrate ITIL 4 into their existing frameworks and achieve significant improvements in their IT service management (ITSM) practices.

Case Study 1: Financial Services Firm

- **Challenge:** A large financial services firm was looking to adopt ITIL 4 to improve the efficiency and effectiveness of its IT services. However, the organization was hesitant to completely overhaul its existing processes and tools, which had been in place for many years.
- **Strategy:** The firm decided to take a phased approach, starting with a thorough assessment of its current ITSM practices. The assessment identified several areas for improvement, including incident management, change management, and problem management. The firm then prioritized these areas based on their potential impact and feasibility, and began implementing ITIL 4 practices incrementally, adapting them to fit the organization's specific context and culture.
- **Outcome:** By building on its existing foundations, the firm was able to successfully adopt ITIL 4 without disrupting its core operations. The implementation led to significant improvements in incident resolution times, change success rates, and overall customer satisfaction. The firm also realized cost savings by eliminating redundant processes and automating manual tasks.

Case Study 2: Healthcare Provider

- **Challenge:** A healthcare provider was struggling with inefficient IT service delivery, resulting in delays, errors, and frustrated users. The organization wanted to implement ITIL 4 to improve service quality, but it was concerned about the potential disruption and cost of a complete overhaul.
- **Strategy:** The healthcare provider opted to leverage its existing electronic health record (EHR) system and other IT tools as a starting point for its ITIL 4 implementation. It conducted a gap analysis to identify areas where its practices fell short of ITIL recommendations and then prioritized those areas for improvement. The provider also invested in training and communication to ensure that staff understood the new practices and were committed to their success.
- **Outcome:** By building on its existing EHR system and other IT tools, the healthcare provider was able to implement ITIL 4 quickly and efficiently. The new practices led to a significant reduction in incident volumes, improved response times, and higher levels of user satisfaction. The organization also saw a decrease in IT-related costs due to improved efficiency and fewer service disruptions.

Case Study 3: Manufacturing Company

- **Challenge:** A global manufacturing company was facing increasing pressure to reduce costs and improve the efficiency of its IT operations. The company decided to adopt ITIL 4 to streamline its processes and optimize resource utilization.
- **Strategy:** The company conducted a value stream mapping exercise to identify areas of waste and inefficiency in its IT service delivery processes. Based on the results of the mapping exercise, the company implemented several improvements, such as automating routine tasks, standardizing processes, and improving communication and collaboration between teams.
- **Outcome:** By building on its existing processes and identifying opportunities for improvement, the manufacturing company was able to reduce its IT operating costs by 15% while also improving service quality and customer satisfaction. The company also achieved greater agility and responsiveness, enabling it to adapt quickly to changing business needs and market demands.

These case studies illustrate the versatility and effectiveness of the "Start Where You Are" principle in different organizational contexts and industries. By leveraging existing strengths, organizations can successfully adopt and adapt ITIL 4 to their unique needs, driving continuous improvement in their IT service management practices and delivering greater value to their customers and stakeholders.

Chapter Summary

In this chapter, we explored the ITIL 4 guiding principle of "Start Where You Are," a practical and efficient approach to implementing service management improvements. This principle emphasizes the importance of building upon your organization's existing strengths and capabilities rather than starting from scratch.

Key points covered in this chapter include:

- **Understanding the Principle:** We delved into the core concept of "Start Where You Are," highlighting its emphasis on practicality, efficiency, and leveraging existing resources to drive improvement.
- **Assessing the Current State:** We discussed the importance of conducting a thorough assessment of your organization's current ITSM practices, processes, and capabilities. We also explored various assessment tools and techniques, such as maturity models, gap analyses, and benchmarking, to identify strengths, weaknesses, and areas for improvement.
- **Risks and Costs of Starting from Scratch:** We highlighted the potential risks and costs associated with disregarding existing practices, such as disruption to services, resistance to change, loss of knowledge, and increased risk of failure.
- **Benefits of Building on Existing Foundations:** We explored the numerous advantages of leveraging existing knowledge, experience, and resources, including reduced learning curves, faster implementation, cost savings, and improved chances of success. We also emphasized how this approach fosters employee ownership and engagement.
- **How to Start Where You Are:** We provided practical guidance and steps on how to implement this principle, from identifying and documenting existing processes to prioritizing improvement initiatives and adapting ITIL 4 practices to your organization's context.
- **Case Studies and Examples:** We shared real-world examples of organizations that successfully applied the "Start Where You Are" principle, showcasing the tangible benefits it can bring across different industries and contexts.

By understanding and applying the "Start Where You Are" principle, you can approach ITIL 4 implementation with a pragmatic and efficient mindset. This allows you to leverage your organization's existing strengths, minimize risks, and achieve a smoother transition to improved service management practices. Remember, the journey towards service excellence is not always about starting anew, but often about building upon the solid foundation you already have.

Progress Iteratively with Feedback

Outline

- Understanding the "Progress Iteratively with Feedback" Principle
- The Benefits of Iterative Progress
- The Role of Feedback
- Practical Steps for Iterative Progress
- Applying the Principle to Different ITIL Practices
- Common Challenges and How to Overcome Them
- Case Studies and Examples
- Chapter Summary

Understanding the "Progress Iteratively with Feedback" Principle

At its core, the "Progress Iteratively with Feedback" principle in ITIL 4 champions a method of continuous improvement where changes are implemented in small, manageable steps, rather than all at once. This is followed by a crucial phase of gathering feedback, learning from the results, and then adjusting the approach before proceeding to the next iteration. This cycle repeats until the desired outcome is achieved.

Contrast with "Big Bang" Approaches:

This iterative approach contrasts sharply with traditional "big bang" methods, where organizations attempt to implement large-scale changes in one fell swoop. While big bang implementations might seem appealing for their potential to deliver immediate and widespread results, they often carry significant risks. These risks include:

- **Disruption:** Large-scale changes can disrupt existing workflows and processes, leading to downtime, errors, and user dissatisfaction.
- **Resistance to Change:** Employees may resist sudden, drastic changes, leading to low morale and lack of adoption.
- **Difficulty in Identifying and Correcting Issues:** With big bang implementations, it can be difficult to pinpoint the source of problems if things go wrong. This can make it challenging to course-correct and may result in costly rework.

Advantages of Iterative Progress:

Iterative progress, on the other hand, offers several advantages:

1. **Reduced Risk:** Smaller, incremental changes are less likely to cause widespread disruption and are easier to roll back if necessary. This allows organizations to experiment and learn without jeopardizing the stability of their services.
2. **Faster Learning and Adaptation:** By gathering feedback after each iteration, organizations can quickly identify what's working and what's not, allowing for rapid adjustments and course corrections. This leads to a more agile and responsive approach to service management.
3. **Increased Stakeholder Engagement:** Involving stakeholders in each iteration of the improvement process fosters a sense of ownership and collaboration. This helps build support for the initiative and ensures that changes align with the needs and expectations of those who will be impacted.
4. **Continuous Improvement:** Iterative progress is a natural fit for the ITIL 4 Continual Improvement Model, which emphasizes the importance of ongoing learning and adaptation. By continuously iterating and incorporating feedback, organizations can create a culture of continuous improvement that drives service excellence.

In summary, the "Progress Iteratively with Feedback" principle provides a more flexible, adaptable, and ultimately more successful approach to service management. By breaking down large initiatives into smaller, manageable steps and regularly gathering feedback, organizations can minimize risk, maximize learning, and ensure that their services are constantly evolving to meet the needs of their customers and stakeholders.

The Benefits of Iterative Progress

Iterative progress is a core tenet of Agile methodologies and a cornerstone of ITIL 4's "Progress Iteratively with Feedback" principle. It offers a pragmatic and flexible approach to change management, enabling organizations to continuously improve their services while mitigating risks and fostering adaptability.

Advantages of Progressing Iteratively:

1. **Reduced Risk:**
   - **Smaller Changes, Smaller Impact:** By breaking down large initiatives into smaller, manageable iterations, organizations can limit the potential impact of any single change. If a change introduces unexpected issues, it's easier to isolate and roll back the specific iteration, minimizing disruption to services and users.
   - **Controlled Experimentation:** Iterative progress allows organizations to experiment with new ideas and approaches in a controlled environment. This enables them to test hypotheses, gather data, and validate assumptions before committing to large-scale changes.
2. **Faster Learning and Adaptation:**
   - **Short Feedback Loops:** Iterative progress creates short feedback loops, enabling organizations to gather feedback quickly and frequently. This feedback provides valuable insights into what's working well and what needs to be improved, allowing for rapid adjustments and course corrections.
   - **Continuous Learning Culture:** Regular feedback and adaptation foster a culture of continuous learning within the organization. Teams become more adept at identifying and addressing problems, leading to improved processes and outcomes over time.
3. **Increased Agility:**
   - **Responding to Change:** In today's fast-paced business environment, the ability to adapt to change is crucial. Iterative progress allows organizations to respond quickly to evolving market conditions, customer demands, and technological advancements.
   - **Flexibility and Adaptability:** By working in smaller iterations, organizations can easily pivot and adjust their plans based on feedback and new information. This flexibility enables them to stay ahead of the curve and remain competitive.
4. **Improved Stakeholder Engagement:**
   - **Building Trust and Collaboration:** Regularly involving stakeholders in the improvement process through feedback and participation builds trust and fosters collaboration. This leads to a greater sense of ownership and shared responsibility for the success of the initiative.
   - **Managing Expectations:** Iterative progress allows organizations to set realistic expectations with stakeholders, demonstrating progress and delivering value incrementally. This can help build support and enthusiasm for the overall initiative.

In Summary:

Iterative progress offers a powerful approach to service management, enabling organizations to reduce risk, accelerate learning, increase agility, and foster stakeholder engagement. By embracing this principle, organizations can continuously improve their services, adapt to changing circumstances, and deliver greater value to their customers and stakeholders.

The Role of Feedback

Feedback is the cornerstone of the "Progress Iteratively with Feedback" principle. It acts as a compass, guiding organizations through the iterative improvement cycle by providing valuable insights into what's working, what's not, and where adjustments are needed.

Critical Role of Feedback in the Iterative Progress Cycle:

In the iterative progress cycle, feedback serves as a constant check and balance. After each iteration, feedback is collected and analyzed to assess the impact of the changes made. This feedback then informs the next iteration, guiding adjustments and refinements to the process or service.

This iterative feedback loop ensures that the improvement process is data-driven and responsive to the needs and expectations of stakeholders. It prevents organizations from getting stuck in a rut or pursuing initiatives that are not delivering the desired results.

Valuable Insights from Feedback:

Feedback provides a wealth of information that can be used to improve IT service management:

- **Identifying Strengths:** Feedback can highlight what is working well, allowing organizations to build upon those strengths and leverage them for further improvement.
- **Uncovering Weaknesses:** Feedback can pinpoint areas where services or processes are falling short, enabling organizations to address those weaknesses and prevent future problems.
- **Understanding Customer and Stakeholder Needs:** Feedback from customers and stakeholders provides valuable insights into their expectations, preferences, and pain points. This information can be used to design and deliver services that better meet their needs.
- **Measuring Progress and Success:** Feedback can be used to measure the effectiveness of improvement initiatives and track progress towards goals. This data-driven approach ensures that efforts are focused on the most impactful areas.

Types of Feedback:

1. **Customer Feedback:** This can be gathered through surveys, interviews, focus groups, social media, or other channels. Customer feedback provides insights into their satisfaction levels, expectations, and suggestions for improvement.
2. **Employee Feedback:** Feedback from employees who are directly involved in service delivery is invaluable. They can provide insights into process bottlenecks, technical issues, and areas where training or support may be needed.
3. **Performance Data:** This includes metrics and key performance indicators (KPIs) that track the performance of IT services and processes. Performance data can reveal trends, patterns, and anomalies that can be used to identify improvement opportunities.

Collecting, Analyzing, and Acting on Feedback Effectively:

To leverage feedback effectively, organizations need to:

- **Collect Feedback Regularly:** Establish regular feedback mechanisms, such as surveys, interviews, or feedback forms, to gather input from stakeholders.
- **Analyze Feedback Systematically:** Analyze feedback data to identify trends, patterns, and common themes. Use this analysis to prioritize improvement initiatives.
- **Act on Feedback:** Implement changes based on the feedback received, communicating the actions taken to stakeholders to close the feedback loop.
- **Track and Measure Results:** Monitor the impact of changes implemented based on feedback to ensure that they are having the desired effect.

Creating a Culture of Open Communication and Feedback:

Fostering a culture of open communication and feedback is essential for the success of the "Progress Iteratively with Feedback" principle. This involves creating an environment where employees feel safe to speak up, share ideas, and raise concerns without fear of retribution. It also means actively seeking feedback from customers and stakeholders and valuing their input.

By creating a culture that embraces feedback, organizations can continuously learn and adapt, driving innovation and improvement in their IT service management practices.

Practical Steps for Iterative Progress

Implementing the "Progress Iteratively with Feedback" principle requires a structured approach that embraces experimentation, learning, and adaptation. Here's a step-by-step guide to help you apply this principle in practice:

1. **Define Goals and Objectives:**
- **Clear Vision:** Start by articulating a clear vision of what you want to achieve through your improvement initiative. This vision should be aligned with your organization's strategic goals and customer needs.
- **SMART Objectives:** Break down the vision into specific, measurable, achievable, relevant, and time-bound (SMART) objectives. This will help you track progress and evaluate success.
2. **Break Down Work into Smaller Iterations:**
- **Manageable Chunks:** Divide the overall initiative into smaller, more manageable iterations or phases. Each iteration should have a clear focus and deliver a tangible outcome.
- **Prioritize:** Prioritize iterations based on their potential impact and feasibility. Start with smaller, less risky changes that can deliver quick wins and build momentum.
3. **Implement Changes:**
- **Controlled Environment:** If possible, test changes in a controlled environment, such as a pilot project or sandbox, before rolling them out to the entire organization.
- **Change Control:** Implement changes in a controlled and coordinated manner, following established change management processes to minimize risk and disruption.
- **Communication:** Clearly communicate the changes being implemented, their purpose, and expected outcomes to all relevant stakeholders.
4. **Gather Feedback:**
- **Diverse Sources:** Collect feedback from a variety of stakeholders, including customers, employees, partners, and suppliers. Use surveys, interviews, focus groups, or other methods to gather diverse perspectives.
- **Quantitative and Qualitative Data:** Collect both quantitative data (e.g., metrics, KPIs) and qualitative data (e.g., opinions, experiences, suggestions) to gain a comprehensive understanding of the impact of the changes.
- **Timely Feedback:** Gather feedback promptly after each iteration so you can make adjustments quickly and efficiently.
5. **Analyze Feedback and Adjust:**
- **Identify Patterns and Themes:** Analyze feedback data to identify patterns, trends, and common themes. Look for areas where the changes are working well, as well as areas where improvements are needed.
- **Root Cause Analysis:** If problems or negative feedback arise, conduct root cause analysis to understand the underlying causes and identify solutions.
- **Incorporate Feedback into Next Iteration:** Use the feedback to adjust your plans and refine your approach for the next iteration.
6. **Repeat:**
- **Continuous Cycle:** Continue the cycle of implementation, feedback, and adjustment until you achieve your desired outcomes. Each iteration should build upon the learnings from the previous ones, leading to continuous improvement.

- **Celebrate Success:** Celebrate milestones and achievements along the way to maintain momentum and motivation.

Additional Tips:

- **Embrace a Growth Mindset:** Encourage a culture of experimentation and learning from mistakes.
- **Be Flexible and Adaptable:** Be prepared to adjust your plans based on feedback and changing circumstances.
- **Communicate Transparently:** Keep stakeholders informed about progress, challenges, and successes throughout the process.
- **Celebrate Small Wins:** Recognize and celebrate small victories along the way to keep morale high and maintain momentum.

By following these practical steps, you can effectively implement the "Progress Iteratively with Feedback" principle in your IT service management initiatives, driving continuous improvement and delivering greater value to your customers and stakeholders.

Applying the Principle to Different ITIL Practices

The "Progress Iteratively with Feedback" principle can be effectively integrated into various ITIL 4 practices, enhancing their effectiveness and adaptability. Let's explore how this principle can be applied in several key practices:

1. Incident Management:

- **Iterative Approach:** Instead of making sweeping changes to the entire incident management process, focus on incremental improvements to specific areas, such as ticket categorization, prioritization, or resolution procedures.
- **Feedback Loop:** Gather feedback from both users and support teams after each iteration. Use this feedback to identify pain points, areas for improvement, and potential solutions. For instance, if users find the incident reporting form too cumbersome, simplify it in the next iteration.

2. Change Management:

- **Phased Implementation:** Break down large changes into smaller, more manageable phases. This allows for better risk management and easier rollback if issues arise.
- **Test and Learn:** Test changes in a controlled environment (like a staging or test environment) before deploying them to production. Gather feedback from testers and users to identify potential problems and make necessary adjustments.

3. Problem Management:

- **Root Cause Analysis Iterations:** Problem management often involves a series of investigations and analyses to identify the root cause of an incident. Each iteration should build upon the previous one, gradually narrowing down the possibilities and leading to a resolution.
- **Feedback from Multiple Sources:** Gather feedback from various sources, such as incident data, error logs, user reports, and subject matter experts, to identify patterns and trends that can help pinpoint the root cause.
- **Kaizen Approach:** Embrace a "kaizen" approach, which means continuous improvement in small, incremental steps. Implement small changes to address the root cause and monitor their effectiveness before moving on to the next iteration.

4. Continual Improvement:

- **The Core of Iteration:** Continual improvement is inherently iterative. It involves a cyclical process of identifying improvement opportunities, planning and implementing changes, measuring their impact, and gathering feedback to inform further improvements.
- **Data-Driven Decisions:** Use data and metrics to assess the effectiveness of improvement initiatives and guide future actions. Track key performance indicators (KPIs) over time to identify trends and patterns that can inform decision-making.
- **Iterative Learning:** Learn from each iteration and adjust your approach accordingly. Continuously refine your improvement process based on feedback and results.

Example: Incident Management Improvement

1. **Identify a pain point:** Users complain about long wait times when calling the service desk.
2. **Break down the problem:** Analyze call volume data, staffing levels, and call handling procedures to identify potential causes of the delay.
3. **Implement a change:** Implement a new call routing system that automatically prioritizes calls based on urgency and routes them to the most appropriate agent.
4. **Gather feedback:** Survey users and service desk agents to gather feedback on the new system.
5. **Analyze and adjust:** Based on feedback, identify areas where the system can be further improved, such as adding more self-service options or refining the call routing logic.
6. **Repeat:** Implement the improvements and continue gathering feedback to drive ongoing optimization of the incident management process.

By applying the "Progress Iteratively with Feedback" principle, organizations can continuously refine and improve their IT service management practices, ensuring that they remain aligned with business needs, deliver value to customers, and adapt to the ever-changing IT landscape.

Common Challenges and How to Overcome Them

Embracing the "Progress Iteratively with Feedback" principle can be a significant cultural shift for some organizations. As with any change, there will be challenges to overcome. Recognizing these common obstacles and employing effective strategies can pave the way for a smoother transition and greater success in implementing this ITIL 4 principle.

Common Challenges:

1. **Resistance to Change:**
- People are naturally resistant to change, especially when it disrupts established routines and familiar ways of working. Employees may fear the unknown, worry about their ability to adapt, or simply prefer the comfort of the status quo.
- **Overcoming Resistance:**
  - **Communication:** Clearly communicate the reasons for the change, the benefits it will bring, and how it will impact employees.
  - **Involvement:** Involve employees in the planning and implementation process, giving them a voice and a sense of ownership.
  - **Training and Support:** Provide adequate training and support to help employees learn new skills and adapt to new processes.
  - **Celebrate Success:** Recognize and celebrate small wins along the way to build momentum and reinforce positive change.
2. **Lack of Resources:**
- Iterative progress often requires additional resources, such as time, budget, and personnel. Organizations may struggle to allocate these resources, especially when faced with competing priorities.
- **Overcoming Resource Constraints:**

- Prioritization: Prioritize improvement initiatives based on their potential impact and feasibility.
- Resource Optimization: Look for ways to optimize existing resources, such as automating tasks, streamlining processes, and leveraging external expertise.
- Phased Implementation: Break down large initiatives into smaller, more manageable phases that can be implemented with available resources.

3. Difficulty Measuring Progress:
- It can be challenging to measure the progress and impact of iterative improvements, especially when dealing with intangible benefits like improved customer satisfaction or increased employee morale.
- Overcoming Measurement Challenges:
  - Establish Clear Metrics: Define clear and measurable metrics that align with the goals of the improvement initiative.
  - Track Progress Regularly: Monitor the metrics regularly to track progress and identify areas where adjustments are needed.
  - Use Multiple Data Sources: Collect data from various sources, such as surveys, interviews, and performance data, to gain a comprehensive understanding of the impact of changes.

Additional Tips and Strategies:

- Build a Culture of Experimentation and Learning: Encourage a mindset of continuous learning and experimentation, where it's okay to make mistakes and learn from them.
- Empower Teams: Give teams the autonomy and authority to make decisions and implement changes within their areas of responsibility.
- Celebrate Small Wins: Recognize and celebrate even small successes to maintain momentum and motivation.
- Communicate Transparently: Keep stakeholders informed about progress, challenges, and successes throughout the improvement process.

By proactively addressing these challenges and adopting a flexible and adaptive approach, organizations can successfully implement the "Progress Iteratively with Feedback" principle and achieve lasting improvements in their IT service management practices.

Case Studies and Examples

The "Progress Iteratively with Feedback" principle has proven its value in real-world scenarios across various industries. Let's examine some case studies that showcase the successful application of this principle and its positive impact on IT service management (ITSM) practices.

Case Study 1: Large Telecommunications Company

- Challenge: A large telecommunications company was experiencing high incident volumes and long resolution times, leading to customer dissatisfaction. They had a complex incident management process with multiple handoffs and delays.
- Strategy: The company adopted an iterative approach to improvement, focusing on one aspect of the incident management process at a time. They started by simplifying the incident categorization system, making it easier for agents to classify and prioritize incidents. They then implemented a new knowledge management system to provide agents with quick access to relevant information, reducing resolution times. After each change, they collected feedback from agents and customers, using that feedback to refine the next iteration of the process.
- Outcome: By progressing iteratively and incorporating feedback, the company was able to reduce incident resolution times by 25% and improve customer satisfaction scores by 10%. The iterative approach also allowed them to identify and address underlying problems more effectively, leading to a further reduction in incident volumes.

Case Study 2: Retail Chain

- **Challenge:** A national retail chain was experiencing difficulties rolling out new software updates to its stores, resulting in downtime and lost sales. The company's change management process was slow and cumbersome, with multiple layers of approvals required.
- **Strategy:** The company decided to adopt a more agile approach to change management, implementing changes in smaller batches and testing them in a pilot group of stores before full deployment. They also established a feedback loop with store managers to gather input on the impact of changes and identify potential issues.
- **Outcome:** The iterative approach allowed the company to identify and resolve issues early on, reducing the risk of disruptions during full deployment. The faster change cycle also enabled the company to respond more quickly to market trends and customer demands, ultimately leading to increased sales and improved customer satisfaction.

Case Study 3: Government Agency

- **Challenge:** A government agency was struggling to implement a new ITIL-based service management framework due to resistance from employees who were accustomed to their old ways of working. The agency was also concerned about the potential disruption that a large-scale implementation could cause.
- **Strategy:** The agency decided to adopt a phased implementation approach, starting with a few key ITIL practices and gradually expanding the implementation over time. They also invested in extensive training and communication to ensure that employees understood the benefits of the new framework and were prepared for the changes.
- **Outcome:** By progressing iteratively and engaging employees throughout the process, the agency was able to successfully implement the ITIL framework with minimal disruption. The phased approach allowed them to address any issues that arose along the way and make adjustments as needed. The new framework led to improved service quality, increased efficiency, and greater alignment between IT and the agency's overall mission.

Key Takeaways:

These case studies demonstrate the effectiveness of the "Progress Iteratively with Feedback" principle in diverse organizational contexts. By breaking down large initiatives into smaller steps, gathering feedback, and continuously adapting their approach, organizations can achieve significant improvements in their ITSM practices, enhance service quality, and drive business value.

Chapter Summary

In this chapter, we explored the ITIL 4 guiding principle "Progress Iteratively with Feedback," a cornerstone of effective service management. We delved into the concept of iterative progress, contrasting it with traditional "big bang" approaches, and highlighting the numerous benefits of this method.

Here's a recap of the key points:

- **The Core Concept:** You learned that iterative progress involves making small, incremental changes and gathering feedback along the way, fostering a continuous cycle of learning and adaptation.
- **Benefits of Iterative Progress:** We discussed the advantages of this approach, including reduced risk, faster learning and adaptation, increased agility, and improved stakeholder engagement. By making smaller changes and gathering feedback regularly, organizations can minimize disruption, quickly identify and correct issues, and adapt to changing needs more effectively.
- **The Role of Feedback:** We emphasized the critical role of feedback in the iterative process. Feedback provides valuable insights into what's working and what needs to be improved, allowing for course corrections and continuous refinement of services. We discussed different types of

feedback, such as customer, employee, and performance data, and how to collect, analyze, and act on it effectively.

- **Practical Steps:** We provided a step-by-step guide on how to implement the "Progress Iteratively with Feedback" principle in practice, from defining goals and objectives to breaking down work into smaller iterations, implementing changes, gathering feedback, analyzing and adjusting, and repeating the cycle.
- **Applying the Principle:** We illustrated how this principle can be applied to various ITIL practices, such as incident management, change management, problem management, and continual improvement. By incorporating iterative progress and feedback loops into these practices, organizations can achieve continuous improvement and enhanced service delivery.
- **Common Challenges and Solutions:** We discussed common challenges faced in implementing this principle, like resistance to change, lack of resources, and difficulty measuring progress. We also offered practical tips and strategies for overcoming these challenges, such as fostering a culture of experimentation and learning, empowering teams, and establishing clear metrics.
- **Case Studies:** We shared real-world examples of organizations that successfully applied this principle, showcasing its benefits in different industries and contexts. These examples demonstrated how iterative progress with feedback can lead to significant improvements in service quality, efficiency, and customer satisfaction.

By understanding and applying the "Progress Iteratively with Feedback" principle, you can transform your organization's approach to IT service management. Embrace the power of continuous improvement, leverage feedback as a guiding force, and empower your teams to adapt and evolve in the face of ever-changing business needs and technologies.

Collaborate and Promote Visibility

Outline

- Understanding the "Collaborate and Promote Visibility" Principle
- The Importance of Collaboration in Service Management
- Barriers to Collaboration
- Strategies for Fostering Collaboration
- The Importance of Visibility in Service Management
- Tools and Techniques for Promoting Visibility
- Collaboration and Visibility in Practice
- Case Studies and Examples
- Chapter Summary

Understanding the "Collaborate and Promote Visibility" Principle

The "Collaborate and Promote Visibility" principle is a fundamental tenet of ITIL 4, emphasizing the power of teamwork and transparency in achieving successful service management. It encourages organizations to break down silos, foster open communication, and share information freely to create a collaborative and high-performing environment.

The Core Concept: Working Together and Sharing Information

Collaboration, at its core, is about working together effectively to achieve shared goals. In the context of IT service management, this involves breaking down barriers between teams, departments, and even external partners. It's about fostering an environment where individuals feel empowered to share their knowledge, expertise, and perspectives, leading to better decision-making and more effective problem-solving.

Promoting visibility, on the other hand, is about making information readily available and transparent to all relevant stakeholders. This includes not only sharing data and metrics but also providing insights into processes, workflows, and decision-making rationale. When information is visible, it enables informed decision-making, proactive problem-solving, and continuous improvement.

How Collaboration Breaks Down Silos, Builds Trust, and Fosters Shared Responsibility:

- **Breaking Down Silos:** Collaboration helps break down the barriers that often exist between different teams and departments. By working together, individuals gain a better understanding of each other's roles, challenges, and perspectives. This shared understanding fosters empathy, reduces conflict, and promotes a more cohesive and integrated approach to service management.
- **Building Trust:** Open communication and collaboration build trust among team members and stakeholders. When people feel that their voices are heard and their contributions are valued, they are more likely to trust their colleagues and work together towards common goals.
- **Fostering a Culture of Shared Responsibility:** Collaboration creates a sense of shared responsibility for service outcomes. When everyone is working together towards a common goal, they are more likely to take ownership of their roles and responsibilities and hold themselves accountable for results.

How Visibility Enables Informed Decision-Making, Proactive Problem-Solving, and Continuous Improvement:

- **Informed Decision-Making:** When information is readily available and transparent, decision-makers have a clearer understanding of the situation and can make more informed choices. This leads to better decisions that are more likely to achieve the desired outcomes.
- **Proactive Problem-Solving:** Visibility into processes, workflows, and performance data enables teams to identify potential problems early on and take proactive measures to prevent them from escalating into major incidents. This can save time, resources, and reduce the impact on customers and stakeholders.
- **Continuous Improvement:** Transparency and visibility into performance data enable organizations to track progress, identify areas for improvement, and measure the effectiveness of their efforts. This creates a feedback loop that drives continuous improvement and ensures that services are constantly evolving to meet the needs of customers and the business.

By embracing the "Collaborate and Promote Visibility" principle, organizations can create a more open, transparent, and collaborative environment. This not only improves the efficiency and effectiveness of IT service management but also fosters a culture of trust, shared responsibility, and continuous improvement.

The Importance of Collaboration in Service Management

Collaboration is the cornerstone of successful IT service management (ITSM). It goes beyond simple communication; it is the active, purposeful, and cooperative effort between individuals and teams to achieve shared goals. In ITSM, collaboration transcends traditional boundaries, fostering unity between IT and other departments and spanning across the entire service value chain.

Benefits of Collaboration in ITSM:

1. **Improved Efficiency and Effectiveness:**
   - **Streamlined Workflows:** Collaboration eliminates redundancies, optimizes resource allocation, and ensures smooth handoffs between teams, leading to faster and more efficient service delivery.
   - **Knowledge Sharing:** Collaborative environments promote the exchange of knowledge, skills, and expertise, enabling teams to learn from each other and develop better solutions.
   - **Shared Ownership:** When individuals work together towards a common goal, they feel a greater sense of ownership and accountability, leading to higher quality outcomes.
2. **Faster Problem Resolution:**
   - **Diverse Perspectives:** Collaboration brings together individuals with different skill sets and perspectives, enabling a more comprehensive understanding of problems and faster identification of solutions.
   - **Collective Problem-Solving:** By pooling their knowledge and experience, teams can collaboratively troubleshoot complex issues and arrive at effective resolutions more quickly.
   - **Reduced Downtime:** Swift problem resolution minimizes downtime, reduces the impact on business operations, and improves customer satisfaction.
3. **Increased Innovation:**
   - **Cross-Pollination of Ideas:** Collaboration fosters a creative environment where ideas are freely exchanged and challenged. This cross-pollination of ideas can spark innovation and lead to the development of new and improved services.
   - **Diverse Skill Sets:** Bringing together individuals with different backgrounds and expertise can lead to the generation of novel solutions and approaches.
   - **Openness to Experimentation:** Collaborative environments encourage experimentation and risk-taking, which are essential for innovation and growth.
4. **Enhanced Customer Satisfaction:**
   - **Understanding Customer Needs:** Collaboration between IT and customer-facing teams ensures that IT services are aligned with customer needs and expectations.

- ○ **Seamless Customer Experience:** Collaboration across the service value chain ensures a seamless and consistent customer experience, from initial engagement to service delivery and support.
- ○ **Faster Response to Feedback:** Collaborative teams can respond more quickly to customer feedback and address any issues or concerns promptly.

5. **Stronger Relationships with Stakeholders:**
   - ○ **Building Trust and Transparency:** Open communication and collaboration foster trust and transparency between IT and stakeholders.
   - ○ **Shared Understanding:** Working together on shared goals creates a sense of partnership and alignment, leading to stronger relationships.
   - ○ **Increased Buy-In:** Stakeholders who feel involved and heard are more likely to support IT initiatives and embrace change.

Breaking Down Silos Between IT and Other Departments:

Collaboration is key to breaking down silos that often exist between IT and other departments. By working together, IT can better understand the needs and priorities of the business, while other departments can gain a deeper appreciation for the value that IT brings to the organization. This leads to improved alignment, more effective decision-making, and a shared focus on achieving business objectives.

Collaboration Across the Entire Service Value Chain:

Collaboration is not just important within IT teams; it's essential across the entire service value chain. From strategizing and designing new services to transitioning, operating, and improving them, collaboration ensures that all stakeholders are involved and their perspectives are considered. This holistic approach to collaboration leads to more customer-centric services, efficient operations, and continuous improvement.

Barriers to Collaboration

Collaboration is essential for IT service management success, yet various obstacles can hinder its effective implementation. Recognizing and addressing these barriers is crucial for fostering a collaborative environment that empowers teams to deliver value and achieve shared goals.

Common Barriers to Collaboration:

1. **Lack of Trust:**
   - ○ **Description:** When team members or departments lack trust in each other, they are less likely to share information openly, seek help, or collaborate effectively. This can lead to misunderstandings, miscommunication, and a reluctance to work together.
   - ○ **Impact:** Lack of trust can hinder problem-solving, slow down decision-making, and create a culture of blame and defensiveness, ultimately impacting service quality and customer satisfaction.

2. **Conflicting Priorities:**
   - ○ **Description:** Different teams and departments often have competing priorities and goals. This can lead to conflicts over resource allocation, timelines, and decision-making, hindering collaboration efforts.
   - ○ **Impact:** Conflicting priorities can create silos, where teams focus on their own goals rather than the overall objectives of the organization. This can lead to inefficiencies, duplication of effort, and missed opportunities for collaboration.

3. **Communication Breakdowns:**
   - ○ **Description:** Poor communication, whether due to lack of clarity, inadequate channels, or language barriers, can lead to misunderstandings, delays, and errors.
   - ○ **Impact:** Communication breakdowns can disrupt workflows, hinder problem-solving, and erode trust between teams, ultimately impacting service delivery and customer satisfaction.

4. **Organizational Culture:**
   - **Description:** An organizational culture that does not value collaboration, rewards individual achievement over teamwork, or fosters a competitive environment can stifle collaborative efforts.
   - **Impact:** A non-collaborative culture can create a disjointed and fragmented organization, where teams work in isolation, knowledge is not shared, and innovation is stifled.
5. **Inadequate Tools and Technology:**
   - **Description:** Lack of access to appropriate collaboration tools, such as communication platforms, document sharing tools, or project management software, can hinder communication and collaboration efforts.
   - **Impact:** Inadequate tools can lead to inefficiencies, delays, and frustration among team members, making it difficult to work together effectively.

Addressing Barriers to Collaboration Proactively:

To foster a collaborative environment, organizations must proactively address these barriers:

- **Building Trust:** Create a culture of openness, transparency, and mutual respect. Encourage open communication, recognize and reward teamwork, and address conflicts constructively.
- **Aligning Priorities:** Ensure that individual, team, and departmental goals are aligned with the overall strategic objectives of the organization. Regularly communicate these goals and priorities to all stakeholders.
- **Enhancing Communication:** Establish clear communication channels, provide training on effective communication skills, and use tools that facilitate seamless information sharing and collaboration.
- **Fostering a Collaborative Culture:** Promote a culture that values teamwork, recognizes and rewards collaboration, and celebrates collective achievements.
- **Investing in Collaboration Tools:** Provide teams with the necessary tools and technologies to collaborate effectively, such as communication platforms, project management software, and knowledge sharing tools.

By actively addressing these barriers, organizations can create a more collaborative and supportive environment that empowers teams to work together effectively, deliver high-quality services, and achieve their shared goals.

Strategies for Fostering Collaboration

Fostering a culture of collaboration requires intentional effort and a multi-faceted approach. Here are practical tips and strategies to promote collaboration within IT teams and across your organization:

1. **Encourage Open Communication and Feedback:**
- **Create Safe Spaces:** Foster an environment where employees feel safe to express their ideas, opinions, and concerns without fear of judgment or retribution. This can be achieved through regular team meetings, one-on-one conversations, and anonymous feedback channels.
- **Active Listening:** Practice active listening, where you genuinely pay attention to what others are saying, seek to understand their perspectives, and ask clarifying questions.
- **Constructive Feedback:** Provide constructive feedback that focuses on specific behaviors or actions, rather than personal attacks. Use feedback as an opportunity for learning and growth.
- **Regular Communication:** Establish regular communication channels, such as team meetings, newsletters, or online forums, to keep everyone informed and connected.
2. **Establish Clear Roles and Responsibilities:**
- **Role Clarity:** Clearly define the roles and responsibilities of each team member, ensuring that everyone understands what is expected of them and how their work contributes to the overall goals.

- **Avoid Overlap and Gaps:** Ensure that there is no overlap or gaps in responsibilities to avoid confusion and duplication of effort.
- **Accountability:** Hold individuals accountable for their assigned tasks and responsibilities, providing support and guidance as needed.
- **Regular Reviews:** Regularly review roles and responsibilities to ensure they remain relevant and aligned with changing business needs.

3. **Create a Shared Understanding of Goals and Priorities:**
- **Communicate the Vision:** Clearly articulate the organization's vision, mission, and goals, ensuring that everyone understands the "big picture" and how their work contributes to it.
- **Set Team Goals:** Establish clear team goals that are aligned with the overall organizational objectives. Ensure that these goals are specific, measurable, achievable, relevant, and time-bound (SMART).
- **Regularly Review and Adjust:** Regularly review and adjust goals and priorities as needed to adapt to changing circumstances and feedback.
- **Use Visual Aids:** Use visual tools like roadmaps, Kanban boards, or dashboards to track progress and visualize goals.

4. **Foster a Culture of Trust and Mutual Respect:**
- **Lead by Example:** Leaders and managers should model collaborative behavior, demonstrating trust and respect towards their team members.
- **Value Diversity:** Recognize and celebrate the diversity of perspectives and experiences within the team.
- **Encourage Collaboration:** Create opportunities for team members to work together on projects, share knowledge, and learn from each other.
- **Recognize and Reward Collaboration:** Acknowledge and reward collaborative efforts, both formally and informally.

5. **Utilize Collaboration Tools and Technologies:**
- **Communication Platforms:** Use tools like Slack, Microsoft Teams, or Zoom to facilitate real-time communication and collaboration across teams and locations.
- **Project Management Tools:** Use tools like Asana, Trello, or Jira to track progress, manage tasks, and collaborate on projects.
- **Document Sharing Tools:** Use platforms like Google Drive, Dropbox, or SharePoint to share documents and collaborate on them in real-time.
- **Knowledge Management Systems:** Use tools like Confluence or Guru to create a centralized repository of knowledge that can be easily accessed and shared.

6. **Celebrate Successes and Recognize Contributions:**
- **Public Recognition:** Acknowledge and celebrate team achievements and individual contributions publicly, through announcements, awards, or other forms of recognition.
- **Positive Feedback:** Provide regular positive feedback to team members, highlighting their strengths and contributions.
- **Team-Building Activities:** Organize team-building activities and social events to foster camaraderie and build relationships.

By implementing these strategies, organizations can create a culture of collaboration that empowers teams to work together effectively, overcome challenges, and achieve shared goals. This, in turn, will lead to improved service delivery, increased customer satisfaction, and enhanced business performance.

The Importance of Visibility in Service Management

Visibility is the cornerstone of informed decision-making and proactive problem-solving in IT service management (ITSM). It refers to the ability to see and understand the various components, activities, and performance of IT services and the underlying processes. By shedding light on the inner workings of the service value chain, visibility empowers organizations to make data-driven decisions, identify and address issues early on, build trust with stakeholders, and drive continuous improvement.

Benefits of Visibility in ITSM:

1. **Improved Decision-Making:**
- **Real-time Information:** Visibility provides access to real-time data and metrics on service performance, resource utilization, and customer satisfaction. This information enables IT leaders and managers to make informed decisions based on accurate and up-to-date information.
- **Data-Driven Insights:** Visibility tools and dashboards can aggregate and analyze data from multiple sources, uncovering patterns and trends that might not be obvious otherwise. These insights can inform strategic decisions, optimize resource allocation, and drive service improvements.

2. **Proactive Problem-Solving:**
- **Early Warning Signals:** Visibility into the service value chain allows IT teams to identify potential issues before they escalate into major incidents. By detecting anomalies, bottlenecks, or deviations from service levels, teams can proactively address problems and prevent disruptions to service delivery.
- **Root Cause Analysis:** Visibility tools can help trace the root cause of incidents and problems, enabling faster resolution and preventing recurrence. This can significantly reduce downtime, improve service availability, and enhance customer satisfaction.

3. **Enhanced Transparency:**
- **Building Trust:** Transparency into processes, performance, and decision-making builds trust with stakeholders, including customers, employees, and partners. When stakeholders understand how IT services are delivered and how decisions are made, they are more likely to have confidence in the IT organization.
- **Open Communication:** Visibility fosters open communication and collaboration among teams and stakeholders. By sharing information freely, organizations can create a culture of trust and accountability, where everyone is working towards the same goals.

4. **Increased Accountability:**
- **Clearly Defined Roles and Responsibilities:** Visibility into roles and responsibilities ensures that everyone knows what is expected of them and who is accountable for specific tasks and outcomes.
- **Performance Tracking:** By tracking individual and team performance, organizations can identify areas where additional support or training is needed, as well as recognize and reward high performers.
- **Continuous Improvement:** Visibility into performance data enables organizations to measure the effectiveness of their processes and identify areas for improvement. This helps create a feedback loop that drives continuous improvement and ensures that services meet evolving needs.

Visibility as an Enabler of Continuous Improvement:

Visibility is a key enabler of continual improvement. By providing insights into the performance and effectiveness of IT services, it allows organizations to identify areas for optimization, streamline processes, and eliminate waste. Visibility tools can also help track the progress of improvement initiatives, ensuring that they are delivering the desired results.

In conclusion, visibility is a critical element of ITIL 4, empowering organizations to make informed decisions, solve problems proactively, build trust with stakeholders, and drive continuous improvement. By investing in visibility tools and practices, organizations can create a more transparent, efficient, and customer-centric approach to IT service management.

Tools and Techniques for Promoting Visibility

Visibility is not just a concept; it's something that can be achieved through the strategic use of various tools and techniques. These tools and techniques can empower both IT teams and stakeholders with the information they need to make informed decisions, collaborate effectively, and drive continuous improvement.

1. **Dashboards and Reports:**
- **Purpose:** Dashboards and reports provide a visual representation of key performance indicators (KPIs) and other relevant data. They offer a quick and easy way to monitor service health, track progress towards goals, and identify areas for improvement.
- **Examples:**
    - **Service Desk Dashboard:** Displays metrics such as ticket volume, resolution times, and customer satisfaction ratings.
    - **Incident Management Dashboard:** Tracks the number of open incidents, their severity, and the time taken to resolve them.
    - **Change Management Dashboard:** Shows the status of change requests, their impact, and the success rate of changes.
- **Key Benefits:**
    - Real-time visibility into service performance.
    - Easy identification of trends and patterns.
    - Facilitates data-driven decision-making.
    - Enables proactive problem-solving and performance optimization.
2. **Service Portals:**
- **Purpose:** Service portals provide a central point of access for users to request services, report incidents, check the status of their requests, and access self-service resources such as knowledge articles and FAQs.
- **Examples:**
    - **Employee Self-Service Portal:** Allows employees to request IT services, report problems, and track their requests.
    - **Customer Self-Service Portal:** Enables customers to access product information, submit support tickets, and check the status of their orders.
- **Key Benefits:**
    - Empowers users to find information and resolve issues on their own.
    - Reduces the workload on service desk agents.
    - Improves customer satisfaction by providing 24/7 access to support.
    - Streamlines service request and incident management processes.
3. **Collaboration Platforms:**
- **Purpose:** Collaboration platforms facilitate communication, knowledge sharing, and teamwork within and across teams. They provide a centralized space for discussions, document sharing, task management, and real-time collaboration.
- **Examples:**
    - **Microsoft Teams**
    - **Slack**
    - **Google Workspace**
    - **Asana**
- **Key Benefits:**
    - Breaks down silos and promotes cross-functional collaboration.
    - Improves communication and information sharing.
    - Facilitates knowledge transfer and problem-solving.
    - Enhances team productivity and efficiency.
4. **Knowledge Management Systems:**
- **Purpose:** Knowledge management systems (KMS) are centralized repositories of information, knowledge, and expertise related to IT services. They enable users to find answers to their questions, access troubleshooting guides, and learn from the experience of others.
- **Examples:**
    - **ServiceNow Knowledge Base**
    - **Confluence**
    - **SharePoint**
- **Key Benefits:**

- Improves the efficiency of service desk agents by providing them with quick access to relevant information.
- Empowers users to resolve issues on their own through self-service.
- Promotes knowledge sharing and collaboration within the organization.
- Reduces the time and cost of resolving incidents and requests.

By strategically implementing these tools and techniques, organizations can significantly enhance visibility in their IT service management practices. This increased transparency fosters a culture of collaboration, enables data-driven decision-making, and ultimately leads to improved service quality, customer satisfaction, and business outcomes.

Collaboration and Visibility in Practice

Collaboration and visibility are not just abstract concepts; they are practical tools that can significantly enhance the effectiveness of various ITIL practices. Let's explore how these principles can be applied in three key areas of IT service management:

1. Incident Management:

- **Collaboration:** When an incident occurs, effective collaboration between different teams is crucial for swift resolution. This could involve the service desk, technical support, application teams, and even external vendors. Collaboration tools like shared communication channels, incident management systems, and knowledge bases facilitate real-time information sharing and coordination.
- **Visibility:** Providing visibility into the incident management process is key to managing user expectations and building trust. This can be achieved through:
    - **Status Updates:** Regularly communicating the status of incidents to affected users, keeping them informed about progress and estimated resolution times.
    - **Self-Service Portals:** Allowing users to track the progress of their incidents and access relevant information, such as known errors and workarounds.
    - **Post-Incident Reviews:** Conducting post-incident reviews (PIRs) with relevant teams to identify root causes, learn from mistakes, and prevent future incidents. These reviews should be transparent and involve all relevant stakeholders.

2. Change Management:

- **Collaboration:** Change management requires collaboration between different teams, including IT, business, and change advisory boards (CABs). This collaboration ensures that changes are aligned with business goals, assessed for risk, and implemented in a controlled manner.
- **Visibility:** Visibility is crucial in change management to ensure that all stakeholders are aware of upcoming changes and their potential impact. This can be achieved through:
    - **Change Calendars:** Publishing schedules of upcoming changes so that stakeholders can plan accordingly.
    - **Impact Assessments:** Conducting thorough impact assessments to identify potential risks and communicate them to stakeholders.
    - **Change Notifications:** Sending timely notifications to affected users and stakeholders about the status and progress of changes.

3. Problem Management:

- **Collaboration:** Problem management often involves collaboration between different teams, such as technical support, development, and operations. This collaboration is essential for identifying root causes, developing solutions, and preventing future incidents.

- **Visibility:** Visibility into the problem management process helps ensure that problems are prioritized effectively and that progress towards resolution is transparent. This can be achieved through:
  - **Problem Tracking Systems:** Using a problem management system to track the status of problems, their root causes, and the actions being taken to resolve them.
  - **Knowledge Sharing:** Documenting known errors and workarounds in a knowledge base to facilitate knowledge sharing and faster resolution of similar incidents in the future.
  - **Root Cause Analysis (RCA):** Conducting thorough RCA to identify the underlying causes of problems and implement preventive measures.

By embracing collaboration and visibility, organizations can create a more proactive, responsive, and customer-centric approach to IT service management. This not only improves the efficiency and effectiveness of IT operations but also builds trust and strengthens relationships with stakeholders.

Case Studies and Examples

The "Collaborate and Promote Visibility" principle has been instrumental in transforming IT service management (ITSM) practices across diverse organizations. Let's examine a few real-world examples that illustrate the power of collaboration and visibility in action:

Case Study 1: Global Financial Institution

- **Challenge:** A global financial institution faced siloed communication between IT teams, leading to delayed incident resolution and frustrated customers.
- **Strategy:** The institution implemented a unified communication platform, enabling real-time collaboration between service desk agents, technical support teams, and application owners. They also created a knowledge base accessible to all teams, fostering information sharing and reducing the need for repetitive troubleshooting.
- **Outcome:** The collaborative approach reduced incident resolution times by 30%. Increased visibility into the incident management process improved customer satisfaction, as users were kept informed of progress through the service portal.

Case Study 2: Healthcare Provider

- **Challenge:** A healthcare provider was struggling to manage changes effectively due to a lack of communication and coordination between IT and clinical teams. This often resulted in unexpected disruptions to patient care.
- **Strategy:** The provider established a cross-functional change advisory board (CAB) that included representatives from both IT and clinical departments. They also implemented a visual change calendar that provided clear visibility into upcoming changes and their potential impact on patient care.
- **Outcome:** The collaborative change management process led to a 50% reduction in change-related incidents. Enhanced visibility allowed clinical teams to prepare for changes, minimizing disruptions to patient care and improving overall safety.

Case Study 3: E-Commerce Company

- **Challenge:** An e-commerce company experienced frequent website outages during peak shopping periods, impacting sales and customer satisfaction. Lack of visibility into system performance hindered proactive problem management.
- **Strategy:** The company implemented a real-time monitoring and analytics dashboard that provided IT teams with a comprehensive view of system health, performance metrics, and potential bottlenecks. They also established a dedicated "war room" where IT teams could collaborate in real-time during incidents, ensuring quick resolution.

- **Outcome:** Proactive monitoring and collaboration enabled the company to detect and address potential issues before they caused outages. This resulted in a 99.9% uptime during peak periods, leading to increased sales and improved customer loyalty.

Case Study 4: Government Agency

- **Challenge:** A government agency faced difficulties in ensuring compliance with data protection regulations. The lack of visibility into data access and usage made it difficult to track and control sensitive information.
- **Strategy:** The agency implemented a data governance framework that defined clear roles and responsibilities for data management. They also deployed a data loss prevention (DLP) solution to monitor and control the movement of sensitive data.
- **Outcome:** Enhanced visibility into data access and usage enabled the agency to ensure compliance with regulations and mitigate the risk of data breaches. This not only protected sensitive information but also strengthened public trust in the agency.

Key Takeaways:

These case studies illustrate the tangible benefits of collaboration and visibility in IT service management. By breaking down silos, promoting open communication, leveraging collaboration tools, and increasing transparency, organizations can achieve significant improvements in service quality, efficiency, customer satisfaction, and compliance. The "Collaborate and Promote Visibility" principle is not just a theoretical concept; it's a practical approach that can transform the way organizations deliver IT services.

Chapter Summary

In this chapter, we delved into the ITIL 4 guiding principle "Collaborate and Promote Visibility," emphasizing its importance in creating a high-functioning and customer-centric service management environment. We explored how collaboration breaks down silos, fosters trust, and promotes shared responsibility, while visibility empowers informed decision-making, proactive problem-solving, and continuous improvement.

Key points from this chapter include:

- **The Importance of Collaboration:** We discussed the numerous benefits of collaboration, including improved efficiency and effectiveness, faster problem resolution, increased innovation, enhanced customer satisfaction, and stronger stakeholder relationships.
- **Barriers to Collaboration:** We identified common barriers to collaboration, such as lack of trust, conflicting priorities, communication breakdowns, organizational culture, and inadequate tools and technology. Recognizing these barriers is the first step towards addressing them.
- **Strategies for Fostering Collaboration:** We provided practical tips and strategies for promoting collaboration, including encouraging open communication and feedback, establishing clear roles and responsibilities, creating a shared understanding of goals, fostering trust, utilizing collaboration tools, and celebrating successes.
- **The Importance of Visibility:** We highlighted the benefits of visibility, such as improved decision-making, proactive problem-solving, enhanced transparency, and increased accountability. Visibility empowers organizations to identify areas for improvement, address issues before they escalate, and build trust with stakeholders.
- **Tools and Techniques for Promoting Visibility:** We explored various tools and techniques that can be used to increase visibility, including dashboards and reports, service portals, collaboration platforms, and knowledge management systems.
- **Collaboration and Visibility in Practice:** We provided concrete examples of how collaboration and visibility can be applied in different ITIL practices, such as incident management, change management, and problem management.

- **Case Studies:** We shared real-world case studies of organizations that successfully applied the "Collaborate and Promote Visibility" principle to improve their ITSM practices, showcasing the tangible benefits it can bring to diverse industries and contexts.

By fostering a culture of collaboration and promoting visibility, organizations can break down silos, empower teams, and create a more customer-centric and value-driven approach to IT service management. This not only leads to improved service delivery and customer satisfaction but also contributes to the overall success and resilience of the organization.

Think and Work Holistically

Outline

- Understanding the "Think and Work Holistically" Principle
- The Holistic Approach in Service Management
- Systems Thinking
- Breaking Down Silos
- Collaboration and Communication
- Integration and Optimization
- Applying Holistic Thinking in ITIL Practices
- Common Challenges and How to Overcome Them
- Case Studies and Examples
- Chapter Summary

Understanding the "Think and Work Holistically" Principle

The "Think and Work Holistically" principle in ITIL 4 is a guiding light that promotes a comprehensive and interconnected view of IT service management (ITSM). It encourages organizations to move beyond a narrow, siloed perspective and embrace a broader understanding of the complex interactions between various elements within the service value system (SVS).

Core Concept: An Interconnected System, Not Isolated Parts

At its core, this principle emphasizes that IT service management is not a collection of isolated parts, but rather an interconnected system. Every component, process, and stakeholder within the SVS is linked to others, and changes in one area can have ripple effects throughout the entire system.

Therefore, to effectively manage and improve IT services, it's crucial to adopt a holistic mindset. This means considering the broader context, understanding the interdependencies between different elements, and making decisions that optimize the entire system, not just individual parts.

Encouraging a Broader Perspective:

The "Think and Work Holistically" principle encourages a broader perspective that goes beyond technical details and individual processes. It prompts organizations to consider the following:

- **The Big Picture:** How do individual IT services contribute to the overall goals and objectives of the organization?
- **Interdependencies:** How do different IT services and processes interact and depend on each other?
- **Stakeholder Needs:** How do different stakeholders (customers, employees, partners, suppliers) perceive and experience IT services?
- **Value Creation:** How can IT services be optimized to create the greatest value for customers and stakeholders?
- **Impact of Change:** How will changes in one area of the SVS affect other areas?

By adopting a broader perspective, organizations can make more informed decisions, identify and address root causes of problems, and optimize their IT service management capabilities for maximum value delivery.

Benefits of a Holistic Approach:

- **Improved Decision-Making:** A holistic approach enables better decision-making by considering the broader context and potential consequences of different options. It helps avoid unintended consequences and ensures that decisions are aligned with the overall goals of the organization.
- **Better Problem-Solving:** A holistic approach helps identify the root causes of problems, rather than just treating the symptoms. By understanding the complex interactions within the SVS, organizations can develop more effective and sustainable solutions.
- **Enhanced Service Delivery:** A holistic approach to service management leads to more efficient and effective processes, improved customer satisfaction, and greater value creation. It helps organizations deliver services that are aligned with customer needs, meet performance targets, and contribute to business success.
- **Increased Adaptability:** By understanding the interconnectedness of the SVS, organizations can better anticipate and respond to changes in the business environment or customer needs. This allows them to remain agile and maintain service continuity in the face of disruption.

In conclusion, the "Think and Work Holistically" principle is a powerful tool for improving IT service management. It encourages organizations to look beyond individual processes and components and embrace a systems thinking approach. By understanding the interconnectedness of the SVS and adopting a broader perspective, organizations can make better decisions, solve problems more effectively, and deliver exceptional service experiences that drive business value.

The Holistic Approach in Service Management

A holistic approach in IT service management (ITSM) means viewing the entire service delivery ecosystem as an interconnected system, rather than a collection of isolated parts. It recognizes that each element within the service value system (SVS) – people, processes, technology, information, and partners – influences and is influenced by others. This interconnectedness necessitates a broader perspective when making decisions and taking actions, ensuring that the impact on the entire system is considered, not just the immediate effects on a single component.

Importance of a Holistic Approach:

- **Identifying Root Causes:** A siloed approach often leads to a focus on surface-level symptoms, resulting in temporary fixes that fail to address the underlying issues. A holistic approach, on the other hand, encourages digging deeper to uncover the root causes of problems. This enables organizations to implement more effective and sustainable solutions that prevent recurring issues and improve overall service quality.
- **Optimizing Processes:** When processes are viewed in isolation, optimization efforts may focus on individual steps, potentially creating bottlenecks or inefficiencies elsewhere in the value stream. A holistic approach allows for end-to-end optimization, ensuring that changes in one area do not negatively impact others. This leads to smoother workflows, reduced waste, and improved service delivery.
- **Delivering Value to Customers:** A holistic approach ensures that IT services are designed and delivered with a focus on the customer's overall experience and desired outcomes. By understanding the interdependencies between different service components, organizations can create seamless and integrated service experiences that truly meet customer needs.
- **Improved Decision-Making:** A holistic approach leads to better decision-making by considering the broader context and potential consequences of different options. This helps avoid unintended consequences and ensures that decisions align with the organization's strategic goals.

Examples of Suboptimal Outcomes from a Siloed Approach:

1. **Inefficient Processes:** In a siloed environment, teams may optimize their own processes without considering the impact on other teams or the overall service delivery. This can lead to fragmented workflows, unnecessary handoffs, and delays, resulting in inefficient and costly processes.

2. **Misaligned Goals:** When departments operate in silos, their goals may not be aligned with the overall objectives of the organization. This can lead to conflicting priorities, wasted resources, and missed opportunities. For example, a development team focused solely on delivering new features might neglect the need for robust security measures, leading to increased risk for the organization.
3. **Frustrated Customers:** A siloed approach can result in a disjointed customer experience. Customers may have to contact multiple departments to resolve a single issue or receive conflicting information from different sources. This can lead to frustration, dissatisfaction, and ultimately, customer churn.

In Summary:

A holistic approach to IT service management is crucial for achieving optimal results. By considering the interconnectedness of the service value system and adopting a broader perspective, organizations can identify and address root causes, optimize processes, and deliver exceptional service experiences that meet the needs of customers and stakeholders.

Systems Thinking

Systems thinking is a holistic approach to analysis that focuses on the way that a system's constituent parts interrelate and how systems work over time and within the context of larger systems. In the context of ITIL 4, systems thinking provides a framework for understanding the complex interactions and interdependencies within the service value system (SVS).

The Concept of Systems Thinking:

At its core, systems thinking involves shifting our perspective from individual components to the entire system. Instead of focusing on isolated events or actions, we consider how different parts of the system interact and influence each other. This involves recognizing that:

- **The whole is greater than the sum of its parts:** A system is not simply a collection of individual components; it is the interactions and relationships between those components that create the system's behavior.
- **Cause and effect are not linear:** In complex systems, cause and effect are often non-linear and can be separated by time and space. Actions taken in one part of the system can have unintended consequences in other areas.
- **Feedback loops are important:** Feedback loops, both positive and negative, play a crucial role in regulating system behavior. Understanding these loops is essential for managing and improving complex systems.

Applying Systems Thinking to IT Service Management:

Systems thinking can be applied to IT service management (ITSM) in several ways:

- **Understanding the Service Value System:** The SVS is a complex system with many interconnected elements. Systems thinking helps IT professionals understand how these elements interact and influence each other, enabling them to identify leverage points for improvement and anticipate the impact of changes.
- **Identifying Root Causes of Problems:** Systems thinking encourages looking beyond the immediate symptoms of a problem to identify the underlying root causes. This can lead to more effective and sustainable solutions that address the root causes rather than just treating the symptoms.
- **Optimizing Processes:** By understanding how processes interact and influence each other, IT professionals can optimize the entire service value chain, not just individual processes. This can lead to improved efficiency, effectiveness, and customer satisfaction.

- **Managing Risk:** Systems thinking helps identify potential risks and vulnerabilities within the SVS. By understanding the interdependencies between different components, organizations can better anticipate and mitigate risks.
- **Fostering Collaboration:** Systems thinking promotes collaboration and communication between different teams and stakeholders. By working together and sharing information, they can gain a shared understanding of the system and its dynamics, leading to better decision-making and improved service delivery.

Benefits of Systems Thinking:

- **Improved Decision-Making:** Systems thinking enables IT professionals to make more informed decisions by considering the broader context and potential consequences of their actions.
- **Better Problem-Solving:** Systems thinking helps identify the root causes of problems, leading to more effective and sustainable solutions.
- **Enhanced Service Delivery:** By optimizing the entire service value chain, systems thinking can improve service quality, efficiency, and customer satisfaction.
- **Increased Adaptability:** Systems thinking helps organizations anticipate and respond to changes in the business environment, ensuring that IT services remain relevant and valuable.
- **Improved Collaboration:** Systems thinking fosters collaboration and communication between different teams and stakeholders, leading to a more cohesive and effective IT organization.

By embracing systems thinking, IT professionals can move beyond a narrow, reactive approach to service management and adopt a more holistic, proactive, and value-driven approach. This can lead to significant improvements in service quality, customer satisfaction, and business performance.

Breaking Down Silos

Silos, in the context of IT service management (ITSM), refer to the isolation of teams or departments within an organization. These silos can be physical, where teams work in separate locations, or functional, where teams focus solely on their specific tasks and responsibilities without considering the bigger picture.

Challenges of Siloed Thinking and Working in ITSM:

1. **Lack of Communication and Collaboration:** Silos create barriers to communication and collaboration, hindering information sharing and knowledge transfer between teams. This can lead to misunderstandings, duplicated efforts, and delays in resolving issues.
2. **Misaligned Goals and Priorities:** When teams operate in silos, their goals and priorities may not be aligned with the overall objectives of the organization or the needs of customers. This can lead to conflicting priorities, wasted resources, and suboptimal outcomes.
3. **Reduced Innovation:** Silos stifle innovation by limiting the cross-pollination of ideas and perspectives. When teams work in isolation, they miss out on opportunities to learn from each other and develop creative solutions.
4. **Inefficient Processes:** Silos can lead to inefficient processes, as each team develops its own way of working without considering the impact on other teams or the overall service delivery process.
5. **Negative Impact on Customer Satisfaction:** Siloed thinking can result in a fragmented customer experience, where customers have to navigate through multiple touchpoints and receive conflicting information. This can lead to frustration, dissatisfaction, and ultimately, customer churn.

How Silos Create Barriers:

- **Lack of Trust:** Silos can breed mistrust and competition between teams, as individuals focus on protecting their own turf rather than collaborating for the greater good.
- **Limited Visibility:** When teams work in isolation, they may not have visibility into the work of other teams, leading to a lack of understanding of how their actions impact the overall service delivery process.

- **Communication Barriers:** Silos can create communication barriers, such as different jargon, conflicting priorities, and a lack of shared understanding.
- **Organizational Culture:** A hierarchical organizational structure or a culture that rewards individual achievement over teamwork can reinforce siloed behavior.

Strategies for Breaking Down Silos:

1. **Promote Cross-Functional Collaboration:** Encourage teams to work together on projects, share knowledge and resources, and participate in joint problem-solving sessions.
2. **Establish Shared Goals:** Ensure that individual, team, and departmental goals are aligned with the overall objectives of the organization. This creates a shared sense of purpose and encourages collaboration towards common goals.
3. **Create a Culture of Open Communication:** Foster a culture of open communication and transparency, where employees feel comfortable sharing information, asking questions, and challenging assumptions.
4. **Implement Collaboration Tools:** Provide teams with the necessary tools and technologies to collaborate effectively, such as communication platforms, document sharing tools, and project management software.
5. **Reward Collaboration:** Recognize and reward collaborative efforts, both formally and informally. This reinforces the importance of teamwork and encourages a collaborative mindset.
6. **Flatten Hierarchies:** Consider flattening the organizational structure to empower employees, encourage autonomy, and facilitate cross-functional collaboration.

By actively breaking down silos and fostering a culture of collaboration, organizations can create a more integrated, efficient, and customer-centric approach to IT service management. This can lead to improved service quality, increased customer satisfaction, and enhanced business performance.

Collaboration and Communication

Collaboration and communication are the lifeblood of a holistic approach to IT service management (ITSM). They serve as the glue that binds together the various components of the Service Value System (SVS), ensuring that information flows freely, teams work together seamlessly, and everyone is aligned towards common goals.

The Critical Role of Collaboration and Communication in a Holistic Approach:

- **Breaking Down Silos:** Effective communication and collaboration dissolve the barriers that isolate teams and departments. By fostering open dialogue and information sharing, they enable individuals to understand each other's roles, challenges, and perspectives. This shared understanding promotes empathy, reduces conflict, and encourages a more integrated and collaborative approach to service management.
- **Building Trust and Transparency:** Open communication and collaboration build trust among team members and stakeholders. When individuals feel safe to express their ideas, opinions, and concerns without fear of judgment, trust flourishes. Transparency about processes, decisions, and performance data further strengthens this trust, fostering a culture of openness and accountability.
- **Fostering a Shared Understanding:** Clear and consistent communication ensures that everyone understands the organization's goals, priorities, and strategies. This shared understanding aligns efforts, reduces misunderstandings, and enables teams to work together more effectively towards common objectives.
- **Enabling Collective Problem-Solving:** Collaboration brings together diverse perspectives and expertise, enhancing the organization's ability to solve complex problems. By working together, teams can leverage their collective knowledge and experience to identify root causes, develop creative solutions, and implement effective improvements.

- **Driving Continuous Improvement:** Open communication and collaboration create a feedback loop that fuels continuous improvement. By sharing ideas, challenges, and successes, teams can learn from each other and identify opportunities for optimization.

Examples of Collaboration Tools and Techniques:

- **Communication Platforms:** Tools like Slack, Microsoft Teams, or Google Chat provide real-time communication channels for teams to collaborate, share information, and stay connected.
- **Project Management Tools:** Platforms like Asana, Trello, or Jira enable teams to track tasks, collaborate on projects, and manage deadlines.
- **Video Conferencing Tools:** Zoom, Google Meet, or Microsoft Teams facilitate virtual meetings and face-to-face communication, fostering collaboration across geographical boundaries.
- **Knowledge Management Systems:** Platforms like Confluence, SharePoint, or Guru serve as central repositories for knowledge articles, FAQs, and best practices, promoting knowledge sharing and self-service.
- **Collaboration Spaces:** Physical or virtual spaces where teams can gather to brainstorm ideas, share knowledge, and work together on projects.
- **Regular Meetings and Stand-Ups:** Scheduling regular team meetings, cross-functional meetings, and stand-ups to discuss progress, challenges, and next steps.
- **Feedback Mechanisms:** Implementing surveys, feedback forms, or suggestion boxes to collect input from employees and customers.

In Summary:

Collaboration and communication are the cornerstones of a successful and holistic IT service management strategy. They empower organizations to break down silos, build trust, foster a shared understanding, and drive continuous improvement. By investing in collaborative tools and fostering a culture of open communication, organizations can unlock the full potential of their workforce and deliver exceptional service experiences that exceed customer expectations.

Integration and Optimization

Integration and optimization are essential for maximizing the value derived from the information and technology dimension of ITIL 4. Integration refers to the seamless connection and interoperability of different IT service management (ITSM) processes, tools, and systems. Optimization focuses on refining and improving the efficiency and effectiveness of these integrated elements.

Importance of Integrating Different Processes and Tools:

- **Seamless Service Delivery:** Integration creates a unified platform where different ITSM processes, such as incident management, problem management, change management, and request fulfillment, can work together seamlessly. This ensures a smooth and efficient flow of work, reduces manual handoffs, and eliminates the need for duplicate data entry.
- **Avoidance of Duplication of Effort:** When systems and processes are not integrated, there's a risk of duplication of effort, where different teams may be working on the same issue or task without knowing it. Integration eliminates this redundancy, saving time and resources.
- **Streamlined Workflows:** Integration enables the automation of workflows across different systems and processes. This reduces the need for manual intervention, accelerates task completion, and improves overall operational efficiency.
- **Improved Data Accuracy:** By integrating data from different sources, organizations can ensure data consistency, accuracy, and completeness. This is essential for making informed decisions, tracking performance, and identifying areas for improvement.
- **Enhanced Visibility:** Integration provides a holistic view of IT services and processes, allowing organizations to track performance, identify bottlenecks, and proactively address issues.

Examples of Integration Tools and Technologies:

- **Enterprise Service Bus (ESB):** An ESB is a software architecture model that provides a standardized way for different applications to communicate with each other. It acts as a central hub for message routing, transformation, and protocol mediation.
- **Application Programming Interfaces (APIs):** APIs are sets of rules and specifications that allow different software applications to communicate and exchange data. They enable integration between different systems, such as ITSM tools, CRM systems, and ERP systems.
- **Integration Platforms as a Service (iPaaS):** iPaaS solutions provide a cloud-based platform for integrating applications and data. They offer pre-built connectors, data mapping tools, and workflow automation capabilities to simplify the integration process.
- **Robotic Process Automation (RPA):** RPA bots can be used to automate repetitive tasks that involve interaction with multiple systems. This can free up human resources for more complex activities and improve efficiency.
- **Workflow Automation Tools:** These tools allow organizations to automate workflows across different systems and processes, reducing manual effort and improving accuracy.
- **Data Lakes and Warehouses:** These centralized repositories store data from various sources, enabling integrated reporting and analysis.

In Summary:

Integration and optimization are key to unlocking the full potential of information and technology in IT service management. By seamlessly connecting processes and tools, automating workflows, and ensuring data accuracy, organizations can achieve a higher level of efficiency, effectiveness, and customer satisfaction. Investing in integration and optimization is a strategic move that can transform IT service management and deliver significant benefits to the organization.

Applying Holistic Thinking in ITIL Practices

The "Think and Work Holistically" principle is not just a theoretical concept; it's a practical approach that can be applied to various ITIL practices, enhancing their effectiveness and impact. Let's explore how this principle can be implemented in four key ITIL practices:

1. Incident Management:

- **Holistic Approach:** Instead of solely focusing on resolving individual incidents, consider the broader impact on other services and processes. For example, a network outage might not only affect internet access but also disrupt email, VoIP calls, and other critical services.
- **Collaboration:** Collaborate with other teams, such as network, security, and application teams, to identify and address the root cause of the incident. This helps prevent similar incidents from occurring in the future and minimizes the overall impact on the organization.
- **Communication:** Keep all relevant stakeholders informed about the incident, its impact, and the progress of resolution. This builds trust and transparency, ensuring everyone is aware of the situation and can take appropriate action.

2. Change Management:

- **Holistic Impact Assessment:** Before implementing any change, conduct a thorough assessment of its potential impact on the entire IT environment. Consider not only the technical aspects but also the impact on users, processes, and other services.
- **Stakeholder Involvement:** Involve all relevant stakeholders in the change process, including IT teams, business users, and customers. This ensures that their perspectives are considered and that the change aligns with their needs and expectations.
- **Risk Management:** Identify and assess the risks associated with the change, and develop mitigation strategies to minimize the potential for disruption.

3. Problem Management:

- **Root Cause Analysis:** Go beyond fixing individual incidents and focus on identifying the root cause of problems. This involves analyzing patterns and trends in incident data, investigating potential causes, and implementing preventive measures to avoid future occurrences.
- **Systems Thinking:** Consider the problem in the context of the broader service environment. Look for interdependencies and potential cascading effects that could impact other services or processes.
- **Collaboration:** Collaborate with different teams to gather information, share knowledge, and develop solutions. This ensures a comprehensive and coordinated approach to problem resolution.

4. Continual Improvement:

- **Value Stream Perspective:** Instead of focusing on isolated improvements to individual processes, take a value stream perspective. Analyze the entire end-to-end flow of work and information, identify bottlenecks or inefficiencies, and implement improvements that optimize the entire value stream.
- **Measurement and Feedback:** Use metrics and feedback from customers and stakeholders to assess the effectiveness of improvement initiatives and identify areas for further optimization.
- **Holistic Culture:** Foster a culture of continuous improvement that encourages everyone in the organization to think holistically, identify opportunities for improvement, and contribute to creating a more efficient and effective service delivery system.

Example: A Holistic Approach to Incident Management

Imagine a scenario where a web server crashes, causing a critical business application to become unavailable. A siloed approach might simply focus on restarting the server to restore service quickly. However, a holistic approach would involve:

- **Collaborating** with the application team to understand the potential impact of the outage on business operations.
- **Analyzing** logs and performance data to identify the root cause of the crash, which could be a software bug, a hardware failure, or a configuration issue.
- **Working** with the network team to investigate any potential network-related issues that might have contributed to the crash.
- **Communicating** the status of the incident and expected resolution time to affected users and stakeholders.
- **Implementing** a temporary workaround, if possible, to minimize the impact of the outage.
- **Developing** a permanent solution to address the root cause and prevent future occurrences.

By taking a holistic approach, the IT team can not only resolve the immediate incident but also prevent similar incidents from happening in the future, improving overall service reliability and customer satisfaction.

Common Challenges and How to Overcome Them

Embracing a holistic approach to IT service management (ITSM) requires a shift in mindset and culture, which can be challenging for some organizations. Here are common obstacles encountered during this transition and strategies to overcome them:

1. **Resistance to Change:**
- **Challenge:** Employees accustomed to working in silos may resist collaborating and sharing information. They might fear losing control, turf wars, or increased workload.
- **Solution:**

- Communication: Clearly communicate the reasons for the change, emphasizing the benefits of a holistic approach for both the organization and individual employees.
- Gradual Implementation: Start with small, manageable changes and gradually expand the scope of collaboration.
- Incentivize Collaboration: Recognize and reward collaborative behavior, creating a positive reinforcement loop.
- Leadership Buy-In: Ensure leadership visibly champions and participates in collaborative efforts, setting an example for others to follow.

2. Lack of Resources:

- Challenge: Adopting a holistic approach may require additional resources, such as time for collaboration, training on new tools and processes, or hiring additional staff.
- Solution:
    - Prioritize Investments: Identify the most critical areas where a holistic approach will yield the greatest benefits and allocate resources accordingly.
    - Optimize Existing Resources: Look for ways to streamline processes, automate tasks, and leverage existing tools to maximize efficiency.
    - Cross-Training: Encourage cross-training and skill development to build a more versatile and adaptable workforce.

3. Cultural Barriers:

- Challenge: Deep-seated organizational culture can be a major barrier to change. If the culture values competition over collaboration or discourages risk-taking and experimentation, it can hinder the adoption of a holistic approach.
- Solution:
    - Leadership: Leaders must champion the cultural shift, modeling collaborative behaviors and emphasizing the importance of teamwork.
    - Change Management: Implement a structured change management process to address cultural barriers and resistance to change.
    - Training and Development: Provide training and development opportunities to help employees develop the skills and mindset needed for collaboration and systems thinking.

Practical Tips and Strategies:

- Create a Shared Vision: Develop a clear and compelling vision for a holistic approach to ITSM that everyone in the organization can understand and support. Communicate this vision regularly and consistently.
- Provide Training and Support: Offer training programs on systems thinking, collaboration skills, and the use of relevant tools and technologies. Provide ongoing support and coaching to reinforce new behaviors.
- Implement Collaboration Tools: Choose and implement collaboration platforms, knowledge management systems, and communication tools that facilitate seamless information sharing and teamwork.
- Celebrate Successes and Recognize Contributions: Publicly acknowledge and reward individuals and teams who demonstrate collaborative behaviors and contribute to the success of the holistic approach.
- Measure and Communicate Progress: Track progress towards the adoption of a holistic approach and communicate results to stakeholders. This helps build momentum and reinforces the value of the initiative.
- Continuous Feedback and Adaptation: Establish feedback loops to gather input from employees, customers, and partners. Use this feedback to continuously refine and improve the approach.

By proactively addressing these challenges and implementing these strategies, organizations can successfully transition to a holistic approach to IT service management, unlocking the full potential of their people, processes, and technologies to deliver exceptional service experiences and achieve their business goals.

Case Studies and Examples

The "Think and Work Holistically" principle has been instrumental in transforming the ITSM practices of various organizations, resulting in improved service delivery, increased efficiency, and enhanced customer satisfaction. Let's delve into a few real-world examples that showcase the practical application and benefits of this principle.

Case Study 1: Global E-commerce Retailer

- **Challenge:** A large e-commerce retailer was experiencing frequent website outages and slow response times, leading to lost sales and customer frustration. The IT department was working in silos, focusing on individual components like servers, networks, and applications, without considering their interdependencies or the overall impact on the customer experience.
- **Strategy:** The company embraced the "Think and Work Holistically" principle by implementing a service-oriented approach. They mapped out their entire e-commerce value stream, identifying bottlenecks and dependencies between different components. They then established cross-functional teams that included representatives from IT, marketing, sales, and customer service to collaborate on issue resolution and service improvement.
- **Outcome:** The holistic approach led to a significant reduction in website downtime and improved response times. The cross-functional teams were able to identify and address root causes of problems more effectively, leading to a more stable and reliable e-commerce platform. Customer satisfaction scores also improved, as customers experienced a more seamless and responsive online shopping experience.

Case Study 2: Manufacturing Company

- **Challenge:** A manufacturing company was struggling with inefficient IT service delivery due to fragmented processes and a lack of communication between different IT teams. This resulted in delays, errors, and increased costs.
- **Strategy:** The company adopted a holistic view of their IT service management by mapping out their key value streams, such as incident management, change management, and request fulfillment. They identified areas where processes were redundant or disjointed and implemented a more integrated approach. They also established a common platform for communication and collaboration between teams, ensuring that everyone had access to the same information and could work together to resolve issues quickly.
- **Outcome:** The holistic approach led to a streamlined IT service delivery process, with reduced wait times, faster resolution times, and improved accuracy. By breaking down silos and fostering collaboration, the company was able to achieve significant cost savings and improve the overall efficiency of its IT operations.

Case Study 3: Healthcare Organization

- **Challenge:** A healthcare organization faced challenges in maintaining the availability and reliability of its electronic health record (EHR) system, which was critical for patient care. Different IT teams were responsible for different components of the system, leading to a lack of coordination and communication.
- **Strategy:** The organization adopted a holistic approach by creating a cross-functional team dedicated to managing the EHR system as a whole. This team included representatives from infrastructure, applications, security, and clinical departments. They established clear roles and responsibilities, implemented a shared communication platform, and developed a comprehensive service management plan that addressed all aspects of the EHR system's lifecycle.
- **Outcome:** The holistic approach significantly improved the availability and reliability of the EHR system. By working together and sharing information, the team was able to proactively identify and address potential issues before they impacted patient care. This resulted in improved patient

outcomes, increased staff satisfaction, and reduced costs associated with system downtime and errors.

Key Takeaways:

These case studies demonstrate the power of the "Think and Work Holistically" principle in transforming IT service management. By breaking down silos, fostering collaboration, and considering the broader impact of decisions and actions, organizations can achieve significant improvements in service quality, efficiency, and customer satisfaction. This holistic approach is essential for navigating the complexities of modern IT environments and delivering value in an increasingly interconnected world.

Chapter Summary

In this chapter, we explored the ITIL 4 guiding principle "Think and Work Holistically," emphasizing its importance in creating a comprehensive and integrated approach to IT service management (ITSM). By understanding the interconnectedness of the service value system (SVS) and adopting a broader perspective, organizations can achieve significant improvements in service delivery, efficiency, and customer satisfaction.

Key takeaways from this chapter include:

- **The Holistic Approach:** We discussed how a holistic approach involves viewing IT service management as an interconnected system, recognizing the interdependencies between different components, processes, and stakeholders. This broader perspective leads to better decision-making, problem-solving, and value creation.
- **Systems Thinking:** We introduced the concept of systems thinking, emphasizing the importance of understanding the complex relationships within the SVS. By applying systems thinking, organizations can identify leverage points for improvement, anticipate unintended consequences, and make more informed decisions.
- **Breaking Down Silos:** We discussed the challenges of siloed thinking and working, which can create barriers to communication, collaboration, and innovation. We provided strategies for breaking down silos, such as promoting cross-functional collaboration, establishing shared goals, and creating a culture of open communication.
- **Collaboration and Communication:** We highlighted the critical role of collaboration and communication in enabling a holistic approach. Effective collaboration breaks down silos, builds trust, and fosters a shared understanding of goals and priorities. We also provided examples of collaboration tools and techniques that can facilitate communication and knowledge sharing.
- **Integration and Optimization:** We explained the importance of integrating different ITSM processes and tools to create a seamless and efficient service delivery system. Integration helps avoid duplication of effort, streamline workflows, and improve data accuracy.
- **Applying Holistic Thinking in ITIL Practices:** We illustrated how the "Think and Work Holistically" principle can be applied to various ITIL practices, such as incident management, change management, problem management, and continual improvement.
- **Common Challenges and Solutions:** We discussed common challenges organizations face when adopting a holistic approach, such as resistance to change, lack of resources, and cultural barriers. We provided practical tips and strategies to overcome these challenges, emphasizing the importance of leadership buy-in, communication, training, and the use of appropriate tools.
- **Case Studies:** We shared real-world examples of organizations that successfully implemented a holistic approach to ITSM, highlighting the positive outcomes they achieved in terms of improved service delivery, efficiency, and customer satisfaction.

By embracing the "Think and Work Holistically" principle, organizations can move beyond a siloed, reactive approach to service management and adopt a more integrated, proactive, and value-driven approach. This shift in mindset can lead to significant improvements in service quality, customer satisfaction, and overall business performance.

Keep It Simple and Practical

Outline

- Understanding the "Keep It Simple and Practical" Principle
- The Value of Simplicity in Service Management
- Practicality vs. Complexity
- Avoiding Overengineering and Overcomplication
- Streamlining Processes and Workflows
- Leveraging Automation and Self-Service
- Balancing Simplicity with Functionality
- Applying the Principle Across the SVS
- Case Studies and Examples
- Chapter Summary

Understanding the "Keep It Simple and Practical" Principle

The "Keep It Simple and Practical" (KISS) principle in ITIL 4 is a guiding philosophy that emphasizes the importance of designing and delivering IT services in a straightforward and user-friendly manner. It's a reminder that complexity often breeds confusion, inefficiency, and increased risk. By embracing simplicity and practicality, organizations can create IT services that are easier to understand, use, and maintain, ultimately leading to better outcomes for both customers and the business.

Core Concept: Avoiding Unnecessary Complexity

At its core, the KISS principle advocates for avoiding unnecessary complexity in IT service management (ITSM). This means:

- **Streamlining Processes:** Eliminating redundant steps, reducing bureaucracy, and focusing on activities that directly contribute to value creation.
- **Simplifying Tools and Technologies:** Choosing tools and technologies that are easy to use, intuitive, and require minimal training.
- **Using Clear and Concise Language:** Avoiding technical jargon and using plain language in documentation, communication, and training materials.
- **Minimizing Customization:** Customizing solutions only when absolutely necessary, as excessive customization can lead to complexity and make it difficult to maintain and upgrade services.
- **Standardization:** Whenever possible, standardize processes and tools to reduce complexity and create consistency across the organization.

How Simplicity and Practicality Contribute to Efficiency, Effectiveness, and Customer Satisfaction:

- **Efficiency:** Simple processes and tools are easier to understand and follow, reducing the risk of errors and delays. This leads to faster and more efficient service delivery.
- **Effectiveness:** By focusing on the essential features and functionalities that meet customer needs, organizations can avoid overengineering and deliver solutions that are more likely to achieve their intended outcomes.
- **Customer Satisfaction:** Simple and intuitive services are easier for customers to use and understand, leading to a more positive experience and higher satisfaction levels.
- **Reduced Costs:** Simple solutions are often less expensive to develop, implement, and maintain than complex ones. This can lead to significant cost savings for the organization.
- **Improved Agility:** Simple solutions are easier to adapt and modify as needs and circumstances change, allowing organizations to respond more quickly to new challenges and opportunities.

Balancing Simplicity with Functionality:

It's important to note that the KISS principle does not mean sacrificing functionality or quality. It's about finding the most straightforward and efficient way to achieve desired outcomes. This involves striking a balance between simplicity and functionality, ensuring that services meet the needs of customers and stakeholders without becoming overly complex.

In some cases, a certain level of complexity may be unavoidable, particularly for highly specialized or technical services. However, even in these cases, organizations should strive to simplify processes and interfaces as much as possible, making them accessible and easy to use for all users.

By embracing the KISS principle, organizations can create IT services that are not only effective and efficient but also user-friendly and easy to maintain. This leads to a better overall experience for both customers and IT staff, ultimately driving business value and success.

The Value of Simplicity in Service Management

Simplicity is a powerful ally in the pursuit of IT service management (ITSM) excellence. By prioritizing clarity, ease of use, and streamlined processes, organizations can unlock a multitude of benefits that positively impact their bottom line, operational efficiency, and customer satisfaction.

Benefits of Simplicity in ITSM:

1. **Reduced Costs:**
   - **Development and Implementation:** Simple solutions often require less time and fewer resources to develop and implement, resulting in lower upfront costs.
   - **Maintenance:** Simple systems are easier to maintain and upgrade, requiring less ongoing effort and resources. This translates to lower operational costs over the long run.
   - **Training:** Intuitive tools and processes require less training for employees and customers, saving time and money.
2. **Improved Efficiency:**
   - **Streamlined Processes:** Simplicity eliminates unnecessary steps, redundancies, and bureaucracy from workflows. This streamlines processes, reduces the risk of errors, and accelerates service delivery.
   - **Reduced Cognitive Load:** Simple processes are easier for employees to understand and follow, leading to faster task completion and improved productivity.
   - **Clear Communication:** Simple and concise language in documentation, instructions, and communications minimizes confusion and misunderstandings, ensuring everyone is on the same page.
3. **Increased User Adoption:**
   - **Intuitive Tools:** User-friendly tools and interfaces encourage adoption and reduce the need for extensive training.
   - **Ease of Use:** When processes are straightforward and easy to follow, employees are more likely to embrace them and use them effectively.
   - **Positive User Experience:** Simple, intuitive solutions create a positive user experience, leading to higher satisfaction and greater engagement.
4. **Enhanced Agility:**
   - **Adaptability:** Simple solutions are easier to adapt and modify as business needs and technologies evolve. This flexibility enables organizations to respond quickly to changing circumstances and maintain their competitive edge.
   - **Innovation:** A culture of simplicity encourages experimentation and innovation, as it is easier to test and implement new ideas when processes and tools are not overly complex.

Risks of Complexity:

Complexity, on the other hand, can be detrimental to IT service management:

- **Increased Costs:** Complex solutions often require more resources to develop, implement, and maintain. They may also be prone to errors and require more frequent troubleshooting and support.
- **Confusion and Misunderstandings:** Complex processes and tools can be difficult to understand and use, leading to confusion, errors, and delays.
- **Resistance to Change:** Employees may resist complex changes, fearing that they will be unable to adapt or that the changes will disrupt their work.
- **Decreased Agility:** Complex systems are often rigid and difficult to change, hindering an organization's ability to respond quickly to evolving needs.

In conclusion, the "Keep It Simple and Practical" principle is not just a slogan; it's a practical approach that can significantly improve the effectiveness, efficiency, and user experience of IT service management. By embracing simplicity, organizations can streamline processes, reduce costs, foster innovation, and deliver greater value to their customers.

Practicality vs. Complexity

In IT service management, there's often a tension between practicality and complexity. While complex solutions may seem impressive on paper, they can often lead to unintended consequences and hinder the overall effectiveness of ITSM. Understanding the difference between practicality and complexity is crucial for making informed decisions and creating solutions that truly benefit the organization and its customers.

Practicality in ITSM:

Practicality in ITSM refers to solutions that are focused on addressing real-world problems and delivering tangible benefits to the organization and its customers. Practical solutions are:

- **User-Centric:** They are designed with the end user in mind, prioritizing ease of use, intuitiveness, and a seamless experience.
- **Efficient:** They streamline workflows, eliminate unnecessary steps, and minimize waste, resulting in faster and more efficient service delivery.
- **Effective:** They solve the problem at hand and deliver the desired outcomes, whether that's reducing downtime, improving customer satisfaction, or increasing productivity.
- **Maintainable:** They are easy to maintain and update, requiring minimal effort and resources over time.
- **Cost-Effective:** They provide good value for money, balancing the cost of implementation and maintenance with the benefits they deliver.

Complexity in ITSM:

Complexity in ITSM refers to solutions that are overly elaborate, convoluted, and difficult to understand or use. Complex solutions may:

- **Be Overengineered:** They may include unnecessary features or functionalities that add little value but increase complexity.
- **Require Extensive Training:** They may have steep learning curves, requiring extensive training and documentation for users to understand and utilize them effectively.
- **Be Difficult to Maintain:** Complex systems can be challenging to maintain, requiring specialized expertise and resources to troubleshoot and update.
- **Introduce Risks:** Complexity can increase the risk of errors, failures, and security vulnerabilities.
- **Inhibit Agility:** Complex solutions can be difficult to adapt and modify, hindering an organization's ability to respond to changing needs.

Balancing Practicality with Functionality:

Achieving the right balance between practicality and functionality is key to successful IT service management. It's about finding the simplest solution that effectively addresses the problem at hand while delivering the required features and capabilities.

Here's how organizations can strike this balance:

- **Focus on Outcomes:** Start by clearly defining the desired outcomes and the problems you are trying to solve. This will help you avoid getting sidetracked by unnecessary features or complexity.
- **Prioritize Usability:** Ensure that solutions are user-friendly and intuitive, even if it means sacrificing some advanced features or functionality.
- **Involve Users in Design:** Gather feedback from users and stakeholders throughout the design process to ensure that solutions meet their needs and are easy to use.
- **Start Simple, Iterate:** Start with a simple solution and gradually add complexity only as needed. This iterative approach allows for flexibility and adaptation based on feedback and real-world experience.
- **Regularly Review and Simplify:** Periodically review your processes, tools, and technologies to identify opportunities for simplification. Eliminate unnecessary steps, automate tasks, and consolidate systems whenever possible.

By embracing practicality and avoiding unnecessary complexity, organizations can create IT service management solutions that are efficient, effective, and user-friendly. This not only improves service quality and customer satisfaction but also reduces costs and enhances the organization's agility and responsiveness.

Avoiding Overengineering and Overcomplication

Overengineering and overcomplication are common pitfalls in IT service management (ITSM), where solutions are often designed to be more complex than necessary. This can lead to increased costs, slower development, and difficulties in maintenance and adoption. By following the "Keep It Simple and Practical" principle, organizations can avoid these pitfalls and create more efficient and effective ITSM solutions.

Practical Tips and Strategies:

1. **Start with a Clear Understanding of the Problem or Need:**
- **Define the Problem:** Before jumping into solutions, clearly define the problem or need you are trying to address. What are the specific pain points or challenges you are facing? What outcomes are you hoping to achieve?
- **Gather Requirements:** Engage with stakeholders, including end-users, to gather detailed requirements. What features and functionalities are essential? What are the "must-haves" vs. the "nice-to-haves"?
- **Scope the Solution:** Based on the problem definition and requirements, clearly define the scope of the solution. Avoid the temptation to add unnecessary features or functionalities that go beyond the core need.
2. **Focus on Desired Outcomes, Not Just Technical Details:**
- **Outcome-Oriented Approach:** Shift your focus from technical details to the desired outcomes. What specific benefits or results are you hoping to achieve with the solution? How will it improve service delivery, enhance customer satisfaction, or reduce costs?
- **Measure Success by Outcomes:** Define clear metrics and key performance indicators (KPIs) that will measure the success of the solution in terms of outcomes, not just technical specifications.
- **Keep the Big Picture in Mind:** Ensure that the solution aligns with the organization's overall goals and strategy, and that it contributes to the creation of value for customers and stakeholders.
3. **Choose the Simplest Solution that Meets the Requirements:**

- **Occam's Razor:** Apply the principle of Occam's Razor, which states that the simplest explanation is often the best. Avoid overcomplicating solutions by choosing the most straightforward approach that meets the defined requirements.
- **Minimum Viable Product (MVP):** Consider developing a minimum viable product (MVP) first, which includes only the essential features and functionalities. This allows you to test the concept and gather feedback before investing in more complex features.

4. **Avoid Adding Unnecessary Features or Functionality:**

- **Resist the Temptation:** Avoid the temptation to add "bells and whistles" that are not directly related to the core purpose of the solution. These extra features may seem appealing but can add unnecessary complexity and cost.
- **Focus on User Needs:** Prioritize features and functionalities that directly address user needs and pain points.
- **Regularly Review and Refine:** Continuously review the solution to identify any features or functionalities that are underutilized or not adding value. Consider removing or simplifying them to streamline the solution.

5. **Involve Users and Stakeholders in the Design Process:**

- **Gather Feedback:** Engage with users and stakeholders throughout the design process to gather their feedback and insights. This helps ensure that the solution is practical, user-friendly, and meets their needs.
- **Usability Testing:** Conduct usability testing with representative users to identify any potential usability issues and gather feedback on the overall user experience.

6. **Regularly Review and Simplify Existing Processes and Tools:**

- **Continuous Improvement:** Regularly review existing processes and tools to identify opportunities for simplification and optimization. Eliminate unnecessary steps, automate tasks, and consolidate systems whenever possible.
- **Technology Refresh:** Evaluate and update technologies regularly to ensure that they remain current and do not become a source of unnecessary complexity.
- **Document and Communicate Changes:** Clearly document any changes or simplifications made to processes and tools, and communicate them effectively to all relevant stakeholders.

By following these tips and strategies, organizations can avoid overengineering and overcomplication in their IT service management practices. This leads to simpler, more efficient, and more effective solutions that deliver greater value to customers and stakeholders.

Streamlining Processes and Workflows

Streamlining processes and workflows is a fundamental aspect of the "Keep It Simple and Practical" principle. It involves critically examining existing processes, eliminating unnecessary steps, automating repetitive tasks, and standardizing procedures to improve efficiency, reduce errors, and enhance the overall service experience.

How to Streamline Processes and Workflows:

1. **Eliminate Unnecessary Steps:**

- **Value Stream Mapping:** Utilize value stream mapping to visualize the entire workflow and identify steps that do not directly contribute to value creation for the customer. These non-value-adding steps should be eliminated or reduced.
- **Critical Analysis:** Question the purpose and necessity of each step in the process. Ask yourself, "Does this step add value? Is it essential for achieving the desired outcome?"
- **Lean Principles:** Apply lean principles, such as eliminating waste (e.g., delays, rework, unnecessary approvals), optimizing flow, and empowering employees to identify and remove bottlenecks.

2. **Automate Repetitive Tasks:**

- **Identify Automation Opportunities:** Look for tasks that are repetitive, rule-based, and time-consuming. These are prime candidates for automation.
- **Leverage Technology:** Use automation tools and technologies, such as robotic process automation (RPA), workflow automation software, and artificial intelligence (AI), to automate these tasks.
- **Focus on High-Value Activities:** Free up employees from mundane, repetitive tasks so they can focus on more complex and value-adding activities, such as problem-solving, innovation, and customer engagement.
3. **Standardize Procedures:**
- **Document Standard Operating Procedures (SOPs):** Create clear and concise SOPs that outline the steps involved in each process. This ensures consistency, reduces the risk of errors, and facilitates knowledge transfer.
- **Train Employees:** Provide training to ensure that employees understand and follow the SOPs.
- **Regularly Review and Update:** Review and update SOPs regularly to reflect changes in processes, technologies, or business needs.

Use of Process Mapping and Analysis Tools:

Process mapping and analysis tools can be invaluable in identifying bottlenecks and inefficiencies in workflows.

- **Process Flow Diagrams:** Visual representations of the steps in a process, highlighting decision points, handoffs, and potential areas for improvement.
- **Swimlane Diagrams:** Show the different roles and responsibilities involved in a process, helping to identify areas where collaboration can be improved.
- **Value Stream Maps:** Visualize the entire value stream, including the flow of information, materials, and value, revealing bottlenecks and opportunities for optimization.
- **Data Analysis:** Analyze process data, such as cycle times, error rates, and throughput, to identify areas where performance can be improved.

Importance of Involving Process Users:

Involving process users in the improvement process is crucial for success. They possess valuable insights into how the process works in practice, where the pain points are, and what improvements could be made. Their involvement can also help build buy-in and ensure that the changes are adopted and embraced.

In Summary:

By streamlining processes and workflows through the elimination of unnecessary steps, automation of repetitive tasks, and standardization of procedures, organizations can achieve significant improvements in efficiency, effectiveness, and customer satisfaction. The use of process mapping and analysis tools can further enhance these efforts by identifying bottlenecks and opportunities for optimization. Most importantly, involving process users in the improvement process ensures that the changes are practical, relevant, and sustainable.

Leveraging Automation and Self-Service

Automation and self-service are two powerful tools that can significantly streamline and simplify IT service management (ITSM). By reducing manual intervention, automating repetitive tasks, and empowering users to help themselves, organizations can improve efficiency, reduce costs, and enhance the overall customer experience.

How Automation and Self-Service Simplify ITSM and Improve Efficiency:

- **Reduced Manual Effort:** Automation takes over repetitive, rule-based tasks that were previously performed by humans. This frees up IT staff to focus on more complex and value-adding activities, such as problem-solving, innovation, and strategic planning.
- **Faster Response Times:** Automated processes can execute tasks much faster than humans, leading to quicker resolution of incidents, fulfillment of service requests, and delivery of information. This improves service levels and enhances customer satisfaction.
- **Increased Accuracy and Consistency:** Automation eliminates the risk of human error, ensuring that tasks are performed consistently and accurately every time. This improves data quality, reduces rework, and enhances the reliability of IT services.
- **24/7 Availability:** Self-service portals and chatbots can provide support and information to users around the clock, even outside of normal business hours. This improves accessibility and convenience for users, especially those in different time zones.
- **Cost Savings:** Automation and self-service can significantly reduce operational costs by minimizing the need for manual labor, streamlining processes, and preventing errors.

Examples of Automation Tools and Technologies:

- **Chatbots:** AI-powered chatbots can interact with users in natural language, answering questions, providing guidance, and resolving simple issues. They can be integrated into various channels, such as websites, messaging apps, and social media platforms.
- **Robotic Process Automation (RPA):** RPA bots can mimic human actions to automate repetitive tasks, such as data entry, form filling, and report generation. They can interact with multiple systems and applications, streamlining complex workflows.
- **Workflow Automation Software:** These tools allow organizations to automate and orchestrate business processes, routing tasks to the appropriate teams or individuals, tracking progress, and ensuring compliance with policies and procedures.
- **AI-Powered Virtual Assistants:** These intelligent assistants can understand and respond to user requests, providing personalized support and recommendations.
- **Self-Healing Systems:** These systems can automatically detect and resolve issues, reducing the need for manual intervention and minimizing downtime.

Importance of Designing User-Friendly Self-Service Portals and Knowledge Bases:

Self-service portals and knowledge bases are essential components of an effective self-service strategy. However, their success depends on how well they are designed.

- **Easy to Use:** The interface should be intuitive and user-friendly, with clear navigation and search functionality. Users should be able to find the information they need quickly and easily.
- **Relevant Information:** The content should be accurate, up-to-date, and relevant to the user's needs. It should be organized in a logical way and presented in a clear and concise format.
- **Multiple Channels:** Self-service should be available through multiple channels, such as web portals, mobile apps, and chatbots, to cater to different user preferences.
- **Feedback Mechanisms:** Provide mechanisms for users to provide feedback on the self-service experience, such as surveys, ratings, or comments. This feedback can be used to continuously improve the self-service offerings.
- **Integration with Other Systems:** The self-service portal should be integrated with other relevant systems, such as the ITSM tool or the knowledge management system, to provide users with a seamless experience.

By designing user-friendly self-service portals and knowledge bases, organizations can empower users to help themselves, reduce the burden on the service desk, and improve overall customer satisfaction.

Balancing Simplicity with Functionality

Striking the right balance between simplicity and functionality is a continuous challenge in IT service management (ITSM). While the "Keep It Simple and Practical" principle emphasizes the benefits of simplicity, it doesn't mean sacrificing essential features or capabilities. It's about finding the sweet spot where solutions are both effective and easy to use.

The Challenge of Balancing Simplicity with Functionality:

- **Conflicting Goals:** Simplicity and functionality can sometimes seem like opposing forces. Simpler solutions may be easier to use and maintain, but they may lack the advanced features or customization options that some users require. On the other hand, highly functional solutions may be more powerful but also more complex, leading to longer learning curves and increased risk of errors.
- **Diverse Stakeholder Needs:** Different stakeholders may have different priorities and preferences. Some may value simplicity and ease of use above all else, while others may demand advanced features and customization options. Balancing these diverse needs can be a challenge.
- **Evolving Technologies:** The rapid pace of technological change can also make it difficult to maintain simplicity. New features and capabilities are constantly emerging, and there's a temptation to incorporate them all into IT services, leading to increased complexity.

Understanding Trade-offs and Making Informed Decisions:

To achieve the right balance, it's important to understand the trade-offs between simplicity and complexity and make informed decisions based on the specific needs of the organization and its stakeholders. This involves:

- **Clearly Defining Requirements:** Thoroughly analyze and understand the requirements for the IT service. What are the core functionalities that must be delivered? What are the nice-to-haves that could be added later?
- **Prioritizing User Needs:** Put user needs at the center of the design process. Focus on creating solutions that are easy to use and understand, even if it means sacrificing some advanced features.
- **Iterative Development:** Adopt an iterative approach to development, starting with a minimum viable product (MVP) and gradually adding features based on user feedback and testing.
- **Regular Reviews:** Regularly review and assess the complexity of IT services. Identify areas where simplification can be made without compromising functionality or quality.

The Role of Continuous Improvement:

Continuous improvement plays a crucial role in achieving and maintaining the right balance between simplicity and functionality. By regularly evaluating and refining processes, tools, and technologies, organizations can:

- **Identify Opportunities for Simplification:** Uncover areas where processes can be streamlined, tasks automated, or tools consolidated.
- **Optimize Functionality:** Enhance the functionality of IT services while minimizing complexity by focusing on features that deliver the most value to users.
- **Adapt to Change:** As technologies and business needs evolve, continually adapt and refine IT services to maintain their simplicity and relevance.

In Summary:

Balancing simplicity with functionality is an ongoing challenge in IT service management. By understanding the trade-offs, making informed decisions, and embracing continuous improvement, organizations can create IT services that are both effective and user-friendly, delivering value to customers and stakeholders while minimizing complexity and risk.

Applying the "Keep It Simple and Practical" Principle Across the SVS

The "Keep It Simple and Practical" (KISS) principle can be woven into every stage of the Service Value System (SVS), enhancing efficiency, promoting user-friendliness, and optimizing value delivery. Here's how:

1. Service Strategy:

- **Goal Setting:** Instead of overly ambitious plans, set clear, achievable goals that focus on delivering tangible value to customers and stakeholders. Break down complex objectives into smaller, more manageable steps.
- **Prioritization:** Prioritize initiatives based on their potential impact and feasibility, avoiding overcommitment and ensuring resources are used effectively.
- **Communication:** Clearly communicate the service strategy to stakeholders in a concise and easy-to-understand manner, ensuring everyone is aligned and understands the value proposition.

2. Service Design:

- **User-Centric Design:** Involve end-users in the design process to ensure that services are intuitive, easy to use, and meet their needs.
- **Streamlined Service Catalog:** Keep the service catalog concise and well-organized, avoiding unnecessary complexity or confusing options.
- **Standard Service Offerings:** Whenever possible, create standardized service offerings with clear descriptions, SLAs, and pricing models.

3. Service Transition:

- **Phased Implementation:** Instead of a "big bang" rollout, implement changes in a controlled and phased manner. This allows for testing, feedback, and adjustments before full deployment, minimizing disruption and risk.
- **Change Control:** Maintain a robust change management process to ensure that changes are properly assessed, authorized, and implemented in a way that minimizes disruption and risk.
- **Clear Communication:** Communicate changes clearly and effectively to all stakeholders, providing them with adequate notice, training, and support.

4. Service Operation:

- **Process Optimization:** Continuously review and streamline operational processes to eliminate waste, automate repetitive tasks, and reduce manual effort.
- **Standard Operating Procedures (SOPs):** Create clear and concise SOPs that are easy to understand and follow. Review and update SOPs regularly to ensure they remain relevant.
- **Automation:** Leverage automation tools to automate repetitive tasks, such as ticket routing, password resets, and data entry. This frees up service agents to focus on more complex and value-adding activities.

5. Continual Improvement:

- **Root Cause Analysis (RCA):** Conduct thorough RCA to identify and address the root causes of complexity, such as unnecessary process steps, redundant systems, or confusing user interfaces.
- **Simplification Initiatives:** Launch specific initiatives to simplify processes, tools, and technologies. This could involve consolidating systems, reducing customization, or standardizing procedures.
- **Feedback Loops:** Establish feedback loops with customers and stakeholders to gather input on areas where complexity could be reduced or processes could be streamlined.

In Summary:

By applying the "Keep It Simple and Practical" principle throughout the Service Value System, organizations can create a more efficient, effective, and user-friendly ITSM environment. This leads to improved service quality, increased customer satisfaction, and reduced costs, ultimately contributing to the overall success of the organization.

Case Studies and Examples

The "Keep It Simple and Practical" (KISS) principle has been adopted by numerous organizations across various industries to streamline their IT service management (ITSM) practices, leading to remarkable improvements in efficiency, cost reduction, and customer satisfaction.

Case Study 1: Large Telecommunications Company

- **Challenge:** A large telecommunications company was struggling with a complex and cumbersome incident management process that involved multiple manual steps, lengthy approval chains, and outdated tools. This led to delays in incident resolution, increased costs, and frustrated customers.
- **Strategy:** The company embraced the KISS principle by simplifying and automating its incident management process. They eliminated unnecessary approval steps, implemented a user-friendly self-service portal for incident reporting, and leveraged automation tools to triage and assign incidents based on priority and expertise.
- **Outcome:** By streamlining the incident management process, the company was able to reduce incident resolution times by 40%, decrease support costs by 20%, and significantly improve customer satisfaction. The simplified process also made it easier for new employees to onboard and contribute quickly.

Case Study 2: Healthcare Provider

- **Challenge:** A healthcare provider was using a complex and customized electronic health record (EHR) system that was difficult to use and prone to errors. The system required extensive training for new staff, and its complexity often led to delays in patient care.
- **Strategy:** The provider adopted the KISS principle by replacing the customized EHR system with a simpler, more intuitive commercial solution. The new system required less training, was easier to use, and had fewer opportunities for errors. The provider also standardized clinical workflows and developed clear and concise documentation to support the new system.
- **Outcome:** The simplified EHR system led to a significant reduction in errors and improved the efficiency of clinical workflows. Staff members were able to access patient information more quickly and easily, leading to faster and more effective patient care. The improved usability of the system also boosted staff morale and job satisfaction.

Case Study 3: Government Agency

- **Challenge:** A government agency was burdened with a complex network infrastructure that was difficult to manage and maintain. The agency was experiencing frequent outages, slow performance, and high support costs.
- **Strategy:** The agency applied the KISS principle by consolidating its network infrastructure, eliminating redundant systems, and standardizing configurations. They also implemented automation tools to simplify routine maintenance tasks and monitor network performance.
- **Outcome:** The simplified network infrastructure led to a significant reduction in outages and improved performance. The automation of maintenance tasks freed up IT staff to focus on more strategic initiatives, and the standardized configurations made it easier to troubleshoot and resolve issues.

Case Study 4: Software Development Company

- **Challenge:** A software development company was struggling to manage the growing complexity of its software development projects. The company's development process was overly bureaucratic, with numerous approval steps and documentation requirements. This slowed down development cycles and hampered innovation.
- **Strategy:** The company adopted an agile development methodology, which emphasizes iterative development, continuous feedback, and collaboration. They also implemented a simplified project management tool that focused on essential features and eliminated unnecessary bureaucracy.
- **Outcome:** The agile approach and simplified tools allowed the company to accelerate its development cycles and deliver new features and products more quickly. The focus on collaboration and feedback also improved communication between teams and fostered a more innovative culture.

These case studies demonstrate the diverse applications and tangible benefits of the "Keep It Simple and Practical" principle in IT service management. By prioritizing simplicity and practicality, organizations can streamline processes, reduce costs, improve efficiency, enhance user adoption, and foster innovation. The KISS principle is not just a theoretical concept; it's a practical tool that can drive significant improvements in IT service delivery and overall business performance.

Chapter Summary

In this chapter, we explored the ITIL 4 guiding principle "Keep It Simple and Practical." We emphasized the importance of simplicity in creating efficient, effective, and user-friendly IT service management (ITSM) solutions.

Key takeaways from this chapter include:

- **The Value of Simplicity:** Simplicity in ITSM leads to numerous benefits, including reduced costs, improved efficiency, increased user adoption, and enhanced agility. Simple solutions are easier to understand, implement, maintain, and adapt to changing needs.
- **Practicality vs. Complexity:** We contrasted the concepts of practicality and complexity, highlighting that practical solutions focus on solving real-world problems and delivering tangible benefits, while complex solutions often lead to overengineering and unnecessary complications.
- **Avoiding Overengineering and Overcomplication:** We offered practical tips for avoiding overengineering, such as starting with a clear understanding of the problem, focusing on desired outcomes, choosing the simplest solution, involving users in the design process, and regularly reviewing and simplifying existing processes and tools.
- **Streamlining Processes and Workflows:** We discussed how to streamline processes by eliminating unnecessary steps, automating repetitive tasks, and standardizing procedures. We also highlighted the use of process mapping and analysis tools and the importance of involving process users in the improvement process.
- **Leveraging Automation and Self-Service:** We explained how automation and self-service can simplify ITSM and improve efficiency by reducing manual effort, speeding up response times, and increasing accuracy. We also emphasized the importance of designing user-friendly self-service portals and knowledge bases.
- **Balancing Simplicity with Functionality:** We acknowledged the challenge of balancing simplicity with functionality and the need to understand the trade-offs involved. We stressed the importance of making informed decisions based on specific organizational and stakeholder needs, prioritizing user needs, and using continuous improvement to refine and optimize solutions.

By applying the "Keep It Simple and Practical" principle throughout the Service Value System (SVS), organizations can create a more streamlined, efficient, and user-centric ITSM environment. This leads to improved service quality, enhanced customer satisfaction, reduced costs, and increased agility, ultimately contributing to the organization's overall success.

Optimize and Automate

Outline

- Understanding the "Optimize and Automate" Principle
- The Importance of Optimization in Service Management
- Optimization Techniques
- The Role of Automation in Service Management
- Types of Automation
- Benefits of Automation
- Risks and Challenges of Automation
- Balancing Optimization and Automation
- Applying the Principle Across the SVS
- Case Studies and Examples
- Chapter Summary

Understanding the "Optimize and Automate" Principle

The "Optimize and Automate" principle in ITIL 4 underscores a dual approach to service management improvement:

1. **Optimization:** Continuously improving and refining resources, processes, and capabilities to maximize their effectiveness and efficiency.
2. **Automation:** Leveraging technology to streamline repetitive, manual tasks, freeing up human resources for more complex and value-adding activities.

Core Concept: Continuous Improvement and Technological Leverage

This principle recognizes that resources, both human and technical, are valuable assets that should be used to their fullest potential. Optimization involves eliminating waste, reducing redundancy, and fine-tuning processes to achieve optimal performance. Automation complements optimization by automating tasks that can be performed more efficiently and accurately by machines, allowing human resources to focus on activities that require creativity, problem-solving, and decision-making.

How Optimization and Automation Lead to Improved Outcomes:

- **Efficiency:** Optimization streamlines processes and eliminates bottlenecks, while automation reduces manual effort and accelerates task completion. This combined effect leads to significant improvements in efficiency, allowing organizations to do more with less.
- **Effectiveness:** Optimization ensures that processes are aligned with desired outcomes and that resources are utilized effectively. Automation reduces the risk of human error, ensuring that tasks are performed consistently and accurately, leading to better results.
- **Cost Savings:** By eliminating waste, streamlining processes, and reducing manual effort, both optimization and automation contribute to cost savings. This can be achieved through lower labor costs, reduced rework, and optimized resource utilization.

Finding the Right Balance: Enhancing, Not Replacing, Human Capabilities

The "Optimize and Automate" principle does not advocate for complete automation at the expense of human involvement. Instead, it emphasizes the importance of finding the right balance between optimization and automation.

Automation should be seen as a tool to enhance human capabilities, not replace them. While technology excels at repetitive, rule-based tasks, humans are still needed for complex problem-solving, decision-making, and creative thinking. By automating mundane tasks, organizations can free up their employees to focus on higher-value activities that require uniquely human skills.

Furthermore, it's important to maintain human oversight and control over automated processes to ensure that they function as intended and do not create unintended consequences. Regular monitoring and evaluation are crucial to identify any potential issues and make necessary adjustments.

By finding the right balance between optimization and automation, organizations can create a more efficient, effective, and human-centered approach to IT service management. This not only leads to improved service delivery and customer satisfaction but also empowers employees and fosters a culture of continuous improvement and innovation.

The Importance of Optimization in Service Management

Optimization is a critical aspect of ITIL 4's "Optimize and Automate" principle. It represents the ongoing pursuit of improving efficiency, effectiveness, and value delivery within IT service management (ITSM). By continuously refining and enhancing processes, workflows, technologies, and resource utilization, organizations can ensure that their IT services are operating at peak performance and delivering maximum value to customers and stakeholders.

Significance of Optimization in ITSM:

- **Enhanced Efficiency:** Optimization eliminates waste and redundancies, streamlines workflows, and maximizes the use of resources. This leads to faster service delivery, quicker response times, and improved overall efficiency.
- **Improved Effectiveness:** By optimizing processes and tools, organizations can ensure that IT services consistently meet or exceed customer expectations and align with business goals. This leads to better outcomes, increased customer satisfaction, and enhanced business value.
- **Cost Reduction:** Optimization often results in significant cost savings. By identifying and eliminating waste, streamlining processes, and maximizing resource utilization, organizations can reduce operational expenses and improve their bottom line.
- **Continuous Improvement:** Optimization is not a one-time event; it's a continuous process of identifying and implementing improvements. By constantly seeking ways to do things better, organizations can stay ahead of the curve, adapt to changing needs, and maintain their competitive edge.

Applying Optimization to Various Aspects of Service Management:

Optimization can be applied to all aspects of service management, including:

- **Processes:** Analyzing and streamlining processes to eliminate bottlenecks, reduce cycle times, and improve quality.
- **Workflows:** Optimizing the flow of work between different teams and departments to ensure smooth handoffs, reduce delays, and improve collaboration.
- **Technology:** Evaluating and upgrading technology solutions to improve performance, scalability, and security.
- **Resources:** Optimizing the allocation and utilization of human resources, infrastructure, and financial resources to maximize value creation.

Examples of Optimization Techniques:

- **Eliminating Waste:** Identifying and removing non-value-adding activities, such as unnecessary approvals, redundant data entry, or excessive documentation.

- **Streamlining Processes:** Simplifying complex processes by reducing the number of steps, standardizing procedures, and automating tasks where possible.
- **Improving Resource Utilization:** Analyzing resource utilization data to identify underutilized resources and reallocate them to areas where they can be used more effectively.
- **Lean Practices:** Adopting Lean principles, such as continuous improvement, value stream mapping, and just-in-time delivery, to identify and eliminate waste.
- **Data Analysis:** Leveraging data analytics to identify trends, patterns, and outliers that can inform optimization decisions.

In Summary:

Optimization is a continuous journey, not a destination. By embracing a culture of optimization and using a variety of techniques, organizations can ensure that their IT services are constantly evolving and improving to meet the ever-changing needs of their customers and stakeholders. This commitment to optimization not only drives efficiency and effectiveness but also creates a competitive advantage and ensures the long-term success of IT service management.

Optimization Techniques

Optimization is the continuous pursuit of improving efficiency, effectiveness, and value within IT Service Management (ITSM). Various techniques and methodologies can be employed to achieve this goal. Here's an overview of some prominent optimization approaches:

1. **Lean Principles:**

Lean principles, derived from lean manufacturing, focus on maximizing customer value while minimizing waste. Key lean principles relevant to ITSM optimization include:

- **Identifying and Eliminating Waste:** This involves identifying and eliminating activities that consume resources but do not add value to the customer. Common types of waste include delays, defects, overproduction, inventory, unnecessary motion, and underutilized talent.
- **Improving Flow:** This focuses on ensuring a smooth and continuous flow of work through the value stream, minimizing interruptions, delays, and bottlenecks.
- **Empowering Employees:** Lean emphasizes empowering employees at all levels to identify and solve problems, encouraging a culture of continuous improvement.
2. **Six Sigma Methodologies:**

Six Sigma is a data-driven methodology that aims to improve process quality by reducing defects and variation. It utilizes statistical tools and techniques to analyze processes, identify root causes of problems, and implement solutions.

- **DMAIC (Define, Measure, Analyze, Improve, Control):** This five-step process is used to improve existing processes.
- **DMADV (Define, Measure, Analyze, Design, Verify):** This five-step process is used to design new processes or products.
- **Statistical Process Control (SPC):** A tool used to monitor process performance and identify variations that may require corrective action.
3. **Theory of Constraints (TOC):**

The Theory of Constraints focuses on identifying and addressing bottlenecks in processes. It emphasizes that every system has at least one constraint, and improving the system's overall performance requires identifying and eliminating these constraints.

- **Five Focusing Steps:**
    1. Identify the constraint.

2. Exploit the constraint.
3. Subordinate everything else to the constraint.
4. Elevate the constraint.
5. If in the previous steps a constraint has been broken, go back to step 1.

4. **Value Stream Mapping (VSM):**

Value Stream Mapping is a lean technique used to visualize and analyze the flow of materials and information required to deliver a product or service. It helps identify waste and bottlenecks, enabling targeted improvement efforts.

- **Current State Map:** This map documents the current state of the value stream, including process steps, cycle times, inventory levels, and information flow.
- **Future State Map:** This map envisions the ideal state of the value stream after improvements have been implemented.
- **Implementation Plan:** This plan outlines the steps required to move from the current state to the future state.

Example: Optimizing Incident Management with Lean Principles

1. **Identify Waste:** Analyze the incident management process and identify non-value-adding activities, such as delays in ticket assignment, unnecessary escalations, or redundant approvals.
2. **Improve Flow:** Streamline the workflow by eliminating unnecessary steps, automating approvals, and implementing clear escalation procedures.
3. **Empower Employees:** Encourage service desk agents to take ownership of incident resolution, providing them with the tools and training they need to resolve issues quickly and effectively.

By applying these optimization techniques, organizations can significantly improve the efficiency, effectiveness, and value of their IT service management processes, ultimately leading to better service delivery and increased customer satisfaction.

The Role of Automation in Service Management

Automation, a key component of the "Optimize and Automate" principle, is a game-changer in IT service management (ITSM). By leveraging technology to take over routine, manual tasks, organizations can unlock a new level of efficiency, accuracy, and speed in service delivery.

Streamlining Processes, Reducing Manual Effort, and Improving Efficiency:

Automation acts as a force multiplier in ITSM, enabling teams to achieve more with less. It eliminates the need for human intervention in repetitive and time-consuming tasks, freeing up valuable resources to focus on higher-value activities. This not only improves efficiency but also reduces the risk of human error, ensuring consistent and reliable service delivery.

Here's how automation achieves this:

- **Streamlining Processes:** Automation tools can orchestrate complex workflows, seamlessly integrating different systems and applications to automate end-to-end processes. This reduces manual handoffs, eliminates bottlenecks, and accelerates service delivery.
- **Reducing Manual Effort:** By automating repetitive tasks, such as data entry, form filling, and report generation, automation frees up IT staff from mundane work, allowing them to focus on more strategic and complex activities that require human judgment and expertise.
- **Improving Efficiency:** Automated processes can execute tasks much faster and more accurately than humans, leading to quicker resolution of incidents, faster fulfillment of requests, and improved service levels.

How Automation is Used in ITSM:

Automation can be applied to various aspects of IT service management, including:

- **Performing Repetitive Tasks:** Automation can handle routine tasks like password resets, software installations, and data backups, freeing up IT staff from repetitive manual work.
- **Enforcing Policies:** Automation can ensure compliance with policies and procedures by automatically validating requests, enforcing approval workflows, and generating audit trails.
- **Triggering Actions Based on Predefined Conditions:** Automation can be used to trigger actions based on specific events or conditions. For example, a monitoring tool can automatically trigger an alert when a server's CPU usage exceeds a certain threshold, allowing IT teams to proactively address the issue before it impacts service availability.

Examples of Automation Use Cases in IT Service Management:

1. **Incident Routing:** Automatically categorizing and routing incidents to the appropriate support teams based on predefined rules. This ensures that incidents are assigned to the right experts for faster resolution.
2. **Password Resets:** Automating the password reset process, allowing users to reset their passwords through self-service portals or chatbots without needing to contact the service desk.
3. **Service Request Fulfillment:** Automating the fulfillment of standard service requests, such as provisioning new user accounts or granting access to applications.
4. **Server Monitoring and Maintenance:** Automating server monitoring and maintenance tasks, such as patching, backups, and performance optimization.
5. **Software Deployment:** Automating the deployment of software updates and patches, reducing the risk of errors and ensuring consistent configurations across the environment.

By embracing automation, organizations can transform their IT service management practices, achieving greater efficiency, accuracy, and speed in service delivery. This not only improves customer satisfaction but also empowers IT teams to focus on higher-value activities that drive innovation and business growth.

Types of Automation in IT Service Management

Automation in ITSM is not a one-size-fits-all concept. It encompasses a wide array of technologies and tools, each with unique capabilities and applications. Understanding these different types can help organizations choose the right solutions for their specific needs and achieve their automation goals.

1. **Robotic Process Automation (RPA):**

RPA is a software technology that uses "bots" or "software robots" to mimic human actions and automate repetitive, rule-based tasks. These bots can interact with various applications and systems, just like a human would, to perform tasks such as:

- **Data Entry:** Entering data into forms, spreadsheets, or databases.
- **Data Extraction:** Extracting information from documents, emails, or websites.
- **Report Generation:** Creating and distributing reports based on predefined templates.
- **System Maintenance:** Performing routine system maintenance tasks, such as restarting services or clearing logs.

RPA is particularly useful for automating tasks that involve interacting with legacy systems that lack modern APIs or integration capabilities.

2. **Workflow Automation:**

Workflow automation tools automate the flow of work between different systems and applications. They can trigger actions based on specific events or conditions, route tasks to the appropriate teams or individuals, and track progress throughout the workflow.

- **Examples:**
  - **Ticket Routing:** Automatically routing incident or service requests to the appropriate support teams based on predefined rules.
  - **Approval Workflows:** Automating the approval process for change requests or purchase orders.
  - **Notification and Escalation:** Automatically notifying stakeholders about important events or escalating issues based on predefined criteria.

Workflow automation can significantly improve efficiency and reduce errors by eliminating manual handoffs and ensuring that tasks are completed consistently and in a timely manner.

3. **Artificial Intelligence (AI) and Machine Learning (ML):**

AI and ML are advanced technologies that enable systems to learn from data and make decisions or predictions. They can be used to enhance the capabilities of automation tools, making them more intelligent and adaptable.

- **Examples in ITSM:**
  - **Intelligent Chatbots:** Chatbots that can understand natural language queries and provide personalized responses.
  - **Predictive Analytics:** Analyzing historical data to predict future trends, such as potential system failures or service demand spikes.
  - **Anomaly Detection:** Identifying unusual patterns or events that may indicate a security breach or performance issue.

AI and ML can significantly improve the accuracy and efficiency of automation, enabling organizations to proactively address issues, personalize service experiences, and make data-driven decisions.

4. **Chatbots and Virtual Agents:**

Chatbots and virtual agents are AI-powered tools that can interact with users in natural language, simulating human conversation. They can be used to provide instant support, answer questions, guide users through self-service processes, and escalate complex issues to human agents.

- **Benefits:**
  - **24/7 Availability:** Provide support to users around the clock, even outside of business hours.
  - **Reduced Wait Times:** Handle simple queries instantly, reducing wait times for users and freeing up human agents for more complex issues.
  - **Improved Customer Satisfaction:** Provide a convenient and personalized experience for users.
  - **Cost Savings:** Reduce the cost of providing customer support by automating routine tasks.

By leveraging these different types of automation technologies, organizations can transform their IT service management practices, achieving greater efficiency, accuracy, and responsiveness while freeing up human resources to focus on higher-value activities.

Benefits of Automation in ITSM

Automation is a powerful tool that can revolutionize IT service management (ITSM). By strategically implementing automation, organizations can reap numerous benefits that positively impact their bottom line, operational efficiency, and overall service quality.

1. **Reduced Costs:**

- **Labor Savings:** Automating repetitive, manual tasks reduces the need for human intervention, freeing up valuable staff resources for more complex and strategic activities. This can lead to significant savings in labor costs.
- **Error Reduction:** Human errors are costly, often leading to rework, delays, and customer dissatisfaction. Automation eliminates these errors, reducing the associated costs.
- **Improved Resource Utilization:** Automation optimizes the utilization of IT resources, such as servers, storage, and network bandwidth, by ensuring they are used efficiently and effectively. This can lead to cost savings in infrastructure and maintenance.

2. **Improved Efficiency and Productivity:**

- **Faster Task Completion:** Automated processes can complete tasks much faster than humans, accelerating service delivery and response times. This improves overall efficiency and productivity.
- **Streamlined Workflows:** Automation eliminates bottlenecks and manual handoffs, streamlining workflows and reducing delays.
- **Increased Throughput:** Automation enables IT teams to handle a higher volume of tasks without increasing headcount, improving the overall throughput of the service desk and other ITSM functions.

3. **Increased Accuracy and Consistency:**

- **Error Elimination:** Automation eliminates the risk of human error, ensuring consistent and accurate execution of tasks. This improves data quality, reduces rework, and enhances service reliability.
- **Standardized Processes:** Automation enforces standardized procedures, ensuring that tasks are performed consistently across the organization. This improves quality control and reduces the risk of non-compliance.
- **Improved Decision-Making:** Automated systems can provide accurate and timely data for decision-making, helping IT leaders make informed choices based on real-time information.

4. **Faster Response Times:**

- **24/7 Availability:** Automated systems can operate around the clock, providing instant responses to incidents, requests, and queries, even outside of business hours. This improves service availability and responsiveness.
- **Immediate Action:** Automation can trigger immediate actions in response to specific events or conditions, such as automatically restarting a failed service or escalating a critical incident.

5. **Enhanced Customer Satisfaction:**

- **Faster Resolution:** Automation speeds up incident resolution and request fulfillment, reducing wait times for customers and improving their experience.
- **Self-Service:** Automated self-service portals and chatbots empower customers to resolve issues and find information on their own, providing a convenient and personalized experience.
- **Proactive Communication:** Automation can be used to proactively communicate with customers, providing updates on incident status, service requests, or upcoming changes.

6. **Improved Employee Morale:**

- **Job Enrichment:** By automating mundane and repetitive tasks, organizations can free up employees to focus on more challenging and rewarding work, leading to increased job satisfaction and engagement.
- **Professional Development:** Automation can provide employees with opportunities to learn new skills and develop their careers, as they move from manual tasks to more strategic and analytical roles.
- **Reduced Stress:** By automating repetitive and time-consuming tasks, employees can experience reduced stress and burnout, leading to improved morale and well-being.

In Summary:

Automation is a powerful tool that can transform IT service management. By reducing costs, improving efficiency, increasing accuracy, and enhancing customer satisfaction, automation can help organizations achieve their service management goals and deliver greater value to their customers and stakeholders. As technology continues to advance, the potential for automation in ITSM will only grow, offering new and exciting opportunities for innovation and improvement.

Risks and Challenges of Automation

While automation offers numerous benefits for IT service management (ITSM), it is important to be aware of the potential risks and challenges that come with its implementation. Careful planning and consideration are necessary to mitigate these risks and ensure that automation is used effectively and responsibly.

1. Job Displacement:

- **Concern:** One of the primary concerns surrounding automation is the potential displacement of jobs. As machines become more capable of performing tasks traditionally done by humans, there is a fear that jobs may be lost, leading to unemployment and social disruption.
- **Mitigation:** Organizations need to approach automation strategically, focusing on automating repetitive, mundane tasks that can be done more efficiently by machines. This frees up human employees to focus on more complex, value-adding activities that require creativity, problem-solving, and human interaction. Upskilling and reskilling programs can also help employees transition to new roles within the organization.

2. Over-Reliance on Technology:

- **Concern:** Over-reliance on automation can create a dependency on technology that can be risky. If automated systems fail or malfunction, it can lead to significant disruptions in service delivery and business operations.
- **Mitigation:** Organizations should implement redundancy and failover mechanisms to ensure that critical services are not solely dependent on automated systems. Regular testing and maintenance of automated processes are also crucial to identify and address any potential issues. Additionally, it's important to maintain human oversight of automated systems and have manual procedures in place for critical tasks.

3. Lack of Human Oversight:

- **Concern:** Without proper human oversight, automated processes can run amok, leading to errors, inconsistencies, and unintended consequences. This can be particularly problematic in complex systems with multiple dependencies.
- **Mitigation:** Organizations should establish clear governance frameworks and control mechanisms for automated processes. Regular audits and reviews can help identify potential issues and ensure that automation aligns with organizational goals and values. It's also important to maintain human involvement in critical decision-making processes and ensure that there are mechanisms for human intervention when needed.

4. Potential for Errors or Unintended Consequences:

- **Concern:** Even well-designed automated systems can make mistakes or produce unintended consequences. This can be due to faulty algorithms, incorrect data inputs, or unforeseen circumstances.
- **Mitigation:** Thorough testing and validation of automated processes are essential to identify and fix errors before they cause problems. Organizations should also have robust monitoring and alerting systems in place to detect any anomalies or unexpected behavior. Continuous improvement and feedback loops are also crucial for refining and optimizing automated processes.

5. Resistance to Change:

- **Concern:** Employees may resist automation due to fear of job loss, lack of understanding of new technologies, or concerns about the impact on their work routines.

- **Mitigation:** Clear communication and transparency are key to addressing resistance to change. Organizations should explain the benefits of automation, provide training and support to help employees adapt, and address any concerns or anxieties they may have. Involving employees in the design and implementation of automation can also increase their buy-in and acceptance.

By proactively addressing these risks and challenges, organizations can successfully harness the power of automation to improve their ITSM practices, enhance efficiency, reduce costs, and deliver better service experiences.

Balancing Optimization and Automation

The "Optimize and Automate" principle in ITIL 4 emphasizes the complementary nature of optimization and automation. However, finding the right balance between these two approaches is crucial for maximizing their benefits and avoiding potential pitfalls.

The Importance of Finding the Right Balance:

Optimization and automation are not mutually exclusive; they work best in tandem. Optimization focuses on improving processes and workflows, while automation leverages technology to execute those processes more efficiently. A balanced approach ensures that automation is applied strategically to the right tasks, while human expertise is retained for critical decision-making and problem-solving.

- **Over-Automation:** Over-reliance on automation can lead to rigidity, reduced flexibility, and a loss of human touch in service delivery. It can also create a false sense of security, as automated systems may not be able to handle unexpected situations or exceptions.
- **Under-Optimization:** Neglecting optimization before automation can lead to the automation of inefficient or ineffective processes, amplifying existing problems and wasting resources.

Enhancing Human Capabilities, Not Replacing Them:

Automation should be viewed as a tool to enhance human capabilities, not replace them. By automating repetitive, time-consuming tasks, organizations can free up their employees to focus on more complex and value-adding activities, such as problem-solving, innovation, and customer engagement. This not only improves efficiency but also enhances job satisfaction and employee engagement.

Need for Human Oversight and Decision-Making:

While automation can handle many routine tasks, there are certain areas where human oversight and decision-making remain essential. This includes:

- **Complex Problem-Solving:** When unexpected issues arise, or when problems require creative solutions, human expertise is invaluable. Automated systems may lack the context, intuition, and critical thinking skills needed to resolve complex problems.
- **Decision-Making:** Important decisions, especially those with ethical or financial implications, should not be left solely to machines. Human judgment and experience are necessary to ensure that decisions align with organizational values and goals.
- **Customer Interactions:** While chatbots and virtual agents can handle many routine inquiries, complex or sensitive customer interactions often require the empathy, understanding, and problem-solving skills of a human agent.

Continuously Evaluating and Adjusting the Balance:

The optimal balance between optimization and automation is not static. It needs to be continuously evaluated and adjusted as technologies and business needs evolve. Organizations should regularly assess the impact of automation on their processes, workflows, and workforce. They should also stay informed about new automation technologies and identify opportunities to further optimize and automate their IT service management practices.

By striking the right balance between optimization and automation, organizations can harness the power of technology to enhance their service management capabilities while retaining the human touch that is essential for delivering exceptional customer experiences.

Applying the "Optimize and Automate" Principle Across the SVS

The "Optimize and Automate" principle has far-reaching implications for the entire Service Value System (SVS). By weaving optimization and automation into each stage of the SVS, organizations can create a more efficient, effective, and adaptable service management ecosystem. Here's how this principle can be applied in practice:

1. Service Strategy:

- **Optimization:** Optimize resource allocation by analyzing demand patterns, forecasting future needs, and aligning resources with strategic priorities. For instance, use data analytics to identify peak usage times and allocate resources accordingly.
- **Automation:** Automate portfolio management processes, such as tracking project progress, managing budgets, and generating reports. This frees up time for strategic planning and decision-making.

2. Service Design:

- **Optimization:** Streamline the service design process by using standardized templates, reusable components, and collaborative design tools.
- **Automation:** Utilize automation tools to simulate user scenarios, test service functionality, and identify potential bottlenecks or performance issues early in the design phase.

3. Service Transition:

- **Optimization:** Optimize the transition process by standardizing deployment procedures, defining clear roles and responsibilities, and implementing rigorous testing and validation protocols.
- **Automation:** Automate deployment and release processes to reduce manual effort, minimize errors, and accelerate time-to-market. This can involve using tools for automated code deployment, configuration management, and testing.

4. Service Operation:

- **Optimization:** Continuously monitor and analyze service performance data to identify areas for improvement. Optimize incident, problem, and change management processes to reduce resolution times and improve efficiency.
- **Automation:** Implement automation tools to streamline incident routing, problem diagnosis, change approvals, and other repetitive tasks. Use chatbots or virtual agents to handle routine user inquiries and provide self-service options.

5. Continual Improvement:

- **Optimization:** Regularly review and assess the effectiveness of IT services and processes, identifying opportunities for further optimization. Use techniques like value stream mapping, process mining, and root cause analysis to pinpoint areas for improvement.
- **Automation:** Leverage automation to collect and analyze large volumes of data, providing valuable insights into service performance, customer satisfaction, and operational efficiency. Use this data to drive continuous improvement initiatives and measure the impact of changes.

Examples of Optimization and Automation in Practice:

- **Service Strategy:** Automating the generation of service portfolio reports, enabling faster and more accurate decision-making.
- **Service Design:** Using automated testing tools to simulate user interactions and identify usability issues early in the design process.
- **Service Transition:** Automating the deployment of software updates to multiple environments, reducing the risk of errors and ensuring consistency.
- **Service Operation:** Using chatbots to provide instant support to users, freeing up service desk agents to handle more complex issues.
- **Continual Improvement:** Analyzing incident data to identify recurring problems and implementing automation to prevent future occurrences.

By integrating optimization and automation throughout the SVS, organizations can create a more efficient, effective, and adaptable IT service management system. This enables them to deliver high-quality services, meet customer expectations, and achieve their strategic goals in an increasingly complex and dynamic business environment.

Case Studies and Examples

The "Optimize and Automate" principle has been embraced by organizations across various industries, leading to remarkable transformations in their IT service management (ITSM) capabilities. Here are a few real-world examples that highlight the practical benefits and impact of this principle:

Case Study 1: Financial Services Firm

- **Challenge:** A global financial services firm faced challenges with manual, error-prone processes for handling customer onboarding and account maintenance requests. This led to delays, high operational costs, and customer dissatisfaction.
- **Strategy:** The firm implemented robotic process automation (RPA) to automate these repetitive tasks, freeing up employees to focus on more complex activities that require human judgment and interaction. They also optimized their workflows by eliminating unnecessary steps and approvals, streamlining the overall process.
- **Outcome:** The automation and optimization efforts resulted in a 60% reduction in processing time for customer requests, a 30% decrease in operational costs, and a significant improvement in customer satisfaction ratings. The firm also saw a reduction in employee turnover, as staff were no longer burdened with repetitive tasks and could focus on more engaging work.

Case Study 2: Healthcare Provider

- **Challenge:** A healthcare provider was struggling with a high volume of IT incidents, causing delays in patient care and frustration among clinical staff. The manual incident management process was time-consuming and prone to errors.
- **Strategy:** The provider implemented an AI-powered incident management system that could automatically categorize and prioritize incidents based on their urgency and impact. The system also utilized machine learning algorithms to identify patterns and trends in incident data, allowing for proactive problem management.
- **Outcome:** The automation of incident management resulted in a 50% reduction in incident resolution times, leading to faster restoration of services and improved patient care. The predictive analytics capabilities of the system helped identify potential problems before they caused disruptions, further enhancing service availability and reliability.

Case Study 3: Government Agency

- **Challenge:** A government agency was tasked with processing a large volume of citizen requests for information and services. The manual processing of these requests was time-consuming, prone to errors, and led to significant delays.
- **Strategy:** The agency developed a self-service portal that allowed citizens to submit requests online, track their status, and access relevant information. They also implemented workflow automation to streamline the processing of requests, automatically routing them to the appropriate departments and notifying citizens of progress.
- **Outcome:** The self-service portal and workflow automation reduced the processing time for citizen requests by 75%. This improved the agency's responsiveness and customer satisfaction, while also freeing up staff resources for other important tasks.

Case Study 4: Manufacturing Company

- **Challenge:** A manufacturing company was facing challenges with managing its IT assets, including tracking inventory, software licenses, and maintenance contracts. The manual processes were time-consuming, error-prone, and difficult to scale.
- **Strategy:** The company implemented an IT asset management (ITAM) system that automated the discovery, tracking, and management of IT assets. The system also provided real-time insights into asset utilization, helping the company optimize its IT investments and reduce costs.
- **Outcome:** The automated ITAM system enabled the company to gain better control over its IT assets, reduce the risk of compliance violations, and optimize its IT spending. The system also freed up IT staff from manual tasks, allowing them to focus on more strategic initiatives.

Key Takeaways:

These case studies demonstrate that the "Optimize and Automate" principle can be applied in a variety of organizational contexts and industries, leading to significant improvements in efficiency, effectiveness, cost savings, and customer satisfaction. By embracing optimization and automation, organizations can transform their IT service management practices and deliver exceptional value to their stakeholders in the digital age.

Chapter Summary

In this chapter, we explored the ITIL 4 guiding principle "Optimize and Automate." We highlighted the importance of continuous improvement and the strategic use of technology to streamline processes, reduce manual effort, and enhance overall service management efficiency.

Key takeaways from this chapter:

- **Understanding Optimization and Automation:** We discussed how these two concepts work hand-in-hand, with optimization focusing on improving processes and automation using technology to execute those processes more effectively.
- **The Importance of Optimization:** We emphasized the significance of optimization in ITSM for enhancing efficiency, effectiveness, and cost savings. It's a continuous process that applies to all aspects of service management, including processes, workflows, technology, and resources.
- **Optimization Techniques:** We explored various optimization techniques, such as Lean principles, Six Sigma methodologies, the Theory of Constraints (TOC), and Value Stream Mapping (VSM), providing you with a toolbox for continuous improvement.
- **The Role of Automation:** We discussed how automation can streamline processes, reduce manual effort, and improve efficiency in ITSM. We explained how automation can be used to perform repetitive tasks, enforce policies, and trigger actions based on predefined conditions.
- **Types of Automation:** We delved into different automation technologies and tools, including Robotic Process Automation (RPA), workflow automation, artificial intelligence (AI), machine learning (ML), and chatbots, highlighting their unique capabilities and applications in ITSM.

- **Benefits of Automation:** We discussed the numerous benefits of automation, such as reduced costs, improved efficiency and productivity, increased accuracy, faster response times, enhanced customer satisfaction, and improved employee morale.
- **Risks and Challenges of Automation:** We addressed potential risks and challenges associated with automation, including job displacement, over-reliance on technology, lack of human oversight, and errors. We also emphasized the importance of mitigating these risks through strategic planning and implementation.
- **Balancing Optimization and Automation:** We stressed the importance of finding the right balance between optimization and automation, ensuring that technology enhances human capabilities rather than replacing them. We highlighted the need for human oversight and decision-making in critical areas.
- **Applying the Principle Across the SVS:** We provided examples of how to apply the "Optimize and Automate" principle in various stages of the Service Value Chain, from service strategy to continual improvement.

By understanding the importance of optimization and automation, as well as the various techniques and tools available, you can create a more efficient, effective, and adaptable ITSM environment that delivers greater value to your organization and its customers. Remember, optimization and automation are not just about technology; they're about a mindset of continuous improvement and leveraging technology to empower people to do their best work.

Section D:
The ITIL Service Value System (SVS)

Understanding the Service Value Chain

Outline

- Introduction to the Service Value Chain (SVC)
- The Six Value Chain Activities
- The Flow of Value
- The Service Value Chain and the ITIL Practices
- Applying the Service Value Chain in Practice
- Example: Incident Management through the Service Value Chain
- Chapter Summary

Introduction to the Service Value Chain (SVC)

The Service Value Chain (SVC) sits at the heart of ITIL 4's Service Value System (SVS), acting as the engine that drives the creation and delivery of value through IT-enabled services. It is a fundamental concept in ITIL 4, providing a flexible operating model for how organizations can respond to demand and facilitate value realization throughout the entire lifecycle of a service.

Central Role in the SVS:

The SVC is the core component of the SVS, connecting all other elements of the system, including the guiding principles, governance, practices, and continual improvement. It provides a structured framework for understanding how all these elements interact and contribute to value creation.

Key Operating Model for Creating, Delivering, and Managing Value:

The SVC is not just a theoretical model; it's a practical tool that organizations can use to manage their IT services effectively. It provides a step-by-step guide for how to:

1. **Identify and Understand Demand:** The SVC starts with understanding the needs and demands of customers and stakeholders. This involves gathering requirements, analyzing trends, and anticipating future needs.
2. **Plan and Design Services:** Based on the identified demand, services are planned and designed to meet the specific needs of customers and stakeholders. This includes defining service requirements, designing service solutions, and developing service level agreements (SLAs).
3. **Build and Implement Services:** Once the services are designed, they are built and implemented, ensuring that they meet the defined specifications and quality standards. This involves developing the necessary infrastructure, procuring resources, and testing the service.
4. **Deliver and Support Services:** The final step is to deliver and support the services to customers and stakeholders. This involves managing incidents and requests, fulfilling service orders, and ensuring that services meet agreed-upon service levels.
5. **Continually Improve Services:** The SVC is a continuous cycle of improvement. Organizations should regularly assess the performance of their services, gather feedback from customers and

stakeholders, and implement improvements to enhance service quality, efficiency, and effectiveness.

Flexibility and Adaptability:

One of the key strengths of the SVC is its flexibility. It is not a rigid, one-size-fits-all model. Organizations can adapt and tailor the SVC to fit their specific needs, industry, and context. The activities in the SVC can be performed in different sequences or in parallel, depending on the specific circumstances.

Dynamic and Iterative Nature:

The SVC is not a linear process; it's a dynamic and iterative cycle. Organizations should continuously revisit and refine their approach to each activity, incorporating feedback and learning from experience to drive continuous improvement. This iterative nature allows organizations to adapt quickly to changing circumstances and ensure that their services remain relevant and valuable.

By understanding the SVC and its role within the SVS, organizations can gain a deeper understanding of how to create, deliver, and manage value through IT-enabled services. This knowledge can empower them to optimize their service management practices, improve customer satisfaction, and achieve their business goals.

The Six Value Chain Activities

The ITIL 4 Service Value Chain (SVC) is comprised of six interconnected activities that guide the end-to-end creation and delivery of value. These activities are not sequential steps, but rather flexible components that can be adapted and combined to suit the specific needs of an organization. Let's explore each activity in detail:

1. **Plan:**
   - **Purpose:** To ensure a shared understanding of the vision, direction, and priorities for all four dimensions of service management (organizations and people, information and technology, partners and suppliers, value streams and processes). This activity lays the groundwork for value creation by aligning service management with overall business objectives.
   - **Inputs:** Strategic objectives, stakeholder requirements, market trends, resource constraints, risk assessments.
   - **Outputs:** Strategic plans, roadmaps, policies, budgets, resource allocation plans.
   - **Key Activities:** Strategy development, portfolio management, demand management, financial management, risk management.
   - **Value Creation:** By aligning IT services with strategic goals, the "Plan" activity ensures that efforts are focused on initiatives that deliver the most value to the business and its customers.
2. **Improve:**
   - **Purpose:** To ensure continual improvement of products, services, and practices across the entire service value chain. This activity focuses on learning from experience, identifying opportunities for improvement, and implementing changes to enhance service quality, efficiency, and effectiveness.
   - **Inputs:** Performance data, customer feedback, incident reports, problem records, change records.
   - **Outputs:** Improvement plans, action items, lessons learned, knowledge articles.
   - **Key Activities:** Problem management, incident analysis, root cause analysis, trend analysis, service level management.
   - **Value Creation:** By identifying and addressing issues and inefficiencies, the "Improve" activity helps to ensure that services are continuously optimized to deliver maximum value.
3. **Engage:**
   - **Purpose:** To build and maintain strong relationships with stakeholders, understand their needs and expectations, and ensure their active participation in the service management process.
   - **Inputs:** Stakeholder requirements, feedback, communication plans, relationship management plans.

- **Outputs:** Stakeholder engagement plans, communication materials, feedback reports.
- **Key Activities:** Stakeholder identification and analysis, communication and collaboration, relationship management, customer satisfaction surveys.
- **Value Creation:** By understanding and addressing stakeholder needs, the "Engage" activity ensures that services are designed and delivered in a way that creates value for all parties involved.

4. **Design and Transition:**

- **Purpose:** To ensure that products and services are designed and transitioned to live environments effectively. This involves translating stakeholder requirements into service designs, developing and testing new solutions, and managing the transition from development to production.
- **Inputs:** Service requirements, design specifications, architectural models, test plans, deployment plans.
- **Outputs:** Service designs, prototypes, test results, deployment packages, release notes.
- **Key Activities:** Service design, service validation and testing, release and deployment management, change management.
- **Value Creation:** By designing and transitioning high-quality services, the "Design and Transition" activity ensures that services meet customer expectations and deliver the desired value.

5. **Obtain/Build:**

- **Purpose:** To ensure that the necessary service components are available when and where they are needed. This includes sourcing components from external suppliers, developing components internally, and managing the lifecycle of service assets.
- **Inputs:** Service requirements, procurement plans, supplier contracts, asset management plans.
- **Outputs:** Procured components, developed components, updated asset records, supplier performance reports.
- **Key Activities:** Procurement, supplier management, asset management, inventory management.
- **Value Creation:** By ensuring the timely and cost-effective availability of service components, the "Obtain/Build" activity enables the efficient delivery of services.

6. **Deliver and Support:**

- **Purpose:** To ensure that services are delivered and supported according to agreed specifications and service levels. This involves managing incidents, fulfilling service requests, and providing ongoing support to users.
- **Inputs:** Service requests, incident reports, service level targets, operational procedures.
- **Outputs:** Resolved incidents, fulfilled service requests, service performance reports, customer satisfaction data.
- **Key Activities:** Incident management, request fulfillment, service desk operations, event management, access management.
- **Value Creation:** By delivering reliable and high-quality services, the "Deliver and Support" activity directly contributes to customer satisfaction and the realization of business value.

Interdependencies Between Activities:

The activities in the Service Value Chain are highly interconnected and interdependent. For example:

- The "Plan" activity informs the "Design and Transition" activity by defining the service requirements and strategic goals.
- The "Engage" activity provides valuable feedback to the "Improve" activity, which in turn helps to refine the "Plan" and "Design and Transition" activities.
- The "Obtain/Build" activity ensures that the resources needed for "Deliver and Support" are available.
- The "Deliver and Support" activity generates data that is used by the "Improve" activity to identify opportunities for improvement.

This intricate web of interdependencies highlights the importance of a holistic approach to IT service management. By understanding how the different activities in the SVC interact and influence each other, organizations can optimize their service delivery processes, maximize value creation, and achieve their strategic objectives.

The Flow of Value

The Service Value Chain (SVC) is a dynamic and iterative framework that guides the transformation of demands and opportunities into valuable outcomes for customers and stakeholders. Let's delve into how value flows through the SVC, exploring the transformation of inputs into outputs at each stage and how these outputs collectively contribute to value creation.

Transformation of Inputs into Outputs:

- **Plan:** The demand or opportunity is analyzed, and plans are developed to address it. The output of this activity is a strategic plan, which outlines the objectives, scope, and approach for creating and delivering the service.
- **Improve:** The strategic plan is refined based on feedback and performance data. The output of this activity is an improved plan, which incorporates lessons learned and identifies opportunities for further optimization.
- **Engage:** Stakeholders are engaged to understand their needs and expectations. The output of this activity is a shared understanding of requirements and expectations, which informs the design and delivery of the service.
- **Design and Transition:** The service is designed, developed, and tested based on the defined requirements. The output of this activity is a well-designed and tested service ready for deployment.
- **Obtain/Build:** The necessary resources, such as infrastructure, software, and skills, are obtained or built to support the service. The output of this activity is a set of available resources ready to be utilized for service delivery.
- **Deliver and Support:** The service is delivered and supported according to agreed-upon service levels. The output of this activity is a reliable and high-quality service that meets or exceeds customer expectations.

Value Creation through the SVC:

The value created by the SVC is not a single output but the cumulative effect of all the outputs generated at each stage.

- **Plan and Improve:** These activities ensure that services are aligned with business goals and customer needs, maximizing the potential for value creation.
- **Engage:** This activity ensures that the voice of the customer is heard and incorporated into service design and delivery, leading to a more customer-centric and valuable experience.
- **Design and Transition:** These activities ensure that services are well-designed, thoroughly tested, and smoothly transitioned into production, minimizing disruptions and ensuring a positive user experience.
- **Obtain/Build:** This activity ensures that the right resources are available at the right time, enabling efficient and effective service delivery.
- **Deliver and Support:** This activity ensures that services are delivered and supported according to agreed-upon standards, providing a reliable and high-quality experience that meets or exceeds customer expectations.

In Summary:

The Service Value Chain is a dynamic framework that illustrates how value is created, delivered, and managed throughout the entire lifecycle of an IT service. By understanding the flow of value through the SVC and the role of each activity, organizations can optimize their service management practices, improve customer satisfaction, and achieve their business goals.

The Service Value Chain and the ITIL Practices

The 34 ITIL management practices serve as the "tools" that organizations can leverage to carry out the activities of the Service Value Chain (SVC) effectively. Each practice contributes specific capabilities and expertise that support one or more activities within the SVC. However, it's important to note that the relationship between practices and activities is not rigidly defined. Practices can be flexibly applied across the value chain, depending on the specific needs and context of each organization.

How ITIL Practices Support SVC Activities:

Let's examine how some key ITIL practices can be applied within each value chain activity:

1. **Plan:**
   - **Strategy Management:** Helps define the organization's overall service management strategy, ensuring alignment with business goals.
   - **Portfolio Management:** Guides decision-making about which services to offer, invest in, and retire.
   - **Demand Management:** Understands and influences customer demand for services, ensuring that capacity meets demand.
   - **Risk Management:** Identifies and assesses risks to the organization's ability to create and deliver value through services.
2. **Improve:**
   - **Continual Improvement:** Establishes a framework for identifying and implementing improvements to services and processes.
   - **Measurement and Reporting:** Defines and tracks key performance indicators (KPIs) to measure progress and identify areas for improvement.
   - **Problem Management:** Identifies and addresses root causes of incidents to prevent recurrence.
   - **Service Level Management:** Ensures that services are delivered according to agreed-upon service levels.
3. **Engage:**
   - **Relationship Management:** Builds and maintains strong relationships with customers and stakeholders.
   - **Business Analysis:** Analyzes business needs and requirements to identify opportunities for new or improved services.
   - **Service Desk:** Provides a single point of contact for users to report issues and request assistance.
4. **Design and Transition:**
   - **Service Design:** Designs new or changed services, taking into account customer needs, business requirements, and technical feasibility.
   - **Service Validation and Testing:** Ensures that new or changed services meet the defined requirements and perform as expected.
   - **Change Enablement:** Manages the process of transitioning new or changed services into the live environment.
   - **Release Management:** Plans, schedules, and controls the deployment of new or changed services.
5. **Obtain/Build:**
   - **Supplier Management:** Manages relationships with suppliers to ensure that they deliver the required goods and services.
   - **Infrastructure and Platform Management:** Manages the infrastructure and platforms on which services are built and delivered.
   - **Software Development and Management:** Develops and maintains software applications that support service delivery.
6. **Deliver and Support:**
   - **Service Request Management:** Handles requests for standard services, such as password resets or access provisioning.

- **Incident Management:** Restores normal service operation as quickly as possible when incidents occur.
- **Monitoring and Event Management:** Monitors the performance and availability of services and infrastructure, and proactively detects and responds to events.
- **Service Configuration Management:** Maintains accurate and up-to-date information about configuration items (CIs).

Flexibility in Applying Practices:

While some practices may be more closely associated with specific value chain activities, it's important to recognize that the practices are not rigidly tied to them. Organizations can adapt and apply the practices flexibly across the value chain based on their specific needs and context. For example, the Problem Management practice can be used not only to improve the "Deliver and Support" activity but also to inform the "Design and Transition" activity by identifying design flaws or potential problems before services are deployed.

By understanding how the ITIL practices can be leveraged across the Service Value Chain, organizations can create a more integrated and effective approach to IT service management, ensuring that every activity contributes to the creation and delivery of value.

Applying the Service Value Chain in Practice

The Service Value Chain (SVC) is not just a theoretical model; it's a practical tool that organizations can use to guide their IT service management (ITSM) initiatives and drive continuous improvement. Here's how to apply the SVC in real-world scenarios:

Practical Guidance for Applying the SVC:

1. **Visualize Your Value Streams:** Start by mapping out your key value streams, such as incident resolution, request fulfillment, or new service development. Use the SVC activities as a framework to identify the steps involved in each value stream. This visual representation will help you understand the flow of work, identify bottlenecks, and pinpoint areas for improvement.
2. **Identify Opportunities for Optimization:** Analyze each activity in the SVC and look for opportunities to optimize processes, reduce waste, and improve efficiency. For example, in the "Obtain/Build" activity, you might identify opportunities to streamline procurement processes or optimize inventory management.
3. **Measure and Monitor Performance:** Define key performance indicators (KPIs) for each activity in the SVC, such as average resolution time for incidents, customer satisfaction ratings, or time-to-market for new services. Regularly track these metrics to measure performance and identify areas where improvements are needed.
4. **Align with Business Goals:** Ensure that your SVC activities are aligned with your organization's strategic goals and objectives. This involves understanding the needs of your customers and stakeholders and ensuring that your services are delivering the value they expect.
5. **Foster Collaboration:** The SVC is a collaborative framework that requires active participation from all stakeholders. Encourage cross-functional collaboration between IT, business, and other relevant departments. This will help ensure that everyone is working together to create and deliver value.
6. **Embrace Continual Improvement:** The SVC is not a static model; it's a dynamic and iterative process. Regularly review and assess your SVC, incorporate feedback from stakeholders, and continuously look for ways to improve your service delivery.

Using the SVC to Identify Improvement Opportunities, Optimize Processes, and Measure Effectiveness:

- **Identifying Improvement Opportunities:** By mapping out your value streams and analyzing the flow of work and information, you can identify bottlenecks, redundancies, and other inefficiencies.

This allows you to prioritize improvement initiatives and focus your efforts on areas that will have the greatest impact.

- **Optimizing Processes:** The SVC provides a framework for analyzing and optimizing processes at each stage of the value chain. By applying lean principles and other improvement methodologies, you can streamline workflows, eliminate waste, and improve overall efficiency.
- **Measuring Effectiveness:** By tracking key performance indicators (KPIs) for each value chain activity, you can measure the effectiveness of your service delivery and identify areas where further improvements are needed.

Creating a Customer-Centric and Value-Driven Approach:

The SVC promotes a customer-centric and value-driven approach to IT service management. By focusing on the end-to-end delivery of value, from understanding customer needs to providing ongoing support, organizations can ensure that their services are aligned with customer expectations and deliver the desired outcomes. This customer-centric approach fosters trust, loyalty, and ultimately, business success.

Example: Incident Management through the Service Value Chain

Incident Management, a critical process in ITIL, can be comprehensively understood and optimized by aligning it with the activities of the Service Value Chain (SVC). Let's walk through a typical incident management scenario and see how each SVC activity contributes to its effective resolution and prevention of future occurrences.

1. **Deliver and Support:**
- **Trigger:** A user experiences an issue with their email service and reports it to the service desk. This is the initial *demand* that triggers the incident management process within the SVC.
- **Activities:**
   - **Incident Logging:** The service desk agent records the incident details, including the user's information, the nature of the problem, and its impact on the user's work.
   - **Initial Support:** The agent attempts to resolve the issue using known solutions or workarounds.
   - **Escalation:** If the agent cannot resolve the issue, it is escalated to a higher level of support.
2. **Engage:**
- **Activities:**
   - **Investigation and Diagnosis:** The technical support team investigates the incident, gathers additional information from the user, and analyzes logs and system data to diagnose the root cause.
   - **Communication:** The support team keeps the user informed about the progress of the investigation and any potential workarounds.
3. **Design and Transition:**
- **Activities:**
   - **Solution Implementation:** Once the root cause is identified, the support team develops and implements a solution to resolve the incident. This may involve applying a patch, reconfiguring a system, or providing additional training to the user.
   - **Testing:** The solution is tested to ensure that it resolves the issue without causing any unintended consequences.
   - **Deployment:** The solution is deployed to the live environment and the service is restored.
4. **Improve:**
- **Activities:**
   - **Problem Management:** If the incident is a symptom of a recurring problem, a problem record is created to investigate the root cause and prevent future occurrences.
   - **Knowledge Management:** The knowledge gained during incident resolution is captured and documented in a knowledge base, making it available to other support agents for future reference.

- ○ **Post-Incident Review:** A review is conducted to assess the effectiveness of the incident management process and identify opportunities for improvement.

The Service Value Chain's Contribution to Effective Incident Management:

The Service Value Chain provides a holistic framework for incident management, ensuring that:

- **Demand is Captured and Prioritized:** The "Deliver and Support" activity ensures that incidents are promptly identified, logged, and prioritized based on their impact and urgency.
- **Stakeholders are Engaged:** The "Engage" activity ensures that users and stakeholders are kept informed about the progress of incident resolution and their feedback is gathered to improve the process.
- **Solutions are Designed and Implemented:** The "Design and Transition" activity ensures that solutions are developed and implemented effectively, minimizing disruption and restoring service as quickly as possible.
- **Root Causes are Addressed:** The "Improve" activity ensures that lessons learned from incidents are used to identify and address underlying problems, preventing future occurrences and improving overall service quality.

By viewing incident management through the lens of the Service Value Chain, organizations can ensure a more coordinated, customer-centric, and value-driven approach to resolving incidents and preventing future disruptions.

Chapter Summary

In this chapter, we delved into the Service Value Chain (SVC), the central element of ITIL 4's Service Value System. We explored how the SVC provides a dynamic and flexible operating model for creating, delivering, and managing value through IT-enabled services.

Here's a recap of the key takeaways:

- **The Core of Value Creation:** The SVC is the heart of ITIL 4, guiding the end-to-end creation and delivery of value through its six interconnected activities. It provides a structured framework for understanding how all elements of the Service Value System work together to achieve this goal.
- **The Six Activities:** We explored each of the six SVC activities in detail:
  - ○ **Plan:** Strategizing and coordinating activities.
  - ○ **Improve:** Ensuring continual improvement.
  - ○ **Engage:** Understanding stakeholder needs.
  - ○ **Design and Transition:** Designing and transitioning services effectively.
  - ○ **Obtain/Build:** Ensuring component availability.
  - ○ **Deliver and Support:** Ensuring service delivery and support.
- **The Flow of Value:** We illustrated how value flows through the SVC, starting with a demand or opportunity and transforming into a valuable outcome for customers and stakeholders through the interconnected activities.
- **The SVC and ITIL Practices:** We discussed how the 34 ITIL practices support and enable the activities within the SVC, providing a toolbox of resources and capabilities for each stage of the value chain.
- **Applying the SVC in Practice:** We provided practical guidance on how to use the SVC to visualize value streams, identify improvement opportunities, optimize processes, and measure the effectiveness of service delivery. We emphasized the importance of collaboration, feedback, and continuous improvement in maximizing the value of IT services.

By understanding the SVC and its role in the SVS, organizations can gain a deeper appreciation for the interconnected nature of IT service management. This knowledge can empower them to optimize their processes, enhance service quality, and deliver greater value to their customers and stakeholders. As we progress through this book, we will explore how the SVC interacts with other key components of the ITIL 4 framework, such as governance, practices, and continual improvement.

Governance

Outline

- Introduction to Governance in ITIL 4
- Purpose and Objectives of Governance
- Governance in the Service Value System (SVS)
- Three Lines of Defense Model
- Governance Structures and Roles
- Governance Activities
- Governance and Risk Management
- Governance and Continual Improvement
- Challenges and Best Practices in Governance
- Chapter Summary

Introduction to Governance in ITIL 4

Governance is a system by which organizations are directed and controlled. It encompasses the structures, processes, and mechanisms that ensure an organization's activities align with its objectives, comply with relevant laws and regulations, and create value for stakeholders.

ITIL 4's Definition of Governance:

In the context of ITIL 4, governance is defined as "the means by which an organization is directed and controlled." It entails evaluating, directing, monitoring, and communicating with stakeholders about how the organization uses its resources to fulfill its objectives.

How ITIL 4 Governance Applies to IT Service Management:

ITIL 4 governance provides a framework for ensuring that IT services are not only delivered efficiently and effectively but also in a way that supports the organization's overall strategic goals and objectives. It helps answer questions like:

- Are IT services aligned with business priorities?
- Are resources being used effectively?
- Are risks being managed appropriately?
- Are decisions being made in a transparent and accountable manner?

Importance of Governance in Ensuring Alignment with Strategy and Objectives:

Effective governance is essential for aligning IT services with the organization's broader strategy and objectives. It provides the mechanisms for:

- **Setting Strategic Direction:** Governance bodies, such as steering committees or boards, are responsible for setting the strategic direction for IT, ensuring that it aligns with the organization's overall goals.
- **Prioritizing Investments:** Governance helps prioritize IT investments based on their potential impact on business outcomes, ensuring that resources are allocated to the most valuable initiatives.
- **Monitoring Performance:** Governance bodies track and evaluate the performance of IT services against agreed-upon targets, identifying areas for improvement and holding individuals accountable for results.

Role of Governance in Decision-Making, Risk Management, and Resource Allocation:

Governance plays a crucial role in several key areas of IT service management:

- **Decision-Making:** Governance bodies establish decision-making processes and provide oversight to ensure that decisions are made in a transparent, consistent, and accountable manner.
- **Risk Management:** Governance helps identify, assess, and mitigate IT-related risks, ensuring that the organization has a proactive approach to risk management and can respond effectively to potential threats.
- **Resource Allocation:** Governance oversees the allocation of resources, such as budget, personnel, and technology, to ensure that they are used effectively and efficiently to support the delivery of IT services.

By establishing a strong governance framework, organizations can ensure that IT services are aligned with business needs, risks are managed effectively, and resources are utilized optimally. This leads to improved service quality, enhanced customer satisfaction, and greater business value.

Purpose and Objectives of Governance

Governance in ITIL 4 is not merely about control and oversight; it's a strategic function aimed at maximizing the value that IT delivers to the organization and its stakeholders. It sets the direction for IT service management, ensures alignment with business goals, and fosters a culture of transparency, accountability, and continuous improvement.

The key purposes and objectives of governance in ITIL 4 include:

1. **Ensuring Value Delivery:**
- **Customer-Centricity:** Governance ensures that IT services are designed and delivered with a focus on meeting customer needs and expectations, ultimately providing value in the form of improved experiences, increased satisfaction, and positive outcomes.
- **Business Alignment:** Governance mechanisms ensure that IT services align with the organization's strategic goals and objectives. This means that IT investments are prioritized based on their potential impact on business outcomes, such as revenue growth, cost reduction, or risk mitigation.
2. **Aligning IT Services with Strategic Goals and Objectives:**
- **Strategic Planning:** Governance involves developing and maintaining a strategic plan for IT that aligns with the overall business strategy. This plan outlines the goals, priorities, and roadmap for IT services, ensuring they support the organization's broader objectives.
- **Performance Measurement:** Governance establishes key performance indicators (KPIs) and metrics to track the effectiveness and efficiency of IT services. This allows for regular evaluation of performance against strategic goals and identification of areas for improvement.
3. **Managing IT-Related Risks and Ensuring Compliance:**
- **Risk Assessment and Mitigation:** Governance involves identifying, assessing, and mitigating risks associated with IT services, such as security breaches, data loss, system failures, and compliance violations. This includes developing risk management plans, implementing security controls, and ensuring adherence to relevant regulations and standards.
- **Compliance Management:** Governance ensures that IT services comply with relevant laws, regulations, and industry standards, protecting the organization from legal and reputational risks.
4. **Optimizing Resource Utilization and Ensuring Accountability:**
- **Resource Allocation:** Governance oversees the allocation of IT resources, such as budget, personnel, and technology, to ensure they are used effectively and efficiently to support the delivery of value.

- **Performance Management:** Governance holds individuals and teams accountable for their performance, ensuring that IT investments deliver the expected returns and contribute to business goals.
- **Transparency and Accountability:** Governance promotes transparency in decision-making and resource allocation, fostering a culture of accountability and responsibility.
5. **Fostering a Culture of Transparency, Collaboration, and Continual Improvement:**
- **Open Communication:** Governance encourages open communication and collaboration between IT and business stakeholders, ensuring that IT decisions are aligned with business needs and that stakeholders are kept informed about IT performance and risks.
- **Feedback Loops:** Governance establishes feedback mechanisms to gather input from stakeholders, enabling continuous improvement of IT services and processes.
- **Learning Culture:** Governance fosters a culture of learning and experimentation, encouraging IT teams to try new approaches, learn from their mistakes, and continuously improve their practices.

By fulfilling these purposes and objectives, governance acts as a compass, guiding the IT organization towards the successful delivery of value-driven services that align with the overall strategic goals of the organization. It ensures that IT is not just a cost center but a strategic enabler of business success.

Governance in the Service Value System (SVS)

Governance within the ITIL 4 Service Value System (SVS) is a dynamic and integral function that operates as the compass guiding the entire system. It's the mechanism that ensures the SVS is not only efficient but also aligns with the organization's strategic goals and objectives. Let's examine how governance interplays with the various components of the SVS.

How Governance Functions Within the SVS:

- **Guiding Principles:** Governance acts as the custodian of the ITIL guiding principles, ensuring that decisions and actions throughout the SVS adhere to these core values. It promotes a focus on value, collaboration, holistic thinking, and continuous improvement.
- **Practices:** Governance provides the structure and oversight to enable the effective implementation and operation of the 34 ITIL management practices. It defines roles, responsibilities, and decision-making processes to ensure that practices are executed consistently and in alignment with the overall strategy.
- **Service Value Chain:** Governance influences and is influenced by each stage of the Service Value Chain. It ensures that the value chain activities are aligned with strategic goals, that risks are managed effectively, and that resources are allocated optimally.

Governance as the Oversight and Decision-Making Mechanism:

Governance provides the oversight and decision-making mechanisms needed to steer the SVS in the right direction. It establishes a framework for:

- **Evaluating:** Assessing the organization's current state, identifying risks and opportunities, and evaluating the effectiveness of IT services.
- **Directing:** Setting the strategic direction for IT service management, defining priorities, and allocating resources.
- **Monitoring:** Tracking the performance of IT services and processes, ensuring that they meet agreed-upon targets and objectives.
- **Communicating:** Providing transparent and regular communication to stakeholders about IT performance, risks, and plans.

Role of Governance in Each Stage of the Service Value Chain:

- **Plan:** Governance defines the overall strategy and objectives for IT service management. It establishes the criteria for selecting services to be offered, determines investment priorities, and sets performance targets.
- **Improve:** Governance oversees the continual improvement process, ensuring that lessons learned from incidents, problems, and changes are incorporated into future decision-making. It also approves improvement plans and monitors their progress.
- **Engage:** Governance ensures that stakeholders are engaged in the service management process. It establishes mechanisms for gathering feedback, managing expectations, and ensuring that IT services meet the needs of customers and the business.
- **Design and Transition:** Governance provides oversight of service design and transition activities, ensuring that new or changed services are aligned with the organization's strategic goals and risk appetite.
- **Obtain/Build:** Governance approves procurement decisions, ensures that suppliers are managed effectively, and oversees the development and acquisition of IT assets.
- **Deliver and Support:** Governance monitors service performance, ensures that service levels are met, and oversees the resolution of incidents and problems. It also provides guidance and support to operational teams.

In Summary:

Governance plays a pivotal role in the ITIL 4 Service Value System. It provides the direction, oversight, and decision-making mechanisms needed to ensure that IT services align with strategic goals, deliver value, and are managed effectively. By integrating governance into every aspect of the SVS, organizations can create a more transparent, accountable, and high-performing IT service management system.

Three Lines of Defense Model

The Three Lines of Defense (3LoD) model is a widely recognized framework for structuring governance, risk management, and internal control activities within an organization. It provides a clear delineation of roles and responsibilities, ensuring a comprehensive and effective approach to managing risks and ensuring compliance.

Introduction to the 3LoD Model:

The 3LoD model divides an organization's risk management and control functions into three distinct but interconnected lines:

1. **First Line of Defense:**
- **Role:** Operational management, which includes individuals and teams directly responsible for delivering products or services.
- **Responsibilities:**
    - Owning and managing risks within their areas of responsibility.
    - Implementing and maintaining controls to mitigate risks.
    - Monitoring and reporting on risk exposures and control effectiveness.
2. **Second Line of Defense:**
- **Role:** Risk management and compliance functions, which are independent of operational management.
- **Responsibilities:**
    - Providing oversight and guidance to the first line on risk management and control activities.
    - Developing and implementing risk management frameworks, policies, and procedures.
    - Monitoring and assessing the effectiveness of the first line's risk management and control activities.
    - Reporting on risk exposures and control effectiveness to senior management and the board.
3. **Third Line of Defense:**

- **Role:** Internal audit, which is independent of both operational management and the second line.
- **Responsibilities:**
  - Providing independent assurance over the effectiveness of governance, risk management, and internal control.
  - Conducting audits to assess the design and operating effectiveness of controls.
  - Reporting findings and recommendations to senior management and the board.

Relationship Between the Three Lines:

The three lines of defense work together to create a comprehensive risk management and control framework. The first line is responsible for managing risks on a day-to-day basis, while the second line provides oversight and guidance. The third line provides independent assurance that the overall governance framework is effective.

Benefits of the 3LoD Model:

- **Clear Roles and Responsibilities:** The 3LoD model clarifies the roles and responsibilities of different functions involved in governance, risk management, and control, avoiding duplication of effort and ensuring accountability.
- **Improved Risk Management:** By clearly defining the roles and responsibilities of each line of defense, the 3LoD model helps to ensure that risks are identified, assessed, and mitigated effectively.
- **Enhanced Governance:** The 3LoD model provides a structured framework for governance, ensuring that decisions are made in a transparent and accountable manner.
- **Increased Assurance:** The third line of defense provides independent assurance that the governance, risk management, and control framework is operating effectively.

By adopting the Three Lines of Defense model, organizations can create a more robust and effective governance framework that supports their strategic objectives, manages risks, and ensures compliance with relevant laws and regulations.

Governance Structures and Roles

Effective governance requires a well-defined structure that outlines the roles and responsibilities of various stakeholders involved in the decision-making process. These structures ensure accountability, transparency, and alignment with strategic objectives in IT service management (ITSM).

Typical Governance Structures Used in ITSM:

1. **Steering Committee:** A cross-functional group of senior leaders and stakeholders responsible for overseeing the overall direction and strategy of IT service management. They make high-level decisions, prioritize investments, and ensure alignment with organizational goals.
2. **Management Board:** A smaller group of executives responsible for the day-to-day management and oversight of IT service management. They review performance, approve budgets, and make tactical decisions.
3. **Advisory Groups:** Specialized groups that provide expertise and advice on specific areas of IT service management, such as security, architecture, or compliance. They may include both internal and external experts.
4. **Change Advisory Board (CAB):** A group responsible for reviewing and approving proposed changes to IT services. They assess the impact of changes, ensure that risks are mitigated, and authorize the implementation of changes.
5. **Service Owner Forum:** A group of service owners who meet regularly to discuss service performance, share best practices, and coordinate service management activities.

Roles and Responsibilities of Key Governance Stakeholders:

- **Executives:** Set the overall strategic direction for the organization, including IT service management goals and objectives. They approve major IT investments and ensure that IT aligns with business priorities.
- **Senior Managers:** Provide leadership and oversight for IT service management, ensuring that services are delivered effectively and efficiently. They make decisions on resource allocation, budget, and policy.
- **IT Managers:** Responsible for the day-to-day management of IT services. They oversee operations, manage teams, and ensure that services meet agreed-upon service levels.
- **Process Owners:** Responsible for the design, implementation, and continuous improvement of specific ITSM processes. They ensure that processes are documented, followed, and aligned with best practices.
- **Service Owners:** Accountable for the overall performance and value delivery of specific services. They work closely with IT managers and process owners to ensure that services meet customer and stakeholder needs.

Importance of Clear Roles and Responsibilities:

Clearly defined roles and responsibilities are crucial for effective governance. They ensure that:

- **Accountability:** Every decision and action has a clear owner, ensuring that individuals are held accountable for their performance and results.
- **Decision-Making:** Decisions are made by the appropriate individuals or groups, with the necessary expertise and authority.
- **Avoiding Conflicts:** Clear roles help avoid conflicts and misunderstandings by ensuring that everyone understands their responsibilities and areas of ownership.
- **Efficient Communication:** Clear roles facilitate communication and collaboration by establishing clear channels for information flow and decision-making.

By establishing a well-defined governance structure with clear roles and responsibilities, organizations can ensure that their IT service management practices are aligned with their strategic goals, that risks are managed effectively, and that resources are used efficiently to deliver value to customers and stakeholders.

Governance Activities

IT governance is not a singular action but a collection of ongoing activities that ensure IT resources are utilized effectively and align with organizational objectives. These activities form the foundation of a robust governance framework, contributing to informed decision-making, risk mitigation, and value creation.

Key Activities Involved in IT Governance:

1. **Setting Strategic Direction and Objectives for IT:**
- **Defining the IT Vision:** Governance bodies articulate a clear vision for how IT will support and enable the organization's overall strategic goals.
- **Setting Objectives:** They establish measurable objectives that guide IT activities and investments, ensuring alignment with business priorities.
- **Developing Roadmaps:** Governance teams create roadmaps that outline the steps and timelines for achieving IT objectives, providing a clear direction for the organization.
2. **Developing and Implementing IT Policies and Standards:**
- **Policy Creation:** Governance bodies establish policies that guide the use of IT resources, ensuring compliance with legal, regulatory, and ethical requirements.
- **Standard Development:** They define standards for technology, processes, and service levels, promoting consistency and efficiency across the organization.
- **Implementation and Enforcement:** Governance mechanisms ensure that policies and standards are communicated to all relevant stakeholders and enforced through regular audits and reviews.

3. **Prioritizing and Approving IT Projects and Initiatives:**
- **Portfolio Management:** Governance bodies oversee the IT project portfolio, evaluating proposed projects against strategic objectives, risk appetite, and resource constraints.
- **Approval Processes:** They establish transparent and objective criteria for approving IT projects, ensuring that investments align with the organization's overall strategy.
- **Resource Allocation:** Governance bodies make decisions about how resources, such as budget and personnel, are allocated to different projects, ensuring that they are used effectively to achieve the desired outcomes.
4. **Monitoring and Evaluating IT Performance:**
- **Performance Measurement:** Governance establishes key performance indicators (KPIs) to track the performance of IT services and processes against defined targets.
- **Regular Reporting:** They receive regular reports on IT performance, highlighting areas of success and areas that need improvement.
- **Performance Reviews:** Governance bodies conduct periodic reviews of IT performance, assessing whether IT services are meeting business needs and delivering value.
5. **Managing IT-Related Risks:**
- **Risk Assessment:** Governance bodies oversee the identification and assessment of IT-related risks, such as security breaches, data loss, system failures, and compliance violations.
- **Risk Mitigation:** They develop and implement risk mitigation strategies to reduce the likelihood and impact of these risks.
- **Risk Monitoring:** They regularly monitor and review the effectiveness of risk mitigation measures and make adjustments as needed.
6. **Ensuring Compliance with Regulations and Standards:**
- **Regulatory Compliance:** Governance ensures that IT services and processes comply with relevant laws, regulations, and industry standards, protecting the organization from legal and reputational risks.
- **Security Compliance:** They oversee the implementation and maintenance of security controls to protect sensitive data and prevent cyberattacks.
- **Audits and Reviews:** Governance bodies conduct regular audits and reviews to ensure that compliance requirements are met.
7. **Communicating with Stakeholders about IT Performance and Risks:**
- **Transparent Communication:** Governance provides transparent and timely communication to stakeholders about IT performance, risks, and plans.
- **Stakeholder Engagement:** They involve stakeholders in decision-making processes and seek their feedback on IT services.
- **Reporting:** They provide regular reports to senior management and the board on IT performance, risks, and compliance.

By actively engaging in these activities, governance bodies can ensure that IT is aligned with the organization's strategic goals, that risks are managed effectively, and that resources are used efficiently to deliver value.

Governance and Risk Management

Governance and risk management are intrinsically linked within the ITIL 4 framework. Effective governance provides the foundation for proactive risk management, while risk management insights inform and influence governance decisions. This symbiotic relationship is crucial for ensuring the stability, resilience, and success of IT service delivery.

The Close Relationship Between Governance and Risk Management:

Governance establishes the overall framework for decision-making, resource allocation, and accountability in IT service management. It sets the tone for how risks are perceived, evaluated, and addressed within the organization. Effective governance ensures that risk management is not an afterthought but an integral part of the decision-making process.

- **Risk-Aware Culture:** Governance plays a crucial role in establishing a risk-aware culture, where risks are identified, assessed, and addressed proactively at all levels of the organization. This involves communicating the importance of risk management, providing training and awareness programs, and fostering an environment where employees feel empowered to report and escalate risks.
- **Risk Appetite:** Governance defines the organization's risk appetite, which is the level of risk it is willing to accept in pursuit of its objectives. This sets the boundaries for risk-taking and guides decision-making around risk mitigation strategies.
- **Risk Management Framework:** Governance establishes a risk management framework that defines the processes, roles, and responsibilities for identifying, assessing, and mitigating risks. This framework provides a structured approach to risk management and ensures that risks are managed consistently and effectively.

How Governance Structures and Activities Establish a Risk-Aware Culture:

Governance structures, such as steering committees and risk management boards, provide a forum for discussing and evaluating IT-related risks. They ensure that risks are considered at the highest levels of the organization and that decisions are made with a full understanding of the potential consequences.

Governance activities, such as risk assessments, policy reviews, and audits, help to embed risk management into the organization's culture and processes. These activities promote a proactive approach to risk management, where risks are identified and addressed before they can cause harm.

Integration of Risk Management into Governance Processes:

Risk management can be integrated into governance processes in several ways:

1. **Risk Assessments:** Conducting regular risk assessments to identify and evaluate potential risks to IT services and infrastructure. This information can be used to inform decision-making and prioritize risk mitigation efforts.
2. **Risk Registers:** Maintaining a risk register that documents identified risks, their likelihood and impact, and the mitigation strategies in place. This provides a central repository of risk information that can be used for reporting and decision-making.
3. **Risk Mitigation Plans:** Developing and implementing risk mitigation plans that outline specific actions to be taken to reduce the probability or impact of identified risks. These plans should be regularly reviewed and updated as new risks emerge or existing risks change.

Examples of Risk Management in Governance:

- A steering committee reviews a proposed IT project and identifies a potential risk of data breaches due to the sensitivity of the data involved. The committee decides to implement additional security controls to mitigate this risk before approving the project.
- A risk management board conducts a risk assessment of the organization's IT infrastructure and identifies a vulnerability in a critical system. The board develops a risk mitigation plan that includes patching the vulnerability, implementing additional security measures, and testing the system to ensure its resilience.
- An internal audit team reviews the organization's incident management process and identifies a risk of delayed response due to a lack of clear escalation procedures. The team recommends that the organization establish clear escalation procedures and provide additional training to service desk staff to ensure timely and effective incident resolution.

By integrating risk management into governance processes, organizations can proactively identify and address potential threats, ensuring that IT services are delivered reliably and securely. This not only protects the organization's assets but also builds trust with customers and stakeholders, who can be confident that their interests are being safeguarded.

Governance and Continual Improvement

Governance and continual improvement are two sides of the same coin in ITIL 4. While governance provides the direction, oversight, and structure for IT service management, continual improvement is the engine that drives ongoing optimization and value creation. Their relationship is symbiotic, with governance providing the framework and support for improvement initiatives, while continual improvement insights inform and refine governance decisions.

How Governance Supports Continual Improvement:

1. **Setting Clear Objectives:** Governance bodies, such as steering committees or management boards, establish clear objectives for continual improvement. These objectives align with the organization's strategic goals and provide a clear direction for improvement efforts.
2. **Providing Resources:** Governance allocates resources, such as budget, personnel, and technology, to support continual improvement initiatives. This ensures that teams have the necessary tools and support to identify and implement improvements effectively.
3. **Monitoring Progress:** Governance regularly monitors the progress of continual improvement initiatives, tracking key performance indicators (KPIs) and metrics to assess their effectiveness. This allows for early identification of potential issues and ensures that improvement efforts remain on track.
4. **Creating a Culture of Improvement:** Governance fosters a culture of continual improvement by recognizing and rewarding those who contribute to positive change. It encourages employees to identify and report improvement opportunities, experiment with new approaches, and learn from mistakes.

The Role of Governance in Reviewing and Approving Improvement Proposals:

Governance bodies play a critical role in reviewing and approving improvement proposals. They assess the potential impact of proposed changes, ensure that they align with strategic goals, and evaluate their potential to deliver value. This oversight helps to prioritize initiatives that offer the greatest benefits and minimize the risk of unintended consequences.

Importance of Feedback Loops Between Governance and Operational Teams:

Effective communication and feedback loops between governance and operational teams are essential for successful continual improvement. Operational teams provide valuable insights into the day-to-day challenges and opportunities for improvement, while governance bodies provide strategic guidance and ensure that improvement efforts are aligned with the organization's overall goals.

Key elements of effective feedback loops include:

- **Regular Reporting:** Operational teams provide regular reports to governance bodies on service performance, improvement initiatives, and lessons learned.
- **Open Communication:** Governance bodies maintain open communication channels with operational teams, providing feedback, guidance, and support.
- **Collaboration:** Governance and operational teams collaborate to identify improvement opportunities, develop solutions, and implement changes.
- **Shared Learning:** Both governance and operational teams learn from each other's experiences, sharing knowledge and best practices to continuously improve IT service management.

Example: Governance Supporting a Major Service Upgrade:

A governance committee approves a proposal to upgrade a critical business application. They allocate a budget, assign resources, and establish timelines for the project. The project team regularly reports to the committee on progress, challenges, and risks. The committee provides feedback and guidance throughout the project, ensuring that it remains on track and delivers the expected value. After the upgrade is completed, the committee conducts a post-implementation review to assess the project's success and identify lessons learned that can be applied to future initiatives.

By working together, governance and operational teams can create a virtuous cycle of continuous improvement, where feedback and learning are used to refine processes, optimize resources, and deliver increasing value to customers and stakeholders.

Challenges and Best Practices in Governance

Implementing effective IT governance is not without its hurdles. Organizations often encounter various challenges that can hinder the successful establishment and operation of a governance framework. However, by understanding these challenges and adopting best practices, organizations can overcome these obstacles and achieve their governance objectives.

Common Challenges in Implementing Effective IT Governance:

1. **Resistance to Change:**
- **Description:** Employees and managers may resist changes to existing processes, roles, and responsibilities, especially if they perceive governance as an additional layer of bureaucracy or a threat to their autonomy.
- **Solution:**
    - **Communication and Education:** Clearly communicate the reasons for implementing governance and the benefits it will bring to the organization. Educate stakeholders about their roles and responsibilities within the governance framework.
    - **Gradual Implementation:** Start with a few key governance activities and gradually expand the scope as the organization becomes more comfortable with the new approach.
    - **Empowerment:** Empower employees to participate in governance processes and provide feedback, giving them a sense of ownership and control.
2. **Lack of Clarity in Roles and Responsibilities:**
- **Description:** If roles and responsibilities are not clearly defined, it can lead to confusion, duplication of effort, and conflicts between different stakeholders.
- **Solution:**
    - **Clear Definitions:** Create clear and concise role descriptions that outline the responsibilities and authority of each governance role.
    - **RACI Matrix:** Use a RACI (Responsible, Accountable, Consulted, Informed) matrix to clarify who is responsible for each governance activity and who needs to be involved in decision-making.
    - **Training:** Provide training to governance stakeholders to ensure that they understand their roles and responsibilities.
3. **Inadequate Communication:**
- **Description:** Poor communication can lead to misunderstandings, misaligned expectations, and resistance to change. It can also hinder the flow of information between different governance levels and stakeholders.
- **Solution:**
    - **Establish Communication Channels:** Create clear communication channels for sharing information, updates, and feedback between governance bodies, IT teams, and business stakeholders.
    - **Regular Meetings:** Schedule regular meetings to discuss governance issues, review performance, and make decisions.

    ○ **Transparency:** Be transparent about governance decisions and their rationale, providing regular updates and reports to stakeholders.

Best Practices for Overcoming Challenges in Governance:

1. **Establish Clear Governance Structures and Roles:**
- Define the roles and responsibilities of each governance body (e.g., steering committee, management board, advisory groups).
- Outline the decision-making processes and authority levels for each body.
- Ensure that roles and responsibilities are communicated clearly to all stakeholders.
2. **Develop and Communicate Clear Policies and Standards:**
- Develop comprehensive IT policies and standards that cover areas such as security, risk management, change management, and procurement.
- Ensure that policies and standards are aligned with the organization's overall strategy and objectives.
- Communicate policies and standards clearly to all relevant stakeholders and provide training as needed.
3. **Involve Stakeholders in Decision-Making Processes:**
- Engage stakeholders early in the governance process to gather their input and feedback.
- Create opportunities for stakeholders to participate in decision-making through committees, forums, or surveys.
- Communicate decisions and their rationale to stakeholders in a transparent and timely manner.
4. **Regularly Monitor and Evaluate IT Performance:**
- Establish key performance indicators (KPIs) to track the performance of IT services and processes.
- Regularly monitor KPIs and compare them to targets.
- Use performance data to identify areas for improvement and make informed decisions about resource allocation and investment priorities.
5. **Foster a Culture of Transparency, Collaboration, and Continuous Improvement:**
- Encourage open communication and feedback between governance bodies, IT teams, and business stakeholders.
- Promote collaboration and knowledge sharing across the organization.
- Create a culture that values continuous improvement and innovation.
- Recognize and reward individuals and teams who contribute to improvement initiatives.

By adopting these best practices, organizations can overcome the challenges of implementing effective IT governance and create a governance framework that supports their strategic goals, manages risks, and delivers value to their customers and stakeholders.

Chapter Summary

In this chapter, we delved into the crucial concept of governance within the ITIL 4 Service Value System (SVS). We explored its role in ensuring alignment with strategic goals, managing risks, facilitating decision-making, and fostering a culture of continual improvement.

Key takeaways from this chapter:

- **Governance as Direction and Control:** We defined governance as the system by which organizations are directed and controlled, ensuring their activities align with objectives, comply with regulations, and create value. In ITIL 4, it's the mechanism ensuring IT services meet the organization's needs.
- **Purpose and Objectives:** We outlined the key purposes and objectives of governance in ITIL 4, which include ensuring IT services deliver value, aligning IT with strategic goals, managing risks, optimizing resources, and fostering transparency and collaboration.

- **Governance in the SVS:** We illustrated how governance functions within the SVS, connecting all its elements – guiding principles, practices, and the service value chain – to ensure effectiveness and alignment with strategic objectives.
- **Three Lines of Defense Model:** We introduced this model as a common framework for organizing governance activities, clearly defining the roles and responsibilities of operational management, risk management and compliance functions, and internal audit.
- **Governance Structures and Roles:** We described typical governance structures like steering committees, management boards, and advisory groups, highlighting the roles and responsibilities of key stakeholders. We stressed the importance of clearly defined roles for accountability and effective decision-making.
- **Governance Activities:** We detailed the key activities involved in IT governance, including setting strategic direction, developing policies and standards, prioritizing projects, monitoring performance, managing risks, ensuring compliance, and communicating with stakeholders.
- **Governance and Risk Management:** We explored the close relationship between governance and risk management, emphasizing that effective governance is essential for proactive risk identification, assessment, and mitigation.
- **Governance and Continual Improvement:** We discussed how governance supports continual improvement by setting objectives, providing resources, monitoring progress, and fostering a culture of improvement. We highlighted the importance of feedback loops between governance and operational teams to ensure effective implementation and learning from past experiences.
- **Challenges and Best Practices:** We addressed common challenges in implementing effective IT governance, such as resistance to change, unclear roles, and inadequate communication. We offered best practices to overcome these, such as establishing clear structures, communicating policies, involving stakeholders, monitoring performance, and fostering a culture of transparency and collaboration.

By understanding and implementing effective governance practices, organizations can ensure their IT services are aligned with strategic objectives, risks are managed proactively, and resources are utilized efficiently, ultimately delivering greater value to customers and stakeholders.

Practices

Outline

- Introduction to ITIL Practices
- General Management Practices
- Service Management Practices
- Technical Management Practices
- Integrating Practices into the Service Value Chain
- Chapter Summary

Introduction to ITIL Practices

ITIL 4 represents a significant evolution from previous versions, notably in its shift from a process-centric approach to a more flexible, holistic model centered on practices. Understanding what ITIL practices are and why they are crucial in this new paradigm is essential for effective implementation and utilization.

What are ITIL Practices?

In ITIL 4, a **practice** is defined as a set of organizational resources designed for performing work or accomplishing an objective. These resources encompass a wide range of elements, including:

- **People:** The skills, knowledge, and experience of individuals and teams.
- **Processes:** Structured sets of activities designed to achieve specific outcomes.
- **Information and Technology:** The data, information systems, and technology tools that support work activities.
- **Partners and Suppliers:** External organizations that contribute to service delivery.
- **Value Streams and Processes:** The end-to-end activities that create and deliver value.

Think of practices as a toolbox of resources that organizations can leverage to achieve their desired outcomes. They provide guidance and structure without being overly prescriptive, allowing for flexibility and adaptation to different contexts.

Why are Practices Important in ITIL 4?

The shift to a practice-based approach in ITIL 4 is a response to the increasing complexity and dynamism of modern IT environments. Practices are more flexible and adaptable than processes, allowing organizations to tailor their approaches to their specific needs and circumstances. They also encourage a more holistic view of service management, recognizing the interconnectedness of different elements within the Service Value System (SVS).

Here's why practices are crucial in ITIL 4:

- **Flexibility:** Practices can be adapted and combined to fit the specific needs of an organization, allowing for greater customization and agility.
- **Focus on Value:** Practices emphasize the importance of delivering value to customers and stakeholders, rather than just following rigid processes.
- **Holistic Approach:** Practices encourage a broader perspective that considers the interdependencies between different elements of the SVS, leading to better decision-making and improved outcomes.
- **Continuous Improvement:** Practices are designed to be continuously improved and evolved, ensuring that they remain relevant and effective in the face of changing business needs and technologies.

Practices vs. Processes: Key Differences

Feature	Practices	Processes
Focus	Resources and capabilities	Steps and activities
Flexibility	High	Low
Adaptability	High	Low
Scope	Broad	Narrow
Orientation	Outcome-oriented	Activity-oriented

While processes are still important in ITIL 4, they are now seen as components of practices rather than the primary focus. Practices provide a broader and more comprehensive approach to service management, encompassing not only processes but also the people, technology, information, and partners needed to deliver value.

In conclusion, ITIL practices are the building blocks of effective IT service management. By understanding the concept of practices and how they differ from processes, organizations can leverage the flexibility and adaptability of ITIL 4 to create a service management system that is tailored to their unique needs and delivers value to their customers and stakeholders.

General Management Practices

ITIL 4 introduces 14 general management practices that are applicable across the entire organization, not just within IT. These practices support various aspects of business operations, ensuring alignment with strategic goals, effective risk management, and continuous improvement.

1. Strategy Management:

- **Purpose:** To formulate and implement an organization's strategies, ensuring alignment with its vision, mission, and objectives.
- **Key Activities:** Strategic planning, portfolio management, resource allocation, performance management, and communication of strategic goals.
- **Value Contribution:** Guides the organization's overall direction and ensures that IT services support strategic objectives.

2. Portfolio Management:

- **Purpose:** To ensure the organization has the right mix of services, projects, and programs to execute its strategy within its constraints.
- **Key Activities:** Identifying, prioritizing, and authorizing investments in services, projects, and programs, managing their lifecycles, and optimizing their value.
- **Value Contribution:** Maximizes the value delivered by IT investments by ensuring alignment with strategic goals and effective resource utilization.

3. Architecture Management:

- **Purpose:** To design and maintain a holistic architecture that supports the organization's strategy and enables the effective and efficient delivery of services.
- **Key Activities:** Defining architecture principles, creating and maintaining architecture models, assessing and mitigating architectural risks, and ensuring compliance with standards and regulations.

- **Value Contribution:** Provides a blueprint for IT services and ensures that they are designed and implemented in a way that supports business needs and goals.

4. Service Financial Management:

- **Purpose:** To manage the financial aspects of IT services, ensuring that they are cost-effective and provide value for money.
- **Key Activities:** Budgeting, accounting, charging, and cost optimization.
- **Value Contribution:** Helps organizations understand the costs and value of their IT services, enabling them to make informed decisions about investments and prioritize initiatives that deliver the greatest return.

5. Workforce and Talent Management:

- **Purpose:** To attract, develop, and retain a skilled and motivated workforce that can effectively support the organization's goals.
- **Key Activities:** Workforce planning, recruitment, onboarding, training, performance management, career development, and succession planning.
- **Value Contribution:** Ensures that the organization has the right people with the right skills in the right roles to deliver high-quality IT services.

6. Continual Improvement:

- **Purpose:** Align practices and services with changing business needs through ongoing improvement.
- **Key Activities:** Identifying improvement opportunities, assessing and prioritizing them, planning and implementing improvements, and measuring their effectiveness.
- **Value Contribution:** Ensures that the SVS remains adaptable, efficient, and delivers increasing value over time.

7. Measurement and Reporting:

- **Purpose:** To monitor, measure, and report on the performance of IT services and processes, providing insights for decision-making and improvement.
- **Key Activities:** Defining metrics and KPIs, collecting data, analyzing trends, and generating reports.
- **Value Contribution:** Provides valuable data and insights that enable informed decision-making, support continual improvement initiatives, and demonstrate the value of IT services to stakeholders.

8. Risk Management:

- **Purpose:** To identify, assess, and manage risks associated with IT services and operations, ensuring that the organization can anticipate and respond effectively to potential threats.
- **Key Activities:** Risk identification, assessment, evaluation, and treatment (mitigation, transfer, acceptance, or avoidance).
- **Value Contribution:** Protects the organization from potential harm and ensures the continuity of IT services.

9. Information Security Management:

- **Purpose:** To protect the confidentiality, integrity, and availability of information assets.
- **Key Activities:** Developing and implementing security policies, conducting risk assessments, implementing security controls, and monitoring for security threats.
- **Value Contribution:** Safeguards sensitive information, protects the organization's reputation, and ensures compliance with regulatory requirements.

10. Knowledge Management:

- **Purpose:** To capture, share, and reuse knowledge and information within the organization, fostering a culture of learning and innovation.
- **Key Activities:** Creating and maintaining a knowledge base, promoting knowledge sharing, and encouraging collaboration.
- **Value Contribution:** Improves decision-making, problem-solving, and efficiency by making relevant knowledge readily available to employees.

11. Organizational Change Management:

- **Purpose:** To manage the people side of change, ensuring that employees are prepared for and supportive of changes in IT services and processes.
- **Key Activities:** Developing and implementing change plans, communicating changes effectively, and addressing resistance to change.
- **Value Contribution:** Helps to minimize disruption and maximize the benefits of change initiatives.

12. Project Management:

- **Purpose:** To ensure that IT projects are delivered successfully, on time, and within budget.
- **Key Activities:** Project planning, execution, monitoring, and closure.
- **Value Contribution:** Ensures that IT projects deliver the desired outcomes and contribute to the organization's goals.

13. Relationship Management:

- **Purpose:** To establish and maintain strong relationships with stakeholders, both internal and external.
- **Key Activities:** Stakeholder identification, engagement, communication, and relationship building.
- **Value Contribution:** Ensures that IT services are aligned with stakeholder needs and expectations.

14. Supplier Management:

- **Purpose:** To manage the relationships with suppliers of IT services and components.
- **Key Activities:** Supplier selection, contract negotiation, performance monitoring, and relationship management.
- **Value Contribution:** Ensures that suppliers deliver high-quality services and components that meet the organization's needs.

By understanding and applying these general management practices, organizations can create a solid foundation for effective IT service management, ensuring that IT services are aligned with business goals, risks are managed proactively, and resources are utilized optimally.

Service Management Practices

The 17 Service Management Practices in ITIL 4 form the core of ITIL's guidance on designing, delivering, and supporting IT services. These practices provide a comprehensive framework for managing the entire service lifecycle, from strategy and design to operation and improvement.

1. Business Analysis:

- **Purpose:** To investigate business situations, identify and evaluate options for improvement, and propose solutions that enable the organization to achieve its desired business outcomes.
- **Key Activities:** Stakeholder analysis, requirements elicitation, solution evaluation, business case development.
- **Value Contribution:** Ensures that IT services are aligned with business needs and deliver value to the organization.

2. Service Catalog Management:

- **Purpose:** To provide and maintain a single source of information about all services offered by the organization, ensuring that accurate and reliable information is available to users and stakeholders.
- **Key Activities:** Creating and maintaining the service catalog, managing service requests, and providing information about service availability, costs, and performance.
- **Value Contribution:** Improves transparency, communication, and understanding of available services, enabling users to make informed decisions and request services efficiently.

3. Service Design:

- **Purpose:** To design new or changed services, taking into account customer and stakeholder needs, business requirements, and technical feasibility.
- **Key Activities:** Service prototyping, service modeling, service level agreement (SLA) design, user experience (UX) design, and risk assessment.
- **Value Contribution:** Ensures that services are designed to meet the needs of users and stakeholders, are fit for purpose, and can be delivered and supported effectively.

4. Service Level Management:

- **Purpose:** To set clear and measurable targets for service levels, monitor performance against these targets, and take corrective action as needed to ensure that services meet or exceed agreed-upon standards.
- **Key Activities:** Defining service levels, negotiating and documenting SLAs, monitoring service performance, reporting on SLA compliance, and reviewing and updating SLAs.
- **Value Contribution:** Ensures that services are delivered according to agreed-upon standards, manages customer expectations, and provides a basis for measuring and improving service performance.

5. Availability Management:

- **Purpose:** To ensure that IT services are available when and where they are needed to meet agreed-upon requirements.
- **Key Activities:** Availability planning, design, monitoring, analysis, and improvement.
- **Value Contribution:** Maximizes the uptime of IT services, minimizes the impact of disruptions, and ensures that services can meet business needs.

6. Capacity and Performance Management:

- **Purpose:** To ensure that IT services can meet current and future demand in a cost-effective manner.
- **Key Activities:** Capacity planning, performance monitoring, analysis, and optimization.
- **Value Contribution:** Ensures that IT services have the necessary capacity to meet demand, perform optimally, and deliver a positive user experience.

7. Service Continuity Management:

- **Purpose:** To enable the organization to continue delivering essential services during and after a disruptive incident.
- **Key Activities:** Business impact analysis (BIA), risk assessment, development of continuity plans, testing, and exercising.
- **Value Contribution:** Minimizes the impact of disruptions on business operations and ensures that critical services can be recovered quickly.

8. Monitoring and Event Management:

- **Purpose:** To systematically observe services and service components, as well as record and report selected changes of state identified as events.
- **Key Activities:** Defining monitoring requirements, implementing monitoring tools, collecting and analyzing event data, and generating alerts and notifications.
- **Value Contribution:** Enables proactive detection and response to potential problems, improving service availability and preventing incidents.

9. Service Desk:

- **Purpose:** To be the single point of contact between the service provider and the users.
- **Key Activities:** Incident logging and categorization, request fulfillment, service information and support, and user communication.
- **Value Contribution:** Provides a central point of contact for users, improves communication, and facilitates faster resolution of issues.

10. Incident Management:

- **Purpose:** Minimize the negative impact of incidents by restoring normal service operation as quickly as possible.
- **Key Activities:** Incident identification, logging, categorization, prioritization, diagnosis, resolution, closure, and communication.
- **Value Contribution:** Ensures service availability and minimizes disruptions to business operations.

11. Service Request Management:

- **Purpose:** To manage the lifecycle of service requests, ensuring that they are fulfilled efficiently and effectively.
- **Key Activities:** Request logging, categorization, prioritization, fulfillment, and closure.
- **Value Contribution:** Provides a structured approach to managing service requests, ensuring that they are handled in a timely and consistent manner.

12. Problem Management:

- **Purpose:** To reduce the likelihood and impact of incidents by identifying and managing the root causes of incidents.
- **Key Activities:** Problem identification, logging, categorization, prioritization, investigation, diagnosis, resolution, and closure.
- **Value Contribution:** Reduces the frequency and impact of incidents, improving service stability and availability.

13. Release Management:

- **Purpose:** To plan, schedule, and control the movement of releases to test and live environments.
- **Key Activities:** Release planning, build and configuration management, testing, deployment, and early life support.
- **Value Contribution:** Ensures that releases are deployed smoothly and without disruption to services.

14. Change Enablement:

- **Purpose:** To maximize the number of successful IT changes by ensuring that risks are properly assessed, authorized, and managed.
- **Key Activities:** Change assessment, authorization, planning, implementation, and review.
- **Value Contribution:** Minimizes the risk of changes causing disruptions to services and ensures that changes are aligned with business needs.

15. Service Validation and Testing:

- **Purpose:** To ensure that services meet agreed-upon requirements and expectations before they are deployed to live environments.
- **Key Activities:** Test planning, test case development, test execution, and test reporting.
- **Value Contribution:** Improves service quality by identifying and fixing defects early in the lifecycle.

16. Service Configuration Management:

- **Purpose:** To ensure that accurate and reliable information about configuration items (CIs) is available when and where it is needed.
- **Key Activities:** CI identification, configuration recording, status accounting, and verification and audit.
- **Value Contribution:** Provides a single source of truth for configuration information, supporting incident management, problem management, and change management.

17. IT Asset Management:

- **Purpose:** To plan and manage the full lifecycle of all IT assets.
- **Key Activities:** Asset identification, tracking, financial management, optimization, and disposal.
- **Value Contribution:** Optimizes the use of IT assets, reduces costs, and ensures compliance with software licenses and contracts.

This overview provides a glimpse into the diverse and interconnected nature of ITIL service management practices. Each practice plays a crucial role in creating, delivering, and supporting IT services that meet the needs of customers and stakeholders. By understanding and applying these practices, organizations can build a robust and effective IT service management system that drives business value and success.

Technical Management Practices

The three Technical Management practices in ITIL 4 focus on the technical aspects of service delivery, ensuring that the underlying infrastructure and platforms are reliable, secure, and performant. They are essential for maintaining the availability, continuity, and functionality of IT services.

1. Deployment Management:

- **Purpose:** To move new or changed hardware, software, documentation, processes, or any other service component to live environments. This practice also encompasses deployments to other environments for testing or staging.
- **Key Activities:**
    - Planning and scheduling deployments
    - Coordinating with different teams involved in the deployment process
    - Building and configuring deployment packages
    - Managing the deployment process and resolving any issues that arise
    - Monitoring and verifying the success of deployments
    - Providing early life support and troubleshooting for deployed components
- **Value Contribution:** Ensures that new or changed service components are deployed smoothly, efficiently, and with minimal disruption to business operations. It also helps to ensure that deployments are properly tested and validated before being released to production.

2. Infrastructure and Platform Management:

- **Purpose:** To manage the infrastructure and platforms (hardware, software, networks, etc.) used to support the delivery of IT services.
- **Key Activities:**
    - Monitoring infrastructure and platform health and performance
    - Maintaining and updating infrastructure and platform components

- ○ Managing capacity and performance to ensure optimal service levels
- ○ Ensuring the availability and reliability of infrastructure and platforms
- ○ Implementing security controls to protect infrastructure and platforms from unauthorized access and threats
- **Value Contribution:** Provides a stable and reliable foundation for IT service delivery, ensuring that services are available, performant, and secure.

3. Software Development and Management:

- **Purpose:** To manage the lifecycle of software applications from design and development to deployment and maintenance.
- **Key Activities:**
  - ○ Requirements gathering and analysis
  - ○ Software design and development
  - ○ Testing and quality assurance
  - ○ Release and deployment management
  - ○ Maintenance and support
  - ○ Version control and configuration management
- **Value Contribution:** Ensures that software applications meet user needs, are reliable and secure, and can be easily maintained and updated.

In summary, the Technical Management practices focus on the technical aspects of IT service management, ensuring that the underlying infrastructure and platforms are reliable, secure, and performant. These practices are essential for supporting the delivery of high-quality IT services that meet the needs of customers and stakeholders. By effectively managing infrastructure, platforms, and software development, organizations can enhance the availability, reliability, and performance of their services, leading to increased customer satisfaction and business value.

Integrating Practices into the Service Value Chain

A key strength of ITIL 4's practice-based approach is its flexibility. The 34 management practices are not confined to specific stages of the Service Value Chain (SVC) but can be applied across the entire chain as needed. This adaptability empowers organizations to tailor their use of practices to their unique circumstances and priorities.

Flexibility of ITIL Practices:

Unlike the more rigid processes of previous ITIL versions, practices in ITIL 4 are adaptable and can be combined, modified, or even created anew to suit an organization's specific needs. This flexibility allows for a more agile and responsive approach to service management, enabling organizations to respond effectively to changing business demands and customer expectations.

Examples of Practices Used Across Multiple SVC Activities:

- **Knowledge Management:**
  - ○ **Plan:** Used to gather and analyze information about customer needs and market trends.
  - ○ **Improve:** Used to capture and share lessons learned from incidents and problems.
  - ○ **Design and Transition:** Used to document service designs, create knowledge articles, and support training activities.
  - ○ **Deliver and Support:** Used to provide self-service support to users and empower service desk agents with relevant information.
- **Risk Management:**
  - ○ **Plan:** Used to assess and prioritize risks to the organization's strategic objectives and service delivery.

- ○ **Design and Transition:** Used to identify and mitigate risks associated with new or changed services.
  - ○ **Obtain/Build:** Used to assess risks associated with suppliers and service components.
  - ○ **Deliver and Support:** Used to monitor and manage risks that may impact service availability and performance.
- **Relationship Management:**
  - ○ **Plan:** Used to establish and maintain relationships with key stakeholders.
  - ○ **Engage:** Used to foster collaboration and communication with stakeholders.
  - ○ **Design and Transition:** Used to ensure that stakeholder needs and expectations are considered in service design and transition.
  - ○ **Deliver and Support:** Used to manage ongoing relationships with customers and resolve any issues or concerns.
- **Continual Improvement:**
  - ○ **Plan:** Used to identify and prioritize improvement opportunities.
  - ○ **Improve:** Used to plan, implement, and evaluate improvement initiatives.
  - ○ **Design and Transition:** Used to incorporate lessons learned into service design and transition processes.
  - ○ **Deliver and Support:** Used to identify and address recurring problems that impact service delivery.

Tailoring the Use of Practices:

The flexibility of ITIL 4 practices allows organizations to tailor their use to their specific needs and context. This means that organizations can:

- **Prioritize Practices:** Focus on the practices that are most relevant and beneficial to their specific goals and challenges.
- **Adapt Practices:** Modify or combine practices to create custom solutions that fit their unique environment.
- **Develop New Practices:** Create new practices that address specific needs not covered by the standard ITIL practices.
- **Integrate with Other Frameworks:** Combine ITIL practices with other frameworks, such as Agile or DevOps, to create a hybrid approach that best suits their needs.

In Summary:

The ITIL 4 practices are versatile tools that can be applied flexibly across the entire Service Value Chain. By understanding the purpose and capabilities of each practice, and by tailoring their use to their specific needs, organizations can create a more agile, responsive, and effective IT service management system. This adaptability is a key strength of ITIL 4, enabling organizations to embrace the principles of service management while tailoring them to their unique context and goals.

Chapter Summary

In this chapter, we explored the ITIL 4 practices, highlighting their role in facilitating the creation and delivery of value within the Service Value System (SVS). We delved into the differences between practices and the more traditional process-focused approach of previous ITIL versions, emphasizing the flexibility and adaptability that practices offer.

Here's a recap of the key points covered:

- **Introduction to ITIL Practices:** We defined ITIL practices as sets of organizational resources designed for performing work or accomplishing an objective. We explained how practices, unlike processes, are more flexible and outcome-oriented, allowing organizations to tailor their implementation to their specific needs.

- **General Management Practices:** We introduced the 14 general management practices that support various aspects of business operations, ensuring alignment with strategic goals, effective risk management, and continuous improvement. We provided examples of their purpose, key activities, and value contributions, such as Continual Improvement for adapting to changing business needs and Measurement and Reporting for data-driven decision-making.
- **Service Management Practices:** We explored the 17 service management practices focusing on the specific activities involved in managing IT services throughout their lifecycle. Examples include Incident Management, which minimizes the impact of service disruptions, and Service Request Management, which ensures efficient handling of user requests.
- **Technical Management Practices:** We discussed the three technical management practices that deal with the technical aspects of IT service management, such as Infrastructure and Platform Management for ensuring availability and reliability. We highlighted their purpose, key activities, and contributions to the overall service performance.
- **Integrating Practices into the Service Value Chain:** We explained how ITIL practices are not tied to specific stages of the Service Value Chain but can be applied flexibly across the entire chain as needed. We provided examples of how different practices, like Knowledge Management and Risk Management, can be utilized in multiple value chain activities, emphasizing the importance of tailoring their use to each organization's specific needs and context.

By understanding the ITIL practices and their flexible application within the Service Value Chain, organizations can effectively leverage these tools to create a more adaptable, value-driven, and customer-centric approach to IT service management. This allows them to respond to changing business needs, deliver high-quality services, and achieve their strategic objectives. In the following chapters, we will delve deeper into the specifics of each practice, providing you with a comprehensive understanding of their implementation and value creation.

Continual Improvement

Outline

- Introduction to Continual Improvement in ITIL 4
- The ITIL Continual Improvement Model
- Key Principles of Continual Improvement
- Continual Improvement and the Service Value Chain (SVC)
- The Role of Measurement and Metrics
- Challenges and Pitfalls in Continual Improvement
- Fostering a Culture of Continual Improvement
- Chapter Summary

Introduction to Continual Improvement in ITIL 4

Continual improvement is a cornerstone of the ITIL 4 framework. It's more than just a practice; it's a mindset, a philosophy, and an ongoing commitment to enhancing the value delivered through IT services. ITIL 4 views continual improvement as a fundamental aspect of the Service Value System (SVS), permeating every activity and decision within the service lifecycle.

Importance of Continual Improvement as a Core Principle:

In today's rapidly changing business landscape, organizations must constantly adapt and evolve to remain competitive. Continual improvement provides the mechanism for this adaptation, ensuring that IT services remain relevant, efficient, and effective in meeting evolving customer and stakeholder needs.

- **Adaptation to Changing Business Needs:** Business requirements and customer expectations are constantly shifting. Continual improvement allows organizations to proactively identify and respond to these changes, ensuring that their IT services remain aligned with business goals and deliver the desired value.
- **Improved Service Quality:** By systematically analyzing performance data, gathering feedback, and implementing improvements, organizations can enhance the quality, reliability, and responsiveness of their IT services. This leads to higher customer satisfaction, increased loyalty, and improved business outcomes.
- **Enhanced Efficiency:** Continual improvement focuses on identifying and eliminating waste, streamlining processes, and optimizing resource utilization. This results in increased efficiency, reduced costs, and better value for money.
- **Driving Innovation:** A culture of continual improvement encourages experimentation, learning, and the adoption of new technologies and practices. This fosters innovation, enabling organizations to stay ahead of the curve and maintain a competitive edge.

Shift Towards a Holistic Approach in ITIL 4:

ITIL 4 represents a significant shift in the approach to continual improvement compared to previous versions. While earlier versions focused primarily on improving IT services, ITIL 4 adopts a more holistic perspective, encompassing all aspects of service management and involving all stakeholders.

This holistic approach recognizes that improvement is not just the responsibility of the IT department but a collective effort that involves everyone in the organization. It emphasizes the importance of collaboration, communication, and a shared commitment to continuous learning and adaptation. This broader perspective ensures that improvement initiatives are aligned with the overall strategic goals of the organization and deliver value to all stakeholders.

In Summary:

Continual improvement is a fundamental principle of ITIL 4 that underpins the entire Service Value System. It is a dynamic and ongoing process that enables organizations to adapt to change, improve service quality, enhance efficiency, and drive innovation. By embracing a holistic approach to continual improvement and involving all stakeholders, organizations can create a culture of learning and adaptation that leads to sustainable success in IT service management.

The ITIL Continual Improvement Model

The ITIL Continual Improvement (CI) Model provides a structured approach to identifying, implementing, and measuring improvements across all areas of IT service management. It is a cyclical process, meaning it is designed to be repeated continuously, with each cycle building upon the lessons learned from previous iterations.

The Seven Steps of the ITIL Continual Improvement Model:

1. **What is the vision?**
- **Purpose:** To define a clear direction for improvement, ensuring that all efforts are aligned with the organization's strategic goals and objectives.
- **Key Activities:**
   - Establishing a shared vision and understanding of what the organization wants to achieve through continual improvement.
   - Identifying the desired outcomes and benefits of the improvement initiative.
   - Defining success criteria and metrics to measure progress.
- **Outputs:**
   - Vision statement
   - Strategic goals and objectives
   - Success criteria and metrics

2. **Where are we now?**
- **Purpose:** To assess the current state of the organization's IT service management practices, identify areas for improvement, and establish a baseline for measuring progress.
- **Key Activities:**
   - Gathering data and information about current performance, processes, and customer satisfaction.
   - Analyzing data to identify trends, patterns, and root causes of problems.
   - Conducting gap analyses to compare current practices against best practices and desired outcomes.
- **Outputs:**
   - Baseline assessment report
   - Gap analysis report
   - Problem statements
   - Improvement opportunities

3. **Where do we want to be?**
- **Purpose:** To define specific, measurable, achievable, relevant, and time-bound (SMART) improvement targets based on the desired outcomes and the current state assessment.
- **Key Activities:**
   - Prioritizing improvement opportunities based on their potential impact and feasibility.
   - Defining clear and specific objectives for each improvement initiative.
   - Establishing metrics and KPIs to measure progress towards the objectives.
- **Outputs:**
   - Improvement plan
   - Prioritized improvement opportunities
   - SMART objectives and targets

      ○ Metrics and KPIs

4. **How do we get there?**
- **Purpose:** To develop a detailed plan for implementing the improvement initiatives, outlining the steps, resources, and timelines required.
- **Key Activities:**
  - Designing solutions to address the identified problems and achieve the improvement targets.
  - Identifying the resources (e.g., budget, personnel, technology) needed for implementation.
  - Developing a project plan that includes timelines, milestones, and responsibilities.
  - Communicating the plan to stakeholders and securing their buy-in.
- **Outputs:**
  - Implementation plan
  - Project plan
  - Communication plan
  - Resource allocation plan

5. **Take Action:**
- **Purpose:** To execute the implementation plan and put the improvement initiatives into action.
- **Key Activities:**
  - Executing the tasks and activities outlined in the implementation plan.
  - Monitoring progress and making adjustments as needed.
  - Communicating progress to stakeholders and addressing any concerns or issues that arise.
- **Outputs:**
  - Implemented improvements
  - Progress reports
  - Lessons learned

6. **Did we get there?**
- **Purpose:** To evaluate the effectiveness of the implemented improvements by measuring performance against the defined targets.
- **Key Activities:**
  - Collecting and analyzing data to measure the impact of the improvements.
  - Comparing actual results to the defined targets.
  - Gathering feedback from stakeholders on the perceived benefits and impact of the changes.
- **Outputs:**
  - Evaluation report
  - Performance data
  - Stakeholder feedback

7. **How do we keep the momentum going?**
- **Purpose:** To ensure that the improvement process is ongoing and sustainable, and that lessons learned are incorporated into future initiatives.
- **Key Activities:**
  - Identifying new improvement opportunities based on the evaluation results and stakeholder feedback.
  - Sharing lessons learned with the wider organization.
  - Updating processes, procedures, and documentation based on the outcomes of the improvement initiative.
  - Celebrating successes and recognizing the contributions of those involved in the improvement process.
- **Outputs:**
  - New improvement initiatives
  - Updated processes and procedures
  - Lessons learned repository
  - Recognition and rewards for contributors

Iterative and Cyclical Nature of the Model:

The ITIL Continual Improvement Model is not a linear process with a defined endpoint. It's a cyclical process where each step informs the next, and the end of one cycle marks the beginning of another. This iterative approach allows organizations to continuously learn, adapt, and improve their IT service management practices.

Feedback and learning from each iteration are crucial for driving the next cycle. The evaluation step (Did we get there?) provides valuable insights into what worked well and what didn't, which can be used to refine future improvement initiatives. This ensures that the organization is constantly evolving and improving its ability to deliver value to its customers and stakeholders.

Key Principles of Continual Improvement

The ITIL 4 Continual Improvement (CI) Model is guided by seven key principles that form the foundation of a successful improvement journey. These principles are not unique to CI but are applicable to all aspects of service management, ensuring that improvement efforts are aligned with the organization's goals, values, and customer-centric approach.

1. **Focus on Value:**
- **Explanation:** Every improvement initiative should aim to create or enhance value for customers and stakeholders. This means identifying what is truly important to them and focusing efforts on areas that deliver the most significant impact.
- **Guidance for CI:** Ensure that improvement projects are selected based on their potential to create value, not just on their technical feasibility or ease of implementation. Define clear success criteria and metrics that measure the value generated by the improvement.
2. **Start Where You Are:**
- **Explanation:** Recognize and build upon existing strengths and capabilities rather than starting from scratch. This means leveraging existing processes, tools, knowledge, and expertise to accelerate the improvement journey.
- **Guidance for CI:** Assess the current state of your IT service management (ITSM) practices, identify areas for improvement, and prioritize actions based on their potential impact and feasibility. Avoid the temptation to reinvent the wheel or implement wholesale changes that may disrupt existing services.
3. **Progress Iteratively with Feedback:**
- **Explanation:** Break down large improvement initiatives into smaller, manageable steps. Implement changes incrementally, gather feedback after each iteration, and use that feedback to refine the next steps. This approach reduces risk, enables faster learning, and ensures that improvement efforts remain aligned with evolving needs.
- **Guidance for CI:** Plan improvement initiatives in a series of iterations, each with clear objectives and measurable outcomes. Gather feedback from stakeholders at each stage, use that feedback to adjust your approach, and celebrate small wins along the way.
4. **Collaborate and Promote Visibility:**
- **Explanation:** Continual improvement is a team effort. Encourage collaboration and open communication between different teams and stakeholders. Share information transparently, create opportunities for feedback, and ensure everyone understands their role in the improvement process.
- **Guidance for CI:** Create cross-functional teams to work on improvement initiatives. Use collaborative tools and platforms to facilitate communication and knowledge sharing. Regularly communicate progress and results to stakeholders to build support and maintain momentum.
5. **Think and Work Holistically:**
- **Explanation:** View improvement initiatives in the context of the broader service value system (SVS). Consider the impact of changes on other processes, services, and stakeholders. Adopt a systems thinking approach to identify potential risks and unintended consequences.

- **Guidance for CI:** Analyze improvement opportunities from a holistic perspective, considering their impact on the entire SVS. Engage stakeholders from different areas of the organization to ensure that improvement efforts are aligned with the overall goals and objectives of the business.

6. **Keep It Simple and Practical:**
- **Explanation:** Avoid unnecessary complexity and focus on practical solutions that are easy to understand, implement, and maintain. Prioritize actions that deliver the greatest value with the least effort.
- **Guidance for CI:** Keep improvement initiatives focused and manageable. Avoid overengineering solutions or implementing changes that are overly complex or difficult to adopt. Strive for simplicity and practicality in all aspects of the improvement process.

7. **Optimize and Automate:**
- **Explanation:** Leverage technology to streamline processes, automate tasks, and optimize resource utilization. Automation can free up valuable human resources, reduce errors, and improve efficiency.
- **Guidance for CI:** Identify opportunities for automation within the improvement process. Use automation tools and technologies to streamline data collection, analysis, and reporting. Automate repetitive tasks to free up time for more strategic activities.

By applying these guiding principles, organizations can ensure that their continual improvement efforts are focused, effective, and aligned with their overall goals and priorities. This leads to a culture of continuous learning and adaptation, where IT services are constantly evolving to meet the changing needs of customers and stakeholders.

Continual Improvement and the Service Value Chain (SVC)

Continual Improvement (CI) is not a separate activity within the ITIL 4 Service Value Chain (SVC); rather, it's an integral part of every activity, a continuous thread that runs through the entire value creation process. It's about fostering a mindset of constantly seeking ways to do things better, whether it's enhancing efficiency, reducing costs, or improving customer satisfaction.

Integration of Continual Improvement into the SVC:

CI is woven into each of the six SVC activities, ensuring that the pursuit of improvement is ongoing and embedded in every aspect of service management:

1. **Plan:**
   - CI involves reviewing and updating strategic plans based on lessons learned from previous initiatives.
   - It ensures that plans are regularly adapted to changing business needs and market conditions.
   - CI also plays a role in identifying and prioritizing improvement opportunities that align with the organization's strategic goals.
2. **Improve:**
   - This activity is the heart of continual improvement.
   - It involves systematically analyzing data, gathering feedback, identifying root causes of problems, and implementing solutions to improve service quality, efficiency, and effectiveness.
   - The "Improve" activity is a continuous cycle of learning and adaptation, where lessons learned are used to inform future improvements.
3. **Engage:**
   - CI is about actively seeking feedback from stakeholders throughout the service lifecycle.
   - This feedback can be used to identify areas where services can be improved and to ensure that changes are aligned with customer expectations.

- Engagement also involves building relationships with stakeholders, fostering a culture of collaboration and continuous improvement.

4. **Design and Transition:**
   - CI is applied in the design and transition of new or changed services.
   - Feedback from pilots and tests is incorporated into service designs to ensure that they meet the needs of users and stakeholders.
   - Processes are continually refined to streamline the transition of services into the live environment.

5. **Obtain/Build:**
   - In this activity, CI involves evaluating supplier performance, identifying opportunities for cost savings or quality improvements, and building internal capabilities to support service delivery.
   - Regular reviews of supplier contracts and performance can lead to improvements in service quality and cost-effectiveness.

6. **Deliver and Support:**
   - CI is applied in the day-to-day operation and support of services.
   - Incident and problem data are analyzed to identify trends and implement preventive measures.
   - Customer feedback is used to identify areas where service delivery can be enhanced.

Examples of Continual Improvement in Each SVC Activity:

- **Plan:** Reviewing and adjusting the IT strategy based on lessons learned from previous projects and changing market conditions.
- **Improve:** Implementing a new incident management tool to streamline the resolution process and reduce downtime.
- **Engage:** Conducting regular customer satisfaction surveys to gather feedback and identify improvement opportunities.
- **Design and Transition:** Incorporating feedback from a pilot group into the design of a new self-service portal before its full release.
- **Obtain/Build:** Negotiating new terms with a supplier to improve service levels and reduce costs.
- **Deliver and Support:** Analyzing incident data to identify recurring problems and implementing solutions to prevent them from happening again.

By integrating continual improvement into every aspect of the Service Value Chain, organizations can create a culture of continuous learning and adaptation, where IT services are constantly evolving to meet the changing needs of customers and stakeholders.

The Role of Measurement and Metrics in Continual Improvement

Measurement and metrics are the backbone of continual improvement in ITIL 4. They provide the objective data and insights necessary to evaluate performance, identify areas for improvement, track progress, and make informed decisions. Without measurement, continual improvement would be based on guesswork and intuition, rather than facts and evidence.

Importance of Measurement and Metrics:

1. **Assess Current Performance:** Metrics provide a snapshot of how well services and processes are performing. They allow organizations to identify areas where they are meeting or exceeding expectations, as well as areas where they are falling short. This baseline assessment is crucial for understanding the starting point and setting realistic goals for improvement.
2. **Identify Improvement Opportunities:** By analyzing performance data and trends, organizations can pinpoint bottlenecks, inefficiencies, and other areas where improvements can be made. This helps prioritize improvement efforts and focus resources where they will have the greatest impact.

3. **Track Progress Towards Goals:** Metrics allow organizations to track progress towards their improvement goals and objectives. By regularly monitoring key performance indicators (KPIs), they can determine whether their efforts are paying off and make adjustments as needed to stay on track.

4. **Evaluate the Effectiveness of Improvement Initiatives:** Metrics are essential for evaluating the effectiveness of improvement initiatives. By comparing performance before and after implementing a change, organizations can measure the impact of the change and determine whether it has achieved the desired results. This allows for data-driven decision-making and helps ensure that improvement efforts are delivering real value.

Key Metrics for Measuring Service Performance:

- **Customer Satisfaction:** This metric measures how satisfied customers are with the services they receive. It can be collected through surveys, feedback forms, or other methods. High customer satisfaction is a key indicator of service quality and can lead to increased loyalty and repeat business.

- **Incident Resolution Time:** This measures the average time it takes to resolve an incident. Faster resolution times indicate a more responsive and efficient service desk and can improve customer satisfaction.

- **Mean Time to Restore Service (MTTR):** The average time it takes to recover from a service outage or disruption. Lower MTTR indicates a more resilient and reliable service.

- **Cost per Service:** This measures the average cost of delivering a particular service. It can be used to identify opportunities for cost optimization and to compare the cost-effectiveness of different service delivery models.

- **Service Availability:** The percentage of time that a service is available to users. Higher availability indicates a more reliable service that meets user needs.

- **Employee Satisfaction:** This measures the satisfaction and engagement of IT staff. Happy and motivated employees are more likely to deliver high-quality services and contribute to continual improvement efforts.

By carefully selecting and tracking relevant metrics, organizations can gain valuable insights into the performance of their IT services, identify areas for improvement, and measure the success of their continual improvement initiatives.

Challenges and Pitfalls in Continual Improvement

Continual improvement is a journey, not a destination. Organizations that embark on this journey often encounter challenges and pitfalls that can hinder their progress and limit the effectiveness of their improvement initiatives. Recognizing and addressing these challenges is crucial for achieving sustainable success.

Common Challenges and Pitfalls:

1. **Lack of Leadership Commitment:**
   - **Challenge:** Without strong leadership commitment, continual improvement initiatives may lack direction, resources, and momentum. Employees may not see the value in improvement efforts if they don't perceive support from the top.
   - **Solution:** Secure leadership buy-in by clearly articulating the benefits of continual improvement, aligning it with strategic goals, and demonstrating the potential return on investment (ROI). Leaders should actively champion the initiative, communicate its importance, and provide the necessary resources and support.

2. **Resistance to Change:**

- Challenge: People are naturally resistant to change, especially when it disrupts established routines and familiar ways of working. Employees may fear the unknown, worry about their ability to adapt, or simply prefer the comfort of the status quo.
- Solution: Address resistance to change through clear communication, involving employees in the improvement process, providing training and support, and celebrating small wins along the way. Create a culture of openness and transparency where employees feel safe to express their concerns and ideas.

3. **Lack of Resources:**
   - Challenge: Continual improvement requires resources, such as time, budget, and personnel. Organizations may struggle to allocate these resources, especially when faced with competing priorities.
   - Solution: Prioritize improvement initiatives based on their potential impact and feasibility. Start with small, achievable projects that can demonstrate quick wins and build momentum. Optimize existing resources by automating tasks, streamlining processes, and leveraging external expertise.

4. **Poorly Defined Metrics:**
   - Challenge: Without clear and measurable metrics, it is difficult to assess the effectiveness of improvement initiatives and track progress towards goals.
   - Solution: Establish a set of relevant and meaningful metrics that align with the organization's strategic goals and objectives. These metrics should be specific, measurable, achievable, relevant, and time-bound (SMART). Regularly track and analyze the metrics to identify trends and areas for improvement.

5. **Focus on Outputs Rather Than Outcomes:**
   - Challenge: Some organizations focus on measuring outputs (e.g., the number of incidents resolved) rather than outcomes (e.g., the impact of incidents on customer satisfaction). This can lead to a narrow focus on efficiency and overlook the broader goal of delivering value.
   - Solution: Shift the focus from outputs to outcomes by defining clear outcome-based goals and measuring progress against those goals. Use customer feedback and business impact assessments to evaluate the true value of improvement initiatives.

Strategies for Overcoming Challenges:

- **Securing Leadership Buy-In:** Clearly articulate the benefits of continual improvement to senior management, highlighting its potential impact on key business metrics.
- **Communicating the Benefits:** Communicate the benefits of continual improvement to all employees, emphasizing how it can improve their work experience, enhance their skills, and contribute to the organization's success.
- **Providing Adequate Resources and Training:** Allocate sufficient resources, such as time, budget, and personnel, to support continual improvement initiatives. Provide training on improvement methodologies and tools to empower employees to participate in the process.
- **Defining Clear and Measurable Goals:** Establish clear, specific, and measurable goals for improvement initiatives. This will help to focus efforts, track progress, and evaluate success.
- **Establishing a Culture of Learning and Experimentation:** Encourage employees to experiment with new ideas, learn from their mistakes, and share their knowledge. Celebrate successes and create a safe space for learning and growth.

By proactively addressing these challenges and implementing these strategies, organizations can create a culture of continual improvement that drives innovation, efficiency, and customer satisfaction.

Fostering a Culture of Continual Improvement

Continual improvement is not merely a process to follow; it is a mindset that must be embedded within the organizational culture. It's about fostering an environment where everyone, from frontline staff to executives, actively participates in identifying and implementing improvements, embraces change, and values learning and experimentation.

The Importance of a Continual Improvement Culture:

A culture of continual improvement is essential for sustaining long-term success in IT service management. It enables organizations to:

- **Adapt to Change:** In the fast-paced digital age, organizations must be agile and adaptable to stay competitive. A continual improvement culture ensures that the organization is constantly evolving and responding to changing business needs and customer expectations.
- **Improve Service Quality:** Continual improvement is the key to enhancing the quality, reliability, and efficiency of IT services. It enables organizations to identify and address issues proactively, optimize processes, and deliver a superior customer experience.
- **Boost Employee Engagement:** A culture that values continuous learning and improvement empowers employees, giving them a sense of ownership and purpose. This leads to increased engagement, higher job satisfaction, and improved productivity.
- **Drive Innovation:** A culture of continual improvement encourages experimentation and risk-taking, fostering a spirit of innovation. It creates a safe space for employees to try new ideas and learn from their mistakes, leading to the development of new and improved services.

The Role of Leadership:

Leadership plays a pivotal role in fostering a culture of continual improvement. Leaders set the tone, create a supportive environment, and model the behaviors they expect from their teams.

Key leadership actions to promote continual improvement:

- **Communicate the Vision:** Clearly articulate the organization's commitment to continual improvement, emphasizing its importance for achieving strategic goals and delivering value to customers.
- **Lead by Example:** Actively participate in improvement initiatives, demonstrate a learning mindset, and be open to feedback.
- **Empower Employees:** Give employees the autonomy and resources to identify and implement improvements within their areas of responsibility.
- **Recognize and Reward:** Celebrate successes and acknowledge the contributions of individuals and teams who drive improvement efforts.

Tips for Fostering a Culture of Continual Improvement:

1. **Encourage Experimentation and Learning from Mistakes:** Create a safe environment where employees feel comfortable trying new ideas and learning from their mistakes. Encourage a growth mindset that sees failure as an opportunity for learning and improvement.
2. **Recognize and Reward Improvement Efforts:** Recognize and reward employees who contribute to improvement initiatives, both formally and informally. This could include bonuses, promotions, public recognition, or simply a sincere thank you.
3. **Provide Opportunities for Training and Development:** Invest in training and development programs that help employees develop the skills and knowledge they need to identify and implement improvements. This could include training on problem-solving, root cause analysis, data analysis, and process improvement methodologies.
4. **Communicate Successes and Lessons Learned:** Regularly share success stories and lessons learned from improvement initiatives with the wider organization. This helps to create a sense of momentum and reinforces the importance of continual improvement.
5. **Make Continual Improvement a Part of Everyone's Job:** Embed continual improvement into the organization's culture by making it part of everyone's job description and performance expectations.

Encourage employees to take ownership of improvement efforts and provide them with the necessary tools and support.

By fostering a culture of continual improvement, organizations can create a dynamic and adaptive environment that continuously strives for excellence. This not only benefits the organization by improving efficiency, reducing costs, and enhancing service quality, but it also creates a more engaging and rewarding work environment for employees.

Chapter Summary

In this chapter, we explored the concept of Continual Improvement, a cornerstone of the ITIL 4 framework and a fundamental aspect of the Service Value System (SVS). We emphasized that continual improvement is not merely a set of processes but a mindset, a philosophy, and an ongoing commitment to enhancing the value delivered through IT services.

Key takeaways from this chapter:

- **Continual Improvement as a Core Principle:** We discussed the importance of continual improvement in adapting to changing business needs, improving service quality, enhancing efficiency, and fostering innovation. We highlighted the shift in ITIL 4 towards a more holistic approach, encompassing all aspects of service management and involving all stakeholders.
- **The ITIL Continual Improvement Model:** We detailed the seven-step cyclical model, explaining the purpose, key activities, and outputs of each step. This model provides a structured framework for organizations to identify and implement improvements in a continuous and iterative manner.
- **Key Principles of Continual Improvement:** We discussed the seven guiding principles that underpin the continual improvement model, emphasizing how they ensure that improvement efforts are aligned with the organization's goals, values, and customer-centric approach.
- **Continual Improvement and the Service Value Chain (SVC):** We illustrated how continual improvement is integrated into each activity of the SVC, from planning and design to delivery and support. We provided examples of how CI can be applied at every stage to enhance value creation.
- **The Role of Measurement and Metrics:** We highlighted the importance of measurement and metrics in driving continual improvement. Metrics enable organizations to assess performance, identify improvement opportunities, track progress, and evaluate the effectiveness of initiatives.
- **Challenges and Pitfalls:** We acknowledged common challenges in implementing continual improvement, such as lack of leadership commitment, resistance to change, limited resources, and poorly defined metrics. We also offered strategies to overcome these obstacles, including securing leadership buy-in, fostering a culture of learning and experimentation, and utilizing relevant metrics.
- **Fostering a Culture of Continual Improvement:** We emphasized the importance of creating a culture where everyone is encouraged to contribute to continuous improvement. We discussed the role of leadership in setting the tone and creating a supportive environment, and provided practical tips for fostering this culture, such as encouraging experimentation, recognizing efforts, and providing training opportunities.

By understanding and applying the concepts discussed in this chapter, organizations can embed continual improvement into their DNA. This will enable them to adapt to change, enhance service quality, drive innovation, and ultimately deliver more value to their customers and stakeholders. Continual improvement is not just a goal; it's an ongoing journey of learning, adapting, and evolving to meet the ever-changing demands of the digital age.

Section E:
ITIL Management Practices

General Management Practices

Outline

- Introduction to General Management Practices
- Strategy Management
- Portfolio Management
- Architecture Management
- Service Financial Management
- Workforce and Talent Management
- Continual Improvement
- Measurement and Reporting
- Risk Management
- Information Security Management
- Knowledge Management
- Organizational Change Management
- Project Management
- Relationship Management
- Supplier Management
- Chapter Summary

Introduction to General Management Practices

The General Management Practices in ITIL 4 form a critical foundation for effective service management. Unlike the more IT-specific Service Management and Technical Management practices, these 14 general practices apply to the entire organization, transcending departmental boundaries and ensuring a holistic approach to managing resources, risks, and relationships.

The Role of General Management Practices in ITIL 4:

General Management Practices are not exclusive to IT departments; they are essential for any organization aiming to deliver value through services. They provide a framework for managing the broader business aspects that underpin successful service delivery. This includes:

- **Strategic Alignment:** General management practices help ensure that IT service management is not an isolated function but an integral part of the overall business strategy. This alignment ensures that IT investments and initiatives are prioritized based on their potential to contribute to the organization's strategic goals.
- **Risk Management:** These practices provide a structured approach to identifying, assessing, and mitigating risks across the organization, not just those related to IT. By addressing risks proactively, organizations can protect their assets, reputation, and ability to deliver value through services.
- **Resource Optimization:** General management practices help organizations optimize the use of their resources, including financial, human, and technological assets. This ensures that resources are allocated efficiently and effectively to support service delivery and achieve desired outcomes.

- **Relationship Management:** These practices emphasize the importance of building and maintaining strong relationships with stakeholders, both internal and external. This includes customers, employees, partners, suppliers, and other relevant parties. Strong relationships foster trust, collaboration, and a shared commitment to value creation.
- **Continual Improvement:** General management practices promote a culture of continuous learning and improvement across the organization. This encourages innovation, adaptability, and a relentless pursuit of excellence in service delivery.

Providing a Foundation for Effective Management:

The General Management Practices form a solid foundation upon which the more specialized Service Management and Technical Management practices can be built. They provide the essential framework for managing the organization as a whole, ensuring that IT service management is aligned with the broader business context and contributes to the achievement of strategic goals.

By mastering these general management practices, organizations can develop a strong operational backbone that enables them to deliver high-quality IT services efficiently and effectively, while managing risks, optimizing resources, and fostering strong relationships with stakeholders. This holistic approach to service management ultimately leads to greater customer satisfaction, increased business value, and sustained competitive advantage.

Strategy Management

Strategy management is the compass of an organization's IT service management (ITSM) approach. It provides direction and ensures that every service and initiative aligns seamlessly with the broader business goals and objectives. In essence, it bridges the gap between IT and business, transforming IT from a mere support function into a strategic enabler of success.

Purpose of Strategy Management:

The primary purpose of strategy management is to:

- **Align IT with Business:** Ensure that IT services are not developed and delivered in isolation but are carefully crafted to support and enhance the organization's overall business strategy. This alignment ensures that IT investments are focused on initiatives that deliver tangible value and contribute to achieving strategic goals.
- **Maximize Value Delivery:** By aligning IT with business objectives, strategy management ensures that resources are allocated to the most valuable initiatives. It helps organizations identify and prioritize investments in services that have the greatest potential to drive business growth, improve customer satisfaction, reduce costs, or mitigate risks.
- **Adaptability and Resilience:** In a constantly changing business environment, strategy management enables organizations to adapt their IT services to evolving needs and market conditions. It ensures that IT remains agile and responsive, capable of supporting new business initiatives and responding to emerging threats or opportunities.

Key Activities of Strategy Management:

1. **Strategic Planning:** This involves defining the organization's IT vision, mission, and strategic objectives. It includes analyzing the internal and external environment, identifying opportunities and threats, and developing a roadmap for how IT will support the organization's overall strategy.
2. **Portfolio Management:** This encompasses the management of the entire lifecycle of IT services and investments, from ideation and prioritization to development, delivery, and retirement. It involves making decisions about which services to offer, how to invest in them, and when to retire them based on their strategic value and performance.

3. **Demand Management:** This involves understanding and influencing customer demand for IT services. It includes forecasting demand, analyzing usage patterns, and adjusting service capacity to ensure that it meets customer needs and expectations.
4. **Financial Management:** This focuses on managing the financial aspects of IT services, ensuring that they are cost-effective and provide value for money. This includes budgeting, cost allocation, and pricing strategies.
5. **Risk Management:** This involves identifying, assessing, and mitigating risks associated with IT services and operations. It includes developing risk management plans, implementing security controls, and ensuring compliance with relevant regulations and standards.

Value Contribution of Strategy Management:

Strategy management ensures that IT services are not just operational necessities but strategic assets that contribute to the organization's success. It ensures that IT investments are aligned with business goals, maximizes value delivery, and enables the organization to adapt to change and remain competitive in the market.

By incorporating strategy management into their IT service management practices, organizations can transform IT from a cost center to a value center, driving innovation, growth, and long-term success.

Portfolio Management

Portfolio management in ITIL 4 is the strategic practice of overseeing all services and projects within an organization, ensuring they are aligned with business goals and deliver optimal value. It's akin to a gardener tending to a diverse collection of plants, each with different needs and growth potential. Portfolio management ensures that the right "plants" (services and projects) are nurtured, given the right resources, and contribute to a flourishing garden (the organization's overall objectives).

The Role of Portfolio Management:

Portfolio management serves as a bridge between strategy and execution. It translates the organization's strategic objectives into a portfolio of services and projects that will best achieve those objectives within the constraints of available resources, risk appetite, and market conditions. This involves:

- **Balancing Risk and Reward:** Portfolio management involves assessing the potential risks and rewards of different investments to create a balanced portfolio that maximizes value while minimizing risk.
- **Optimizing Resource Utilization:** It ensures that resources are allocated efficiently to the most promising services and projects, avoiding overspending and ensuring that investments deliver the expected returns.
- **Alignment with Strategic Goals:** It ensures that all services and projects in the portfolio contribute to the organization's strategic goals and objectives, avoiding wasted effort and ensuring that IT investments are focused on areas that drive business value.
- **Adaptability:** It enables organizations to adapt their service portfolio to changing business needs and market conditions by regularly reviewing and adjusting the portfolio based on performance, risks, and emerging opportunities.

Key Activities of Portfolio Management:

1. **Identifying and Defining Services and Projects:** This involves understanding the organization's current and future service needs, identifying potential new services or projects, and defining their scope, objectives, and requirements.
2. **Prioritizing Investments:** Evaluating and prioritizing services and projects based on their strategic alignment, potential value, risk profile, and resource requirements. This involves using various techniques such as cost-benefit analysis, scoring models, and expert judgment.

3. **Authorizing Investments:** Obtaining formal approval for services and projects that have been prioritized, ensuring that they have the necessary funding, resources, and executive support.
4. **Managing the Service Portfolio Lifecycle:** Overseeing the entire lifecycle of services and projects, from ideation and development to delivery, operation, and retirement. This involves tracking progress, managing risks, and ensuring that services and projects deliver the expected value.
5. **Optimizing Value Delivery:** Continuously evaluating the performance and value of services and projects in the portfolio. Identifying opportunities for improvement, reallocating resources as needed, and retiring services that are no longer viable or aligned with strategic goals.

Value Contribution of Portfolio Management:

Portfolio management is a critical enabler of value creation in IT service management. It helps organizations make informed decisions about their IT investments, ensuring that resources are allocated to the most valuable initiatives that align with strategic goals and deliver tangible benefits to the business. By optimizing the service portfolio, organizations can maximize the return on their IT investments and ensure that their IT services contribute to the achievement of their overall business objectives.

Architecture Management

Architecture management is the practice of designing, planning, and managing the structure of an organization's IT services and infrastructure. It serves as the blueprint that guides how technology is used to support business goals and deliver value. Effective architecture management ensures that the IT landscape is cohesive, efficient, and aligned with the organization's strategic vision.

Importance of Architecture Management in ITIL 4:

- **Holistic Design:** Architecture management takes a holistic view of the IT landscape, considering the relationships and dependencies between various components and services. This ensures that all elements work together seamlessly and efficiently to deliver value to customers.
- **Strategic Alignment:** A well-defined architecture aligns IT with business goals, ensuring that technology investments support the organization's overall strategy and contribute to its success.
- **Scalability and Flexibility:** Architecture management focuses on designing systems that can adapt to changing business needs and scale to accommodate growth. This allows organizations to respond quickly to new opportunities and challenges.
- **Reliability and Performance:** A well-architected system is more reliable and performant, as it is designed with resilience, redundancy, and performance optimization in mind.
- **Cost Efficiency:** Architecture management helps organizations make informed decisions about technology investments, optimizing costs and ensuring that resources are used effectively.

Key Activities of Architecture Management:

1. **Defining Architecture Principles:** Establishing guiding principles that outline the organization's approach to architecture design and management. These principles define the desired characteristics of the IT landscape, such as scalability, flexibility, security, and interoperability.
2. **Creating and Maintaining Architecture Models:** Developing and maintaining detailed models that represent the current and future state of the IT landscape. These models help stakeholders visualize the architecture, understand its components, and assess its alignment with business goals.
3. **Assessing and Mitigating Architectural Risks:** Identifying and evaluating risks associated with the architecture, such as technology obsolescence, security vulnerabilities, and performance bottlenecks. Developing and implementing mitigation strategies to reduce the likelihood and impact of these risks.

4. **Ensuring Compliance with Standards and Regulations:** Ensuring that the architecture complies with relevant standards and regulations, such as industry best practices, security frameworks, and data protection laws.

Value Contribution of Architecture Management:

Architecture management provides a framework for the design and development of IT services, ensuring that they are:

- **Scalable:** Capable of handling increased workloads and accommodating growth.
- **Reliable:** Resistant to failures and able to recover quickly from disruptions.
- **Performant:** Delivering fast and responsive service to users.
- **Adaptable:** Flexible enough to accommodate changing business needs and new technologies.
- **Secure:** Protected from unauthorized access, data breaches, and other security threats.
- **Cost-Effective:** Optimized to minimize costs and maximize the value of IT investments.

By investing in architecture management, organizations can create an IT landscape that is well-structured, aligned with business goals, and capable of delivering the services that customers and stakeholders need. This results in improved service quality, increased efficiency, and reduced risks, ultimately contributing to the organization's overall success.

Service Financial Management

Service Financial Management (SFM) is a crucial practice within ITIL 4, focusing on the financial aspects of IT services. Its purpose is to ensure that the organization's investment in IT services is not only cost-effective but also delivers value proportionate to the costs incurred. SFM provides the financial transparency and control needed for informed decision-making, helping organizations prioritize services, allocate resources efficiently, and ultimately, achieve their strategic objectives.

Purpose of Service Financial Management:

The primary purpose of SFM is to:

- **Understand and Control Costs:** Accurately track and manage the costs associated with IT services, including both direct costs (e.g., hardware, software, personnel) and indirect costs (e.g., overheads, administrative expenses). This understanding allows for better budget planning and cost control.
- **Optimize Value:** Ensure that IT services deliver the expected value to customers and stakeholders in relation to the costs incurred. This involves evaluating the costs and benefits of different services, prioritizing investments, and identifying opportunities for cost optimization.
- **Support Decision-Making:** Provide financial information and insights to support informed decision-making about IT investments, service offerings, and pricing strategies. This enables organizations to allocate resources effectively and prioritize initiatives that deliver the greatest return.
- **Ensure Financial Accountability:** Establish clear accountability for IT spending and ensure that IT services are financially sustainable in the long run. This involves tracking costs, analyzing variances, and reporting on financial performance to stakeholders.

Key Activities of Service Financial Management:

1. **Budgeting:** Developing and managing budgets for IT services, taking into account operational costs, capital expenses, and projected demand.
2. **Accounting:** Recording and reporting financial transactions related to IT services, ensuring accurate and transparent accounting practices.

3. **Charging:** Determining the appropriate pricing models for IT services, whether it's chargeback to internal departments, cost recovery from external customers, or value-based pricing.
4. **Cost Optimization:** Continuously identifying and implementing opportunities to reduce costs without compromising service quality. This may involve streamlining processes, automating tasks, negotiating better contracts with suppliers, or optimizing resource utilization.

Value Contribution of Service Financial Management:

SFM enables organizations to:

- **Make Informed Investment Decisions:** By understanding the costs and benefits of different IT services, organizations can make informed decisions about where to invest their resources.
- **Prioritize Value-Driven Initiatives:** SFM helps prioritize initiatives that deliver the most value to the organization, ensuring that resources are allocated to the most impactful projects.
- **Optimize IT Spending:** By identifying cost-saving opportunities and implementing efficient financial practices, organizations can reduce their IT spending and improve their bottom line.
- **Enhance Transparency and Accountability:** SFM provides transparency into IT costs and performance, ensuring accountability for IT investments and building trust with stakeholders.

By effectively managing the financial aspects of IT services, organizations can ensure that their IT investments deliver value, support business objectives, and contribute to the overall success of the organization.

Workforce and Talent Management

Workforce and Talent Management (WTM) is a vital general management practice in ITIL 4, recognizing the essential role people play in the success of IT service management (ITSM). It focuses on strategically managing and developing an organization's human resources to ensure that they have the right skills, knowledge, and experience to deliver and support high-quality IT services.

Importance of Workforce and Talent Management:

- **Skilled Workforce:** ITSM relies on skilled professionals who understand the complexities of technology, processes, and customer needs. WTM ensures that the organization has the right talent in place to design, develop, deliver, and support IT services effectively.
- **Employee Engagement and Retention:** A motivated and engaged workforce is more productive, innovative, and committed to delivering excellent service. WTM focuses on creating a positive work environment, fostering career development, and providing opportunities for growth to retain top talent.
- **Organizational Agility:** In today's dynamic business landscape, organizations need to be agile and adaptable. WTM helps build a flexible workforce that can quickly respond to changing needs, adopt new technologies, and support business transformation initiatives.
- **Cost Efficiency:** Effective WTM can reduce costs associated with recruitment, onboarding, and turnover. It also ensures that resources are utilized efficiently, with the right people in the right roles, maximizing productivity and minimizing waste.
- **Value Creation:** By ensuring a skilled, engaged, and motivated workforce, WTM directly contributes to the creation and delivery of value through IT services. It enables organizations to provide high-quality services that meet customer expectations and support business goals.

Key Activities of Workforce and Talent Management:

1. **Workforce Planning:** Identifying the organization's current and future workforce needs, considering factors such as strategic goals, technological advancements, and employee turnover.
2. **Recruitment:** Attracting and selecting qualified candidates for IT roles, utilizing various recruitment channels and assessment methods.

3. **Onboarding:** Ensuring new hires are integrated into the organization smoothly and effectively, providing them with the necessary training, resources, and support to become productive team members.
4. **Training and Development:** Providing ongoing training and development opportunities to enhance employees' skills, knowledge, and expertise. This includes technical training, soft skills development, and leadership training.
5. **Performance Management:** Setting clear expectations, providing regular feedback, and conducting performance reviews to assess employee performance and identify areas for improvement.
6. **Career Development:** Helping employees develop their careers within the organization by providing opportunities for advancement, promoting from within, and creating career paths.
7. **Succession Planning:** Identifying and developing high-potential employees to fill critical roles in the future, ensuring continuity of leadership and expertise.

Value Contribution of Workforce and Talent Management:

By implementing effective WTM practices, organizations can:

- **Attract and Retain Top Talent:** Build a highly skilled and motivated workforce that is committed to delivering excellent service.
- **Improve Service Quality:** Ensure that IT services are delivered by qualified professionals who possess the necessary skills and knowledge.
- **Enhance Efficiency:** Optimize resource utilization and streamline processes to reduce costs and improve productivity.
- **Drive Innovation:** Foster a culture of learning and experimentation, encouraging employees to contribute new ideas and improve existing practices.
- **Achieve Strategic Goals:** Ensure that IT services are aligned with the organization's strategic objectives and contribute to its overall success.

Workforce and Talent Management is a critical investment that enables organizations to build a high-performing IT team, deliver exceptional service experiences, and achieve their business goals.

Continual Improvement

Continual improvement is a fundamental principle in ITIL 4, not merely a practice but a mindset woven into the fabric of the Service Value System (SVS). It's the relentless pursuit of better ways to deliver value through IT services. By consistently seeking opportunities to enhance efficiency, effectiveness, and customer satisfaction, organizations can adapt to change, remain competitive, and foster a culture of innovation.

Continual Improvement as a Key Enabler of Value Creation:

In ITIL 4, continual improvement is seen as a catalyst for value creation. It goes beyond fixing problems; it's about continuously seeking opportunities to optimize processes, enhance service quality, and improve customer outcomes.

Continual improvement drives value creation through:

- **Customer Focus:** By regularly gathering and analyzing feedback, organizations can understand and address customer needs more effectively, ensuring that services remain relevant and valuable.
- **Efficiency Gains:** Continual improvement identifies and eliminates waste and inefficiencies in processes, resulting in faster service delivery, reduced costs, and better resource utilization.
- **Quality Enhancement:** Through ongoing analysis of performance data and incident trends, continual improvement allows organizations to proactively identify and address issues before they escalate, improving service quality and reliability.

- **Innovation:** Continual improvement fosters a culture of experimentation and learning, encouraging teams to try new approaches, embrace new technologies, and drive innovation within the organization.

Key Activities of Continual Improvement:

1. **Identifying Improvement Opportunities:** This involves proactively seeking out areas where services, processes, or practices can be enhanced. This can be done through various methods, such as analyzing performance data, conducting surveys and interviews, and observing user behavior.
2. **Prioritizing Improvement Opportunities:** Not all improvement opportunities are created equal. It's essential to prioritize them based on their potential impact, feasibility, and alignment with strategic goals. This ensures that resources are focused on initiatives that will deliver the greatest value.
3. **Planning and Implementing Improvements:** Once improvement opportunities are identified and prioritized, a detailed plan for implementation is created. This includes defining objectives, identifying resources, establishing timelines, and assigning responsibilities. The plan is then put into action, monitoring progress and adjusting as needed to ensure successful implementation.
4. **Measuring Effectiveness:** After implementing improvements, it's crucial to measure their effectiveness to ensure that they are achieving the desired outcomes. This involves tracking relevant metrics and KPIs, analyzing data, and gathering feedback from stakeholders.
5. **Incorporating Lessons Learned:** The final step in the continual improvement cycle is to incorporate lessons learned from the improvement initiative into future actions. This involves documenting successes and failures, identifying best practices, and updating processes and procedures to ensure that the organization continues to learn and evolve.

Value Contribution of Continual Improvement:

Continual improvement ensures that IT services and processes are not static but constantly evolving to meet the changing needs of the business and its customers. This dynamic approach leads to:

- **Increased Efficiency:** Streamlined processes, reduced waste, and optimized resource utilization.
- **Improved Effectiveness:** Services that are better aligned with customer needs and deliver greater value.
- **Enhanced Customer Satisfaction:** A focus on meeting customer expectations and resolving issues promptly.
- **Innovation:** A culture of learning and experimentation that fosters innovation and adaptability.

By embedding continual improvement into its DNA, an organization can create a sustainable competitive advantage, ensuring that its IT services remain relevant, valuable, and responsive to the ever-changing demands of the digital age.

Measurement and Reporting

Measurement and Reporting is a fundamental practice in ITIL 4 that provides the backbone for data-driven decision-making and continual service improvement. It involves the systematic collection, analysis, and presentation of data related to IT services and processes, transforming raw data into actionable insights that drive informed decisions and continuous improvement.

The Role of Measurement and Reporting:

Measurement and reporting play a pivotal role in IT service management by:

- **Providing Visibility:** It shines a light on the performance of IT services and processes, highlighting areas of strength and weakness. This visibility enables organizations to identify trends, patterns, and anomalies that may require attention.

- **Enabling Data-Driven Decision-Making:** Measurement and reporting provide objective data that can be used to make informed decisions about resource allocation, investment priorities, and improvement initiatives. This ensures that decisions are based on evidence rather than gut feeling or intuition.
- **Supporting Continual Improvement:** By tracking key performance indicators (KPIs) and analyzing trends over time, organizations can identify opportunities for improvement and measure the effectiveness of their improvement efforts.
- **Demonstrating Value:** Measurement and reporting can be used to quantify and communicate the value that IT services deliver to the business. This can help justify investments in IT, secure funding for future initiatives, and build credibility with stakeholders.

Key Activities of Measurement and Reporting:

1. **Defining Metrics and KPIs:** Identify the key metrics and KPIs that are most relevant to the organization's goals and objectives. These metrics should be aligned with strategic priorities, customer needs, and industry benchmarks.
2. **Collecting Data:** Gather data from various sources, such as IT service management tools, monitoring systems, surveys, and feedback channels. Ensure that the data is accurate, reliable, and relevant to the chosen metrics.
3. **Analyzing Trends:** Use statistical tools and techniques to analyze data and identify trends, patterns, and correlations. This analysis can reveal insights into the root causes of problems, the effectiveness of processes, and the impact of changes.
4. **Generating Reports:** Create clear and concise reports that summarize the findings of the analysis and present them in a format that is easy to understand and actionable. Reports should be tailored to the needs of different stakeholders, providing them with the information they need to make informed decisions.

Value Contribution of Measurement and Reporting:

- **Data-Driven Decision-Making:** Provides objective data and insights that enable IT leaders and business stakeholders to make informed decisions about IT investments, service offerings, and improvement initiatives.
- **Continual Improvement:** Enables organizations to track progress towards goals, identify areas for improvement, and measure the effectiveness of changes.
- **Demonstrating Value:** Helps communicate the value of IT services to the business by quantifying their impact on key business metrics, such as cost savings, revenue generation, and customer satisfaction.
- **Transparency and Accountability:** Promotes transparency and accountability by providing visibility into IT performance and ensuring that IT services are meeting agreed-upon targets.
- **Stakeholder Engagement:** Engages stakeholders in the improvement process by providing them with relevant data and reports that they can use to monitor progress and provide feedback.

Measurement and Reporting is a critical enabler of ITIL 4's value-driven approach. It provides the foundation for data-driven decision-making, supports continual improvement initiatives, and ensures that IT services are aligned with business goals and deliver tangible benefits to the organization.

Risk Management

Risk management is a critical general management practice in ITIL 4, focusing on the identification, assessment, evaluation, and treatment of risks that could potentially impact the organization's ability to achieve its objectives. It's a proactive approach to dealing with uncertainty, ensuring that risks are managed in a way that aligns with the organization's risk appetite and strategic goals.

Importance of Risk Management in ITIL 4:

IT services and operations are susceptible to various risks, ranging from technical failures and security breaches to natural disasters and human error. These risks can disrupt service delivery, compromise data, incur financial losses, and damage the organization's reputation. Effective risk management is essential for:

- **Protecting the Organization:** By proactively identifying and mitigating risks, organizations can safeguard their assets, reputation, and ability to deliver value through IT services.
- **Enhancing Resilience:** Risk management helps organizations build resilience by preparing them to respond effectively to unexpected events and disruptions.
- **Supporting Decision-Making:** Risk assessments provide valuable insights that inform decision-making about IT investments, service designs, and operational strategies.
- **Improving Service Quality:** By addressing risks that could impact service availability, performance, and security, risk management contributes to improved service quality and customer satisfaction.

Key Activities of Risk Management:

1. **Risk Identification:** This involves systematically identifying potential risks that could affect the organization's IT services and operations. This can be done through various methods, such as brainstorming, risk workshops, historical data analysis, and risk assessment tools.
2. **Risk Assessment:** Once risks are identified, they need to be assessed in terms of their probability of occurrence and potential impact. This involves analyzing the likelihood of the risk event happening and the potential consequences if it does occur.
3. **Risk Evaluation:** This involves evaluating the assessed risks against the organization's risk appetite and tolerance levels. Risks that exceed these thresholds require further attention and mitigation efforts.
4. **Risk Treatment:** This is the process of deciding how to address the identified risks. ITIL 4 outlines four risk treatment options:
   - **Mitigation:** Taking action to reduce the probability or impact of the risk.
   - **Transfer:** Shifting the risk to a third party, such as through insurance or outsourcing.
   - **Acceptance:** Accepting the risk if its potential impact is low or the cost of mitigation is too high.
   - **Avoidance:** Avoiding the activity or situation that creates the risk altogether.

Value Contribution of Risk Management:

By effectively managing risks, organizations can:

- **Protect Assets:** Safeguard critical IT infrastructure, data, and intellectual property from loss, damage, or unauthorized access.
- **Ensure Continuity:** Minimize the impact of disruptions and ensure that essential services can continue to be delivered even in the face of unexpected events.
- **Improve Decision-Making:** Make more informed decisions about IT investments and service designs, taking into account the associated risks.
- **Enhance Reputation:** Demonstrate a commitment to responsible and proactive risk management, building trust with customers, employees, and stakeholders.

Example: Risk Management in Change Management

The Change Management practice heavily relies on risk management principles. Before implementing any change, a risk assessment is conducted to evaluate the potential impact of the change on IT services, infrastructure, and business operations. Based on this assessment, mitigation strategies are put in place to minimize risks and ensure a smooth transition. For example, a change to a critical system might require thorough testing in a staging environment before being deployed to production, and a rollback plan might be developed in case of unexpected issues.

Risk management is not a one-time activity but an ongoing process that needs to be embedded into the organization's culture and practices. By proactively identifying, assessing, and mitigating risks, organizations can create a more resilient and adaptable IT service management system, capable of responding effectively to unexpected events and minimizing their impact on business operations.

Information Security Management

Information Security Management (ISM) is a critical general management practice in ITIL 4. It's the discipline of protecting an organization's information assets from unauthorized access, use, disclosure, disruption, modification, or destruction. In the digital age, where information is a valuable asset and cyber threats are ever-present, effective ISM is essential for maintaining the confidentiality, integrity, and availability of information, ensuring business continuity, and safeguarding the organization's reputation.

Critical Role of Information Security Management:

Information security is not just an IT issue; it's a business-wide concern. A security breach can have devastating consequences for an organization, including financial losses, reputational damage, and legal liabilities. Effective ISM helps to mitigate these risks by:

- **Protecting Confidentiality:** Ensuring that sensitive information, such as customer data, financial records, and intellectual property, is only accessible to authorized individuals and entities.
- **Ensuring Integrity:** Maintaining the accuracy, completeness, and consistency of information, preventing unauthorized modification or alteration.
- **Ensuring Availability:** Making sure that information and systems are available when needed by authorized users, minimizing downtime and disruptions.

Key Activities of Information Security Management:

1. **Developing and Implementing Security Policies:** Creating a comprehensive set of policies that define the organization's approach to information security. These policies should address areas such as access controls, data classification, incident response, and acceptable use.
2. **Conducting Risk Assessments:** Identifying and assessing potential risks to information assets, such as vulnerabilities in systems, threats from malicious actors, and natural disasters. This assessment helps to prioritize risks and allocate resources to the most critical areas.
3. **Implementing Security Controls:** Putting in place technical and organizational measures to mitigate identified risks. This may include access controls, encryption, firewalls, intrusion detection systems, antivirus software, regular backups, and employee training.
4. **Monitoring for Security Threats:** Continuously monitoring systems and networks for signs of suspicious activity or potential security breaches. This involves using tools like intrusion detection systems (IDS), security information and event management (SIEM) systems, and vulnerability scanners.
5. **Incident Response:** Having a well-defined incident response plan in place to quickly and effectively respond to security incidents. This includes procedures for identifying, containing, and eradicating threats, as well as recovering from the incident and preventing future occurrences.
6. **Security Awareness Training:** Educating employees about security risks and best practices, such as identifying phishing emails, creating strong passwords, and reporting suspicious activity.

Value Contribution of Information Security Management:

Effective information security management provides significant value to organizations:

- **Protects Sensitive Information:** Safeguards customer data, financial information, and intellectual property from unauthorized access or disclosure, maintaining customer trust and protecting the organization's reputation.

- **Ensures Business Continuity:** Minimizes the impact of security incidents and ensures that critical business operations can continue even in the event of a disruption.
- **Reduces Costs:** Helps avoid financial losses due to data breaches, downtime, and legal penalties.
- **Complies with Regulations:** Ensures compliance with relevant data protection regulations and standards, such as GDPR and HIPAA.
- **Builds Stakeholder Confidence:** Demonstrates a commitment to protecting information assets, which can boost customer confidence, employee morale, and investor trust.

By prioritizing information security management, organizations can create a more secure and resilient IT environment, safeguard their valuable assets, and maintain the trust of their stakeholders. This is essential for achieving long-term success in today's increasingly digital and interconnected world.

Knowledge Management

Knowledge Management (KM) is a critical general management practice in ITIL 4. It focuses on the systematic handling of an organization's collective knowledge – the information, insights, and expertise that reside within its people, processes, and technologies. By effectively capturing, sharing, and utilizing this knowledge, organizations can improve decision-making, streamline processes, enhance problem-solving, and foster innovation.

Importance of Knowledge Management in ITIL 4:

- **Enhanced Efficiency and Effectiveness:** By making relevant information readily available, KM empowers employees to resolve issues faster, make better decisions, and avoid reinventing the wheel. This leads to improved efficiency, reduced downtime, and better utilization of resources.
- **Improved Decision-Making:** Access to accurate and up-to-date information enables better decision-making at all levels of the organization. KM provides a centralized repository of knowledge, ensuring that everyone has access to the same information and can make decisions based on the collective wisdom of the organization.
- **Faster Problem Resolution:** KM plays a crucial role in incident and problem management. By documenting known errors, workarounds, and solutions, organizations can quickly diagnose and resolve issues, minimizing the impact on service availability and customer satisfaction.
- **Increased Collaboration and Innovation:** KM promotes knowledge sharing and collaboration between teams and individuals. This cross-pollination of ideas can spark innovation, leading to new and improved ways of delivering IT services.
- **Reduced Training Costs:** A well-maintained knowledge base can serve as a valuable training resource for new employees, reducing the need for extensive formal training and accelerating onboarding.

Key Activities of Knowledge Management:

1. **Creating and Maintaining a Knowledge Base:** This involves establishing a central repository for storing and organizing knowledge articles, documents, procedures, and other relevant information. The knowledge base should be easily searchable and accessible to all authorized users.
2. **Promoting Knowledge Sharing:** This involves encouraging employees to share their knowledge and expertise with others. This can be done through various mechanisms, such as wikis, forums, communities of practice, mentoring programs, and knowledge sharing sessions.
3. **Encouraging Collaboration:** KM fosters collaboration by providing a platform for employees to work together on knowledge creation and sharing. This can involve collaborative document editing, online discussions, and joint problem-solving sessions.
4. **Continual Improvement:** KM is an ongoing process that requires continuous review and improvement. This involves regularly updating the knowledge base, evaluating its effectiveness, and identifying opportunities to enhance knowledge capture, sharing, and reuse.

Value Contribution of Knowledge Management:

Knowledge Management provides significant value to organizations by:

- **Improving Decision-Making:** Providing access to accurate and relevant information enables better decision-making at all levels of the organization.
- **Enhancing Problem-Solving:** Facilitating faster and more effective problem resolution by providing access to known solutions and workarounds.
- **Increasing Efficiency:** Streamlining processes and reducing the need for repetitive work by making knowledge easily accessible.
- **Promoting Collaboration and Innovation:** Fostering a culture of knowledge sharing and collaboration, leading to new ideas and improved solutions.
- **Reducing Costs:** Lowering training costs and minimizing downtime by providing readily available knowledge resources.

By investing in knowledge management, organizations can unlock the hidden value of their collective knowledge and expertise, driving continuous improvement and innovation in IT service management.

Organizational Change Management

Organizational Change Management (OCM) is a critical general management practice in ITIL 4. It focuses on the people side of change, recognizing that successful change initiatives require more than just technical adjustments. OCM ensures that employees are prepared for and supportive of changes, minimizing disruptions and maximizing the benefits of change initiatives.

The Role of Organizational Change Management:

In the context of IT service management, OCM plays a vital role in facilitating the smooth and effective implementation of changes to IT services and processes. This includes:

- **Understanding and Addressing Resistance:** Change often triggers resistance due to fear of the unknown, loss of control, or perceived negative impacts. OCM helps identify and address these concerns through communication, education, and involvement of stakeholders in the change process.
- **Minimizing Disruption:** Change can be disruptive to business operations and employee productivity. OCM helps minimize these disruptions by planning the change carefully, communicating it effectively, and providing training and support to employees.
- **Maximizing Benefits:** OCM ensures that the benefits of change initiatives are realized by helping employees adopt new ways of working and ensuring that the changes are aligned with the organization's goals and objectives.
- **Creating a Change-Ready Culture:** OCM fosters a culture of adaptability and openness to change, making it easier for the organization to embrace future changes and continuously improve.

Key Activities of Organizational Change Management:

1. **Develop a Change Plan:** This involves defining the scope and objectives of the change, identifying stakeholders, assessing risks and impacts, and developing a communication and training plan.
2. **Communicate Changes Effectively:** This involves creating a communication strategy that clearly explains the reasons for the change, the benefits it will bring, and the impact it will have on employees. Communication should be timely, transparent, and tailored to different audiences.
3. **Address Resistance to Change:** This involves identifying potential sources of resistance, understanding the underlying reasons, and developing strategies to address them. This may include providing additional training, offering incentives, or addressing concerns directly.
4. **Provide Training and Support:** Offer training programs and resources to help employees learn new skills and processes. Provide ongoing support to help them adapt to the changes and overcome any challenges they may encounter.

5. **Monitor and Evaluate Progress:** Track the progress of the change initiative, measuring its impact on key metrics such as employee satisfaction, productivity, and service quality. Use feedback to make adjustments as needed and ensure that the change is achieving its desired outcomes.

Value Contribution of Organizational Change Management:

Effective OCM helps organizations:

- **Minimize Disruption:** By preparing employees for change and addressing their concerns, OCM helps to minimize disruptions to business operations and maintain productivity.
- **Maximize Benefits:** By ensuring that changes are adopted and embraced by employees, OCM helps to maximize the benefits of change initiatives and achieve desired outcomes.
- **Improve Employee Morale:** By involving employees in the change process and providing them with support, OCM can improve employee morale and engagement.
- **Enhance Adaptability:** OCM helps to create a change-ready culture, making it easier for the organization to embrace future changes and continuously improve.

By incorporating OCM into their ITSM practices, organizations can ensure that changes are implemented smoothly, effectively, and with minimal disruption. This not only benefits the organization by improving efficiency and reducing costs but also creates a more positive and supportive work environment for employees.

Project Management

Project management is an essential practice within ITIL 4, as IT projects are often the vehicles for delivering new or improved services. Effective project management ensures that these projects are executed efficiently, deliver the expected value, and align with the organization's strategic goals.

Importance of Project Management in ITIL 4:

IT projects are unique endeavors with defined start and end dates, aiming to achieve specific objectives. They can range from small-scale enhancements to large-scale transformations. Regardless of size, effective project management is crucial for:

- **Successful Delivery:** Ensuring that projects are completed on time, within budget, and meet the defined requirements.
- **Value Creation:** Project management helps ensure that IT projects deliver the intended benefits and value to the organization and its stakeholders.
- **Risk Mitigation:** Identifying and managing risks associated with projects, minimizing their impact on project outcomes.
- **Resource Optimization:** Allocating resources effectively and efficiently to ensure that projects are completed successfully.
- **Stakeholder Satisfaction:** Managing stakeholder expectations and communication to ensure that projects meet their needs and requirements.

Key Activities of Project Management:

1. **Project Planning:**
- **Defining Scope:** Clearly articulating the goals, objectives, deliverables, and constraints of the project.
- **Creating a Project Plan:** Developing a detailed plan that outlines the tasks, timelines, resources, and dependencies involved in the project.
- **Identifying Risks:** Assessing potential risks that could impact the project's success and developing mitigation strategies.

- **Establishing Communication Plan:** Defining how information will be shared among project team members, stakeholders, and other relevant parties.

2. **Project Execution:**

- **Assigning Tasks and Responsibilities:** Allocating tasks to team members based on their skills and expertise.
- **Managing Resources:** Ensuring that the project has the necessary resources, such as personnel, budget, and tools.
- **Monitoring Progress:** Tracking project progress against the plan, identifying any deviations, and taking corrective action as needed.
- **Communicating with Stakeholders:** Providing regular updates to stakeholders on project status, risks, and issues.

3. **Project Monitoring and Controlling:**

- **Tracking Performance:** Monitoring project performance against established metrics and KPIs.
- **Managing Risks:** Identifying and managing new risks that emerge during the project lifecycle.
- **Managing Issues:** Addressing any problems or obstacles that arise during the project.
- **Adjusting the Plan:** Making necessary adjustments to the project plan based on feedback and changing circumstances.

4. **Project Closure:**

- **Finalizing Deliverables:** Ensuring that all project deliverables are completed and meet quality standards.
- **Documenting Lessons Learned:** Capturing lessons learned from the project and sharing them with the organization to improve future projects.
- **Transitioning to Operations:** Handing over the project deliverables to the operations team for ongoing support and maintenance.

Value Contribution of Project Management:

Project management ensures that IT projects:

- **Deliver Value:** By focusing on outcomes and aligning with strategic goals, project management ensures that IT projects deliver the intended benefits and value to the organization.
- **Meet Deadlines and Budgets:** Effective project planning, monitoring, and control help to ensure that projects are completed on time and within budget.
- **Minimize Risks:** Proactive risk management helps to identify and mitigate potential threats to project success.
- **Improve Stakeholder Satisfaction:** Clear communication and engagement with stakeholders throughout the project lifecycle help to build trust and ensure that their needs are met.

In conclusion, project management is a vital practice in ITIL 4, enabling organizations to deliver successful IT projects that support their strategic goals and create value for their customers and stakeholders. By adhering to the principles of project management, organizations can ensure that their IT investments deliver the desired outcomes and contribute to their overall success.

Relationship Management

Relationship management is a crucial general management practice within the ITIL 4 framework. It emphasizes the significance of building and nurturing positive, collaborative relationships with all stakeholders involved in or impacted by IT services. This practice recognizes that strong relationships are essential for understanding stakeholder needs, managing expectations, and ensuring that IT services deliver value and meet the organization's strategic objectives.

The Role of Relationship Management in ITIL 4:

Relationship Management serves as the bridge between IT and its stakeholders, fostering trust, collaboration, and open communication. It encompasses a wide range of activities aimed at:

- **Understanding Stakeholder Needs:** Actively listening to stakeholders, gathering feedback, and understanding their perspectives to ensure that IT services align with their requirements and expectations.
- **Building Trust and Rapport:** Establishing trust and rapport with stakeholders through open communication, transparency, and responsiveness to their concerns. This creates a foundation for long-term, mutually beneficial relationships.
- **Managing Expectations:** Setting realistic expectations with stakeholders regarding service delivery, performance, and costs. This involves clear communication, transparent agreements, and regular updates on progress and challenges.
- **Resolving Conflicts:** Proactively addressing and resolving conflicts that may arise between IT and stakeholders. This involves active listening, empathy, negotiation, and compromise.
- **Promoting Collaboration:** Encouraging collaboration and cooperation between IT and stakeholders to achieve shared goals. This involves sharing information, working together on projects, and co-creating solutions.

Key Activities of Relationship Management:

1. **Stakeholder Identification:** Identifying all individuals and groups who have an interest in or are affected by IT services. This includes internal stakeholders (e.g., employees, managers, executives) and external stakeholders (e.g., customers, suppliers, partners, regulators).
2. **Stakeholder Engagement:** Engaging with stakeholders to understand their needs, expectations, and concerns. This can be done through various channels, such as surveys, interviews, focus groups, workshops, and regular communication.
3. **Communication:** Establishing and maintaining open communication channels with stakeholders, providing timely and accurate information about IT services, changes, and issues. This includes proactive communication, as well as responding to inquiries and concerns in a timely and professional manner.
4. **Relationship Building:** Developing strong and lasting relationships with stakeholders based on trust, mutual respect, and collaboration. This involves building rapport, understanding their motivations, and working together to achieve common goals.

Value Contribution of Relationship Management:

Effective relationship management ensures that IT services are aligned with stakeholder needs and expectations, leading to:

- **Increased Customer Satisfaction:** When customers feel heard and valued, they are more likely to be satisfied with the services they receive, leading to increased loyalty and repeat business.
- **Improved Stakeholder Engagement:** Engaged stakeholders are more likely to support IT initiatives, provide valuable feedback, and collaborate on improvement efforts.
- **Enhanced Decision-Making:** By understanding stakeholder perspectives, IT leaders can make better decisions about service design, development, and delivery.
- **Reduced Conflicts:** Proactive relationship management helps to prevent conflicts and misunderstandings, leading to a more harmonious and productive work environment.
- **Increased Value Creation:** By aligning IT services with stakeholder needs and expectations, relationship management ensures that IT investments deliver the desired benefits and contribute to the organization's overall success.

Relationship management is not just about keeping stakeholders happy; it's about building strategic partnerships that drive innovation, improve service quality, and create long-term value for the organization. By investing in relationship management, organizations can establish a strong foundation for successful IT service management and achieve their strategic objectives.

Supplier Management

Supplier management is a pivotal practice in ITIL 4, focusing on the effective management of relationships with external vendors who provide IT services and components. It recognizes that in today's interconnected business landscape, organizations often rely on external suppliers for various aspects of their IT operations. This practice ensures that these relationships are managed strategically, maximizing value and minimizing risk for the organization.

Importance of Supplier Management in ITIL 4:

- **Quality Assurance:** Supplier management ensures that the goods and services provided by suppliers meet the organization's quality standards and requirements. This is critical for maintaining the reliability, performance, and security of IT services.
- **Cost Optimization:** By effectively managing supplier relationships, organizations can negotiate favorable terms and conditions, optimize costs, and get the best value for their investment.
- **Risk Mitigation:** Relying on external suppliers can introduce risks, such as service disruptions, data breaches, or financial instability. Supplier management helps to identify and mitigate these risks, protecting the organization from potential harm.
- **Collaboration and Innovation:** Strong relationships with suppliers can foster collaboration and innovation, leading to the development of new and improved services and solutions.
- **Business Continuity:** Effective supplier management ensures the availability and continuity of critical IT services, even in the face of disruptions or supplier-related issues.

Key Activities of Supplier Management:

1. **Supplier Selection:**
- **Needs Assessment:** Clearly defining the organization's needs and requirements for the goods or services being sought.
- **Market Research:** Identifying potential suppliers that can meet those needs and requirements.
- **Supplier Evaluation:** Evaluating potential suppliers based on various criteria, such as their capabilities, experience, financial stability, reputation, and cultural fit.
- **Selection:** Choosing the most suitable supplier based on a comprehensive evaluation of their offerings and capabilities.
2. **Contract Negotiation:**
- **Defining Terms and Conditions:** Clearly defining the terms and conditions of the agreement, including scope of work, service levels, pricing, payment terms, and termination clauses.
- **Negotiation:** Negotiating with the supplier to reach mutually agreeable terms that meet the organization's needs and budget.
- **Contract Drafting and Review:** Drafting a formal contract that reflects the agreed-upon terms and ensuring that it is legally sound and protects the organization's interests.
3. **Performance Monitoring:**
- **Establishing Performance Metrics:** Defining key performance indicators (KPIs) to measure supplier performance, such as service availability, response times, quality metrics, and cost-effectiveness.
- **Regular Monitoring:** Tracking supplier performance against the established KPIs on an ongoing basis.
- **Performance Reviews:** Conducting regular performance reviews with suppliers to discuss performance results, address any issues, and identify opportunities for improvement.
4. **Relationship Management:**
- **Building Trust and Collaboration:** Fostering a positive and collaborative relationship with the supplier based on trust, mutual respect, and open communication.
- **Regular Communication:** Maintaining regular communication with the supplier to discuss performance, address concerns, and explore opportunities for collaboration.
- **Joint Planning:** Involving the supplier in planning and decision-making processes to ensure their perspectives are considered and their needs are met.
- **Continuous Improvement:** Working collaboratively with the supplier to identify and implement opportunities for improvement in the delivery of goods or services.

Value Contribution of Supplier Management:

Effective supplier management ensures that suppliers deliver high-quality services and components that meet the organization's needs, on time and within budget. It also helps to:

- **Reduce Costs:** By negotiating favorable terms and optimizing supplier relationships, organizations can reduce their IT spending.
- **Improve Service Quality:** By monitoring supplier performance and addressing issues proactively, organizations can ensure that their IT services remain reliable and meet customer expectations.
- **Mitigate Risks:** By identifying and mitigating supplier-related risks, organizations can protect themselves from disruptions, data breaches, and other potential threats.
- **Foster Innovation:** By collaborating with suppliers, organizations can tap into their expertise and knowledge to drive innovation and improve their IT services.

In conclusion, supplier management is a critical practice for any organization that relies on external vendors for IT services and components. By effectively managing these relationships, organizations can ensure that they are getting the best value for their investment, minimizing risks, and maximizing the benefits of their IT partnerships.

Chapter Summary

In this chapter, we explored the 14 General Management Practices within the ITIL 4 framework. These practices, drawn from general business management domains, are essential for effective and holistic service management within any organization, not just those focused on IT.

Here are the key takeaways:

- **The Foundation of ITSM:** We emphasized how General Management Practices provide the bedrock for successful IT service management. They ensure alignment with strategic goals, manage risks, optimize resources, nurture relationships, and promote a culture of continuous improvement.
- **Key Practices:** We delved into each of the 14 practices, providing concise descriptions of their purpose, key activities, and the value they contribute to the overall Service Value System.
- **Beyond IT:** We highlighted that these practices are not limited to IT departments but are applicable across the entire organization, fostering a holistic and integrated approach to service management.
- **Strategic Alignment and Value Delivery:** We underscored how practices like Strategy Management and Portfolio Management ensure that IT services directly support broader business objectives and maximize value delivery.
- **Risk Management and Security:** We discussed the critical role of Risk Management and Information Security Management in identifying, assessing, and mitigating risks to protect the organization and ensure the continuity of services.
- **People and Processes:** We explored how Workforce and Talent Management focuses on developing a skilled and engaged workforce, while practices like Continual Improvement and Organizational Change Management ensure adaptability and ongoing optimization of processes.
- **Financial Oversight and Knowledge Sharing:** We covered the importance of Service Financial Management for understanding the costs and value of IT services, as well as Knowledge Management for capturing, sharing, and reusing knowledge within the organization.
- **Project and Relationship Management:** We touched on the significance of Project Management for successful project delivery and Relationship Management for building strong relationships with both internal and external stakeholders.

By mastering these General Management Practices, organizations can create a solid foundation for IT service management success. The concepts covered in this chapter will not only enhance your understanding of ITIL 4 but also equip you with practical tools and strategies for effective service management in your organization.

In the following chapters, we'll delve deeper into the Service Management and Technical Management practices, providing a comprehensive guide to the complete spectrum of ITIL 4 practices and their application in real-world scenarios.

Service Management Practices

Outline

- Introduction to Service Management Practices
- Service Desk
- Incident Management
- Problem Management
- Service Request Management
- Service Level Management
- IT Asset Management
- Monitoring and Event Management
- Service Configuration Management
- Change Enablement
- Release Management
- Service Validation and Testing
- Business Analysis
- Service Catalog Management
- Service Design
- Availability Management
- Capacity and Performance Management
- Service Continuity Management
- Chapter Summary

Introduction to Service Management Practices

Service Management Practices are the cornerstone of ITIL 4, providing the framework and guidance for the effective design, delivery, and support of IT services. These practices shift the focus from rigid processes to a more flexible and holistic approach, encompassing the people, processes, information, and technology involved in managing services throughout their lifecycle.

The Central Role of Service Management Practices:

Service management practices are at the heart of the ITIL 4 Service Value System (SVS). They are the key enablers that help organizations create, deliver, and maintain value for their customers and stakeholders through IT services.

- **End-to-End Management:** These practices cover the entire service lifecycle, from strategy and design to transition, operation, and continual improvement. This ensures that services are managed consistently and effectively throughout their existence.
- **Customer and Business Focus:** The practices are designed to meet the needs of both customers and the business. They help organizations understand customer requirements, design services that deliver value, and ensure that services align with strategic business objectives.
- **Flexibility and Adaptability:** Unlike the prescriptive processes of previous ITIL versions, the practices in ITIL 4 are more flexible and adaptable. They can be tailored to fit the specific needs and context of each organization, allowing for greater agility and responsiveness to changing circumstances.

Importance of Service Management Practices:

Service management practices are essential for ensuring the quality, efficiency, and customer satisfaction of IT services. They provide a structured approach to managing services, enabling organizations to:

- **Improve Service Quality:** By implementing best practices for service design, delivery, and support, organizations can improve the quality and reliability of their services, reducing downtime, errors, and customer complaints.
- **Increase Efficiency:** By streamlining processes, automating tasks, and optimizing resource utilization, service management practices can improve the efficiency of IT operations, leading to cost savings and faster service delivery.
- **Enhance Customer Satisfaction:** By focusing on customer needs and expectations, service management practices can help organizations deliver services that meet or exceed customer requirements, leading to increased satisfaction and loyalty.
- **Align IT with the Business:** By ensuring that IT services align with strategic business objectives, service management practices can help IT become a strategic enabler of business success.

Overview of the 17 ITIL Service Management Practices:

1. **Service Desk:** The single point of contact for users seeking help or information.
2. **Incident Management:** Restores normal service operation as quickly as possible.
3. **Problem Management:** Reduces the likelihood and impact of incidents by identifying and managing their root causes.
4. **Service Request Management:** Handles requests for standard services, such as password resets or access provisioning.
5. **Service Level Management:** Ensures that services are delivered according to agreed-upon service levels.
6. **IT Asset Management:** Manages the lifecycle of IT assets, from acquisition to disposal.
7. **Monitoring and Event Management:** Observes services and service components, and records and reports selected changes of state identified as events.
8. **Service Configuration Management:** Maintains information about configuration items (CIs) and their relationships.
9. **Change Enablement:** Maximizes the number of successful IT changes by ensuring they are properly assessed, authorized, and managed.
10. **Release Management:** Plans, schedules, and controls the movement of releases to test and live environments.
11. **Service Validation and Testing:** Ensures that services meet agreed-upon requirements and expectations.
12. **Business Analysis:** Investigates business situations and identifies options for improvement.
13. **Service Catalog Management:** Provides and maintains a single source of information about all services offered.
14. **Service Design:** Designs new or changed services.
15. **Availability Management:** Ensures that IT services are available when and where they are needed.
16. **Capacity and Performance Management:** Ensures that IT services can meet current and future demand.
17. **Service Continuity Management:** Enables the organization to continue delivering essential services during and after a disruptive incident.

By understanding and applying these service management practices, organizations can create a comprehensive and effective IT service management system that delivers value, improves efficiency, and enhances customer satisfaction.

Service Desk

- **Purpose:** The Service Desk serves as the single point of contact (SPOC) between the service provider (IT organization) and its users (customers, employees, or partners). Its primary goal is to capture and fulfill service requests and resolve incidents in a timely and efficient manner, ensuring customer satisfaction and minimizing disruption to business operations.

- **Key Activities:**
  - **Incident Logging and Categorization:** Receiving, recording, and classifying user-reported incidents based on their type, impact, and urgency.
  - **Request Fulfillment:** Processing and fulfilling service requests, such as password resets, access provisioning, or software installations.
  - **First-Level Support and Troubleshooting:** Providing initial support to users, attempting to resolve simple incidents, and escalating complex issues to specialized teams.
  - **Communication and Coordination:** Keeping users informed about the status of their incidents and requests, coordinating with other IT teams to resolve issues, and managing communication throughout the incident lifecycle.
  - **Knowledge Management:** Utilizing and contributing to a knowledge base to quickly identify solutions, workarounds, and known errors, and to improve the efficiency of incident and request resolution.
  - **Self-Service Support:** Providing access to self-service portals, knowledge bases, and chatbots to empower users to resolve simple issues on their own.
- **Value Contribution:**
  - **Improved User Experience:** Provides a single point of contact for users, ensuring that their issues and requests are addressed promptly and professionally.
  - **Faster Incident Resolution:** Enables faster incident resolution by providing initial support, triaging issues, and escalating them to the appropriate teams.
  - **Increased Efficiency:** Streamlines the handling of incidents and requests, reducing manual effort and improving productivity.
  - **Cost Reduction:** By empowering users with self-service options and automating routine tasks, the service desk can help reduce the overall cost of IT support.
  - **Data Collection and Analysis:** The service desk collects valuable data on incidents, requests, and user feedback, which can be used to identify trends, prioritize improvement initiatives, and measure the effectiveness of IT services.
- **Examples:**
  - A user calls the service desk to report a computer crash.
  - An employee submits a request for a new software license through the self-service portal.
  - A service desk agent uses the knowledge base to resolve a common printer issue.
- **Challenges:**
  - **High Call Volumes:** Managing high call volumes during peak times can be challenging. Implementing self-service options and automation can help alleviate this.
  - **Skill Shortages:** Finding and retaining skilled service desk agents can be difficult. Providing ongoing training and development opportunities can help attract and retain talent.
  - **Communication Barriers:** Effectively communicating technical information to non-technical users can be a challenge. Training agents on communication skills and providing user-friendly knowledge articles can help overcome this.
- **Relationships with Other Practices:**
  - **Incident Management:** The service desk is the primary interface for incident reporting and communication.
  - **Service Request Management:** The service desk is responsible for fulfilling service requests.
  - **Problem Management:** The service desk escalates incidents to the problem management team for root cause analysis.
  - **Knowledge Management:** The service desk uses and contributes to the knowledge base.
- **Metrics:**
  - Average Speed to Answer (ASA)
  - First Call Resolution (FCR) rate
  - Customer Satisfaction (CSAT)
  - Number of incidents and service requests logged
  - Cost per ticket
  - Abandonment rate

Incident Management

- **Purpose:** The core purpose of Incident Management is to minimize the negative impact of incidents on business operations by restoring normal service operation as quickly as possible. This is done while ensuring that service quality is maintained or restored to agreed-upon levels.
- **Key Activities:**
  - **Identification and Logging:** This involves detecting and recording an incident. This can be done through various channels like user reports, automated alerts, or system monitoring tools. The logging process includes capturing essential details such as the nature of the incident, its impact, and the time it was reported.
  - **Categorization and Prioritization:** Incidents are classified based on their type, urgency, and impact. This helps prioritize which incidents need immediate attention and which can be addressed later.
  - **Initial Diagnosis:** A preliminary assessment is performed to understand the nature of the incident and determine if it can be resolved quickly.
  - **Escalation:** If the incident cannot be resolved at the initial stage, it is escalated to a team or individual with the necessary expertise and authority.
  - **Investigation and Diagnosis:** The escalated team conducts a thorough investigation to diagnose the root cause of the incident.
  - **Resolution and Recovery:** Once the root cause is identified, the appropriate solution or workaround is implemented to restore the service.
  - **Closure:** The incident is closed after confirming that the service has been restored and the user is satisfied.
  - **Documentation and Communication:** Throughout the incident lifecycle, proper documentation and communication with relevant stakeholders (users, IT teams, management) are essential.
- **Value Contribution:**
  - **Minimizes Business Impact:** By quickly restoring service operation, incident management reduces the negative impact of disruptions on business operations, productivity, revenue, and customer satisfaction.
  - **Enhances Customer Satisfaction:** Swift resolution of incidents demonstrates a commitment to customer service and helps maintain customer trust and loyalty.
  - **Improves Service Quality:** The data and insights gathered during incident management can be used to identify underlying problems and improve the overall quality and reliability of services.
  - **Supports Continual Improvement:** Incident analysis helps identify trends and patterns, which can then be used to implement preventive measures and drive continuous improvement.
- **Examples:**
  - A server outage causing a critical application to become unavailable.
  - A network failure disrupting internet connectivity for users.
  - A security breach exposing sensitive customer data.
- **Challenges:**
  - **High Incident Volume:** Managing a large number of incidents can be overwhelming. Prioritization and efficient workflows are key to addressing this challenge.
  - **Lack of Information:** Sometimes, limited information may be available about the incident, making diagnosis and resolution difficult.
  - **Communication Gaps:** Poor communication between IT teams and users can lead to delays and frustration.
- **Relationships with Other Practices:**
  - **Problem Management:** Incident management identifies potential problems, triggering problem management activities.

- **Change Enablement:** Changes can often cause incidents, and incident management helps assess the impact of changes.
- **Knowledge Management:** A knowledge base helps service desk agents resolve incidents quickly and efficiently.
- **Metrics:**
  - Mean Time to Restore Service (MTTR)
  - Mean Time Between Failures (MTBF)
  - Number of incidents per period
  - Percentage of incidents resolved within SLAs
  - Customer satisfaction with incident resolution

Problem Management

- **Purpose:** The core purpose of Problem Management is to reduce the likelihood and impact of incidents by identifying and managing the root causes of incidents. It goes beyond just fixing the immediate issue and aims to prevent similar incidents from happening again.
- **Key Activities:**
  - **Problem Identification:** Recognizing that a problem exists, usually triggered by one or more incidents with similar symptoms or root causes.
  - **Problem Logging and Categorization:** Documenting the problem details, categorizing it based on type and impact, and assigning it a priority.
  - **Problem Investigation and Diagnosis:** Performing a detailed analysis of the problem, often involving technical specialists, to determine its underlying cause(s). This might include reviewing incident records, error logs, and system data.
  - **Workaround Implementation (if applicable):** If a permanent solution is not immediately available, a temporary workaround is implemented to reduce the impact on users and services.
  - **Root Cause Analysis (RCA):** A thorough investigation to identify the fundamental cause of the problem, not just the symptoms.
  - **Solution Development and Implementation:** Developing and implementing a permanent solution to address the root cause and prevent future incidents.
  - **Problem Closure:** Closing the problem record after verifying that the solution has been implemented and is effective.
- **Value Contribution:**
  - **Reduced Incident Volume and Impact:** By addressing the root causes of incidents, Problem Management decreases the frequency and severity of disruptions, improving service availability and stability.
  - **Improved Service Quality:** Eliminating underlying problems leads to more reliable and robust services, enhancing overall user satisfaction.
  - **Cost Savings:** Preventing recurring incidents can significantly reduce the costs associated with reactive support, such as overtime pay, customer compensation, and lost productivity.
  - **Proactive Approach:** Problem Management promotes a proactive approach to IT service management, shifting the focus from reacting to incidents to preventing them altogether.
- **Examples:**
  - A series of application crashes is traced back to a faulty software update.
  - Network outages are found to be caused by an incorrectly configured router.
  - A spike in help desk calls is attributed to a lack of user training on a new system.
- **Challenges:**
  - **Complexity:** Identifying root causes can be complex and time-consuming, especially in large and interconnected IT environments.
  - **Resource Constraints:** Problem management often requires specialized skills and resources that may not be readily available.

- ○ **Lack of Information:** Sometimes, there may be limited information available to diagnose the root cause, requiring additional investigation and analysis.
- **Relationships with Other Practices:**
  - ○ **Incident Management:** Problem management is triggered by incidents and works closely with incident management to identify and resolve underlying problems.
  - ○ **Change Enablement:** Changes are a common cause of incidents and problems. Problem management ensures that changes are assessed for potential risks and that any resulting problems are addressed.
  - ○ **Knowledge Management:** Problem management contributes to the knowledge base by documenting known errors and workarounds, helping to prevent similar incidents in the future.
- **Metrics:**
  - ○ Number of problems identified and resolved
  - ○ Mean Time to Resolve (MTTR) problems
  - ○ Percentage of problems resolved within target timeframes
  - ○ Number of incidents linked to known problems
  - ○ Cost savings resulting from problem resolution
  - ○ Reduction in incident volumes due to problem management

Service Request Management

- **Purpose:** The purpose of Service Request Management is to support the agreed quality of a service by handling all pre-defined, user-initiated service requests in an effective and user-friendly manner. It aims to ensure that requests for standard services are fulfilled promptly, efficiently, and according to agreed service level targets.
- **Key Activities:**
  - ○ **Request Logging and Categorization:** Receiving, recording, and classifying service requests based on their type and urgency. This typically involves the use of a service catalog where users can select the required service and provide relevant information.
  - ○ **Request Prioritization and Approval:** Assessing the priority of service requests and obtaining necessary approvals based on predefined criteria. This may involve checking service level agreements (SLAs) and obtaining authorization from relevant managers or stakeholders.
  - ○ **Request Fulfillment:** Fulfilling service requests according to agreed procedures and within defined timeframes. This can involve providing information, granting access, delivering goods, or performing routine tasks.
  - ○ **Request Closure:** Closing the service request after confirming that it has been fulfilled and the user is satisfied.
  - ○ **Communication:** Keeping the user informed about the status of their request throughout the fulfillment process, providing updates and responding to queries.
  - ○ **Continual Improvement:** Regularly reviewing the service request management process, gathering feedback from users, and identifying opportunities for improvement.
- **Value Contribution:**
  - ○ **Enhanced User Experience:** Provides a streamlined and user-friendly process for requesting standard services, making it easier for users to access the services they need.
  - ○ **Improved Efficiency:** Automates routine tasks and standardizes procedures, leading to faster and more efficient fulfillment of service requests.
  - ○ **Increased Productivity:** Enables users to focus on their core tasks by quickly and easily obtaining the services they need to do their jobs.
  - ○ **Cost Reduction:** Minimizes the cost of service delivery by automating tasks and reducing the need for manual intervention.
  - ○ **Data Collection:** Provides valuable data on service demand and usage patterns, which can be used for capacity planning, service improvement, and cost optimization.

- **Examples:**
    - A new employee requests access to various software applications and systems.
    - A user requests a password reset.
    - A customer requests information about a product or service.
    - A manager requests a new laptop for their team.
- **Challenges:**
    - **Lack of Standardization:** Inconsistent or poorly defined processes can lead to delays and errors in service request fulfillment.
    - **Communication Gaps:** Poor communication between users and the service desk can lead to misunderstandings and delays.
    - **Complex Approvals:** Cumbersome approval processes can slow down service delivery and frustrate users.
- **Relationships with Other Practices:**
    - **Service Catalog Management:** The service catalog provides a list of available services and their associated request forms.
    - **Service Level Management:** SLAs define the expected service levels for request fulfillment.
    - **Knowledge Management:** A knowledge base can be used to provide information and support for service requests.
    - **Incident Management:** Some service requests may be reclassified as incidents if they involve a disruption to service.
- **Metrics:**
    - Number of service requests received and fulfilled.
    - Percentage of service requests fulfilled within SLAs.
    - Average time to fulfill service requests.
    - Customer satisfaction with the service request process.
    - Cost per service request.

Service Level Management (SLM)

- **Purpose:** The purpose of Service Level Management is to set clear and achievable agreements about the performance of IT services and ensure that they are delivered according to those agreements. It aims to align IT service performance with the needs of the business and its customers, maximizing the value delivered and fostering trust in IT.
- **Key Activities:**
    - **Defining Service Levels:** Working with customers and stakeholders to determine and document the expected levels of service, including availability, reliability, performance, and responsiveness. This often involves creating Service Level Agreements (SLAs), Operational Level Agreements (OLAs), and Underpinning Contracts (UCs).
    - **Negotiating SLAs:** Engaging in negotiations with customers and stakeholders to reach a mutually agreeable set of service levels that balance business needs with technical feasibility and cost considerations.
    - **Monitoring and Reporting:** Continuously monitoring the performance of IT services against agreed-upon SLAs, collecting and analyzing performance data, and generating reports on service levels and compliance.
    - **Reviewing and Improving SLAs:** Regularly reviewing SLAs with customers and stakeholders to ensure they remain relevant and aligned with changing business needs. Identifying areas for improvement and adjusting service levels as needed.
- **Value Contribution:**
    - **Manages Expectations:** SLM helps set clear expectations with customers and stakeholders about the level of service they can expect, avoiding misunderstandings and disappointment.
    - **Ensures Accountability:** SLAs hold IT service providers accountable for delivering services that meet agreed-upon standards, fostering trust and confidence.

- o **Drives Continual Improvement:** By monitoring and reviewing service performance, SLM identifies areas where services can be improved, leading to enhanced efficiency, effectiveness, and customer satisfaction.
  - o **Supports Decision-Making:** SLM provides data and insights that inform decision-making about IT investments, service offerings, and resource allocation.
- **Examples:**
  - o An IT department establishing an SLA with the HR department that guarantees 99.9% uptime for the payroll system.
  - o A cloud provider agreeing to a specific response time for customer support requests.
  - o A software vendor providing a warranty for the performance and reliability of their product.
- **Challenges:**
  - o **Unrealistic Expectations:** Customers and stakeholders may have unrealistic expectations about service levels that are not feasible or cost-effective to achieve.
  - o **Lack of Communication:** Poor communication between IT and stakeholders can lead to misunderstandings about service levels and expectations.
  - o **Insufficient Data:** Without accurate and reliable performance data, it can be difficult to monitor service levels and identify improvement opportunities.
- **Relationships with Other Practices:**
  - o **Service Design:** SLM provides input into the design of new services, ensuring that they are designed to meet agreed-upon service levels.
  - o **Incident Management:** SLM monitors incident volumes and resolution times to assess the impact of incidents on service levels.
  - o **Problem Management:** SLM identifies trends in incidents and problems that may indicate a need for service improvement.
  - o **Supplier Management:** SLM may be involved in negotiating and managing SLAs with external suppliers.
- **Metrics:**
  - o Percentage of SLAs met
  - o Average response time for incidents and service requests
  - o Customer satisfaction with service levels
  - o Number of service level breaches
  - o Cost of service level breaches
  - o Trends in service performance over time

IT Asset Management

- **Purpose:** The purpose of IT Asset Management (ITAM) is to plan and manage the full lifecycle of all IT assets, both hardware and software. This includes strategic decision-making about asset acquisition, deployment, utilization, maintenance, and disposal. The goal is to optimize the value and cost-effectiveness of IT assets while mitigating risks and ensuring compliance with regulatory requirements.
- **Key Activities:**
  - o **Asset Identification and Discovery:** Identifying and documenting all IT assets within the organization, including hardware, software, licenses, contracts, and other relevant information. This often involves using automated discovery tools to scan the IT environment.
  - o **Asset Tracking and Inventory Management:** Maintaining an accurate and up-to-date inventory of all IT assets, including their location, ownership, status, and configuration.
  - o **Asset Lifecycle Management:** Managing IT assets throughout their lifecycle, from procurement and deployment to maintenance, upgrades, and eventual disposal.
  - o **Software License Management:** Tracking and managing software licenses to ensure compliance with licensing agreements and avoid overspending or underutilization.

- Financial Management: Tracking the financial aspects of IT assets, such as purchase costs, depreciation, and maintenance expenses. This information can be used for budgeting, cost allocation, and investment decision-making.
  - Optimization: Analyzing asset utilization data to identify underutilized assets and optimize their use. This can involve reallocating assets, consolidating resources, or implementing virtualization technologies.
- Value Contribution:
  - Cost Optimization: ITAM helps organizations optimize their IT spending by ensuring that assets are used effectively, eliminating unnecessary purchases, and avoiding overspending on software licenses.
  - Risk Mitigation: By tracking and managing IT assets, organizations can reduce the risk of unauthorized use, software license non-compliance, and data breaches.
  - Improved Decision-Making: ITAM provides accurate and timely information about IT assets, enabling informed decision-making about asset acquisition, deployment, and retirement.
  - Enhanced Efficiency: Automating asset management tasks can streamline processes and reduce manual effort, improving the efficiency of IT operations.
- Examples:
  - Tracking the location and status of laptops across a distributed workforce.
  - Managing software licenses to ensure compliance and avoid over-licensing or under-licensing.
  - Identifying underutilized servers and consolidating them to reduce hardware costs.
  - Implementing a software asset management (SAM) tool to automate license tracking and compliance.
- Challenges:
  - Data Accuracy: Maintaining accurate and up-to-date asset data can be challenging, especially in large and complex IT environments.
  - Lack of Visibility: Gaining visibility into the location and usage of IT assets can be difficult, especially for assets that are mobile or distributed across multiple locations.
  - Complex Licensing Models: Software licensing can be complex and confusing, making it difficult to track compliance and optimize spending.
  - Resistance to Change: Employees may resist ITAM initiatives if they perceive them as intrusive or restrictive.
- Relationships with Other Practices:
  - Service Request Management: ITAM supports the fulfillment of service requests by ensuring that the necessary assets are available.
  - Incident Management: ITAM provides information about the configuration and status of assets, which can help with incident diagnosis and resolution.
  - Problem Management: ITAM data can be used to identify trends and patterns in asset failures, helping to pinpoint root causes of problems.
  - Change Enablement: ITAM helps assess the impact of changes on IT assets and ensure that changes are properly authorized and documented.
- Metrics:
  - Number of assets under management
  - Percentage of assets accurately tracked and inventoried
  - Software license compliance rate
  - Cost savings achieved through asset optimization
  - Return on investment (ROI) for IT asset management initiatives

Monitoring and Event Management

- Purpose: The purpose of Monitoring and Event Management is to systematically observe services and service components (configuration items), and record and report selected changes of state identified as events. The ultimate goal is to detect and respond to events promptly, facilitating early identification of potential problems or incidents, and maintaining service availability and performance.

- **Key Activities:**
  - **Establish Monitoring Requirements:** Define what needs to be monitored, including services, infrastructure components, applications, and events. This involves identifying critical metrics and thresholds for triggering alerts.
  - **Implement Monitoring Tools:** Select and deploy appropriate monitoring tools and technologies, such as network monitoring systems, application performance management (APM) tools, and log analysis software.
  - **Event Detection and Correlation:** Collect data from various sources, detect significant events based on predefined rules and thresholds, and correlate events to identify patterns and trends.
  - **Alerting and Notification:** Generate alerts and notifications for critical events, ensuring that responsible teams are notified promptly so they can take action.
  - **Event Analysis and Reporting:** Analyze event data to identify root causes of problems, trends, and areas for improvement. Generate reports to provide insights into service health and performance.
- **Value Contribution:**
  - **Early Detection of Incidents and Problems:** By detecting events that could lead to incidents or service degradation, Monitoring and Event Management enables proactive problem-solving and preventive maintenance, reducing downtime and minimizing the impact on users.
  - **Improved Service Availability and Performance:** Continuously monitoring service components and identifying potential issues allows organizations to take corrective actions promptly, ensuring high availability and optimal performance of IT services.
  - **Enhanced Visibility and Transparency:** Monitoring and event data provide valuable insights into the health and performance of IT services, allowing for better decision-making and increased transparency with stakeholders.
  - **Cost Reduction:** By preventing incidents and proactively addressing potential problems, organizations can reduce the costs associated with reactive support and downtime.
- **Examples:**
  - A monitoring system detects a high CPU utilization on a server, triggering an alert before it leads to a service outage.
  - An event correlation tool identifies a pattern of recurring errors in a specific application, leading to the discovery of a software bug that needs to be fixed.
  - Network monitoring detects a failed network link, allowing the network team to reroute traffic and minimize the impact on users.
- **Challenges:**
  - **Alert Fatigue:** Too many alerts can overwhelm IT teams and make it difficult to prioritize critical issues. It's important to establish clear escalation procedures and filter out irrelevant or low-priority alerts.
  - **Data Overload:** The sheer volume of event data can be overwhelming. Organizations need to implement effective data analysis tools and techniques to extract meaningful insights.
  - **Tool Integration:** Integrating data from different monitoring tools can be challenging, requiring careful planning and implementation.
- **Relationships with Other Practices:**
  - **Incident Management:** Monitoring and Event Management is often the first step in the incident management process, providing the initial detection of potential incidents.
  - **Problem Management:** Event data can be used to identify recurring problems and their root causes.
  - **Availability Management:** Monitoring and Event Management provides data on service availability, helping to measure and improve service uptime.

- **Capacity and Performance Management:** Monitoring and Event Management provides data on service performance and resource utilization, helping to optimize capacity and ensure that services can meet demand.
- **Metrics:**
  - Number of events detected and correlated
  - Percentage of events that result in incidents
  - Mean time to detect (MTTD) events
  - Mean time to resolve (MTTR) incidents triggered by events
  - Number of false positive and false negative alerts
  - Availability and performance metrics of monitored services

Service Configuration Management (SCM)

- **Purpose:** The purpose of Service Configuration Management is to ensure that accurate and reliable information about the configuration of services, and the configuration items (CIs) that support them, is available when and where it is needed. This includes information on how CIs are configured and the relationships between them. It helps maintain an accurate picture of the IT environment, enabling effective decision-making, change management, and incident resolution.
- **Key Activities:**
  - **Configuration Identification:** Identifying and defining CIs that are relevant to service management. This includes hardware, software, documentation, processes, and any other components that contribute to service delivery.
  - **Configuration Recording:** Documenting the details of each CI, including its attributes, relationships, and dependencies.
  - **Status Accounting:** Tracking and reporting on the status of CIs, including their current state, location, and ownership.
  - **Verification and Audit:** Regularly verifying the accuracy of configuration data and conducting audits to ensure compliance with configuration standards.
  - **Configuration Management System (CMS):** Establishing and maintaining a CMS to store and manage configuration information. This may involve using a Configuration Management Database (CMDB) to store CI data and relationships.
- **Value Contribution:**
  - **Improved Decision-Making:** Accurate configuration information enables informed decision-making about changes, incidents, and problems.
  - **Efficient Change Management:** Understanding the impact of changes on CIs helps to assess risks and plan changes effectively.
  - **Faster Incident and Problem Resolution:** Knowing the configuration of affected services enables faster diagnosis and resolution of incidents and identification of root causes of problems.
  - **Optimized Resource Utilization:** Understanding the relationships between CIs can help to optimize resource allocation and utilization.
  - **Compliance:** SCM helps ensure that IT systems and services are configured in accordance with regulatory requirements and industry standards.
- **Examples:**
  - A CMDB that stores information about all servers, applications, and network devices in an organization's IT environment.
  - A change manager using a CMS to assess the impact of a proposed change on dependent services.
  - A service desk agent using a knowledge base linked to a CMS to quickly identify the configuration of a user's device when troubleshooting an incident.
  - An IT auditor using a CMS to verify that systems are configured according to security standards.
- **Challenges:**

- - ○ **Data Accuracy:** Maintaining accurate and up-to-date configuration data can be challenging due to the dynamic nature of IT environments. Automated discovery tools and regular audits can help address this.
    - ○ **Complexity:** Managing complex configurations and relationships between CIs can be difficult, especially in large organizations. Adopting a structured approach and using visualization tools can help manage complexity.
    - ○ **Resistance to Change:** Employees may resist updating configuration information, viewing it as an additional burden. Communicating the benefits of SCM and providing user-friendly tools can help overcome this resistance.
- **Relationships with Other Practices:**
    - ○ **IT Asset Management:** ITAM provides information about the physical and financial aspects of assets, which is used by SCM to track and manage CIs.
    - ○ **Change Enablement:** SCM provides information about CIs, which is used by change management to assess the impact of changes.
    - ○ **Incident Management:** SCM provides information about CIs, which is used by incident management to diagnose and resolve incidents.
    - ○ **Problem Management:** SCM provides information about CIs, which is used by problem management to identify and resolve root causes of problems.
- **Metrics:**
    - ○ Percentage of CIs under configuration control
    - ○ Accuracy of configuration data
    - ○ Number of unauthorized changes detected
    - ○ Time taken to resolve configuration-related incidents
    - ○ Customer satisfaction with configuration management services

Change Enablement

- **Purpose:** The purpose of Change Enablement is to maximize the number of successful IT changes by ensuring that risks are properly assessed, authorized, and managed. It aims to minimize the negative impact of changes on services while enabling beneficial changes to be implemented quickly and efficiently. This practice ensures that changes align with organizational objectives and are implemented in a controlled and coordinated manner.
- **Key Activities:**
    - ○ **Change Evaluation:** Assessing the potential impact, benefits, and risks of proposed changes. This includes identifying potential conflicts, dependencies, and resource requirements.
    - ○ **Change Prioritization:** Prioritizing changes based on urgency, impact, and risk. This ensures that critical changes are implemented first, while lower-priority changes are scheduled appropriately.
    - ○ **Change Planning:** Developing detailed plans for implementing changes, including timelines, resources, roles, and responsibilities.
    - ○ **Change Approval:** Obtaining authorization for changes from relevant stakeholders, such as Change Advisory Board (CAB) or management.
    - ○ **Change Implementation:** Coordinating and executing the change according to the approved plan, following established procedures and protocols.
    - ○ **Change Review and Closure:** Evaluating the success of the change, documenting lessons learned, and closing the change record.
- **Value Contribution:**
    - ○ **Reduced Risk:** By assessing and mitigating risks, Change Enablement minimizes the negative impact of changes on services, reducing the likelihood of disruptions, outages, or security breaches.
    - ○ **Improved Service Quality:** Controlled changes help maintain the stability and reliability of IT services, ensuring they meet agreed-upon service levels.

- ○ **Faster Time to Market:** Streamlined change processes enable faster implementation of beneficial changes, allowing organizations to adapt quickly to changing business needs and market conditions.
  - ○ **Enhanced Collaboration:** Change Enablement fosters collaboration between IT teams, business stakeholders, and other parties involved in the change process, ensuring everyone is aligned and informed.
- **Examples:**
  - ○ Implementing a new software patch to address a security vulnerability.
  - ○ Upgrading a server operating system to improve performance.
  - ○ Changing the configuration of a network device.
  - ○ Implementing a new business process that requires IT system changes.
- **Challenges:**
  - ○ **Resistance to Change:** Employees may resist changes due to fear of disruption or lack of understanding. Effective communication and stakeholder engagement are key to addressing this challenge.
  - ○ **Inadequate Planning:** Poorly planned changes can lead to delays, errors, and unforeseen consequences. Thorough planning and risk assessment are crucial for successful change implementation.
  - ○ **Lack of Visibility:** Lack of visibility into the change process can lead to confusion and miscommunication. Using change management tools and dashboards can provide transparency and improve coordination.
- **Relationships with Other Practices:**
  - ○ **Service Configuration Management (SCM):** Change Enablement relies on accurate configuration data from SCM to assess the impact of changes.
  - ○ **Release Management:** Change Enablement works closely with Release Management to ensure that changes are properly packaged, tested, and deployed.
  - ○ **Incident Management:** Change Enablement helps to prevent incidents caused by changes, and works with Incident Management to investigate and resolve incidents that do occur.
  - ○ **Problem Management:** Change Enablement can help to identify and address problems that may arise from changes.
- **Metrics:**
  - ○ Number of successful changes
  - ○ Percentage of changes implemented on time and within budget
  - ○ Number of incidents caused by changes
  - ○ Mean time to implement (MTTI) changes
  - ○ Change success rate
  - ○ Backlog of changes

Release Management

- **Purpose:** The purpose of Release Management is to ensure that new or changed services and features are released into production environments in a controlled and coordinated way. It focuses on planning, scheduling, testing, deploying, and validating releases to minimize risks and disruptions to ongoing operations. The ultimate goal is to deliver new functionalities or improvements to users smoothly and efficiently, without compromising the stability and availability of existing services.
- **Key Activities:**
  - ○ **Release Planning:** This involves defining the scope and objectives of a release, identifying the required resources, creating a release schedule, and developing a detailed plan for building, testing, and deploying the release.
  - ○ **Release Build and Configuration:** This involves building the release package, configuring the necessary environments (e.g., development, testing, staging, production), and ensuring that all components are properly integrated.

- ○ **Release Testing:** Rigorous testing is performed to ensure that the release meets quality standards, functions correctly, and does not introduce any new issues or vulnerabilities. Different types of testing may be conducted, such as functional testing, performance testing, security testing, and user acceptance testing (UAT).
- ○ **Release Deployment:** This involves the actual deployment of the release package into the production environment. The deployment process should be carefully planned and executed to minimize downtime and disruption to users.
- ○ **Early Life Support (ELS):** Providing support and troubleshooting for the release during its initial period in production to address any unexpected issues or problems that may arise.
- ● **Value Contribution:**
  - ○ **Minimizes Risk and Disruption:** Release Management ensures that releases are thoroughly tested and validated before deployment, reducing the risk of errors, failures, and disruptions to services.
  - ○ **Accelerates Time to Market:** Streamlined release processes enable faster delivery of new or changed services, allowing organizations to respond quickly to market demands and competitive pressures.
  - ○ **Improves Quality and Reliability:** Rigorous testing and validation processes ensure that released services meet quality standards and perform reliably.
  - ○ **Enhances Customer Satisfaction:** By delivering new functionalities and improvements smoothly and efficiently, Release Management contributes to a positive customer experience.
  - ○ **Supports Continual Improvement:** The lessons learned from each release are documented and used to improve future release processes, fostering a culture of continuous improvement.
- ● **Examples:**
  - ○ **Software Release:** Deploying a new version of a software application with enhanced features or bug fixes.
  - ○ **Infrastructure Upgrade:** Rolling out a new server or network infrastructure to improve performance or capacity.
  - ○ **Security Patch Deployment:** Applying security patches to protect systems and data from vulnerabilities.
- ● **Challenges:**
  - ○ **Coordination:** Coordinating multiple teams and stakeholders involved in the release process can be challenging.
  - ○ **Testing:** Ensuring adequate testing coverage and quality can be difficult, especially for complex releases.
  - ○ **Environment Management:** Managing different environments (e.g., development, testing, staging, production) and ensuring consistency can be a challenge.
  - ○ **Rollback and Recovery:** Having a robust rollback plan in case of failed deployments is crucial but can be complex to execute.
- ● **Relationships with Other Practices:**
  - ○ **Change Enablement:** Release Management is often triggered by a change request and works closely with Change Enablement to ensure that changes are properly assessed and authorized before deployment.
  - ○ **Service Validation and Testing:** Release Management relies on Service Validation and Testing to ensure that releases meet quality standards and functional requirements.
  - ○ **Deployment Management:** Release Management collaborates with Deployment Management to plan and execute the deployment of releases into the production environment.
  - ○ **Service Desk:** Release Management communicates with the Service Desk to ensure that they are aware of upcoming releases and can provide support to users during the transition.
- ● **Metrics:**
  - ○ Number of successful releases
  - ○ Percentage of releases completed on time and within budget

- Number of incidents caused by releases
- Mean time to restore service (MTTR) for release-related incidents
- User satisfaction with releases

Service Validation and Testing

- **Purpose:** The purpose of Service Validation and Testing (SV&T) is to ensure that new or changed IT services meet the agreed-upon requirements and quality standards before they are released into the live environment. This practice aims to confirm that services are fit for purpose and fit for use, minimizing the risk of service disruptions, errors, or performance issues once deployed.
- **Key Activities:**
  - **Test Planning:** Defining the scope, objectives, and approach for testing, identifying test cases, and creating test schedules and resource plans.
  - **Test Environment Setup:** Preparing and configuring test environments that accurately replicate the production environment, including data, configurations, and dependencies.
  - **Test Design:** Developing test cases that cover all functional and non-functional requirements, including performance, security, usability, and compatibility.
  - **Test Execution:** Executing test cases in the test environment, documenting results, and identifying any defects or issues.
  - **Defect Management:** Tracking, prioritizing, and resolving defects identified during testing.
  - **Test Reporting:** Generating test reports that summarize the results of testing, including the number of test cases executed, pass/fail rates, and any outstanding issues.
  - **User Acceptance Testing (UAT):** Involving users in testing to confirm that the service meets their needs and expectations.
- **Value Contribution:**
  - **Reduced Risk of Service Disruptions:** By thoroughly testing services before deployment, SV&T helps identify and address issues early, reducing the risk of service disruptions, errors, and performance issues in the live environment.
  - **Improved Service Quality:** SV&T ensures that services meet agreed-upon quality standards and requirements, leading to increased customer satisfaction and trust.
  - **Faster Time to Market:** Effective SV&T can accelerate the release of new or changed services by identifying and resolving issues early in the development cycle.
  - **Cost Savings:** Preventing production issues through rigorous testing can save significant costs associated with fixing problems in the live environment.
- **Examples:**
  - **Functional Testing:** Testing whether a new software application performs the functions it was designed to do correctly.
  - **Performance Testing:** Testing how a service performs under different load conditions to ensure it can handle the expected demand.
  - **Security Testing:** Testing a service to identify vulnerabilities that could be exploited by attackers.
  - **Usability Testing:** Testing a service with representative users to ensure that it is intuitive and easy to use.
- **Challenges:**
  - **Test Environment Management:** Maintaining accurate and up-to-date test environments that mirror production can be difficult.
  - **Test Data Management:** Creating and managing realistic test data can be time-consuming and challenging.
  - **Time Constraints:** Balancing the need for thorough testing with the pressure to release new services quickly.
- **Relationships with Other Practices:**
  - **Service Design:** SV&T provides feedback to Service Design on the testability of new or changed services.

- o **Change Enablement:** SV&T ensures that changes are tested and validated before implementation.
    - o **Release Management:** SV&T provides assurance that releases are ready for deployment into production.
    - o **Incident Management:** SV&T helps prevent incidents by identifying and fixing defects before they cause service disruptions.
    - o **Problem Management:** SV&T helps identify potential problems by analyzing test results and patterns of defects.
- **Metrics:**
    - o Number of test cases executed
    - o Pass/fail rates for test cases
    - o Number of defects identified and resolved
    - o Time taken to execute test cases
    - o Cost of testing
    - o Customer satisfaction with the service after deployment

Business Analysis

- **Purpose:** The purpose of Business Analysis is to investigate business situations, identify and evaluate options for improvement, and propose solutions that enable the organization to achieve its desired business outcomes. It acts as a bridge between business needs and IT solutions, ensuring that IT services align with strategic goals and deliver value to customers and stakeholders.
- **Key Activities:**
    - o **Stakeholder Analysis:** Identifying and engaging with stakeholders who have an interest in the outcome of the analysis. Understanding their needs, expectations, and concerns.
    - o **Requirements Elicitation:** Gathering, analyzing, and documenting requirements for new or changed services. This involves using techniques like interviews, workshops, surveys, and document analysis.
    - o **Solution Evaluation:** Assessing the feasibility, viability, and desirability of different solution options based on technical, financial, and organizational constraints.
    - o **Business Case Development:** Developing a business case that outlines the costs, benefits, risks, and impact of the proposed solution. This provides a justification for investment and helps secure approval for implementation.
- **Value Contribution:**
    - o **Alignment with Business Goals:** Business Analysis ensures that IT services are designed and delivered in a way that supports the organization's strategic goals and objectives.
    - o **Customer Focus:** By understanding and prioritizing customer needs, Business Analysis helps to ensure that services are designed to meet or exceed customer expectations.
    - o **Informed Decision-Making:** By providing a comprehensive analysis of options and their potential impact, Business Analysis enables informed decision-making about IT investments.
    - o **Risk Management:** Business Analysis helps identify and assess potential risks associated with different solutions, allowing for proactive risk mitigation.
    - o **Value Optimization:** By focusing on the desired outcomes of the business, Business Analysis helps ensure that IT services deliver maximum value to customers and stakeholders.
- **Examples:**
    - o Analyzing the impact of a new customer relationship management (CRM) system on sales and marketing processes.
    - o Assessing the feasibility of implementing a new self-service portal for IT support.
    - o Developing a business case for a cloud migration project.
    - o Gathering requirements for a new mobile application that will streamline field service operations.
- **Challenges:**

- ○ **Stakeholder Management:** Managing diverse and sometimes conflicting stakeholder expectations can be challenging.
  - ○ **Requirements Elicitation:** Gathering complete and accurate requirements can be difficult, especially when dealing with complex or ambiguous business needs.
  - ○ **Solution Evaluation:** Assessing the feasibility and viability of different options can be complex and involve trade-offs between different criteria.
  - ○ **Business Case Development:** Creating a compelling business case that clearly articulates the value proposition of the proposed solution can be challenging.
- **Relationships with Other Practices:**
  - ○ **Strategy Management:** Business Analysis aligns with the organization's overall strategy and objectives.
  - ○ **Service Design:** Business Analysis provides the requirements that inform service design.
  - ○ **Project Management:** Business Analysis contributes to the project planning and execution phases.
  - ○ **Relationship Management:** Business Analysis involves engaging with stakeholders to understand their needs and expectations.
- **Metrics:**
  - ○ Number of business requirements identified and documented.
  - ○ Percentage of projects with a clearly defined business case.
  - ○ Stakeholder satisfaction with the business analysis process.
  - ○ Time taken to complete business analysis activities.
  - ○ Success rate of projects based on business analysis recommendations.

Service Catalog Management

- **Purpose:** The purpose of Service Catalog Management is to provide and maintain a single source of consistent information on all operational services (and those being prepared to be run operationally) and to ensure that it is available to those authorized to access it. It is designed to ensure accurate, up-to-date, and readily available information about all the services that an organization offers, enabling customers and stakeholders to make informed decisions about their service needs.
- **Key Activities:**
  - ○ **Defining and Designing the Service Catalog:** Determining the structure, format, and content of the service catalog, including service descriptions, options, pricing, and terms of use.
  - ○ **Populating the Service Catalog:** Adding new services to the catalog, updating existing service information, and removing retired services.
  - ○ **Managing Service Catalog Data:** Ensuring that the information in the service catalog is accurate, complete, and up-to-date. This includes managing service relationships, dependencies, and versions.
  - ○ **Service Catalog Publication and Access Control:** Publishing the service catalog in a format that is easily accessible to authorized users, such as a web portal or mobile app. Implementing access controls to ensure that only authorized users can view or request services.
  - ○ **Service Catalog Review and Improvement:** Regularly reviewing the service catalog to ensure its accuracy, relevance, and usability. Gathering feedback from users and stakeholders and making improvements as needed.
- **Value Contribution:**
  - ○ **Improved Transparency and Communication:** The service catalog provides a clear and transparent view of the services available to customers and stakeholders, improving communication and understanding.

- ○ **Enhanced Customer Experience:** A well-organized and user-friendly service catalog makes it easier for customers to find and request the services they need, improving their overall experience.
  - ○ **Increased Efficiency:** The service catalog can streamline the service request process by providing a standardized way for users to request services, reducing the need for manual intervention and back-and-forth communication.
  - ○ **Better Decision-Making:** By providing detailed information about services, their costs, and their performance, the service catalog enables customers and stakeholders to make informed decisions about their service needs.
- **Examples:**
  - ○ A company's IT department publishes a service catalog on its intranet, listing all available IT services, such as software installation, hardware repair, and network access.
  - ○ A cloud provider offers a service catalog that describes its various cloud computing services, such as virtual machines, storage, and databases, along with their pricing and service level agreements (SLAs).
  - ○ A university's IT department maintains a service catalog that lists services for students, faculty, and staff, such as email, Wi-Fi access, and software downloads.
- **Challenges:**
  - ○ **Keeping the Catalog Up-to-Date:** As IT services evolve, it can be challenging to keep the service catalog current and accurate. Automated tools and regular reviews can help address this.
  - ○ **Ensuring Data Accuracy:** Inaccurate or incomplete service catalog data can lead to user confusion and frustration. Establishing clear data management processes and utilizing data validation tools can improve data quality.
  - ○ **Balancing Detail and Simplicity:** Providing enough detail to be informative while keeping the catalog simple and user-friendly can be a challenge. User testing and feedback can help find the right balance.
- **Relationships with Other Practices:**
  - ○ **Service Portfolio Management:** Service Catalog Management is a key component of Service Portfolio Management, which oversees the entire portfolio of services.
  - ○ **Service Request Management:** The service catalog is used to initiate service requests.
  - ○ **Service Level Management:** SLAs for services are often published in the service catalog.
  - ○ **Knowledge Management:** The service catalog can be linked to a knowledge base to provide additional information and support for services.
- **Metrics:**
  - ○ Accuracy of service catalog data
  - ○ User satisfaction with the service catalog
  - ○ Number of service requests initiated through the service catalog
  - ○ Percentage of services with up-to-date information in the catalog
  - ○ Time taken to update service catalog information

Service Design

- **Purpose:** The purpose of Service Design is to create new services or design significant changes to existing services. It encompasses the activities required to conceptualize, develop, and prepare IT services for transition into the live environment. The primary goal is to ensure that services are designed with a focus on meeting customer and stakeholder needs, aligning with the organization's strategic objectives, and achieving the desired outcomes in a cost-effective and efficient manner.
- **Key Activities:**
  - ○ **Defining Service Requirements:** Understanding and documenting the functional and non-functional requirements of the service, including performance, reliability, availability, security, and usability. This involves collaborating with stakeholders to gather their input and expectations.

- o **Service Modeling:** Creating conceptual and technical models of the service, including its components, architecture, processes, and interactions with other services and systems. This helps visualize the service and identify potential issues or dependencies.
- o **Service Level Agreement (SLA) Design:** Developing SLAs that define the expected level of service, performance metrics, and responsibilities of both the service provider and the customer.
- o **Service Design Package (SDP):** Creating a comprehensive document that captures all the design details, including requirements, architecture, processes, SLAs, and any other relevant information.
- o **Risk Assessment:** Identifying and assessing potential risks associated with the service design and implementing appropriate mitigation strategies.
- o **Prototyping and Testing:** Creating prototypes or pilot versions of the service to test functionality, usability, and performance before full deployment.
- o **Design Review and Approval:** Reviewing the service design with stakeholders, incorporating feedback, and obtaining approval before proceeding to the transition phase.
- **Value Contribution:**
  - o **Customer Focus:** Service Design ensures that services are designed with the customer at the forefront, focusing on their needs, expectations, and desired outcomes.
  - o **Value Co-creation:** By involving stakeholders in the design process, Service Design fosters collaboration and ensures that the final service design meets the needs of all parties involved.
  - o **Risk Mitigation:** By identifying and addressing potential risks early in the service lifecycle, Service Design minimizes the likelihood of problems arising during service delivery.
  - o **Efficiency and Effectiveness:** A well-designed service is more likely to be efficient, effective, and easy to manage, leading to reduced costs and improved performance.
- **Examples:**
  - o Designing a new self-service portal for employees to access IT support.
  - o Redesigning an existing incident management process to improve response times and resolution rates.
  - o Developing a new mobile application for customers to access banking services.
- **Challenges:**
  - o **Balancing Requirements:** Balancing the often conflicting requirements of different stakeholders can be challenging.
  - o **Managing Complexity:** Designing complex services that integrate with multiple systems and technologies can be a challenge.
  - o **Ensuring Usability:** Creating services that are intuitive and easy to use for all users can be difficult.
  - o **Keeping Up with Technology:** Staying current with the latest technologies and trends in service design can be demanding.
- **Relationships with Other Practices:**
  - o **Service Strategy:** Service Design is informed by the service strategy, which defines the overall direction and objectives for service management.
  - o **Service Transition:** Service Design provides the blueprint for service transition, ensuring that new or changed services are implemented smoothly and effectively.
  - o **Service Operation:** Service Design considers the operational requirements of services, ensuring that they can be supported and maintained efficiently.
  - o **Continual Improvement:** Service Design incorporates lessons learned from previous service implementations to continuously improve the design process.
- **Metrics:**
  - o Customer satisfaction with the service design
  - o Number of design errors or defects identified
  - o Time taken to complete the design process
  - o Cost of service design
  - o Number of service design changes required after implementation

Availability Management

- **Purpose:** The purpose of Availability Management is to ensure that IT services deliver the agreed levels of availability to meet the needs of customers and users. It focuses on minimizing downtime, preventing disruptions, and ensuring that services can be accessed and used when required. Availability management also plays a crucial role in maintaining business continuity and reducing the impact of service interruptions.
- **Key Activities:**
  - **Availability Planning:** Defining availability requirements for IT services based on business needs and customer expectations. This includes setting targets for uptime, downtime, and recovery time objectives (RTOs).
  - **Availability Design:** Designing IT services and infrastructure with availability in mind. This involves implementing redundancy, failover mechanisms, and other measures to ensure that services can continue operating even if components fail.
  - **Availability Monitoring:** Continuously monitoring the availability and performance of IT services to detect potential issues before they impact users. This includes collecting data on uptime, downtime, response times, and error rates.
  - **Availability Analysis and Reporting:** Analyzing availability data to identify trends, patterns, and root causes of availability issues. This information is used to generate reports for stakeholders and inform improvement initiatives.
  - **Availability Improvement:** Implementing corrective and preventive actions to improve service availability based on analysis and feedback. This may involve addressing root causes of problems, upgrading infrastructure, or implementing new technologies.
- **Value Contribution:**
  - **Increased Uptime:** Availability Management helps ensure that IT services are available when needed, minimizing downtime and maximizing productivity.
  - **Improved Reliability:** By preventing and mitigating disruptions, Availability Management increases the reliability of IT services, building customer trust and confidence.
  - **Enhanced Business Continuity:** Availability Management supports business continuity by ensuring that critical services can be recovered quickly in the event of an outage or disruption.
  - **Cost Reduction:** By preventing downtime and service disruptions, Availability Management can significantly reduce the costs associated with lost productivity, customer dissatisfaction, and regulatory penalties.
- **Examples:**
  - Ensuring that a company's e-commerce website is available 24/7 to process customer orders.
  - Designing a backup and disaster recovery plan for a critical business application to ensure it can be recovered quickly in the event of a failure.
  - Monitoring the uptime of a network infrastructure and proactively addressing any issues that could lead to outages.
- **Challenges:**
  - **Complexity:** IT environments can be complex, making it difficult to identify and address all potential causes of downtime.
  - **Cost:** Implementing redundancy and other availability measures can be expensive.
  - **Unpredictability:** Some events, such as natural disasters or cyberattacks, can be difficult to predict and prevent.
  - **Balancing Availability and Performance:** Increasing availability can sometimes lead to trade-offs with performance, requiring careful optimization to achieve the right balance.
- **Relationships with Other Practices:**
  - **Service Level Management:** Availability Management works closely with SLM to define and monitor availability targets.

- Incident Management: Availability Management helps to prevent incidents by identifying and addressing potential problems.
- Problem Management: Availability Management collaborates with Problem Management to investigate and resolve the root causes of availability issues.
- Change Enablement: Availability Management assesses the impact of changes on service availability.
- Capacity and Performance Management: Availability Management works with Capacity and Performance Management to ensure that services have enough capacity to meet demand and perform optimally.
- Metrics:
  - Uptime Percentage
  - Downtime Duration
  - Mean Time to Repair (MTTR)
  - Mean Time Between Failures (MTBF)
  - Availability Service Level Agreement (SLA) compliance
  - Number of availability-related incidents

Capacity and Performance Management

- Purpose: The purpose of Capacity and Performance Management is to ensure that IT services can meet current and future demand in a cost-effective and timely manner. This involves balancing the performance of services against the cost of providing them, with the ultimate goal of delivering an optimal user experience.
- Key Activities:
  - Capacity Planning: Forecasting future demand for IT services and determining the resources (e.g., hardware, software, network bandwidth, personnel) required to meet that demand. This involves analyzing historical data, understanding usage patterns, and considering business growth projections.
  - Performance Monitoring: Continuously monitoring the performance of IT services and infrastructure components to identify bottlenecks, trends, and anomalies. This may involve using monitoring tools to collect data on response times, throughput, resource utilization, and error rates.
  - Performance Analysis: Analyzing performance data to identify root causes of performance issues, such as inefficient code, inadequate resources, or misconfigurations. This analysis helps inform decisions about capacity adjustments, tuning, or upgrades.
  - Capacity and Performance Tuning: Adjusting system configurations, optimizing software code, and reallocating resources to improve performance and address bottlenecks.
  - Reporting: Regularly reporting on capacity and performance metrics to stakeholders, providing insights into service health and identifying areas for improvement.
- Value Contribution:
  - Optimal User Experience: Capacity and Performance Management ensures that IT services have sufficient capacity to meet demand, resulting in fast response times, minimal delays, and a positive user experience.
  - Cost Optimization: By balancing performance with cost, Capacity and Performance Management helps organizations avoid overprovisioning of resources and optimize their IT spending.
  - Improved Reliability: Proactive capacity planning and performance monitoring help to identify potential issues before they impact service availability, leading to more reliable and resilient IT services.
  - Data-Driven Decision Making: Capacity and Performance Management provides data and insights that inform decisions about capacity upgrades, technology investments, and service optimization.

- o **Business Alignment:** By ensuring that IT services can meet the demands of the business, Capacity and Performance Management contributes to the overall success of the organization.
- **Examples:**
  - o A cloud provider analyzing usage patterns to predict future demand for its virtual machines and storage services.
  - o A web hosting company monitoring website performance to identify bottlenecks and optimize server configurations.
  - o A software development team conducting performance testing to ensure that a new application can handle the expected load.
  - o An IT department creating a capacity plan to determine the resources needed to support a new business initiative.
- **Challenges:**
  - o **Predicting Future Demand:** Accurately forecasting future demand can be challenging due to uncertainties in business growth and changing user behavior.
  - o **Complexity:** IT environments can be complex, with numerous interconnected components, making it difficult to identify and address performance bottlenecks.
  - o **Cost of Capacity:** Adding capacity can be expensive, and organizations need to balance the cost of providing adequate capacity with the risk of performance degradation.
  - o **Monitoring Overhead:** Continuously monitoring IT services and infrastructure can consume significant resources and introduce overhead.
- **Relationships with Other Practices:**
  - o **Availability Management:** Capacity and Performance Management work together to ensure that services are available and performing optimally.
  - o **Incident Management:** Performance issues can trigger incidents, and incident data can be used to identify potential performance bottlenecks.
  - o **Problem Management:** Capacity and Performance Management helps to identify and address underlying problems that contribute to performance issues.
  - o **Change Enablement:** Capacity and Performance Management assesses the impact of changes on service performance.
  - o **Supplier Management:** Capacity and Performance Management may be involved in negotiating and managing performance-related SLAs with external suppliers.
- **Metrics:**
  - o Response time
  - o Throughput
  - o Utilization
  - o Error rates
  - o Apdex score (Application Performance Index)
  - o Transaction success rate
  - o Resource utilization (CPU, memory, disk, network)
  - o User satisfaction with performance

Service Continuity Management

- **Purpose:** The purpose of Service Continuity Management (SCM) is to ensure that the availability and performance of services are maintained at sufficient levels in case of a significant disruption. It aims to minimize the impact of incidents and disasters on business operations, allowing the organization to recover quickly and continue delivering critical services to customers and stakeholders.
- **Key Activities:**
  - o **Business Impact Analysis (BIA):** Identifying critical business processes and the impact of their disruption on the organization. This involves assessing the financial, operational, and reputational consequences of potential disruptions.

- Risk Assessment and Management: Evaluating the risks that could disrupt service delivery, such as natural disasters, cyberattacks, or supplier failures. This includes analyzing the likelihood and impact of each risk and developing mitigation strategies.
- Service Continuity Strategy Development: Creating strategies for maintaining or restoring services in the event of a disruption. This includes identifying alternative workarounds, backup systems, and recovery procedures.
- Continuity Plan Development: Developing detailed plans that outline the steps to be taken to recover from a disruption. These plans should include roles and responsibilities, communication procedures, and recovery timelines.
- Testing and Exercising: Regularly testing and exercising continuity plans to ensure their effectiveness and identify areas for improvement. This can involve tabletop exercises, simulations, or full-scale tests.
- Maintenance and Review: Keeping continuity plans up-to-date and aligned with changing business needs and IT environments. Regularly reviewing and revising plans based on lessons learned from testing and actual disruptions.

- **Value Contribution:**
  - Reduced Business Impact: SCM minimizes the financial, operational, and reputational impact of disruptions, ensuring that critical services can be maintained or restored quickly.
  - Enhanced Resilience: By preparing for and responding effectively to disruptions, SCM enhances the organization's resilience and ability to cope with unexpected events.
  - Improved Customer and Stakeholder Confidence: Demonstrating a commitment to service continuity can build trust and confidence among customers and stakeholders.
  - Regulatory Compliance: SCM helps organizations comply with regulatory requirements related to business continuity and disaster recovery.

- **Examples:**
  - A bank developing a continuity plan to ensure that customers can access their accounts and make transactions in the event of a data center outage.
  - A healthcare provider implementing backup power and redundant systems for their electronic health record (EHR) system to ensure patient care is not disrupted.
  - A manufacturing company establishing alternate supply chain routes and procedures to mitigate the risk of disruptions due to natural disasters or supplier failures.

- **Challenges:**
  - Underestimation of Risk: Organizations may underestimate the likelihood or impact of potential disruptions, leading to inadequate continuity plans.
  - Lack of Testing and Maintenance: Continuity plans that are not regularly tested and updated may not be effective when needed.
  - Resource Constraints: Implementing comprehensive continuity measures can be costly and resource-intensive.
  - Coordination: Coordinating service continuity efforts across multiple departments and stakeholders can be challenging.

- **Relationships with Other Practices:**
  - Risk Management: SCM relies on risk management to identify and assess potential risks to service continuity.
  - Availability Management: SCM works closely with Availability Management to ensure that service availability targets are met even during disruptions.
  - Supplier Management: SCM may involve establishing continuity arrangements with suppliers to ensure that critical services can be maintained in the event of supplier-related issues.
  - Incident Management: SCM provides guidance on how to respond to incidents that could lead to a disruption.
  - Information Security Management: SCM considers security risks and integrates security controls into continuity plans.

- **Metrics:**
  - Recovery Time Objective (RTO)

- o Recovery Point Objective (RPO)
- o Number of successful tests and exercises
- o Cost of downtime due to disruptions
- o Customer satisfaction during and after disruptions

Chapter Summary

In this chapter, we delved into the seventeen Service Management Practices of ITIL 4, a core set of guidelines designed to ensure effective and efficient delivery of IT services. These practices span the entire service lifecycle, from strategizing and designing services to their daily operation and continual improvement.

Here are the key takeaways:

- **Service Management Practices (SMPs):** We emphasized the importance of SMPs in ITIL 4, focusing on their role in the end-to-end management of IT services. These practices offer a flexible, holistic approach, encompassing all the necessary components for successful service delivery.
- **Key Practices Explored:** We provided detailed descriptions for each of the 17 SMPs, including their purpose, key activities, value contribution, examples, challenges, relationships with other practices, and relevant metrics. This comprehensive overview allows for a deeper understanding of each practice's unique role in the Service Value System.

Some notable examples include:

- **Service Desk:** The single point of contact between users and IT, vital for incident reporting, service requests, and communication.
- **Incident and Problem Management:** These practices work in tandem to restore service operation and address underlying issues, respectively, minimizing disruptions and improving service quality.
- **Service Level Management:** Sets clear performance targets for services, ensuring alignment with customer expectations and driving continuous improvement.
- **Change Enablement:** Manages the change process to maximize successful IT changes while minimizing risks and disruptions.
- **Service Design and Transition:** These practices focus on the creation and implementation of new or changed services, ensuring they meet requirements and are smoothly introduced into the live environment.
- **Availability, Capacity, and Continuity Management:** These practices ensure services are available, reliable, and can meet current and future demand, even in the face of disruptions.
- **Business Analysis and Service Catalog Management:** These practices bridge the gap between IT and business, ensuring services align with business needs and are easily accessible to users.
- **Other Practices:** We also covered IT Asset Management, Monitoring and Event Management, Service Configuration Management, Release Management, and Service Validation and Testing, highlighting their unique roles in optimizing IT service delivery.

By understanding and applying these Service Management Practices, organizations can build a robust and adaptable IT service management system. This comprehensive approach leads to improved service quality, enhanced customer satisfaction, reduced costs, and increased efficiency, ultimately contributing to the organization's success.

Technical Management Practices

Outline

- Introduction to Technical Management Practices
- Deployment Management
- Infrastructure and Platform Management
- Software Development and Management
- The Interplay of Technical and Service Management Practices
- Chapter Summary

Introduction to Technical Management Practices

While ITIL 4 emphasizes a holistic approach to service management, it recognizes the critical role that technology plays in delivering value to customers and stakeholders. The three Technical Management practices in ITIL 4 provide the framework and guidance for managing the technical aspects of service delivery, ensuring that the underlying infrastructure, platforms, and software are reliable, secure, and performant.

Role of Technical Management Practices in ITIL 4:

These practices focus on the technical expertise and capabilities required to build, deploy, and maintain the technology components that underpin IT services. They address the specific challenges and complexities of managing modern IT environments, including infrastructure, platforms, software development, and deployment. By ensuring the smooth functioning and evolution of these technical elements, Technical Management Practices contribute significantly to the overall Service Value System (SVS).

Ensuring Reliability, Security, and Performance:

Technical Management Practices are essential for maintaining the reliability, security, and performance of IT services. This involves:

- **Reliability:** Ensuring that services are available when needed, meet performance expectations, and recover quickly from disruptions.
- **Security:** Protecting information and technology assets from unauthorized access, use, disclosure, disruption, modification, or destruction.
- **Performance:** Monitoring and optimizing the performance of IT systems and services to meet agreed-upon service levels.

By focusing on these critical aspects, Technical Management Practices contribute to a stable and resilient IT environment, enabling organizations to deliver high-quality services that meet the needs of customers and stakeholders.

Brief Introduction to the Three Technical Management Practices:

1. **Deployment Management:** This practice focuses on planning, managing, and controlling the movement of releases into production and other environments. It ensures that new or changed services are deployed smoothly, efficiently, and with minimal disruption to business operations.
2. **Infrastructure and Platform Management:** This practice oversees the management of the infrastructure and platforms (hardware, software, networks, etc.) that support the delivery of IT services. It ensures the availability, reliability, and performance of these underlying components.

3. **Software Development and Management:** This practice encompasses the entire lifecycle of software applications, from design and development to deployment and maintenance. It ensures that software applications are developed efficiently, meet user needs, and are integrated seamlessly with other IT services.

Contribution to the Service Value Chain:

Technical Management Practices directly contribute to several activities within the Service Value Chain:

- **Obtain/Build:** Deployment Management and Infrastructure and Platform Management play a key role in acquiring and building the necessary infrastructure and platforms to support service delivery.
- **Design and Transition:** Software Development and Management, along with Deployment Management, ensure that new or changed services are designed, developed, tested, and deployed effectively.
- **Deliver and Support:** All three technical management practices contribute to ensuring the ongoing availability, performance, and security of IT services, which are essential for delivering and supporting services to customers and stakeholders.

By mastering these Technical Management Practices, organizations can build a robust and adaptable IT infrastructure that supports their service management goals. This allows them to respond to changing business needs, deliver high-quality services, and achieve their strategic objectives.

Deployment Management

- **Purpose:** The purpose of Deployment Management is to move new or changed components to live environments (or other controlled environments such as testing or staging) while minimizing disruption to services and ensuring a seamless transition. This practice ensures that new or updated hardware, software, documentation, processes, or other components are installed, configured, and operationalized correctly, contributing to the overall reliability and availability of IT services.
- **Key Activities:**
    - **Planning and Scheduling Deployments:** This involves defining the scope of the deployment, identifying the required resources, creating a detailed deployment plan with timelines, and scheduling the deployment to minimize impact on users.
    - **Coordinating with Relevant Teams:** Effective communication and collaboration with all teams involved in the deployment process, such as development, testing, infrastructure, and operations, are crucial for ensuring a smooth and successful deployment.
    - **Building and Configuring Deployment Packages:** This involves preparing all the necessary components for deployment, including software packages, configuration files, scripts, and documentation. The goal is to create a well-defined and tested package that can be deployed consistently across different environments.
    - **Managing the Deployment Process and Resolving Issues:** This includes executing the deployment plan, monitoring progress, identifying and resolving any issues that may arise during the deployment, and ensuring that the deployment is completed successfully within the agreed-upon timeframe.
    - **Monitoring and Verifying Success:** After deployment, the system is monitored to ensure it functions as expected and meets the defined requirements. Verification processes confirm that the deployment was successful and did not introduce any unexpected problems.
    - **Providing Early Life Support:** This involves providing additional support and troubleshooting during the initial period after deployment to address any issues that may arise and ensure a smooth transition to normal operation.
- **Value Contribution:**

- ○ **Minimized Disruption:** Deployment Management minimizes the risk of service disruptions and downtime by ensuring that deployments are carefully planned, tested, and executed in a controlled manner.
- ○ **Faster Time to Market:** Streamlined and efficient deployment processes enable faster delivery of new or changed services, allowing organizations to respond quickly to market demands and gain a competitive edge.
- ○ **Improved Reliability and Availability:** Thorough testing and validation of deployment packages ensures that services are reliable and available when needed, enhancing customer satisfaction and trust.
- ○ **Cost Reduction:** By preventing deployment failures and minimizing downtime, Deployment Management can significantly reduce the costs associated with rework, troubleshooting, and lost productivity.

Deployment Management is a key enabler of value creation within the ITIL 4 SVS, ensuring that new or changed components are integrated into the live environment seamlessly and efficiently, ultimately contributing to the delivery of reliable, high-quality IT services.

Infrastructure and Platform Management

Infrastructure and Platform Management (IPM) is a technical management practice in ITIL 4 that focuses on overseeing, controlling, and maintaining the technology underpinnings of an organization's IT services. This includes hardware, software, networks, and any other technology-related elements that contribute to service delivery.

Purpose of Infrastructure and Platform Management:

The purpose of IPM is to provide a stable, reliable, and secure foundation for IT services. It aims to ensure that the underlying technology infrastructure and platforms are:

- **Available:** Accessible and operational when needed by users and other services.
- **Reliable:** Functioning consistently and correctly, minimizing downtime and disruptions.
- **Performant:** Delivering adequate speed, responsiveness, and capacity to meet user expectations and agreed-upon service levels.
- **Secure:** Protected from unauthorized access, data breaches, and other security threats.
- **Scalable:** Capable of expanding or contracting to meet changing demands.
- **Maintainable:** Easy to maintain, update, and troubleshoot.

Key Activities of Infrastructure and Platform Management:

1. **Monitoring Infrastructure and Platform Health:** Continuously monitoring the status, health, and performance of infrastructure and platform components. This includes using monitoring tools to collect and analyze data on metrics such as CPU utilization, memory usage, disk space, network traffic, and application response times.
2. **Maintaining and Updating Components:** Performing regular maintenance activities, such as patching, updates, backups, and configuration changes, to ensure the smooth operation and security of the infrastructure and platforms.
3. **Managing Capacity and Performance:** Planning and managing the capacity of infrastructure and platforms to meet current and future demand. This involves analyzing utilization trends, forecasting future needs, and taking proactive measures to ensure sufficient capacity and performance to meet service level agreements (SLAs).
4. **Ensuring Availability and Reliability:** Implementing measures to ensure the availability and reliability of infrastructure and platforms, such as redundancy, failover mechanisms, disaster recovery plans, and proactive maintenance.

5. **Implementing Security Controls:** Protecting infrastructure and platforms from unauthorized access, data breaches, and other security threats. This involves implementing access controls, firewalls, intrusion detection systems, encryption, and other security measures.

Value Contribution of Infrastructure and Platform Management:

By effectively managing infrastructure and platforms, organizations can:

- **Ensure Service Availability:** Minimize downtime and ensure that services are available when needed by users.
- **Improve Service Performance:** Optimize infrastructure and platforms to deliver fast, responsive, and reliable services.
- **Enhance Security:** Protect information assets and mitigate the risk of security breaches, data loss, and other disruptions.
- **Optimize Costs:** By managing capacity effectively and implementing efficient maintenance practices, organizations can reduce infrastructure costs and improve resource utilization.
- **Support Business Agility:** A flexible and scalable infrastructure enables organizations to adapt quickly to changing business needs and market demands.

Infrastructure and Platform Management is a critical practice for organizations that rely on technology to deliver value to their customers and stakeholders. By ensuring the reliability, availability, performance, and security of their IT infrastructure and platforms, organizations can create a solid foundation for delivering high-quality IT services and achieving their strategic objectives.

Software Development and Management

Software Development and Management (SDM) is a vital technical management practice in ITIL 4 that focuses on the entire lifecycle of software applications, from conception to retirement. Its purpose is to ensure that software applications are developed, deployed, and maintained effectively to meet the evolving needs of users and the organization, ultimately contributing to the delivery of value through IT services.

Purpose of Software Development and Management:

The primary purpose of SDM is to:

- **Meet User and Business Needs:** Ensure that software applications are designed and developed to address specific user requirements and support broader business objectives. This involves understanding user needs, gathering requirements, and translating them into functional and technical specifications.
- **Deliver High-Quality Software:** Establish and maintain rigorous quality standards throughout the software development lifecycle. This includes implementing quality assurance processes, conducting thorough testing, and addressing defects and issues promptly.
- **Efficiently Manage Software Assets:** Effectively manage the lifecycle of software applications, from development and deployment to maintenance and retirement. This involves managing software licenses, ensuring compatibility with other systems, and planning for upgrades and replacements.
- **Support Innovation:** Foster a culture of innovation in software development, encouraging the use of new technologies and methodologies to improve efficiency, functionality, and user experience.
- **Align with ITIL Practices:** Integrate software development and management activities with other ITIL practices, such as Change Enablement, Release Management, and Service Validation and Testing.

Key Activities of Software Development and Management:

1. **Requirements Gathering and Analysis:** Understanding and documenting the functional and non-functional requirements of the software application. This involves engaging with users and stakeholders to gather their input, prioritize requirements, and define the scope of the project.
2. **Software Design and Development:** Creating a detailed design for the software application, including its architecture, user interface, and data models. Developing the software code, conducting unit and integration testing, and ensuring that the software meets the defined requirements.
3. **Testing and Quality Assurance:** Thoroughly testing the software application to ensure that it functions correctly, meets performance standards, and is free of defects. This includes functional testing, performance testing, security testing, and user acceptance testing.
4. **Release and Deployment Management:** Planning, scheduling, and controlling the release and deployment of the software application into the live environment. This involves coordinating with other IT teams, managing risks, and ensuring a smooth transition.
5. **Maintenance and Support:** Providing ongoing maintenance and support for the software application, including bug fixes, updates, patches, and user support.
6. **Version Control and Configuration Management:** Managing different versions of the software application and tracking changes to its configuration. This ensures that changes are documented, tested, and deployed in a controlled manner.

Value Contribution of Software Development and Management:

By implementing effective SDM practices, organizations can:

- **Deliver High-Quality Software:** Ensure that software applications are reliable, secure, and meet user needs, leading to increased productivity, efficiency, and customer satisfaction.
- **Accelerate Time to Market:** Streamline the software development lifecycle, allowing organizations to deliver new or updated applications faster.
- **Optimize Costs:** Reduce the cost of software development and maintenance by preventing errors, improving efficiency, and optimizing resource utilization.
- **Enhance Collaboration:** Foster collaboration between development, operations, and other teams, leading to better communication, faster issue resolution, and improved service delivery.
- **Drive Innovation:** Encourage the use of new technologies and methodologies to improve software development and delivery processes.

Software Development and Management is a critical practice for organizations that rely on software applications to support their business operations. By adopting a holistic and disciplined approach to SDM, organizations can ensure that their software applications are developed, deployed, and maintained effectively, delivering value to users and stakeholders.

The Interplay of Technical and Service Management Practices

In the ITIL 4 framework, the Technical Management and Service Management practices are not isolated entities but rather interconnected gears that work together to deliver and maintain valuable IT services. While Technical Management focuses on the technology aspects, Service Management concentrates on the service delivery and customer-facing elements. However, their functions are deeply intertwined, and their collaboration is essential for achieving a seamless and efficient IT service management system.

Deep Intertwining of Technical and Service Management Practices:

The Technical Management practices lay the groundwork for the successful execution of Service Management practices. Without reliable infrastructure, well-maintained platforms, and robust software development, it would be impossible to design, deliver, and support services that meet customer needs and expectations. Conversely, Service Management practices provide the guidance and structure needed to ensure that technology investments align with business goals and deliver value.

Examples of Interplay:

1. **Deployment Management and Release Management:** Deployment Management ensures the smooth and efficient transition of new or changed services into the live environment, supporting the successful execution of Release Management, which focuses on the overall coordination and planning of releases.
2. **Infrastructure and Platform Management and Availability Management:** Infrastructure and Platform Management ensures that the underlying infrastructure is available, reliable, and performant, directly contributing to the goals of Availability Management, which focuses on maximizing service uptime and minimizing disruptions.
3. **Software Development and Management and Change Enablement:** Software Development and Management ensures the quality and functionality of software applications, while Change Enablement assesses the risk and impact of changes to those applications, ensuring that changes are implemented safely and effectively.

Importance of a Holistic Approach:

A holistic approach that considers both technical and service aspects is crucial for delivering high-quality IT services. Organizations must recognize the interdependencies between these practices and foster collaboration between technical and service management teams. This integrated approach ensures that:

- **Technical solutions align with business needs:** Technology investments are not made in isolation but are carefully chosen and implemented to support specific service goals and business objectives.
- **Services are designed for maintainability and supportability:** Technical teams consider the operational and support requirements during the design and development of services, making them easier to manage and maintain.
- **Changes are implemented smoothly:** Collaboration between technical and service management teams ensures that changes are thoroughly tested, risks are mitigated, and deployments are coordinated to minimize disruption.
- **Problems are resolved effectively:** By working together, technical and service management teams can quickly identify and address root causes of problems, leading to improved service quality and reliability.
- **Continuous Improvement is fostered:** A holistic approach encourages feedback and collaboration between technical and service management teams, enabling them to identify and implement opportunities for improvement across the entire service lifecycle.

By embracing a holistic approach that combines technical expertise with service management best practices, organizations can create a more efficient, effective, and customer-centric IT service management system.

Chapter Summary

In this chapter, we explored the Technical Management practices in ITIL 4, a crucial part of the framework that focuses on the technology aspects of service delivery. These practices ensure the underlying infrastructure, platforms, and software are robust and reliable, ultimately contributing to the success of the overall Service Value System.

Key takeaways from this chapter include:

- **Technical Management in ITIL 4:** We emphasized how the Technical Management practices focus on the technical expertise and capabilities needed to build, deploy, and maintain the technological components underpinning IT services, contributing to the stability and resilience of the IT environment.

- **Deployment Management:** This practice is all about smoothly and efficiently moving new or changed components into live environments (and other testing environments) while minimizing disruption to services. We detailed its key activities like planning, coordinating, building, deploying, monitoring, and providing early life support, highlighting how it ensures reliable service delivery.
- **Infrastructure and Platform Management:** We explained how this practice oversees the health, maintenance, capacity, availability, and security of the technology infrastructure. By proactively managing these elements, organizations can guarantee service availability, performance, and security, forming a stable foundation for IT services.
- **Software Development and Management:** This practice guides the entire lifecycle of software applications from conception to retirement. It encompasses key activities like requirements gathering, design, development, testing, deployment, maintenance, and version control, ensuring applications effectively meet user needs and business objectives.
- **Interplay of Practices:** We emphasized the interconnected nature of Technical and Service Management practices, showing how they rely on each other to achieve IT service management goals. We provided examples of how these practices collaborate, such as Deployment Management supporting Release Management, Infrastructure and Platform Management working with Availability Management, and Software Development and Management collaborating with Change Enablement.

Understanding and effectively implementing Technical Management practices is crucial for any organization that relies on technology to deliver value. By ensuring the reliability, availability, performance, and security of their IT infrastructure and applications, organizations can create a solid foundation for IT service delivery and achieve their strategic objectives. In the following chapters, we will delve into the practical application of ITIL 4 in real-world scenarios, providing you with further insights and guidance for successful implementation.

Section F:
ITIL 4 and Practical Implementation

Adopting ITIL 4 in Your Organization

Outline

- Understanding the Need for ITIL 4 Adoption
- Overcoming Challenges in ITIL 4 Adoption
- Key Steps in ITIL 4 Adoption
- Assessing Your Organization's Readiness
- Planning Your ITIL 4 Implementation
- Implementing ITIL 4 Practices
- Measuring and Demonstrating Success
- Sustaining ITIL 4 Adoption
- Tips for Successful ITIL 4 Adoption
- Chapter Summary

Understanding the Need for ITIL 4 Adoption

In today's rapidly evolving digital landscape, organizations face mounting pressures to deliver high-quality IT services that meet the ever-changing needs of their customers and stakeholders. ITIL 4, the latest iteration of the IT Infrastructure Library, offers a comprehensive framework and a set of best practices to address these challenges and drive service excellence.

Business Benefits of Adopting ITIL 4:

- **Improved Service Quality:** ITIL 4 provides a structured approach to service management, encompassing all aspects of the service lifecycle. By implementing ITIL 4 practices, organizations can improve the quality and reliability of their services, reduce downtime, and enhance customer satisfaction.
- **Increased Efficiency:** ITIL 4 emphasizes the optimization and automation of processes, enabling organizations to streamline workflows, reduce manual effort, and improve operational efficiency. This can lead to cost savings, faster service delivery, and increased productivity.
- **Enhanced Customer Satisfaction:** ITIL 4 places a strong emphasis on understanding and meeting customer needs. By adopting a customer-centric approach, organizations can design and deliver services that better meet customer expectations, leading to increased satisfaction and loyalty.
- **Alignment with Business Goals:** ITIL 4 helps align IT services with the organization's overall business strategy and objectives. This ensures that IT investments are focused on initiatives that deliver tangible value and contribute to the organization's success.
- **Adaptability and Resilience:** ITIL 4 recognizes the need for agility and adaptability in the face of rapid technological change and evolving business needs. It provides a flexible framework that can be tailored to the specific needs of each organization, enabling them to respond quickly to new challenges and opportunities.

Challenges Faced in IT Service Management:

- **Increasing Complexity:** Modern IT environments are becoming increasingly complex, with a growing number of interconnected systems, applications, and devices. This complexity makes it challenging to manage IT services effectively and ensure their reliability and performance.
- **Evolving Customer Expectations:** Customers are demanding faster, more personalized, and more convenient service experiences. Meeting these evolving expectations requires IT organizations to be agile and responsive, continuously improving their services and adapting to new technologies and trends.
- **Need for Agility and Adaptability:** The pace of technological change is accelerating, and organizations need to be able to quickly adopt new technologies and adapt their IT services to stay competitive. This requires a flexible and agile approach to IT service management.
- **Cost Pressures:** Organizations are under constant pressure to reduce costs and do more with less. IT service management needs to be cost-effective and demonstrate a clear return on investment.
- **Skills Shortages:** There is a growing shortage of skilled IT professionals, making it difficult for organizations to find and retain the talent they need to deliver and support IT services.

How ITIL 4 Addresses These Challenges:

ITIL 4 provides a comprehensive framework and a set of best practices that can help organizations address these challenges and achieve their service management goals.

- **Managing Complexity:** ITIL 4's holistic approach and focus on value streams help organizations manage the complexity of modern IT environments by breaking down silos, promoting collaboration, and focusing on end-to-end service delivery.
- **Meeting Evolving Expectations:** ITIL 4's emphasis on customer centricity and continual improvement helps organizations understand and adapt to changing customer needs and expectations, ensuring that services remain relevant and valuable.
- **Enabling Agility and Adaptability:** ITIL 4's flexible framework and adaptable practices allow organizations to respond quickly to changing business needs and adopt new technologies without disrupting existing services.
- **Optimizing Costs:** ITIL 4's focus on optimization and automation helps organizations streamline processes, reduce manual effort, and improve efficiency, leading to cost savings and a better return on investment.
- **Developing Talent:** ITIL 4 provides a framework for developing the skills and competencies needed for effective IT service management, helping organizations to build a skilled and motivated workforce.

By adopting ITIL 4, organizations can transform their IT service management practices, improve service quality, enhance efficiency, and deliver greater value to their customers and stakeholders.

Overcoming Challenges in ITIL 4 Adoption

Adopting ITIL 4, like any significant organizational change, can present various challenges. However, with a proactive and well-planned approach, these challenges can be overcome, paving the way for a successful ITIL 4 implementation. Let's delve into the common obstacles and outline strategies to navigate them effectively.

Common Challenges in ITIL 4 Adoption:

1. **Resistance to Change:**
- **Description:** Employees may resist adopting ITIL 4 due to fear of the unknown, concerns about increased workload, or simply a preference for familiar ways of working.
- **Solutions:**

- **Communicate Early and Often:** Clearly articulate the reasons for adopting ITIL 4, highlighting its benefits for both the organization and individual employees. Explain how it will improve service quality, efficiency, and customer satisfaction.
- **Involve Stakeholders:** Engage employees and stakeholders in the planning and implementation process. Seek their input, address their concerns, and make them feel like they are part of the solution.
- **Provide Training and Support:** Offer comprehensive training programs to equip employees with the knowledge and skills they need to understand and apply ITIL 4 concepts. Provide ongoing support and coaching to help them adapt to the new ways of working.

2. **Lack of Resources:**

- **Description:** Implementing ITIL 4 may require additional resources, such as budget for training and tools, time for process redesign, and personnel for implementation and support. Organizations may struggle to allocate these resources, especially when faced with competing priorities.
- **Solutions:**
  - **Build a Strong Business Case:** Clearly articulate the business benefits of adopting ITIL 4, such as improved service quality, reduced costs, and increased customer satisfaction. Use this business case to justify the investment in resources.
  - **Prioritize Investments:** Identify the most critical ITIL 4 practices and processes to implement first, based on their potential impact and alignment with strategic goals. Start small and gradually expand as resources become available.
  - **Optimize Existing Resources:** Look for ways to leverage existing resources and tools, rather than investing in new ones. Consider partnering with external consultants or service providers to fill any gaps in expertise.

3. **Difficulty Integrating with Existing Processes and Tools:**

- **Description:** ITIL 4 may not always align perfectly with an organization's existing processes, tools, and culture. Integrating ITIL 4 practices into the existing environment can be challenging, requiring careful planning and change management.
- **Solutions:**
  - **Assess and Adapt:** Conduct a thorough assessment of existing processes and tools to identify areas of compatibility and incompatibility with ITIL 4. Adapt ITIL 4 practices to fit the organization's specific context and needs, rather than trying to force-fit them.
  - **Phased Implementation:** Implement ITIL 4 in phases, starting with practices that are most compatible with existing processes and tools. This will minimize disruption and allow the organization to gradually adapt to the new framework.
  - **Integration Planning:** Develop a detailed integration plan that outlines how ITIL 4 practices will be integrated with existing processes and tools. Consider using integration platforms or middleware to bridge any gaps.

Additional Strategies and Tips:

- **Securing Leadership Buy-In and Commitment:** Leadership support is crucial for the success of any major change initiative. Secure buy-in from senior management by highlighting the strategic benefits of ITIL 4 and demonstrating its potential impact on business outcomes.
- **Communicating the Benefits of ITIL 4 to Stakeholders:** Clearly communicate the benefits of ITIL 4 to all stakeholders, including IT staff, business users, customers, and partners. Explain how ITIL 4 can help the organization achieve its goals, improve service quality, and enhance customer satisfaction.
- **Starting Small and Scaling Gradually:** Don't try to implement all ITIL 4 practices at once. Start with a few key practices that address the organization's most pressing needs and gradually expand the implementation as you gain experience and resources.
- **Focusing on Quick Wins and Demonstrating Early Successes:** Identify and prioritize initiatives that can deliver quick wins and demonstrate the tangible benefits of ITIL 4. This will help build momentum and support for the broader adoption effort.

By proactively addressing these challenges and implementing these strategies, organizations can overcome the obstacles to ITIL 4 adoption and achieve a successful implementation that delivers real value to the business.

Key Steps in ITIL 4 Adoption

Adopting ITIL 4 is a journey that requires a well-structured and phased approach. It's not just about implementing new processes and tools; it's about transforming your organization's culture and mindset to embrace a more customer-centric and value-driven approach to IT service management. Here's an outline of the key steps involved in this transformative journey:

1. **Assessing Organizational Readiness:**
   - **Understanding the Current State:** Before embarking on an ITIL 4 adoption journey, it's crucial to assess your organization's current state of IT service management (ITSM). This involves evaluating existing processes, tools, skills, and culture to identify strengths, weaknesses, and areas for improvement.
   - **Identifying Key Stakeholders:** Engage with key stakeholders across the organization, including IT staff, business leaders, customers, and partners. Understand their expectations, concerns, and priorities regarding IT service management.
   - **Evaluating Readiness:** Assess the organization's readiness for change, considering factors such as leadership commitment, employee engagement, and available resources.
   - **Determining the Scope of Adoption:** Decide which ITIL 4 practices and processes are most relevant to your organization's needs and priorities. This will help you tailor the implementation to your specific context.
2. **Planning the Implementation:**
   - **Develop an Implementation Roadmap:** Create a detailed plan that outlines the steps, timelines, and milestones for implementing ITIL 4. This roadmap should be aligned with the organization's strategic goals and take into account the findings of the readiness assessment.
   - **Allocate Resources:** Identify the resources needed for successful implementation, including budget, personnel, training, and tools.
   - **Define Roles and Responsibilities:** Clearly define the roles and responsibilities of individuals and teams involved in the implementation process.
   - **Establish Communication and Change Management Plans:** Develop plans for communicating the ITIL 4 adoption initiative to stakeholders and managing the change process effectively.
3. **Implementing ITIL 4 Practices:**
   - **Phased Approach:** Implement ITIL 4 practices in a phased and controlled manner, starting with the most critical or impactful areas. This allows for learning and adjustment along the way, minimizing disruption to operations.
   - **Pilot Projects:** Consider piloting new practices in a limited scope before rolling them out across the entire organization. This allows you to test the effectiveness of the practices and make necessary adjustments.
   - **Customization:** Adapt ITIL 4 practices to fit your organization's specific needs and context. Avoid a "one-size-fits-all" approach and tailor the practices to your unique culture and processes.
4. **Measuring and Demonstrating Success:**
   - **Define Metrics:** Establish key performance indicators (KPIs) and metrics to measure the success of your ITIL 4 implementation. These metrics should be aligned with your organization's goals and objectives and should track both the efficiency and effectiveness of your services.
   - **Track Progress:** Regularly monitor and report on the selected metrics to track progress towards your goals. This data will help you identify areas where further improvements are needed.
   - **Communicate Results:** Share the results of your ITIL 4 implementation with stakeholders, highlighting the positive impact it has had on service quality, efficiency, and customer satisfaction.
5. **Sustaining Adoption:**

- **Embed ITIL 4 into the Culture:** Make ITIL 4 an integral part of your organization's culture by promoting continuous learning, encouraging feedback, and celebrating successes.
- **Regular Reviews:** Conduct regular reviews of your ITIL 4 practices to ensure they remain relevant and effective. Update processes, tools, and documentation as needed to reflect changing business needs and technology advancements.
- **Governance:** Establish a governance structure for IT service management to ensure that ITIL 4 practices are aligned with strategic goals and that resources are allocated effectively.

By following these key steps and approaching ITIL 4 adoption as a continuous journey, organizations can successfully transform their IT service management capabilities, deliver greater value to their customers and stakeholders, and achieve their strategic objectives.

Assessing Your Organization's Readiness

A successful ITIL 4 implementation hinges on a thorough assessment of your organization's readiness. This is a crucial first step that allows you to gauge the current state of your IT service management (ITSM) maturity, identify potential challenges, and tailor your implementation plan accordingly. By understanding your organization's strengths, weaknesses, and capacity for change, you can make informed decisions, allocate resources effectively, and set realistic expectations for the adoption process.

Importance of Assessing Organizational Readiness:

- **Identifying Strengths and Weaknesses:** A readiness assessment helps you understand your organization's current ITSM capabilities, revealing areas where you excel and areas that need improvement. This knowledge allows you to leverage existing strengths and prioritize areas for development.
- **Managing Expectations:** The assessment provides a realistic picture of the challenges and opportunities that lie ahead, allowing you to set realistic expectations for the ITIL 4 implementation timeline, resource requirements, and potential benefits.
- **Tailoring the Implementation:** The assessment results inform your implementation plan, ensuring that it's tailored to your organization's specific needs and context. This increases the likelihood of a successful and sustainable adoption.
- **Securing Buy-In:** Involving stakeholders in the assessment process helps to build consensus and support for the ITIL 4 initiative. It ensures that their perspectives are considered and that they are invested in the success of the implementation.
- **Risk Mitigation:** The assessment helps identify potential risks and obstacles to adoption, allowing you to develop mitigation strategies proactively. This minimizes disruptions and increases the chances of a smooth transition.

How to Conduct a Readiness Assessment:

A comprehensive readiness assessment typically involves the following steps:

1. **Identify Key Stakeholders and Their Expectations:**
   - **Who:** Identify all individuals and groups who have an interest in or will be affected by the ITIL 4 implementation. This includes IT staff, business leaders, customers, partners, and other relevant stakeholders.
   - **What:** Understand their expectations, concerns, and priorities regarding IT service management. What are their pain points? What benefits do they expect to see from ITIL 4 adoption?
2. **Evaluate the Current State of ITSM Practices:**
   - **Processes and Tools:** Assess the maturity and effectiveness of your existing ITSM processes and tools. Are they documented, standardized, and aligned with best practices?
   - **Skills and Competencies:** Evaluate the skills and competencies of your IT staff. Do they have the knowledge and experience needed to implement and manage ITIL 4 practices?

- Metrics and Reporting: Assess your current measurement and reporting capabilities. Do you have the necessary data and tools to track performance and measure the impact of ITIL 4?
3. **Assess Organizational Culture and Change Readiness:**
   - **Culture Assessment:** Evaluate the organization's culture and its openness to change. Does the culture support collaboration, learning, and continuous improvement? Are employees willing to embrace new ways of working?
   - **Change Management Readiness:** Assess the organization's change management capabilities. Do you have a structured change management process in place? Are employees trained and equipped to manage change effectively?
4. **Identify Available Resources and Budget:**
   - **Resource Inventory:** Identify the resources that are available to support the ITIL 4 implementation, including budget, personnel, and technology.
   - **Gap Analysis:** Compare available resources with the estimated requirements for implementation. Identify any resource gaps and develop plans to address them.

By conducting a thorough readiness assessment, you can gain a clear understanding of your organization's strengths, weaknesses, and readiness for change. This information is invaluable for developing a tailored implementation plan that maximizes the chances of success and ensures that your ITIL 4 adoption delivers the desired benefits.

Planning Your ITIL 4 Implementation

A successful ITIL 4 implementation requires meticulous planning to ensure a smooth transition, minimize disruptions, and maximize the benefits. A well-structured implementation plan acts as a roadmap, guiding the organization through the adoption process and ensuring that all necessary steps are taken to achieve the desired outcomes.

Key Elements of an ITIL 4 Implementation Plan:

1. **Defining the Scope and Objectives:**
- **Clear Objectives:** Start by defining clear and specific objectives for your ITIL 4 implementation. What do you hope to achieve? Do you want to improve service quality, reduce costs, enhance customer satisfaction, or achieve a specific maturity level?
- **Scope Definition:** Clearly define the scope of your implementation. Will you be adopting all ITIL 4 practices or focusing on specific areas? Which departments or teams will be involved?
- **Measurable Goals:** Establish measurable goals and targets to track progress and evaluate the success of the implementation. This could include metrics like incident resolution times, service availability, or customer satisfaction ratings.
2. **Selecting the ITIL Practices to be Adopted:**
- **Prioritization:** Not all ITIL 4 practices will be equally relevant or applicable to your organization. Prioritize the practices that align with your strategic goals and address your most pressing challenges.
- **Customization:** Consider how the practices can be adapted or tailored to fit your organization's specific needs and context.
- **Phased Approach:** Plan to implement the practices in a phased manner, starting with those that offer the quickest wins or have the greatest impact on your goals.
3. **Developing a Detailed Implementation Roadmap:**
- **Timeline:** Create a detailed timeline that outlines the start and end dates for each phase of the implementation. This will help you track progress and ensure that the project stays on schedule.
- **Milestones:** Define specific milestones for each phase, such as completion of training, implementation of new tools, or achievement of performance targets.
- **Dependencies:** Identify any dependencies between different activities or phases of the implementation. This will help you anticipate potential bottlenecks and adjust your plan accordingly.

- **Resource Allocation:** Allocate resources, such as budget, personnel, and technology, to each phase of the implementation.
4. **Identifying Resource Requirements and Securing Budget:**
- **Resource Assessment:** Conduct a thorough assessment of the resources required for the implementation, including:
    - **Financial Resources:** Budget for training, tools, consultants, and other expenses.
    - **Human Resources:** Staffing needs for project management, implementation, training, and ongoing support.
    - **Technological Resources:** Software licenses, hardware, and other technology infrastructure needed to support the new practices.
- **Budget Approval:** Secure approval for the necessary budget from senior management or other relevant stakeholders.
5. **Establishing Communication and Change Management Plans:**
- **Communication Plan:** Develop a comprehensive communication plan to keep stakeholders informed about the progress of the ITIL 4 implementation, its benefits, and the expected impacts. This includes regular updates, presentations, training sessions, and Q&A forums.
- **Change Management Plan:** Establish a structured change management process to manage the transition to ITIL 4. This involves identifying potential risks and impacts, developing mitigation strategies, and communicating the changes effectively to minimize disruption and resistance.

By following these key steps and developing a comprehensive implementation plan, organizations can lay the groundwork for a successful ITIL 4 adoption journey. This structured approach ensures that the implementation is aligned with strategic goals, resources are allocated effectively, and stakeholders are engaged and informed throughout the process.

Implementing ITIL 4 Practices

Implementing ITIL 4 practices is not a one-size-fits-all endeavor. Each organization has unique needs, resources, and constraints. Therefore, a phased and controlled approach is essential for successful adoption, ensuring minimal disruption and maximum benefit.

How to Implement ITIL 4 Practices in a Phased and Controlled Manner:

1. **Prioritize Practices:** Not all ITIL 4 practices need to be implemented simultaneously. Begin by identifying the practices that are most relevant to your organization's strategic goals and pain points. Prioritize those that offer the greatest potential for improvement and quick wins.
2. **Start Small:** Don't try to implement all the prioritized practices at once. Start with a pilot project or a small-scale implementation to test the waters. This allows you to learn, adapt, and refine the practices before rolling them out across the entire organization.
3. **Gradual Expansion:** Once you have successfully implemented the pilot project, gradually expand the adoption of ITIL 4 practices to other areas of the organization. This phased approach minimizes disruption and allows you to learn from each implementation, incorporating feedback and making adjustments as needed.
4. **Continual Improvement:** ITIL 4 is not a destination, but a journey of continuous improvement. Regularly review and assess the effectiveness of the implemented practices, gather feedback from stakeholders, and identify opportunities for further optimization.

Guidance on Adapting ITIL 4 Practices:

- **Customization:** ITIL 4 practices are not prescriptive templates; they are flexible guidelines that can be adapted to fit your organization's specific needs and context. Tailor the practices to align with your existing processes, tools, and culture.

- **Integration:** Consider how the new ITIL 4 practices will integrate with your existing ITSM framework and other processes. Avoid creating silos; instead, strive for seamless integration and collaboration between different practices.
- **Scalability:** Design your implementation in a way that can be scaled up or down as needed. Start small and gradually expand as you gain experience and resources.

Importance of Training and Communication:

- **Training:** Provide comprehensive training to all relevant stakeholders on the ITIL 4 framework, its concepts, and the specific practices being implemented. This will ensure that everyone understands the new ways of working and is equipped with the necessary skills to apply them.
- **Communication:** Clearly communicate the goals, benefits, and expected outcomes of the ITIL 4 adoption initiative to all stakeholders. Keep them informed about progress, challenges, and successes throughout the implementation process.
- **Buy-In:** Obtain buy-in and commitment from senior leadership and key stakeholders. Their support is crucial for the successful adoption of ITIL 4.

Importance of Pilot Projects:

- **Testing and Validation:** Pilot projects allow you to test the effectiveness of new practices in a controlled environment before rolling them out across the organization. This helps identify potential issues and refine the practices before they impact the entire organization.
- **Learning Opportunity:** Pilot projects provide a valuable learning opportunity, allowing you to gather feedback from users and stakeholders and make necessary adjustments.
- **Building Confidence:** Successful pilot projects can build confidence in the ITIL 4 framework and demonstrate its value to the organization, paving the way for broader adoption.

Importance of Regular Reviews and Adjustments:

- **Continuous Improvement:** ITIL 4 is a framework for continuous improvement. Regularly review and assess the effectiveness of implemented practices, identify areas for improvement, and make necessary adjustments to ensure that the practices remain relevant and effective over time.
- **Feedback Loop:** Establish feedback loops with stakeholders to gather their input and suggestions for improvement. This will help you tailor the practices to their specific needs and ensure that they deliver the desired value.

By following these guidelines and embracing a phased, adaptable, and iterative approach, organizations can successfully implement ITIL 4 practices and achieve lasting improvements in their IT service management capabilities.

Measuring and Demonstrating Success

Implementing ITIL 4 is a significant investment for any organization. To ensure the initiative's success and demonstrate its value to stakeholders, it's crucial to establish a robust measurement and reporting system. This system should track progress, evaluate outcomes, and provide insights into the effectiveness of ITIL 4 practices in achieving business goals.

Importance of Measuring and Demonstrating Success:

- **Evidence-Based Decision-Making:** Metrics provide objective data that can be used to evaluate the success of ITIL 4 implementation and inform future decisions. They help identify areas where the implementation is working well and areas that need further improvement.
- **Justification of Investments:** Clear metrics and reports demonstrating the positive impact of ITIL 4 on service quality, efficiency, and customer satisfaction can justify investments and secure funding for future initiatives.

- **Stakeholder Communication:** Regularly communicating performance data to stakeholders helps build trust and transparency, showcasing the value that IT services are delivering to the business.
- **Continual Improvement:** Metrics allow organizations to track progress over time and identify trends, enabling them to continuously refine their ITIL 4 practices and drive ongoing improvement.

Establishing Key Performance Indicators (KPIs) and Metrics:

Choosing the right KPIs and metrics is essential for effectively measuring and demonstrating success. Consider the following steps:

1. **Align with Strategic Goals:** KPIs should be closely aligned with the organization's strategic goals and objectives. This ensures that IT service management is focused on delivering value that matters to the business.
2. **Consider Stakeholder Needs:** Identify the metrics that are most important to different stakeholders, such as customers, employees, and executives. This will ensure that the measurement system captures the perspectives of all key stakeholders.
3. **Focus on Outcomes, Not Just Outputs:** While output metrics (e.g., number of incidents resolved) are important, it's crucial to also track outcome metrics that measure the impact of services on business outcomes (e.g., customer satisfaction, revenue growth).
4. **Choose Measurable Metrics:** Select metrics that can be objectively measured and tracked over time. This ensures that the data is reliable and can be used to make informed decisions.
5. **Regularly Review and Refine:** KPIs and metrics should not be static. Regularly review them to ensure they remain relevant and aligned with changing business needs.

Examples of KPIs for Measuring ITIL 4 Success:

Category	KPI Examples
Service Quality	Customer satisfaction ratings, Net Promoter Score (NPS), First Contact Resolution (FCR) rate, Mean Time to Restore Service (MTTR)
Efficiency	Incident resolution time, Service request fulfillment time, Cost per ticket, Resource utilization
Customer Satisfaction	Customer satisfaction surveys, Feedback ratings, Repeat business rate, Net Promoter Score (NPS)
Financial Performance	Return on investment (ROI) for ITIL initiatives, Cost savings from automation and optimization, Revenue generated from IT services

By establishing a robust measurement and reporting system based on relevant KPIs, organizations can gain valuable insights into the performance of their IT services, demonstrate their value to stakeholders, and drive continuous improvement in their IT service management practices.

Sustaining ITIL 4 Adoption

Adopting ITIL 4 is not a one-time event; it's an ongoing journey of continuous improvement and adaptation. To ensure that the benefits of ITIL 4 are realized and sustained over the long term, organizations need to embed the framework into their culture, processes, and governance structures. This requires a sustained effort and a commitment to learning, adaptation, and evolution.

Importance of Sustaining ITIL 4 Adoption:

Sustaining ITIL 4 adoption is crucial for several reasons:

- **Maintaining Momentum:** Initial enthusiasm for ITIL 4 may fade over time, especially if employees feel overwhelmed by the changes or don't see immediate results. Sustained adoption ensures that the momentum of the initial implementation is maintained, keeping the focus on continuous improvement and preventing backsliding into old habits.
- **Adapting to Change:** The business environment and technology landscape are constantly evolving. Sustained adoption ensures that ITIL 4 practices are regularly reviewed and updated to remain relevant and effective in the face of change.
- **Maximizing Value:** ITIL 4 is a value-driven framework, and sustaining adoption ensures that organizations continue to reap the benefits of improved service quality, efficiency, and customer satisfaction.
- **Building a Culture of Improvement:** Sustained adoption fosters a culture of continual improvement, where everyone in the organization is committed to learning, adapting, and evolving their practices to deliver better outcomes.

Strategies for Embedding ITIL 4:

1. **Continuous Training and Development:**
- **Regular Training:** Provide ongoing training to ensure that employees have the necessary skills and knowledge to apply ITIL 4 practices effectively. This includes training on new practices, refresher courses, and opportunities for professional development.
- **Knowledge Sharing:** Encourage knowledge sharing and collaboration among team members through mentoring, coaching, and communities of practice. This helps to build internal expertise and promotes a culture of learning.
2. **Regular Reviews and Updates of ITIL 4 Practices:**
- **Periodic Reviews:** Regularly review ITIL 4 practices to assess their effectiveness and identify areas for improvement. This can be done through audits, surveys, feedback sessions, and performance analysis.
- **Adapting to Change:** Update ITIL 4 practices as needed to reflect changes in business needs, technology trends, and industry best practices. This ensures that the practices remain relevant and aligned with the organization's goals.
- **Experimentation:** Encourage experimentation with new approaches and technologies to continuously improve and optimize IT service management.
3. **Ongoing Communication and Engagement with Stakeholders:**
- **Transparent Communication:** Regularly communicate with stakeholders about the progress of ITIL 4 adoption, its benefits, and the challenges faced. This helps to build trust and maintain support for the initiative.
- **Feedback Loops:** Establish feedback mechanisms to gather input from stakeholders, such as customers, employees, and partners. Use this feedback to identify areas for improvement and inform future decisions.
4. **Establishing a Formal Governance Structure for IT Service Management:**
- **Governance Bodies:** Establish formal governance bodies, such as a steering committee or a change advisory board (CAB), to oversee the ITIL 4 implementation and ensure its alignment with strategic goals.
- **Roles and Responsibilities:** Clearly define the roles and responsibilities of individuals and teams involved in IT service management, ensuring accountability and effective decision-making.
- **Policies and Procedures:** Develop and implement IT service management policies and procedures that align with ITIL 4 best practices and the organization's specific needs.

By implementing these strategies, organizations can embed ITIL 4 into their culture, processes, and governance structures, ensuring that its benefits are sustained over the long term. This ongoing commitment to continual improvement will help organizations to adapt to change, deliver high-quality services, and achieve their strategic objectives.

Tips for Successful ITIL 4 Adoption

Embarking on an ITIL 4 adoption journey can be a transformative experience for an organization. To ensure success and maximize the benefits of this powerful framework, here are some practical tips and advice:

1. **Start Small and Focus on Quick Wins:**
- **Don't Overwhelm:** Resist the temptation to implement all ITIL 4 practices at once. Start with a few key practices that address your most pressing pain points or align with your strategic priorities.
- **Prioritize Value:** Choose practices that offer the quickest and most tangible benefits to demonstrate the value of ITIL 4 early on. This will help build momentum and secure buy-in for further adoption.
- **Learn and Adapt:** Use the initial implementations as a learning opportunity. Gather feedback, identify areas for improvement, and refine your approach before scaling up.

2. **Involve Stakeholders from the Beginning:**
- **Build a Coalition:** Identify key stakeholders across the organization, including IT staff, business leaders, customers, and partners. Engage them early in the process to get their input, address their concerns, and build support for the initiative.
- **Create a Sense of Ownership:** Involve stakeholders in decision-making, process design, and implementation. This will foster a sense of ownership and increase their commitment to the success of the project.
- **Communicate Regularly:** Keep stakeholders informed about the progress of the ITIL 4 adoption, highlighting achievements and addressing any challenges that arise. This transparency builds trust and fosters collaboration.

3. **Clearly Define Roles and Responsibilities:**
- **RACI Matrix:** Use a RACI (Responsible, Accountable, Consulted, Informed) matrix to clearly define the roles and responsibilities of each individual and team involved in the ITIL 4 implementation. This helps avoid confusion, duplication of effort, and conflicts.
- **Governance Structure:** Establish a formal governance structure to oversee the implementation and ensure that it aligns with the organization's strategic goals.
- **Accountability:** Hold individuals accountable for their roles and responsibilities, providing them with the necessary authority and resources to succeed.

4. **Be Flexible and Adaptable:**
- **Tailor ITIL 4 to Your Needs:** ITIL 4 is a flexible framework. Adapt the practices and processes to fit your organization's unique culture, structure, and processes. Don't try to force-fit a standard approach; instead, tailor it to your specific needs.
- **Embrace Change:** Be prepared to adapt your plans and approaches as you learn and gain experience with ITIL 4. The implementation process is an opportunity for continuous learning and improvement.

5. **Measure and Communicate Progress:**
- **Establish KPIs:** Define clear and measurable KPIs that align with your ITIL 4 objectives. These KPIs should track both the efficiency and effectiveness of your IT services and processes.
- **Regular Reporting:** Track and report on KPIs regularly to monitor progress and identify areas for improvement.
- **Communicate Results:** Share the results of your ITIL 4 implementation with stakeholders, highlighting the positive impact it has had on service quality, efficiency, and customer satisfaction.

6. **Celebrate Successes and Learn from Failures:**
- **Recognize Achievements:** Celebrate successes and milestones along the way to maintain momentum and motivation.
- **Learn from Mistakes:** Don't be afraid to make mistakes. Learn from them, adjust your approach, and move forward.
- **Continuous Improvement:** View ITIL 4 adoption as a journey of continuous improvement. Don't settle for the status quo; always strive to find ways to do things better.

By following these tips and embracing a mindset of learning, adaptation, and continuous improvement, organizations can successfully navigate the ITIL 4 adoption journey and achieve lasting benefits in their IT service management practices.

Chapter Summary

In this chapter, we delved into the practical aspects of adopting ITIL 4 within your organization. We explored the compelling reasons to embrace this framework, the common challenges you might encounter, and the strategic steps to navigate a successful implementation.

Here's a recap of the key points:

- **The Need for ITIL 4:** We discussed the numerous benefits ITIL 4 brings to the table, including improved service quality, increased efficiency, enhanced customer satisfaction, and stronger alignment with business goals. We also acknowledged the common challenges faced by organizations in IT service management, such as increasing complexity and evolving customer expectations, highlighting how ITIL 4 can help address these issues.
- **Overcoming Adoption Challenges:** We outlined common obstacles to ITIL 4 adoption, such as resistance to change, lack of resources, and integration difficulties. We provided practical strategies for overcoming these challenges, emphasizing the importance of building a strong business case, securing leadership buy-in, clear communication, and a phased implementation approach.
- **Key Steps to Success:** We outlined the five key steps involved in adopting ITIL 4:
    1. **Assessing Organizational Readiness:** Understanding your current state and identifying strengths, weaknesses, and stakeholder expectations.
    2. **Planning the Implementation:** Developing a detailed roadmap with clear objectives, timelines, resource allocation, and communication plans.
    3. **Implementing ITIL 4 Practices:** Adopting a phased approach, starting small, and customizing practices to fit your organization's specific needs.
    4. **Measuring and Demonstrating Success:** Establishing KPIs and metrics to track progress, evaluate outcomes, and communicate the value of ITIL 4 to stakeholders.
    5. **Sustaining Adoption:** Embedding ITIL 4 into your organizational culture through continuous training, regular reviews, and ongoing communication and engagement.
- **Practical Tips:** We shared additional tips for successful ITIL 4 adoption, including focusing on quick wins, involving stakeholders, defining clear roles, being flexible, and celebrating successes.

By following these key steps and incorporating the tips and strategies discussed, your organization can embark on a successful ITIL 4 adoption journey. Remember, ITIL 4 is not a rigid framework but a flexible guide. Adapt it to your unique context, involve your stakeholders, and focus on continuous improvement to realize the full potential of ITIL 4 in transforming your IT service management practices.

Measuring and Demonstrating Success

Outline

- The Importance of Measuring Success in ITIL 4 Adoption
- Defining Metrics and Key Performance Indicators (KPIs)
- Types of Metrics
- Balanced Scorecard Approach
- Reporting and Communicating Success
- Challenges in Measuring and Demonstrating Success
- Overcoming Challenges: Best Practices
- Chapter Summary

The Importance of Measuring Success in ITIL 4 Adoption

Measurement is not just a post-implementation exercise in ITIL 4; it is an integral part of the adoption process. It provides the objective data and insights necessary to evaluate the effectiveness of ITIL 4 practices, track progress towards goals, and justify the investment made in service management.

Critical Role of Measurement:

1. **Validation of Effectiveness:**
   - **Measuring Outcomes, Not Just Outputs:** ITIL 4 emphasizes a shift from focusing on outputs (e.g., number of incidents resolved) to outcomes (e.g., customer satisfaction, reduced downtime). Measurement helps track these outcomes, validating the effectiveness of ITIL 4 in achieving desired business results.
   - **Evidence-Based Decision Making:** By tracking relevant metrics, organizations can make informed decisions about their ITIL 4 initiatives. This includes identifying what's working well and what needs adjustment, prioritizing future investments, and adapting strategies for continued improvement.
2. **Tracking Progress and Identifying Improvement Areas:**

- **Baselining Performance:** Measurement establishes a baseline of current performance, allowing organizations to track progress over time and identify areas where performance has improved or declined.
- **Pinpointing Bottlenecks:** Analyzing data collected through measurement helps pinpoint bottlenecks and inefficiencies in processes, services, and practices.
- **Data-Driven Improvement:** Measurement provides objective data that can be used to prioritize and implement improvement initiatives, ensuring that efforts are focused on areas that will have the most significant impact.
3. **Justifying Investments in IT Service Management:**

- **Demonstrating ROI:** By tracking the impact of ITIL 4 on key metrics like cost savings, efficiency gains, and customer satisfaction, organizations can demonstrate the return on investment (ROI) for their ITSM initiatives. This is crucial for securing continued funding and support from stakeholders.
- **Building Credibility:** Measurement provides evidence-based proof of the value that IT services deliver to the business, enhancing the credibility of the IT department and fostering trust with stakeholders.
- **Strategic Alignment:** By demonstrating how IT service management contributes to the achievement of strategic goals, organizations can strengthen the alignment between IT and the business, ensuring that IT investments are focused on areas that drive business value.

The Need for a Balanced Approach:

Measuring success in ITIL 4 adoption requires a balanced approach that considers both quantitative and qualitative measures. While quantitative metrics provide objective data on performance and outcomes, qualitative measures, such as customer feedback and employee surveys, offer valuable insights into the user experience and the impact of IT services on the organization's culture and processes.

By incorporating both types of measures, organizations can gain a comprehensive understanding of the effectiveness of their ITIL 4 implementation and make well-rounded decisions about future improvement initiatives. This balanced approach ensures that IT service management is not only efficient and effective but also customer-centric and aligned with the broader goals and values of the organization.

Defining Metrics and Key Performance Indicators (KPIs)

Defining clear and measurable metrics and Key Performance Indicators (KPIs) is a foundational step in establishing a robust measurement and reporting system for ITIL 4. The right metrics provide valuable insights into the effectiveness and efficiency of IT services, guiding decision-making, enabling continual improvement, and demonstrating the value delivered to the organization.

Importance of Defining Clear and Measurable Metrics and KPIs:

- **Clarity and Focus:** Well-defined metrics and KPIs provide clear targets for improvement efforts, ensuring that everyone in the organization understands what is being measured and why it matters.
- **Objective Assessment:** Measurable metrics provide objective data that can be used to assess performance, track progress, and make informed decisions. They eliminate subjectivity and provide a common language for evaluating success.
- **Accountability:** KPIs hold individuals and teams accountable for their performance, creating a sense of ownership and responsibility for achieving results.
- **Continuous Improvement:** Metrics provide the feedback loop necessary for continual improvement. By tracking performance over time, organizations can identify trends, pinpoint areas for improvement, and measure the impact of their efforts.

Choosing the Right Metrics:

Selecting the right metrics is crucial for effectively measuring and demonstrating the value of IT services. Consider the following factors:

- **Alignment with Strategic Goals:** Metrics should be directly linked to the organization's strategic goals and objectives. This ensures that IT service management efforts are focused on delivering value that matters to the business.
- **Customer Focus:** Metrics should reflect the needs and expectations of customers. This may include measures of customer satisfaction, service availability, and response times.
- **Value Drivers:** Identify the key drivers of value for IT services. These could include cost savings, revenue generation, improved productivity, or enhanced customer experience. Choose metrics that reflect these value drivers.
- **Measurability:** Select metrics that can be easily and accurately measured. This ensures that the data collected is reliable and can be used to make informed decisions.
- **Actionability:** Choose metrics that provide actionable insights. Metrics that simply measure activity without providing insights into how to improve are of limited value.

Characteristics of Good Metrics (SMART):

- **Specific:** Clearly defined and focused on a particular aspect of performance.
- **Measurable:** Quantifiable and can be tracked over time.
- **Achievable:** Realistic and attainable with the available resources.
- **Relevant:** Aligned with the organization's goals and objectives.
- **Time-Bound:** Associated with a specific timeframe for achievement.

The Need for Regular Review and Updates:

Business needs and priorities can change over time, and metrics should be reviewed and updated regularly to ensure they remain relevant and aligned with the organization's goals. Regular review also allows for identifying new metrics that may be more appropriate for measuring the evolving value of IT services.

By defining clear and measurable metrics and KPIs, organizations can create a robust measurement and reporting system that supports informed decision-making, drives continual improvement, and demonstrates the value of IT services to the business.

Types of Metrics

To effectively measure and demonstrate the success of ITIL 4 adoption, it's important to understand the different types of metrics that can be employed. These metrics provide insights into various aspects of service management, from the technical performance of infrastructure to the overall impact on business outcomes.

1. **Technology Metrics:**
- **Purpose:** These metrics focus on measuring the performance, availability, and reliability of IT infrastructure and components. They are essential for monitoring the health of the technical environment and identifying potential issues before they impact service delivery.
- **Examples:**
  - **Server Uptime:** The percentage of time a server is operational and available for use.
  - **Network Latency:** The time it takes for a packet of data to travel between two points on a network.
  - **Incident Response Time:** The average time taken to respond to and resolve incidents.
  - **Error Rates:** The frequency of errors or failures in IT systems or components.
  - **Mean Time Between Failures (MTBF):** The average time between failures for a particular component or system.
  - **Mean Time to Repair (MTTR):** The average time it takes to repair a failed component or system.
2. **Process Metrics:**
- **Purpose:** These metrics assess the efficiency and effectiveness of IT processes, such as incident management, change management, and problem management. They help identify bottlenecks, inefficiencies, and areas for improvement.
- **Examples:**
  - **Change Success Rate:** The percentage of successful changes implemented without causing incidents or service disruptions.
  - **Average Time to Resolve Problems:** The average time taken to identify and resolve the root cause of a problem.
  - **First Contact Resolution (FCR) Rate:** The percentage of incidents resolved on the first contact with the service desk.
  - **Request Fulfillment Rate:** The percentage of service requests that are fulfilled within agreed-upon timeframes.
  - **Backlog Management:** The number of open incidents, problems, or requests in the queue.
3. **Service Metrics:**
- **Purpose:** These metrics evaluate the quality and performance of IT services from the customer's perspective. They focus on how well services meet customer needs and expectations.
- **Examples:**
  - **Customer Satisfaction (CSAT):** The percentage of customers who are satisfied with the service.
  - **Net Promoter Score (NPS):** A measure of customer loyalty and willingness to recommend the service.

- - **Service Level Agreement (SLA) Compliance:** The percentage of time that service levels are met.
  - **User Experience Ratings:** Feedback from users on their experience with the service, including ease of use, responsiveness, and overall satisfaction.
4. **Business Metrics:**
- **Purpose:** These metrics measure the impact of IT services on the overall business performance. They provide a link between IT and business goals, demonstrating the value that IT services deliver to the organization.
- **Examples:**
  - **Return on Investment (ROI):** The financial return on an investment in IT services.
  - **Cost Savings:** The amount of money saved through the implementation of ITIL 4 practices and processes.
  - **Revenue Growth:** The increase in revenue attributed to IT services.
  - **Productivity Improvement:** The increase in employee productivity resulting from the use of IT services.
  - **Customer Acquisition and Retention:** The number of new customers acquired or existing customers retained due to improved service quality.

By utilizing a combination of these metrics, organizations can gain a comprehensive understanding of the performance and impact of their IT services. This data-driven approach enables them to make informed decisions, prioritize improvement initiatives, and demonstrate the value of IT service management to stakeholders.

Balanced Scorecard Approach

The Balanced Scorecard (BSC) is a strategic management framework that translates an organization's vision and strategy into a set of actionable objectives and performance measures. While not explicitly part of ITIL 4, the BSC aligns well with ITIL's focus on value creation and can be a powerful tool for measuring and demonstrating the success of IT service management initiatives.

Introduction to the Balanced Scorecard:

The Balanced Scorecard goes beyond traditional financial metrics, incorporating four key perspectives to provide a more holistic view of organizational performance:

1. **Financial Perspective:** This perspective focuses on the financial health and performance of the organization, including metrics such as revenue, profitability, return on investment (ROI), and cost savings.
2. **Customer Perspective:** This perspective focuses on customer satisfaction and perception of value, including metrics such as customer satisfaction ratings, Net Promoter Score (NPS), and market share.
3. **Internal Process Perspective:** This perspective focuses on the efficiency and effectiveness of internal processes, including metrics such as cycle times, error rates, throughput, and resource utilization.
4. **Learning and Growth Perspective:** This perspective focuses on the organization's ability to learn, adapt, and innovate, including metrics such as employee satisfaction, training effectiveness, and new product or service development.

Mapping ITIL 4 Metrics to the Balanced Scorecard:

ITIL 4 metrics can be effectively mapped to the four perspectives of the Balanced Scorecard to demonstrate the value of IT services to the business. Here's an example:

Balanced Scorecard Perspective	ITIL 4 Metrics
Financial Perspective	Cost per ticket, ROI for IT projects, Cost savings from automation
Customer Perspective	Customer satisfaction ratings, Net Promoter Score (NPS), Service level agreement (SLA) compliance
Internal Process Perspective	Mean time to resolve (MTTR) incidents, Change success rate, Availability and reliability metrics
Learning and Growth Perspective	Employee satisfaction surveys, Training completion rates, Number of new service offerings launched

By mapping ITIL 4 metrics to the Balanced Scorecard, organizations can show how IT service management contributes to achieving broader business goals. For example, reduced incident resolution times (Internal Process Perspective) can lead to improved customer satisfaction (Customer Perspective), which in turn can drive revenue growth (Financial Perspective).

Benefits of Using the Balanced Scorecard Approach:

- **Holistic View:** The Balanced Scorecard provides a comprehensive view of organizational performance, not just financial results.
- **Strategic Alignment:** It helps align IT service management initiatives with the organization's overall strategy and objectives.
- **Improved Communication:** The Balanced Scorecard provides a common language for communicating the value of IT services to stakeholders.
- **Performance Management:** It helps organizations identify areas for improvement and track progress towards goals.

By adopting a Balanced Scorecard approach to measurement, organizations can ensure that their IT service management efforts are focused on delivering value, not just achieving technical targets. This can lead to improved service quality, enhanced customer satisfaction, and greater business success.

Reporting and Communicating Success

Effectively reporting and communicating the results of ITIL 4 adoption is essential to demonstrate its value, gain stakeholder buy-in, and drive continuous improvement. It's not just about presenting data; it's about translating that data into meaningful insights that resonate with different audiences and inform decision-making.

Importance of Effective Reporting and Communication:

- **Demonstrating Value:** Reporting provides concrete evidence of the benefits ITIL 4 has brought to the organization. It showcases improvements in service quality, efficiency, customer satisfaction, and other key metrics, justifying the investment in the framework.
- **Building Trust and Transparency:** Transparent reporting builds trust with stakeholders by demonstrating accountability and commitment to improvement. It also fosters a sense of shared responsibility for service management success.
- **Driving Continuous Improvement:** Reporting highlights areas where further improvement is needed, providing valuable insights for prioritizing future initiatives and optimizing resources.
- **Informing Decision-Making:** Decision-makers need accurate and timely information to make informed choices about IT investments, service offerings, and resource allocation. Reporting provides them with the data they need to evaluate options and make strategic decisions.

- **Engaging Stakeholders:** Effective communication keeps stakeholders informed about the progress and impact of ITIL 4, encouraging their continued support and involvement in the improvement process.

Types of Reports:

1. **Dashboards:** Interactive visual displays that provide real-time insights into key performance indicators (KPIs). Dashboards can be customized to show the most relevant metrics for specific audiences, making it easy for them to quickly grasp the overall status and trends of IT service management.
2. **Scorecards:** Summarize key metrics and performance against targets, often using a traffic light system (red, yellow, green) to indicate performance levels. Scorecards provide a high-level overview of service performance and can be used to communicate with senior management and other stakeholders.
3. **Executive Summaries:** Concise, high-level reports that summarize the most important findings and insights from a detailed analysis. Executive summaries are designed for busy executives who need a quick overview of the situation and recommendations for action.
4. **Detailed Reports:** Provide in-depth analysis of specific aspects of IT service management, such as incident trends, problem root causes, or change success rates. These reports are typically used by IT managers and technical teams to investigate issues, identify trends, and develop improvement plans.

Tips for Tailoring Reports to Different Audiences:

- **Know Your Audience:** Understand the needs, interests, and level of technical knowledge of your audience. Tailor your reports accordingly, focusing on the information that is most relevant and meaningful to them.
- **Use Clear and Concise Language:** Avoid technical jargon and use language that is easy to understand.
- **Visualize Data:** Use charts, graphs, and other visuals to present data in a clear and engaging way. This makes it easier for stakeholders to understand complex information and identify trends.
- **Focus on Key Insights:** Highlight the most important findings and insights from your analysis. What are the key takeaways? What actions need to be taken?
- **Provide Recommendations:** Offer clear and actionable recommendations based on your analysis. This helps stakeholders understand the implications of the data and take appropriate action.

By tailoring your reports and communication to the specific needs of each audience, you can ensure that the message is received, understood, and acted upon. This will help you demonstrate the value of ITIL 4, secure continued support for your initiatives, and drive continuous improvement in your organization's IT service management practices.

Challenges in Measuring and Demonstrating Success

Measuring and demonstrating the success of ITIL 4 implementation can be a complex endeavor. Organizations often encounter various challenges that can hinder their ability to collect meaningful data, analyze it effectively, and communicate the value of ITIL 4 to stakeholders.

Common Challenges:

1. **Lack of Clear Metrics and KPIs:**
- **Description:** One of the primary challenges is the lack of clearly defined metrics and key performance indicators (KPIs). Without a clear understanding of what to measure and how to measure it, organizations may struggle to track progress, evaluate the effectiveness of ITIL 4 practices, and demonstrate value to stakeholders.
- **Solution:** To overcome this challenge, organizations should:

- ○ **Align Metrics with Goals:** Carefully select metrics and KPIs that are aligned with the organization's strategic goals and objectives.
- ○ **Focus on Outcomes:** Prioritize metrics that measure the impact of IT services on business outcomes, such as customer satisfaction, revenue growth, and cost savings.
- ○ **Use Established Frameworks:** Leverage established frameworks, such as the Balanced Scorecard, to ensure a balanced approach that considers financial, customer, internal process, and learning and growth perspectives.

2. **Difficulty in Collecting and Analyzing Data:**

- **Description:** Collecting and analyzing data can be complex and time-consuming, especially in large organizations with multiple systems and data sources. Data may be fragmented, inconsistent, or incomplete, making it difficult to extract meaningful insights.
- **Solution:** To address this challenge, organizations should:
  - ○ **Invest in Data Collection Tools:** Implement tools that can automate data collection from various sources and consolidate it into a central repository.
  - ○ **Establish Data Governance:** Define data ownership, access controls, and quality standards to ensure data accuracy and consistency.
  - ○ **Develop Data Analysis Skills:** Train employees on data analysis techniques to extract meaningful insights from data and identify improvement opportunities.

3. **Resistance to Change from Stakeholders:**

- **Description:** Stakeholders may resist the implementation of new metrics and reporting processes, especially if they are perceived as disruptive or unnecessary. They may also have different expectations about the benefits of ITIL 4, leading to skepticism about the value of measurement efforts.
- **Solution:** To overcome resistance to change, organizations should:
  - ○ **Communicate the Benefits:** Clearly explain the benefits of measurement and reporting, emphasizing how it can improve decision-making, optimize processes, and demonstrate the value of IT services.
  - ○ **Involve Stakeholders:** Involve stakeholders in the process of defining metrics and KPIs, ensuring that their perspectives are considered and that the metrics are relevant to their needs.
  - ○ **Provide Training:** Offer training to stakeholders on how to interpret and use the data generated by the measurement system.
  - ○ **Celebrate Successes:** Highlight and celebrate successes achieved through the use of data and metrics to build momentum and reinforce the value of measurement.

4. **Misaligned Expectations About the Benefits of ITIL 4:**

- **Description:** Stakeholders may have unrealistic expectations about the immediate benefits of ITIL 4 adoption. They may expect rapid improvements in all areas of service management, which can lead to disappointment and frustration if results are not immediately apparent.
- **Solution:** To manage expectations, organizations should:
  - ○ **Set Realistic Goals:** Establish clear and realistic goals for ITIL 4 adoption, focusing on achievable outcomes in a specific timeframe.
  - ○ **Communicate Progress:** Regularly communicate progress towards these goals to stakeholders, highlighting successes and addressing any challenges that arise.
  - ○ **Manage Expectations:** Explain that ITIL 4 is a journey of continuous improvement, and that significant benefits may not be realized overnight.
  - ○ **Focus on Value:** Emphasize the value that ITIL 4 is delivering to the business, even if it's not always reflected in immediate improvements to every metric.

By understanding and proactively addressing these challenges, organizations can overcome the obstacles to measuring and demonstrating the success of their ITIL 4 implementation. This will ensure that they have the data and insights they need to make informed decisions, continuously improve their services, and demonstrate the value of IT service management to the business.

Overcoming Challenges: Best Practices

Measuring and demonstrating the success of ITIL 4 adoption can be challenging, but with a proactive and well-structured approach, organizations can overcome these obstacles and build a robust measurement and reporting system that drives value and improvement.

Best Practices for Measuring and Demonstrating Success:

1. **Establishing a Clear Measurement Framework:**
   - **Define Objectives:** Clearly articulate the goals and objectives of your ITIL 4 implementation. What specific outcomes do you want to achieve? How will you measure success?
   - **Select Relevant Metrics:** Choose metrics and KPIs that align with your objectives and are meaningful to stakeholders. Focus on both outcome-based metrics (e.g., customer satisfaction, business impact) and output-based metrics (e.g., incident resolution times, change success rates).
   - **Establish Baselines:** Measure current performance levels to establish a baseline for comparison and track progress over time.
   - **Set Targets:** Define realistic and achievable targets for each metric. This will give you something to aim for and help you gauge the success of your efforts.
   - **Communicate the Framework:** Clearly communicate the measurement framework to all stakeholders, ensuring that everyone understands what is being measured, why it matters, and how it will be used to inform decision-making.
2. **Investing in Data Collection and Analysis Tools and Capabilities:**
   - **Automated Tools:** Implement tools that can automate the collection and aggregation of data from various sources, such as ITSM tools, monitoring systems, and surveys. This will save time, reduce manual effort, and improve data accuracy.
   - **Data Analytics:** Invest in data analytics tools and expertise to analyze data, identify trends, and uncover insights. This will enable you to make data-driven decisions and prioritize improvement initiatives.
   - **Visualization Tools:** Utilize dashboards, reports, and other visualization tools to present data in a clear and actionable format that is easy for stakeholders to understand.
3. **Communicating the Benefits of ITIL 4 and Managing Stakeholder Expectations:**
   - **Clear Communication:** Clearly communicate the benefits of ITIL 4 to stakeholders, explaining how it can improve service quality, efficiency, and customer satisfaction. Use language that is easy to understand and avoid technical jargon.
   - **Realistic Expectations:** Set realistic expectations about the timeframe and potential impact of ITIL 4 adoption. Explain that it is an ongoing journey of continuous improvement and that results may not be immediate.
   - **Regular Updates:** Provide regular updates on progress, highlighting successes and addressing challenges. This transparency helps build trust and maintain stakeholder engagement.
   - **Focus on Value:** When communicating with stakeholders, focus on the value that ITIL 4 is delivering to the business. Highlight how IT services are contributing to achieving strategic goals and improving business outcomes.
4. **Fostering a Culture of Transparency and Accountability:**
   - **Transparency:** Make measurement data and reports readily available to all relevant stakeholders. This transparency fosters trust and encourages a sense of ownership for improvement initiatives.
   - **Accountability:** Hold individuals and teams accountable for their performance against established metrics. This ensures that everyone is focused on achieving results and contributes to a culture of continuous improvement.
   - **Recognition:** Recognize and reward individuals and teams who achieve their performance targets or contribute significantly to improvement efforts. This reinforces the importance of measurement and encourages a culture of excellence.
5. **Continuously Reviewing and Refining the Measurement and Reporting Process:**

- **Regular Review:** Regularly review your measurement and reporting process to ensure that it remains relevant and effective. Are the metrics still aligned with organizational goals? Are there new metrics that should be tracked? Is the data being collected and analyzed effectively?
- **Feedback:** Seek feedback from stakeholders on the effectiveness of the measurement and reporting process. Use this feedback to identify areas for improvement and make necessary adjustments.
- **Adaptation:** As business needs and technologies evolve, be prepared to adapt your measurement and reporting process accordingly. New metrics may need to be introduced, or existing ones may need to be modified to reflect changing priorities.

By implementing these best practices, organizations can overcome the challenges associated with measuring and demonstrating the success of their ITIL 4 implementation. This will ensure that they have the data and insights they need to make informed decisions, continuously improve their services, and demonstrate the value of IT service management to the business.

Chapter Summary

In this chapter, we delved into the crucial aspect of Measuring and Demonstrating Success within the context of ITIL 4 adoption. This phase isn't merely an afterthought; it's an ongoing endeavor vital for ensuring your IT service management efforts are effective and aligned with broader organizational goals.

Key takeaways from this chapter include:

- **The Importance of Measurement:** We emphasized the critical role measurement plays in validating the effectiveness of your ITIL 4 implementation. It's about demonstrating tangible value to the organization, tracking progress, identifying improvement areas, and ultimately justifying your investment in IT service management.
- **Defining Metrics and KPIs:** We discussed the importance of selecting clear, measurable metrics and KPIs that directly align with your organization's strategic goals and objectives. These metrics should reflect the value IT services bring, aiding in continuous improvement. Remember, good metrics are SMART: specific, measurable, achievable, relevant, and time-bound.
- **Types of Metrics:** We explored the different categories of metrics used in ITIL 4: technology metrics (measuring infrastructure performance), process metrics (evaluating process efficiency), service metrics (focusing on customer perspectives), and business metrics (linking IT services to broader business outcomes). We provided numerous examples for each category to help you choose the most relevant ones for your organization.
- **Balanced Scorecard Approach:** We introduced the Balanced Scorecard as a framework for a more holistic view of organizational performance, incorporating financial, customer, internal process, and learning and growth perspectives. We demonstrated how ITIL 4 metrics can be mapped to these perspectives to showcase the broader value IT services provide.
- **Reporting and Communication:** We emphasized the importance of effective reporting and communication to share your ITIL 4 success story with stakeholders. We discussed various report types like dashboards, scorecards, and executive summaries, providing tips for tailoring communication to different audiences.
- **Challenges and Best Practices:** We acknowledged the common challenges organizations face in measuring success, such as lack of clear metrics, data collection difficulties, resistance to change, and misaligned expectations. To overcome these, we offered practical best practices like establishing a clear measurement framework, investing in data tools, effective communication, fostering transparency, and continuous review of the measurement process.

By understanding and applying the principles discussed in this chapter, you can effectively measure and communicate the success of your ITIL 4 adoption, solidifying IT's position as a strategic asset within your organization.

Case Studies and Real-World Examples

Outline

- Introduction to Case Studies
- Case Study 1: ITIL 4 Transformation in a Large Financial Institution
- Case Study 2: Enhancing Customer Experience in a Retail Company
- Case Study 3: Agile ITIL Implementation in a Tech Startup
- Case Study 4: Optimizing IT Operations in a Manufacturing Firm
- Key Takeaways and Lessons Learned
- Chapter Summary

Introduction to Case Studies

The preceding chapters have provided a solid theoretical foundation of ITIL 4, detailing its framework, guiding principles, and practices. However, the true power of ITIL 4 lies in its practical application. Case studies provide invaluable insights into how organizations have successfully leveraged ITIL 4 to overcome challenges, improve their IT service management (ITSM) practices, and ultimately, deliver greater value to their customers and stakeholders.

Purpose of Case Studies:

- **Real-World Application:** Case studies bridge the gap between theory and practice. They demonstrate how abstract concepts and principles can be applied in real-world scenarios, providing tangible examples of how ITIL 4 can be adapted to address specific organizational needs.
- **Illustrating Success Stories:** Case studies showcase the successes and challenges that organizations have encountered in their ITIL 4 adoption journey. By sharing their experiences, they offer valuable lessons and insights that can inspire and guide other organizations.
- **Diverse Contexts:** Case studies often come from various industries and organizational contexts, highlighting the versatility and adaptability of ITIL 4. They demonstrate that ITIL 4 is not a one-size-fits-all solution but a flexible framework that can be tailored to meet the unique needs of different organizations.

Value of Learning from the Experiences of Others:

- **Gaining Insights:** Case studies provide valuable insights into the challenges and opportunities associated with ITIL 4 adoption. By learning from the experiences of others, organizations can anticipate potential pitfalls, identify best practices, and make more informed decisions about their own implementation.
- **Inspiration and Motivation:** Success stories of ITIL 4 implementation can be a source of inspiration and motivation for organizations embarking on their own ITIL journey. They show what is possible when ITIL 4 is applied effectively and encourage organizations to strive for excellence in their service management practices.
- **Peer Learning:** Case studies provide an opportunity for organizations to learn from their peers. They can connect with other organizations that have implemented ITIL 4, share experiences, and learn from each other's successes and failures.
- **Practical Guidance:** Many case studies offer practical tips and recommendations for implementing ITIL 4. This can be valuable guidance for organizations that are new to the framework or are struggling with specific challenges.

In the following sections, we will explore several case studies that illustrate the practical application of ITIL 4 in different organizational contexts. These case studies will highlight the specific challenges that organizations faced, the strategies they employed to overcome them, and the outcomes they achieved through their ITIL 4 adoption. By learning from these examples, you can gain valuable insights and inspiration for your own ITIL 4 journey, ensuring that your implementation is successful and delivers lasting benefits to your organization.

Case Study 1: ITIL 4 Transformation in a Large Financial Institution

Challenges Faced by the Organization:

GlobalFin, a leading financial institution with a vast network of branches and a diverse range of IT services, was grappling with numerous challenges:

- **Siloed IT Departments:** Different IT departments operated independently, leading to poor communication, duplicated efforts, and inconsistent service delivery.
- **Inefficient Processes:** Many IT processes were manual, paper-based, and prone to errors and delays.
- **Lack of Visibility:** There was limited visibility into service performance, making it difficult to identify and address issues proactively.
- **Poor Customer Satisfaction:** Customers complained of slow response times, unresolved issues, and a lack of transparency in the service process.
- **Misalignment with Business Goals:** IT investments were not always aligned with the organization's strategic goals, resulting in wasted resources and missed opportunities.

ITIL 4 Practices and Principles Adopted:

GlobalFin recognized that a fundamental transformation was needed to improve its IT service management. They decided to adopt ITIL 4, embracing its key principles and practices to address their challenges:

- **Service Value System (SVS):** GlobalFin implemented the SVS as a guiding framework, focusing on the end-to-end creation and delivery of value through IT services.
- **Customer Centricity:** They adopted a customer-centric approach, prioritizing customer needs and expectations in all service management activities.
- **Value Co-Creation:** GlobalFin actively engaged customers and stakeholders in service design and improvement processes, ensuring that services met their needs and delivered value.
- **Continual Improvement:** They established a culture of continual improvement, encouraging employees to identify and implement opportunities for optimization.
- **Collaboration:** They broke down silos between IT departments, fostering collaboration and communication to improve efficiency and effectiveness.
- **Focus on Value:** All IT initiatives were evaluated based on their potential to deliver value to customers and the business.

Specific Steps Taken During Implementation:

1. **Baseline Assessment:** GlobalFin conducted a comprehensive assessment of their current ITSM practices, identifying strengths, weaknesses, and areas for improvement.
2. **Implementation Roadmap:** They developed a phased implementation roadmap, prioritizing the most impactful ITIL 4 practices and aligning them with their strategic goals.
3. **Phased Implementation:** They started with a pilot implementation of a few key practices, such as incident management and change management. Once these practices were successfully established, they gradually expanded the implementation to other areas.
4. **Training and Communication:** They invested heavily in training and communication to ensure that employees understood the new ITIL 4 concepts and practices and were engaged in the change process.

5. **Measurement and Reporting:** They established a comprehensive measurement and reporting system to track the progress of the implementation and demonstrate its impact on service quality, efficiency, and customer satisfaction.

Outcomes Achieved:

The ITIL 4 transformation at GlobalFin yielded significant results:

- **Improved Service Quality:** Incidents were resolved faster, service availability increased, and customer satisfaction scores improved significantly.
- **Increased Efficiency:** Automated processes, streamlined workflows, and improved collaboration led to a 30% reduction in operational costs.
- **Enhanced Customer Satisfaction:** Customers reported a more positive experience with IT services, thanks to faster response times, more effective communication, and a greater focus on meeting their needs.
- **Better Alignment with Business Goals:** IT investments were more closely aligned with strategic objectives, ensuring that IT was contributing to the organization's overall success.
- **Increased Employee Engagement:** Employees felt more empowered and engaged in their work, as they were encouraged to contribute to the improvement process and share their knowledge and expertise.

This case study demonstrates the transformative power of ITIL 4 when it is implemented in a holistic and customer-centric manner. By embracing the principles of value co-creation, continual improvement, and collaboration, organizations can achieve significant improvements in their IT service management practices and deliver greater value to their customers and stakeholders.

Case Study 2: Enhancing Customer Experience in a Retail Company

Challenges Faced by the Organization:

RetailCo, a large multinational retail company, was facing a growing number of customer complaints regarding their IT support services. Customers were frustrated with long wait times, inefficient issue resolution, and a lack of transparency in the support process. This negative customer experience was starting to impact the company's brand reputation and sales.

- **High Volume of Customer Complaints:** The customer support team was overwhelmed by a high volume of calls and emails, leading to long wait times and delayed responses.
- **Slow Response Times:** The average time to resolve customer issues was lengthy, causing further frustration and dissatisfaction.
- **Difficulty Resolving Issues Effectively:** The support team struggled to diagnose and resolve complex issues, often requiring multiple escalations and interactions with different departments.
- **Lack of Transparency:** Customers felt in the dark about the status of their issues, leading to a lack of trust and confidence in the IT support team.

ITIL 4 Practices and Principles Adopted:

To address these challenges and enhance the customer experience, RetailCo decided to adopt ITIL 4, focusing on the following practices and principles:

- **Incident Management:** Streamlining the incident management process to ensure faster and more efficient resolution of customer issues.
- **Service Request Management:** Improving the service request process to handle customer requests for information or assistance more effectively.
- **Knowledge Management:** Implementing a knowledge management system to capture and share knowledge, enabling faster resolution of common issues and reducing the need for escalations.

- **Self-Service Portal:** Developing a user-friendly self-service portal where customers could easily find answers to common questions, report issues, and track the status of their requests.
- **Customer Feedback:** Actively seeking and analyzing customer feedback to identify pain points and areas for improvement.
- **Focus on Value:** Aligning IT support services with customer needs and expectations, ensuring that they deliver value and contribute to a positive customer experience.

Specific Steps Taken During Implementation:

1. **Establishing a Customer-Focused Service Desk:** RetailCo created a dedicated service desk team that was trained in customer service skills and empowered to resolve customer issues promptly.
2. **Implementing a Knowledge Management System:** A centralized knowledge base was created to store information about common problems and solutions. This enabled support agents to quickly access relevant information and resolve issues more efficiently.
3. **Automating Routine Tasks:** The company implemented automation tools to handle routine tasks such as password resets and account unlocks, freeing up support agents to focus on more complex issues.
4. **Developing a Self-Service Portal:** A user-friendly self-service portal was created, allowing customers to access information, report issues, and track their requests online. This improved customer convenience and reduced the workload on the service desk.
5. **Measuring Customer Satisfaction:** Regular customer satisfaction surveys were conducted to gather feedback and identify areas for improvement.

Outcomes Achieved:

The implementation of ITIL 4 practices and principles led to significant improvements in RetailCo's customer support services:

- **Reduced Complaint Volumes:** The number of customer complaints decreased by 40% as issues were resolved more quickly and efficiently.
- **Improved Response Times:** The average response time for customer inquiries was reduced by 50%, improving customer satisfaction.
- **Higher First-Contact Resolution (FCR) Rates:** The FCR rate increased to 80%, demonstrating that most issues were resolved on the first contact with the service desk.
- **Increased Customer Satisfaction:** Customer satisfaction scores improved significantly as a result of faster response times, more effective issue resolution, and greater transparency.
- **Improved Brand Reputation:** The enhanced customer experience helped to strengthen the company's brand reputation and build customer loyalty.

This case study demonstrates how the adoption of ITIL 4 practices, with a strong focus on customer feedback and value creation, can significantly improve the customer experience and drive positive business outcomes.

Case Study 3: Agile ITIL Implementation in a Tech Startup

Challenges Faced by the Organization:

InnovateTech, a fast-growing tech startup, was experiencing the classic pains of rapid expansion. Their IT service management (ITSM) processes were struggling to keep pace with the increasing demands of new product development, an expanding user base, and evolving customer needs.

- **Rapid Growth:** The company was doubling in size every year, putting a strain on existing IT infrastructure and support processes.

- **Changing Requirements:** The constantly evolving nature of their products and services required a nimble and adaptable ITSM approach.
- **Need for Flexibility and Agility:** Traditional, rigid processes were hindering the company's ability to innovate and respond quickly to market changes.

ITIL 4 Practices and Principles Adopted:

InnovateTech recognized the need for a more agile and flexible approach to ITSM and decided to embrace ITIL 4, specifically tailoring their implementation to incorporate Agile principles and methodologies. They focused on:

- **Iterative Development:** Breaking down large initiatives into smaller, manageable chunks that could be delivered and improved upon quickly.
- **Collaboration:** Fostering cross-functional collaboration between IT, development, and business teams to ensure alignment and faster decision-making.
- **Continuous Feedback:** Establishing short feedback loops to gather input from customers and stakeholders, enabling rapid adaptation and improvement.

Specific Steps Taken During Implementation:

1. **Cross-Functional Teams:** The company created small, autonomous teams composed of members from different departments, each responsible for a specific service or product. This facilitated collaboration, reduced communication barriers, and empowered teams to make decisions quickly.
2. **Short Feedback Loops:** They established regular sprint reviews and retrospectives to gather feedback from customers and stakeholders. This feedback was then used to prioritize and implement improvements in the next iteration.
3. **Visual Management Tools:** The teams used visual management tools like Kanban boards and Scrum boards to track progress, visualize workflows, and identify bottlenecks. This enhanced transparency and promoted a shared understanding of priorities and dependencies.
4. **Automation:** The company leveraged automation tools to streamline repetitive tasks and free up resources for more strategic activities. This included automating incident routing, service request fulfillment, and software deployment processes.

Outcomes Achieved:

The Agile ITIL implementation yielded significant benefits for InnovateTech:

- **Faster Time to Market:** By adopting iterative development and breaking down work into smaller chunks, the company was able to deliver new services and features more quickly, staying ahead of the competition.
- **Improved Responsiveness to Customer Needs:** The short feedback loops and customer-centric approach enabled the company to respond rapidly to changing customer needs and expectations, enhancing customer satisfaction and loyalty.
- **Increased Employee Engagement:** The collaborative and empowering nature of Agile practices increased employee engagement and motivation, leading to a more productive and innovative workforce.
- **Culture of Innovation:** The iterative and feedback-driven approach fostered a culture of continuous improvement and innovation, enabling the company to adapt quickly to changing market conditions and technological advancements.

This case study demonstrates that ITIL 4, when implemented with an Agile mindset, can be highly effective for fast-growing organizations that need a flexible and adaptable approach to IT service management. By focusing on collaboration, feedback, and iterative improvement, InnovateTech was able to overcome the challenges of rapid growth and changing requirements, ensuring that its IT services remained aligned with the needs of its customers and the business.

Case Study 4: Optimizing IT Operations in a Manufacturing Firm

Challenges Faced by the Organization:

ManuCorp, a global manufacturing company with a large and complex IT infrastructure, was facing escalating IT costs, inefficient processes, and a lack of visibility into the performance of its IT services. This hindered their ability to support business growth and deliver value to customers.

- **High IT Costs:** The company's IT budget was growing rapidly, driven by increasing demands for new services, rising maintenance costs, and inefficient resource utilization.
- **Inefficient Processes:** Many IT processes were manual, time-consuming, and prone to errors. This resulted in delays, rework, and lost productivity.
- **Lack of Visibility:** The company lacked a clear understanding of how its IT resources were being used and how IT services were contributing to business outcomes. This made it difficult to justify IT investments and identify areas for improvement.

ITIL 4 Practices and Principles Adopted:

To address these challenges and optimize its IT operations, ManuCorp decided to adopt ITIL 4, focusing on the following practices and principles:

- **Optimize and Automate:** Streamlining processes, eliminating waste, and leveraging automation tools to improve efficiency and reduce costs.
- **Focus on Value:** Shifting the focus from technology outputs to business outcomes, ensuring that IT services deliver tangible value to the organization.
- **Measurement and Reporting:** Implementing a comprehensive measurement and reporting system to track performance, identify improvement opportunities, and demonstrate value.
- **Continual Improvement:** Embracing a culture of continuous improvement, where processes and services are regularly reviewed and enhanced to meet changing business needs.

Specific Steps Taken During Implementation:

1. **Cost-Benefit Analysis:** The company conducted a detailed cost-benefit analysis of its IT services, identifying areas where costs could be reduced and efficiency improved.
2. **Process Optimization:** ManuCorp mapped out its key IT processes, such as incident management, change management, and request fulfillment, and identified opportunities for streamlining and automation.
3. **Automation Implementation:** They implemented automation tools for tasks such as incident routing, password resets, software deployment, and server provisioning, reducing manual effort and improving efficiency.
4. **Performance Measurement:** The company established key performance indicators (KPIs) to track the effectiveness of its IT services and processes. These KPIs were used to monitor progress, identify improvement opportunities, and report on the value delivered by IT to the business.
5. **Continual Improvement:** ManuCorp established a continual improvement program that involved regular reviews of processes, metrics, and feedback from stakeholders. This helped ensure that IT services remained aligned with business needs and continued to deliver value.

Outcomes Achieved:

The adoption of ITIL 4 and the implementation of optimization and automation initiatives led to significant improvements in ManuCorp's IT operations:

- **Reduced IT Costs:** The company achieved a 20% reduction in IT operating costs through process optimization, automation, and better resource utilization.

- **Improved Operational Efficiency:** Automated processes and streamlined workflows resulted in faster service delivery, quicker incident resolution, and improved responsiveness to business needs.
- **Increased Productivity:** By automating repetitive tasks, IT staff were freed up to focus on more strategic and value-adding activities, leading to increased productivity and employee satisfaction.
- **Enhanced Service Quality:** Improved processes, better resource management, and proactive problem-solving led to a significant reduction in service disruptions and improved overall service quality.

This case study demonstrates the power of the "Optimize and Automate" principle in ITIL 4. By adopting a value-driven approach, optimizing processes, and leveraging automation, organizations can achieve significant cost savings, improve operational efficiency, and deliver high-quality IT services that meet the needs of the business.

Key Takeaways and Lessons Learned

The case studies presented in this chapter offer valuable insights into the real-world application of ITIL 4 and the "Optimize and Automate" principle. By examining the challenges faced, strategies employed, and outcomes achieved by different organizations, we can glean valuable lessons that can be applied to other ITIL 4 adoption journeys.

Common Themes and Successful Strategies:

- **Holistic Approach:** All case studies demonstrate the importance of adopting a holistic approach to IT service management. This involves looking beyond individual processes and technologies and considering the entire service value chain, as well as the needs of all stakeholders.
- **Focus on Value:** The organizations in the case studies all prioritized value creation, aligning their IT services with business goals and focusing on delivering tangible benefits to customers and stakeholders.
- **Data-Driven Decision Making:** Measurement and metrics played a crucial role in all cases, providing the data needed to identify improvement opportunities, track progress, and demonstrate the value of ITIL 4.
- **Continual Improvement:** All organizations embraced a culture of continual improvement, regularly reviewing and refining their processes, tools, and technologies to meet evolving needs.
- **Collaboration:** Collaboration between IT teams, business units, and stakeholders was a key factor in the success of these implementations.
- **Flexibility and Adaptability:** The case studies illustrate the importance of tailoring ITIL 4 to the specific context and needs of each organization. There is no one-size-fits-all approach, and organizations need to be flexible and adaptable in their implementation.

Potential Pitfalls to Avoid:

- **Underestimating Complexity:** ITIL 4 implementation can be complex and challenging, especially in large organizations with legacy systems and processes. It's important to have a realistic understanding of the scope of the project and the resources required.
- **Lack of Leadership Commitment:** Without strong leadership commitment and support, ITIL 4 initiatives can easily falter. Leaders need to champion the change, provide resources, and create a culture of continual improvement.
- **Resistance to Change:** Employees may resist ITIL 4 adoption if they don't understand its benefits or feel threatened by the changes. Effective communication, training, and stakeholder engagement are essential to overcome resistance.
- **Ignoring Existing Strengths:** The "Start Where You Are" principle is important. Organizations should not discard their existing processes and tools but build upon them and integrate them with ITIL 4 practices.

Applying Lessons to Other Organizations:

The lessons learned from these case studies can be applied to other organizations considering ITIL 4 adoption. Here are some key takeaways:

- **Start with a clear vision and objectives:** Define what you want to achieve with ITIL 4 and how it will benefit your organization.
- **Conduct a thorough assessment:** Assess your organization's readiness for change and identify areas for improvement.
- **Develop a comprehensive plan:** Create a detailed implementation plan that outlines the steps, timelines, and resources needed.
- **Involve stakeholders:** Engage stakeholders early and often to build support and ensure that the implementation meets their needs.
- **Be flexible and adaptable:** Tailor ITIL 4 to your organization's specific context and be prepared to adjust your approach as needed.
- **Measure and communicate progress:** Track progress towards your goals and communicate the results to stakeholders.
- **Embrace continual improvement:** Make continual improvement an integral part of your IT service management culture.

By learning from the experiences of others and applying these best practices, your organization can successfully adopt ITIL 4 and achieve lasting improvements in your IT service management practices. Remember, ITIL 4 is not a destination; it's a journey of continuous learning and improvement. Embrace the challenge, stay focused on your goals, and leverage the power of ITIL 4 to transform your IT organization and deliver greater value to your customers and stakeholders.

Chapter Summary

In this chapter, we explored the practical application of ITIL 4 through real-world case studies and examples. We examined how organizations across various industries have successfully implemented ITIL 4 principles and practices to overcome challenges, improve their IT service management capabilities, and achieve significant business outcomes.

Key takeaways from this chapter:

- **Case Study 1: ITIL 4 Transformation in a Large Financial Institution:** We saw how GlobalFin, a large financial institution, addressed challenges like siloed departments, inefficient processes, and poor customer satisfaction by adopting a holistic, customer-centric approach with ITIL 4. The implementation resulted in improved service quality, increased efficiency, and enhanced customer satisfaction.
- **Case Study 2: Enhancing Customer Experience in a Retail Company:** We learned how RetailCo, a multinational retailer, leveraged ITIL 4 practices like incident management, service request management, knowledge management, and self-service portals to significantly improve customer satisfaction and brand reputation.
- **Case Study 3: Agile ITIL Implementation in a Tech Startup:** We explored how InnovateTech, a fast-growing tech startup, adopted an Agile approach to ITIL 4 implementation, focusing on iterative development, collaboration, and continuous feedback. This approach enabled them to respond quickly to changing needs, accelerate time to market, and foster a culture of innovation.
- **Case Study 4: Optimizing IT Operations in a Manufacturing Firm:** We saw how ManuCorp, a global manufacturing company, used ITIL 4 to optimize its IT operations, reduce costs, and improve efficiency. They achieved this by implementing automation tools, streamlining processes, and adopting a value-driven approach to service management.

Lessons Learned:

- **Holistic Approach:** A holistic approach that considers the interconnectedness of all elements in the IT service management system is crucial for success.
- **Focus on Value:** Aligning IT services with business goals and focusing on delivering value to customers and stakeholders is essential.
- **Data-Driven Decision Making:** Measurement and metrics provide valuable insights for identifying improvement opportunities and demonstrating the value of ITIL 4.
- **Continual Improvement:** Embracing a culture of continuous improvement is key to adapting to change and achieving long-term success.
- **Collaboration:** Collaboration between IT teams, business units, and stakeholders is essential for successful ITIL 4 implementation.
- **Flexibility and Adaptability:** ITIL 4 should be tailored to the specific context and needs of each organization. There is no one-size-fits-all approach.

By learning from these case studies and embracing the principles of ITIL 4, your organization can also achieve significant improvements in your IT service management practices, enhance customer satisfaction, and drive business value.

Appendices

Appendix A: Glossary of Key Terms

Agile: A set of values and principles for software development that emphasizes collaboration, flexibility, and iterative delivery.

Availability: The ability of a service or other configuration item (CI) to perform its agreed function when required.

Business Impact Analysis (BIA): A process that identifies the critical business processes and the impact that a disruption would have on them.

Change: The addition, modification, or removal of anything that could have a direct or indirect effect on services.

Change Enablement: The practice of maximizing the number of successful IT changes by ensuring that risks are properly assessed, authorized, and managed.

Configuration Item (CI): Any component that needs to be managed in order to deliver an IT service.

Continual Improvement: The ongoing improvement of products, services, and practices.

Customer: A person who defines the requirements for a service and takes responsibility for the outcomes of service consumption.

Event: Any change of state that has significance for the management of a service or other configuration item (CI).

Four Dimensions of Service Management: Organizations and people, information and technology, partners and suppliers, value streams and processes.

Governance: The means by which an organization is directed and controlled.

Guiding Principles: Recommendations that can guide an organization in all circumstances, regardless of changes in its goals, strategies, type of work, or management structure.

Incident: An unplanned interruption to a service or reduction in the quality of a service.

Information Security Management: The practice of protecting information from unauthorized access, use, disclosure, disruption, modification, or destruction.

IT Asset Management (ITAM): The practice of planning and managing the full lifecycle of all IT assets.

ITIL (IT Infrastructure Library): A set of best practices for IT service management.

Knowledge Management: The practice of capturing, storing, sharing, and reusing knowledge and information within the organization.

Mean Time Between Failures (MTBF): The average time between failures of a system or component.

Mean Time to Repair (MTTR): The average time it takes to repair a failed system or component.

Monitoring and Event Management: The practice of systematically observing services and service components, and recording and reporting selected changes of state identified as events.

Organization: A person or a group of people that has its own functions with responsibilities, authorities, and relationships to achieve its objectives.

Outcome: A result for a stakeholder enabled by one or more outputs.

Output: A tangible or intangible deliverable of an activity.

Partner: A person or organization that has a formal relationship or arrangement with another person or organization to provide services.

Problem: A cause, or potential cause, of one or more incidents.

Process: A set of interrelated or interacting activities that transform inputs into outputs.

Release: A version of a service or other configuration item (CI) that is made available for use.

Release Management: The practice of planning, scheduling, and controlling the movement of releases to test and live environments.

Risk: A possible event that could cause harm or loss.

Service: A means of enabling value co-creation by facilitating outcomes that customers want to achieve, without the customer having to manage specific costs and risks.

Service Catalog Management: The practice of providing and maintaining a single source of information about all services offered by the organization.

Service Configuration Management (SCM): The practice of ensuring that accurate and reliable information about configuration items (CIs) and the relationships between them is available when and where it is needed.

Service Continuity Management: The practice of ensuring that the availability and performance of services are maintained at sufficient levels in case of a significant disruption.

Service Desk: The practice of capturing demand for incident resolution and service requests.

Service Design: The practice of designing new or changed services.

Service Level Agreement (SLA): A documented agreement between a service provider and a customer that identifies both the services required and the expected level of service.

Service Request: A request from a user or user's authorized representative that initiates a service action that has been agreed as a normal part of service delivery.

Service Value Chain (SVC): A set of interconnected activities that an organization performs to deliver a valuable product or service to its consumers.

Service Value System (SVS): A model that describes how all the components and activities of an organization work together as a system to enable value creation.

Stakeholder: A person or organization that has an interest or involvement in an organization, product, service, practice, or other entity.

Supplier: A person or organization that provides goods or services to another organization.

Technical Management Practices: Practices that are primarily focused on the management of technology.

Utility: The functionality offered by a product or service to meet a particular need.

Value: The perceived benefits, usefulness, and importance of something.

Value Stream: A series of steps an organization undertakes to create and deliver products and services to consumers.

Warranty: Assurance that a product or service will meet agreed-upon requirements.

Appendix B: ITIL Exam Preparation Tips

Preparing for the ITIL 4 Foundation exam can be a daunting task, but with the right approach and resources, you can increase your chances of success. This appendix provides essential tips and strategies to help you prepare effectively and confidently for the exam.

1. Understand the Exam Structure and Content:

- **Syllabus:** Familiarize yourself with the official ITIL 4 Foundation syllabus. This will outline the key concepts, practices, and terminology that you need to know.
- **Exam Format:** Understand the exam format, which is a multiple-choice test with 40 questions. You need to answer 26 questions correctly to pass (65%).
- **Time Limit:** The exam duration is 60 minutes for candidates taking it in their native language or 75 minutes for those taking it in a second language.

2. Use Multiple Study Resources:

- **The ITIL 4 Foundation Book:** This is the official guide to the ITIL 4 framework. Read it thoroughly and take notes on key concepts.
- **Training Courses:** Consider enrolling in an ITIL 4 Foundation training course. This will provide you with structured learning, expert guidance, and the opportunity to ask questions and clarify doubts.
- **Practice Exams:** Take practice exams to assess your knowledge and identify areas where you need further study. Many online resources offer practice exams and quizzes.
- **Study Guides and Flashcards:** Utilize study guides and flashcards to reinforce key concepts and terminology.
- **Online Resources:** Explore online resources like blogs, articles, and videos that provide additional insights and explanations.

3. Focus on Key Concepts and Terminology:

- **Guiding Principles:** Understand the seven guiding principles of ITIL 4 and how they apply to service management.
- **Four Dimensions:** Grasp the four dimensions of service management and their role in the Service Value System.
- **Service Value Chain:** Understand the six value chain activities and how they contribute to value creation.
- **Practices:** Familiarize yourself with the 34 management practices and their key activities and outcomes.

4. Develop a Study Plan and Schedule:

- **Time Management:** Create a realistic study schedule that allows sufficient time to cover all the topics in the syllabus. Allocate more time to areas where you feel less confident.
- **Study Environment:** Find a quiet and comfortable place where you can focus on your studies without distractions.
- **Active Learning:** Use active learning techniques, such as summarizing concepts in your own words, creating flashcards, and teaching others what you've learned.
- **Practice Regularly:** Take regular practice exams and quizzes to assess your progress and identify areas that need further review.

5. Exam Day Tips:

- **Arrive Early:** Arrive at the exam center early to allow time for check-in and settling in.
- **Read Questions Carefully:** Read each question carefully and make sure you understand what is being asked before choosing an answer.

- **Time Management:** Pace yourself during the exam, ensuring that you have enough time to answer all questions.
- **Don't Panic:** If you encounter a difficult question, don't panic. Move on to the next question and come back to it later if you have time.
- **Review Answers:** Before submitting your answers, take a few minutes to review them and make any necessary corrections.

Remember: The ITIL 4 Foundation exam is designed to test your understanding of the framework, not just your ability to memorize facts. Focus on understanding the concepts, principles, and practices, and how they apply to real-world scenarios. By preparing thoroughly and approaching the exam with confidence, you can increase your chances of success and demonstrate your expertise in IT service management.

Appendix C: Further Reading and Resources

To deepen your understanding of ITIL 4 and stay updated on the latest developments in service management, here's a curated list of further reading and resources:

Official ITIL Resources:

- **AXELOS:** The official website of AXELOS, the custodian of ITIL, offers a wealth of resources, including the latest ITIL publications, white papers, case studies, and information about ITIL certifications.
    - Website: https://www.axelos.com/
- **ITIL 4 Foundation Book:** The official ITIL 4 Foundation publication provides a comprehensive introduction to the framework and its core concepts.
- **ITIL 4 Practice Guides:** These guides offer in-depth guidance on the 34 ITIL practices, including detailed descriptions, activities, inputs, outputs, and metrics.

Additional Recommended Reading:

- **The Phoenix Project:** A DevOps Handbook for IT Professionals by Gene Kim, Kevin Behr, and George Spafford: This novel tells the story of an IT manager who applies DevOps principles to transform his organization, providing valuable insights into Agile and DevOps methodologies.
- **The DevOps Handbook: How to Create World-Class Agility, Reliability, and Security in Technology Organizations** by Gene Kim, Jez Humble, Patrick Debois, and John Willis: This comprehensive guide provides a deep dive into DevOps principles, practices, and case studies.
- **Service Design and Delivery: A Co-Creation Approach** by James Martin: This book offers a detailed look at service design, emphasizing the importance of collaboration and co-creation with customers and stakeholders.

Online Resources:

- **ITIL 4 Community:** The official ITIL community platform provides a space for ITIL professionals to connect, share knowledge, and discuss best practices.
- **Blogs and Articles:** Numerous blogs and online publications cover ITIL 4 topics, providing insights, opinions, and practical tips.
- **Podcasts and Webinars:** Many podcasts and webinars offer valuable information and discussions on ITIL 4 and service management.

ITIL Certifications:

- **ITIL 4 Certification Scheme:** AXELOS offers a comprehensive certification scheme for ITIL 4, including Foundation, Managing Professional, Strategic Leader, and Master levels. These certifications validate your knowledge and expertise in ITIL and can enhance your career prospects.

Note:

The ITIL framework is constantly evolving, so it's important to stay up-to-date with the latest publications, resources, and best practices. Engaging with the ITIL community, attending conferences and webinars, and subscribing to relevant publications can help you stay informed and continue your learning journey.

Appendix D: ITIL Certifications

Earning an ITIL certification is a powerful way to demonstrate your knowledge and expertise in IT service management. It validates your skills, enhances your professional credibility, and can open doors to new career opportunities. The ITIL 4 certification scheme offers a structured path for professional development, catering to individuals at different stages of their careers and with varying levels of experience.

ITIL 4 Certification Scheme:

The ITIL 4 certification scheme is designed to be flexible and adaptable, allowing individuals to tailor their learning journey based on their interests and career goals. It consists of four main levels:

1. **ITIL 4 Foundation:** This is the entry-level certification, providing a basic understanding of the key concepts, terminology, and practices of ITIL 4. It is a prerequisite for all other ITIL certifications.
2. **ITIL 4 Managing Professional (MP):** This level is designed for IT professionals who are responsible for managing IT-enabled services. It consists of four modules:
    - **Create, Deliver and Support (CDS):** Focuses on the practical aspects of service management, covering the service value chain and the practices involved in creating, delivering, and supporting IT services.
    - **Drive Stakeholder Value (DSV):** Explores how to engage and communicate with stakeholders, understand their needs, and ensure that IT services deliver value.
    - **High Velocity IT (HVIT):** Addresses the challenges of managing IT in a fast-paced and agile environment, focusing on practices like DevOps and continuous delivery.
    - **Direct, Plan, and Improve (DPI):** Covers the leadership and management aspects of IT service management, including strategic planning, governance, and continual improvement.
3. **ITIL 4 Strategic Leader (SL):** This level is designed for IT leaders and managers who are responsible for the overall direction and strategy of IT service management. It consists of two modules:
    - **Direct, Plan, and Improve (DPI):** (same as the MP module)
    - **Digital and IT Strategy (DITS):** Focuses on aligning IT strategy with business strategy, developing digital transformation initiatives, and managing the risks and opportunities of digital disruption.
4. **ITIL Master:** This is the highest level of ITIL certification, reserved for experienced IT professionals who have demonstrated mastery of the ITIL framework and its practical application.

Benefits of ITIL Certification:

- **Enhanced Credibility:** ITIL certifications are globally recognized and respected, demonstrating your expertise and commitment to the field of IT service management.
- **Improved Career Prospects:** Certified ITIL professionals are in high demand, and certification can open doors to new career opportunities and advancement.
- **Increased Earning Potential:** Studies have shown that ITIL-certified professionals typically earn higher salaries than their non-certified counterparts.
- **Better Understanding of ITSM:** ITIL certifications provide a deep understanding of IT service management best practices, enabling you to improve the efficiency, effectiveness, and quality of IT services.
- **Improved Problem-Solving Skills:** ITIL provides a framework for analyzing and solving complex IT problems, enhancing your problem-solving skills.
- **Increased Collaboration:** ITIL promotes a collaborative approach to service management, improving communication and teamwork within IT teams and across the organization.

How to Get Certified:

- **Training:** Enroll in an accredited ITIL training course to learn the concepts and practices of ITIL 4.

- **Exam Preparation:** Utilize study guides, practice exams, and other resources to prepare for the certification exam.
- **Exam:** Take the ITIL certification exam at an accredited testing center.

Conclusion:

Investing in ITIL certifications can be a valuable step for IT professionals looking to enhance their skills, knowledge, and career prospects. It demonstrates a commitment to best practices, improves your understanding of IT service management, and can open doors to new opportunities for personal and professional growth.

Conclusion

Throughout the pages of "The ITIL 4 Service Management Handbook," we have embarked on a journey to understand, adopt, and master the ITIL 4 framework. We began by establishing a solid foundation, exploring the fundamental concepts of service management, tracing the evolution of ITIL, and familiarizing ourselves with its key terminology. We then delved into the four dimensions that shape successful service management: Organizations and People, Information and Technology, Partners and Suppliers, and Value Streams and Processes. Each dimension reveals a unique layer of the interconnected ecosystem that drives value creation.

The seven guiding principles of ITIL 4 were our guiding lights, illuminating the path towards a more holistic, customer-centric, and value-driven approach. We learned the importance of focusing on value, starting from where we are, progressing iteratively with feedback, collaborating openly, thinking holistically, keeping things simple, and optimizing through automation.

At the heart of ITIL 4 lies the Service Value System (SVS), the dynamic engine that powers the creation and delivery of value. We explored the intricate workings of the Service Value Chain, the role of governance, the interplay of practices, and the continuous cycle of improvement that keeps the system agile and responsive to change.

We examined the three categories of ITIL practices – General Management, Service Management, and Technical Management – providing a detailed look at their purpose, key activities, and value contributions. We emphasized the flexibility and adaptability of these practices, encouraging you to tailor them to your organization's unique needs and context.

Finally, we explored the practical aspects of implementing ITIL 4, providing guidance on assessing organizational readiness, developing an implementation plan, measuring success, and sustaining adoption. We also shared real-world case studies to showcase how organizations have successfully leveraged ITIL 4 to achieve remarkable improvements in their service management capabilities.

Embracing the ITIL 4 Journey

As you embark on your own ITIL 4 journey, remember that it's not just about implementing a set of processes or tools; it's about embracing a new mindset and culture that prioritizes value, collaboration, and continuous improvement. It's about seeing the big picture, understanding the interdependencies between different elements, and making informed decisions that optimize the entire system.

ITIL 4 is not a destination but an ongoing journey of learning, adaptation, and evolution. Embrace the challenges, celebrate the successes, and never stop seeking new ways to improve. By applying the knowledge and insights gained from this handbook, you can transform your IT service management practices, deliver exceptional value to your customers and stakeholders, and achieve sustained success in the digital age.

The future of IT service management is bright, and ITIL 4 is your guiding star on this exciting journey.